Wittgenstein and Analytic Philosophy

P. M. S. Hacker
Photograph by Joseph Raz

Wittgenstein and Analytic Philosophy

Essays for P. M. S. Hacker

EDITED BY

Hans-Johann Glock
and
John Hyman

OXFORD
UNIVERSITY PRESS

OXFORD
UNIVERSITY PRESS

Great Clarendon Street, Oxford OX2 6DP

Oxford University Press is a department of the University of Oxford.
It furthers the University's objective of excellence in research, scholarship,
and education by publishing worldwide in

Oxford New York

Auckland Cape Town Dar es Salaam Hong Kong Karachi
Kuala Lumpur Madrid Melbourne Mexico City Nairobi
New Delhi Shanghai Taipei Toronto

With offices in

Argentina Austria Brazil Chile Czech Republic France Greece
Guatemala Hungary Italy Japan Poland Portugal Singapore
South Korea Switzerland Thailand Turkey Ukraine Vietnam

Oxford is a registered trade mark of Oxford University Press
in the UK and in certain other countries

Published in the United States
by Oxford University Press Inc., New York

British Library Cataloguing in Publication Data

Data available

Library of Congress Cataloging in Publication Data
Wittgenstein and analytic philosophy : essays for P.M.S. Hacker / edited by Hans-Johann
Glock and John Hyman.
p. cm.
Includes bibliographical references and index.
ISBN 978−0−19−921323−8 (hardback)
1. Wittgenstein, Ludwig, 1889−1951. 2. Analysis (Philosophy) I. Hacker, P. M. S. (Peter
Michael Stephan) II. Glock, Hans-Johann, 1960- III. Hyman, John.
B3376.W564.W55366 2009
192—dc22
2008046050

Typeset by Laserwords Private Limited, Chennai, India
Printed in Great Britain
on acid-free paper by
the MPG Books Group

ISBN 978−0−19−921323−8

10 9 8 7 6 5 4 3 2 1

Contents

Preface

Peter Hacker is the pre-eminent interpreter of Wittgenstein's philosophy, a powerful and sophisticated exponent of Wittgensteinian ideas in the philosophy of language and the philosophy of mind, and a distinguished historian of the analytic tradition.

Hacker studied PPE (Philosophy, Politics and Economics) at Oxford from 1960 to 1963. He was first directed to read Wittgenstein as a D.Phil. student by his supervisor H. L. A. Hart. But it was only in 1966, when he became a tutorial fellow of St John's College, Oxford, that he 'settled down to study Wittgenstein with care', as he put it, partly under the guidance of Anthony Kenny. At that time, he was also stimulated by P. F. Strawson's lectures on Kant. As a result, he was initially interested in topics on which there are significant similarities and differences between Kant and Wittgenstein, notably idealism, the metaphysics of experience and the nature of philosophy itself. Moreover, Hacker found in Wittgenstein's remarks on solipsism surprising echoes of ideas he had encountered in the Schächterite movement in Israel in his teens. As a result, he was also attuned to the Schopenhauerian influences on the *Tractatus*, which appeared alien from a more conventional Anglo-American point of view.[1]

The eventual result of this research, *Insight and Illusion* (1972), took the exploration of the intellectual roots and of the development of Wittgenstein's philosophy to a new level. It also connected Wittgenstein's later ideas with contemporary developments in analytic philosophy, notably the semantic anti-realism that Michael Dummett was developing in Oxford at that time. The revised edition of the book (1986) elaborated and modified the account of Wittgenstein's intellectual development, and of his later ideas on mind, language and the nature of philosophy. To this day, the revised edition of *Insight and Illusion* is probably the best single book on Wittgenstein. It also involved two substantial changes of mind. First, the

---

[1] Hacker describes his early philosophical career in *Philosophical Investigations* 24 (2001), 121–30. He recounts his collaboration with Gordon Baker, and comments on the disagreements that arose between them in 'Gordon Baker's Late Interpretation of Wittgenstein', in G. Kahane, E. Kanterian and O. Kuusela (eds.), *Wittgenstein and his Interpreters* (Oxford: Blackwell: 2007), 88–122.

similarities Hacker had detected between Wittgenstein and Kant were qualified or downplayed. Second, Hacker now stressed the incompatibility between Wittgenstein's opposition to philosophical theorizing and Dummett's anti-realist semantics, indeed the entire project of a systematic theory of meaning for a natural language, which Davidson and Dummett had pioneered.

In the same decade, Hacker subjected contemporary linguistics and formal semantics, especially truth-conditional theories of meaning, to a host of trenchant criticisms in the book *Language, Sense and Nonsense* (1984), which he co-authored with his colleague at St John's, Gordon Baker. The two also challenged the interpretation of Frege that had inspired formal semantics in general and Dummett's work in particular, in *Frege: Logical Excavations* (1984). This book was also highly controversial, but it anticipated many results of the more historically minded revisionism that has come to prevail in Frege scholarship.

Baker and Hacker presented their joint work-in-progress in their famous Friday afternoon graduate seminars, which drew large audiences of graduate students, faculty members and visiting academics. The audience comprised not just Wittgenstein scholars, aficionados and followers, but also 'mainstream' Oxonian philosophers interested in finding out whether the rumours of outrageous heresies could be true. Some were converted to the view that the targets against which Hacker and Baker were directing their fire were indeed nothing but 'houses of cards'; others had their worst fears confirmed. But it was impossible to deny that philosophical ideas of exceptional importance were being studied, in an intense and highly energized debate.

Baker and Hacker had embarked on their most ambitious collaborative project in 1976: a detailed analytical commentary on Wittgenstein's *Philosophical Investigations*. The first two volumes (1980 and 1985) were co-authored, the two later volumes were written by Hacker alone (1990 and 1996). The resulting four-volume work must rank as the major achievement of Wittgenstein scholarship in the last thirty years, together with the Bergen electronic edition of the Wittgenstein *Nachlass*. Composed on a monumental scale, the *Commentary* combines authoritative textual exegesis, acute philosophical insight, encyclopaedic knowledge of the historical background and lucidity of expression. It rapidly became the definitive starting-point for all scholarly approaches to the book, and it will remain so in the foreseeable future. The achievement of the *Analytical Commentary* is acknowledged not just by readers who rely on it in trying to make sense of the *Philosophical Investigations*, and by its many admirers, but also by its critics, for whom it represents the orthodox interpretation of Wittgenstein's philosophy. This orthodoxy has been attacked from many quarters. In response, Hacker has clarified and robustly defended his perspective on Wittgenstein, notably in exchanges with the so-called 'New Wittgensteinians'. The resulting debate has been extremely lively and continues to occupy centre stage in contemporary Wittgenstein studies.[2]

While many scholars distance Wittgenstein—at least the later Wittgenstein—from the analytic tradition, Hacker regards him as the pivotal figure in the development of twentieth-century analytic philosophy. He originally planned to close the final volume of the *Commentary* with a synoptic essay describing Wittgenstein's role in the development of analytic philosophy, but in the event, the depth of his knowledge about the topic and his passionately held views about it defeated the attempt to confine it in this way. Instead he wrote *Wittgenstein's Place in Twentieth-Century Analytic Philosophy*. Like all of Hacker's books, it could not have been written by anyone else. It presents the central ideas of Wittgenstein's evolving work with his usual clarity and aplomb; it tells, in a learned and gripping way, the story of the whole analytic movement from the end of the nineteenth century onwards; it defends the practice of analytic philosophy, as Hacker sees it, against the movement's leading apostates, as he sees them; and it pays a moving homage to the Oxford of Hacker's youth, dispelling popular prejudices and pinpointing the fallacies and distortions on which glib dismissals of 'Oxford' or 'ordinary language' philosophy typically depend.

Hacker's exegetical and historical work has always been guided by his concern for substantive philosophical problems and their solutions, and by his intense desire to expose conceptual confusion and (perhaps not always sharply distinguished from this) intellectual bad faith. We have already mentioned his predominantly critical contribution to the philosophy of language. In recent years he has turned to the philosophy of mind. His work on neuroscience is of particular importance in the current intellectual scene. He had the good fortune of being able to team up with the distinguished

---

[2] See A. Creary and R. Read (eds.), *The New Wittgenstein*, London: Routledge, and Hacker, *Wittgenstein: Connections and Controversies* (Oxford: Clarendon Press, 2001), chs. 4–6; 'Wittgenstein, Carnap and the New American Wittgensteinians', *Philosophical Quarterly* 53 (2003), 1–23.

Australian neuroscientist Max Bennett. Bennett was impressed by one of Hacker's earlier attacks on computational theories of the mind, and he persuaded Hacker to collaborate on a book, *Philosophical Foundations of Neuroscience* (2003). The book recounts the history of neuroscience and its impressive empirical advances. At the same time, it accuses well-known philosophers and neuroscientists of grave conceptual and methodological mistakes. One idea running through the book, which Anthony Kenny also fruitfully explored many years ago, is that in attributing mental acts and abilities to the brain or its parts, cognitive neuroscience commits the fallacy of attributing to part of an animal's body properties which can be meaningfully attributed only to the animal as a whole.[3] Surprisingly, given the prestige that neuroscience enjoys today, the book received rave reviews, and it was the subject of a widely publicized colloquium with Daniel Dennett and John Searle at the 2005 meeting of the APA, which was subsequently published in book form.[4]

Like Wittgenstein, Hacker is firmly convinced that philosophy is radically different from any *Wissenschaft*, that is, from any systematic body of knowledge, whether it be a priori, as in the formal sciences, or empirical, as in the natural sciences, the social and historical sciences or the humanities. 'Philosophy', he has written, is 'not a contribution to human knowledge, but to human understanding—understanding of the forms of our thought and of the conceptual confusions into which we are liable to fall'.[5] His main current project is a three-volume philosophical study of human nature. The scope of the enterprise will not surprise those familiar with Hacker's work. But some may be surprised by the influence on Hacker's thought of Aristotle, partly filtered through Anthony Kenny's studies of Aristotle and Aquinas. The first volume, *Human Nature: The Categorial Framework*, appeared in 2007.

Peter Hacker's pre-eminent position in Wittgenstein studies and his close association with Oxford, both institutionally and intellectually, make it fitting to honour him with a *Festschrift* published by Oxford University Press. Some of the contributors to this volume are outstanding

---

[3] See A. Kenny, 'The Homunculus Fallacy', repr. in Kenny, *The Legacy of Wittgenstein* (Oxford: Blackwell, 1984).

[4] M. Bennett, D. Dennett, P. Hacker and J. Searle, *Neuroscience and Philosophy: Brain, Mind and Language* (New York: Columbia University Press, 2007), with an introduction and conclusion by D. Robinson.

[5] 'Gordon Baker's Late Interpretation of Wittgenstein', 117.

Wittgenstein scholars, some are internationally leading figures in other areas of philosophy, and some combine these distinctions. They are all personally associated with Peter Hacker. More importantly, their essays reflect the variety of his interests and the importance of his contributions to philosophy. We join them in celebrating Peter's seventieth birthday, and in looking forward to many more years of his powerful and exciting intellectual work.[6]

Hans-Johann Glock and John Hyman

---

[6] We would like to thank Dr Javier Kalhat for his help in preparing this volume for publication.

Contributors and Abstracts

John Canfield

John V. Canfield is Emeritus Professor at the University of Toronto. He has written numerous articles on Wittgenstein, and is the author of Wittgenstein: Language and World *(1981),* The Looking-Glass Self *(1990) and* Becoming Human: The Development of Language, Self and Self-Consciousness *(2007). He edited the fifteen-volume collection* The Philosophy of Wittgenstein *(1986) and is co-editor (with Stuart Shanker) of* Wittgenstein's Intentions. *He also edited* The Philosophy of Meaning, Knowledge and Value in the Twentieth Century *(Routledge History of Philosophy, volume 10).*

Back to the Rough Ground: Wittgenstein and Ordinary Language A number of aspects of the connection between Wittgenstein's later philosophy and the talk of Everyman need clarification. John Canfield discusses the source of and cure for the repugnance an appeal to ordinary language often gives rise to; the idea that Wittgenstein sometimes writes in opposition to what attention to ordinary speech dictates; the issue of bi-polarity; intuition; and the role of a philosophical anthropology.

John Cottingham

John Cottingham is Professor of Philosophy at the University of Reading and an Honorary Fellow of St John's College, Oxford. He is (since 1993) Editor of Ratio, *the international journal of analytic philosophy. In 2002–4 he was Stanton Lecturer in the Philosophy of Religion at Cambridge University. His many books include* Descartes *(1986),* The Rationalists *(1988),* Philosophy and the Good Life: Reason and the Passions in Greek, Cartesian and Psychoanalytic Ethics *(1998),* On the Meaning of Life *(2003) and* The Spiritual Dimension *(2005). He is co-translator of* The Philosophical Writings of Descartes, *the standard three-volume Cambridge edition (1985–91), and his edited collections include* Western Philosophy: An Anthology *(1996, 2nd edition 2008).*

The Lessons of Life: Wittgenstein, Religion and Analytic Philosophy In this essay, John Cottingham argues that Wittgenstein's ideas on religion, properly understood, would richly repay the continued attention of philosophers interested in religion. For those who wish to defend the respectability of religious belief, Wittgenstein (once certain misunderstandings of his view are cleared away) turns out to be a far more promising ally than is generally supposed. As for those for whom (as was the case with Wittgenstein himself) religious faith is not a viable option, his ideas may at least help to illuminate the nature of the door which they take to be shut.

Jonathan Dancy

Jonathan Dancy is Professor of Philosophy at the University of Reading and at the University of Texas at Austin. Previously he worked at the University of Keele for twenty-five years. He has written on epistemology, on George Berkeley and, most extensively, on moral philosophy and the philosophy of action. His books include Moral Reasons *(1993),* Practical Reality *(2000) and* Ethics Without Principles *(2004).*

Action, Content and Inference In this essay, Jonathan Dancy tries to take as seriously as possible the idea that an action can be the conclusion of an inference. To this end he considers possible analogies between two relations: that between the believing and the thing believed, and that between the doing and the thing done. He tries to destabilize the second analogy. He also considers the idea that we should distinguish the thing believed from the content of that belief, and asks whether this could help us to construct a defensible notion of the content of an action. But these efforts come to nothing. Along the way he argues that things are not improved by trying to think of an intention as the conclusion of a 'practical inference'.

John Dupré

John Dupré is a philosopher of science whose work has focused especially on issues in many areas of biology. He is currently Professor of Philosophy of Science at the University of Exeter, and since 2002 he has been Director of the Centre for

Genomics in Society (Egenis). He has formerly held posts at Oxford, Stanford and Birkbeck College, London. In 2006 he held the Spinoza Visiting Professorship of Philosophy at the University of Amsterdam. His publications include The Disorder of Things: Metaphysical Foundations of the Disunity of Science *(1993),* Human Nature and the Limits of Science *(2001),* Humans and Other Animals *(2002) and* Darwin's Legacy: What Evolution Means Today *(2003).*

    Hard and Easy Questions about Consciousness In this essay, John Dupré, closely following work by Peter Hacker both alone and in collaboration with the neuroscientist Max Bennett, argues against the intelligibility of the problems about consciousness that are currently exercising a large number of philosophers. The essay concludes with some reflections on the relations between science and philosophy.

Anthony Kenny

Anthony Kenny was for twenty-five years on the staff of Balliol College, Oxford, first as philosophy tutor and then as Master. Subsequently, he was Warden of Rhodes House, President of the British Academy and Chairman of the British Library. He has written more than forty books on philosophical and historical topics, of which the most recent are the four volumes of A New History of Western Philosophy *(2003–7).*

    Cognitive Scientism Anthony Kenny adumbrates some of the Wittgensteinian arguments used in Peter Hacker and Max Bennett's book *Philosophical Foundations of Neuroscience* against the pretensions of cognitive neuroscience to have superannuated philosophical psychology. Against materialist conceptions of mind he argues that the brain is not identical with the mind, but is merely the vehicle of mental capacities and abilities. The essay ends with the question whether Wittgenstein was right to suggest that there may be psychological phenomena that are unmediated by any physical vehicle.

Wolfgang Künne

Wolfgang Künne is Professor of Philosophy at Hamburg University. His doctoral dissertation, supervised by Gadamer in Heidelberg, was on Plato's Parmenides. *His*

Habilitationsschrift *became his first book,* Abstrakte Gegenstände: Semantik und Ontologie *(1983, second edition 2007). He is President of the International Bolzano Society and a full member of the Göttingen Academy of Sciences and of the Academia Europaea (London). He has published widely in the fields of ontology, philosophy of language and epistemology as well as on the origins of analytic philosophy and of phenomenology. His* Conceptions of Truth *was published in 2003. Currently he is writing a commentary on Frege's* Logical Investigations *and a book on Bolzano's life and work.*

Wittgenstein and Frege's Logical Investigations Against the foil of some biographical facts and conjectures, this essay begins with an evaluation of the philosophical content of the Frege–Wittgenstein correspondence, discussing Frege's criticism of a few sentences in the *Tractatus* and Wittgenstein's objections against a few pages in 'The Thought'. Wolfgang Künne then presents what he takes to be Frege's reactions to the Tractarian philosophy of logic in his last published paper, 'Compound Thoughts'. He concludes with an attempt at deflecting some of the early Wittgenstein's criticisms of Frege's philosophy of logic.

Avishai Margalit

Avishai Margalit is Professor Emeritus of Philosophy at the Hebrew University of Jerusalem. He is currently the George Kennan Professor at the Institute for Advanced Study in Princeton. His numerous published works include three written with Moshe Halbertal, Idolatry *(1991),* The Decent Society *(1996) and* The Ethics of Memory *(2002) and one with Ian Buruma,* Occidentalism *(2004).*

Wittgenstein's Knight Move: Hacker on Wittgenstein's Influence on Analytic Philosophy The title of this essay is based on a metaphor that Victor Shklovsky made famous. The idea is that philosophical influence moves in the way the knight moves in chess, partly straight and partly sideways. Avishai Margalit reflects on the notion of philosophical influence by reviewing Peter Hacker's account of Wittgenstein's influence on twentieth-century analytic philosophy in his book *Wittgenstein's Place in Twentieth-Century Analytic Philosophy*, and he tries to determine in what sense, if any, Wittgenstein influenced analytic philosophy.

Stephen Mulhall

Stephen Mulhall is Fellow and Tutor in Philosophy at New College, Oxford. His research interests include Wittgenstein, Heidegger, Kierkegaard and Nietzsche. His most recent publications are Wittgenstein's Private Language *(2006) and* The Conversation of Humanity *(2007).*

Language-Games and Language: Rules, Normality Conditions and Conversation This essay critically evaluates Peter Hacker's treatment of Wittgenstein's notion of a language-game with respect to three main issues: the centrality of rule-following to language use; the relation between grammatical rules and the normal conditions of their application; and the risks inherent in viewing language as a family of language-games.

Bede Rundle

Bede Rundle is an Emeritus Fellow in Philosophy at Trinity College, Oxford. He is the author of Perception, Sensation, and Verification *(1972),* Grammar in Philosophy *(1979),* Wittgenstein and Contemporary Philosophy of Language *(1990),* Facts *(1993),* Mind in Action *(1997) and* Why there is Something Rather than Nothing *(2004). He has also written on logic, ethics, psychology and philosophy of science.*

The Private Language Argument Wittgenstein's argument against the possibility of a private language of sensations may be thought compelling, but it risks coming into conflict with our everyday talk about sensations. By examining the key concept of sameness of sensations, Bede Rundle attempts to show that this conflict is largely apparent, but that a tension remains between the argument's conclusion and our ordinary beliefs.

Severin Schroeder

Severin Schroeder is Lecturer in Philosophy at the University of Reading. He is the author of three books on the philosophy of Wittgenstein: a monograph on the private language argument, Das Privatsprachen-Argument *(1998),* Wittgenstein: The Way Out of the Fly-Bottle *(2006) and* Wittgenstein lesen *(2008). He is the editor of* Wittgenstein and Contemporary Philosophy of Mind *(2001) and of* Philosophy of Literature *(2009).*

Analytic Truths and Grammatical Propositions In this essay, Severin Schroeder defends the traditional account of analytic truth as truth in virtue of meaning against eight current objections. In the second part of the essay, the concept of an analytic statement is compared with Wittgenstein's concept of a grammatical proposition.

Joachim Schulte

Joachim Schulte teaches at the University of Zürich. He has published a number of articles and four books on the philosophy of Wittgenstein: Chor und Gesetz: Wittgenstein im Kontext *(1990),* Wittgenstein: An Introduction *(1992),* Experience and Expression *(1993) and* Wittgenstein: Leben, Werk, Wirkung *(2005). He is a co-editor of critical editions of Wittgenstein's* Tractatus Logico-Philosophicus *(1989) and of* Philosophical Investigations *(2001). In recent years he has worked chiefly on Wittgenstein's middle period.*

'Moses': Wittgenstein on Names A large part of this article is an examination of the manuscript context of the celebrated 'Moses' remark of Wittgenstein's *Philosophical Investigations* (§79). This is meant to help to render plausible Wittgenstein's idea that there is nothing wrong with speaking of the meaning of names. At the same time the examination of Wittgenstein's text may serve to show that his way of conceiving the meaning of names can be seen to have repercussions for our understanding of the notion of meaning in general.

David Wiggins

David Wiggins was Wykeham Professor of Logic in the University of Oxford from 1994 to 2000. He was previously a tutorial fellow in philosophy at New College, Oxford (1960–7); Professor of Philosophy at Bedford College, London; Fellow and Praelector at University College, Oxford; and Professor of Philosophy at Birkbeck College, London. He has written Sameness and Substance *(1980),* Needs, Values, Truth *(1987, 1991, 1998, 2002),* Sameness and Substance Renewed *(2001) and* Ethics: Twelve Lectures on the Philosophy of Morality

(2006). He is a foreign honorary member of the American Academy of Arts and Sciences.

Knowing How To and Knowing That Ryle maintained that there was a distinction between knowing that something is the case and knowing how to do things and that the second kind of knowing should not be assimilated to the first. David Wiggins takes Ryle's part, insisting that it is consistent with Ryle's thesis, and a part of Ryle's thesis, that knowing how to do something can depend on knowing that something (else) is the case, and conversely, that knowing that something is the case can depend on knowing how to do something. The essay steers past alleged confusions in Ryle's position and criticizes Stanley's and Williamson's attempt to understand 'X knows how to φ' exclusively in terms of knowing that something is the case.

Hans Oberdiek

Hans Oberdiek is Henry C. and Charlotte Turner Professor of Philosophy at Swarthmore College where he teaches courses in philosophy of law, moral philosophy, and political philosophy. He has published two books, *Tolerance: Between Forebearance and Acceptance* (2001) and, with Mary Tiles, *Living in a Technological Culture: Human Tools and Human Values* (1995), as well as articles in moral philosophy and legal philosophy.

Wittgenstein provides a fresh look at nearly every topic he touches, with the notable exception of ethics. Further, while there is a "later" Wittgenstein on virtually everything touched upon in the *Tractatus*, there isn't a "later" Wittgenstein on ethics. In his *Lecture on Ethics* (1929) Wittgenstein warns that talking and writing on ethics runs up against the boundaries of language. Yet Wittgenstein's later writings, especially *On Certainty*, as well as the philosophical explorations of G. H. von Wright's *Varieties of Goodness*, show that there is more to ethics than the "early" wittgenstein allowed without sccumbing to the error of thinking that ethics is a branch of either science or logic.

Abbreviations for Works by Wittgenstein

Reference to works by Wittgenstein (including *Nachlass*, lectures, correspondence and dictations) is by abbreviations using the familiar capital letter system. Unless otherwise stated, references are to page numbers of the edition specified.

1. Wittgenstein's Published Works in Order of Composition

NL   *Notes on Logic* [1913], in NB, 93–107.

NM   *Notes Dictated to Moore in Norway* [1914], in NB, 108–19.

NB   *Notebooks 1914–16* [German–English parallel text], ed. G. E. M. Anscombe and G. H. von Wright, tr. G. E. M. Anscombe (Oxford: Blackwell, rev. edn 1979). Cited according to date.

CV   *Culture and Value* [1914–51,German–English parallel text], ed. G. H. von Wright in collaboration with H. Nyman, tr. P. Winch (Oxford: Blackwell, 1980). Page numbers followed by 'e' (e.g. 19e) refer to the facing English translation.

PT   *Proto-Tractatus* [1917–18, German–English parallel text], ed. B. F. McGuinness, T. Nyberg and G. H. von Wright, tr. D. F. Pears and B. F. McGuinness, with an introduction by G. H. von Wright (London: Routledge and Kegan Paul, 1971).

TLP   *Tractatus Logico-Philosophicus* [1922], tr. D. F. Pears and B. F. McGuinness (London: Routledge and Kegan Paul, 1961). References are to numbered sections.

PR   *Philosophical Remarks* [1929–30], ed. R. Rhees, tr. R. Hargreaves and R. White (Oxford: Blackwell, 1975).

BT   *The Big Typescript: TS 213*, ed. and tr. M. Aue and C. G. Luckhardt (Oxford, Blackwell, 2005).

PG   *Philosophical Grammar*, ed. R. Rhees, tr. A. J. P. Kenny (Oxford: Blackwell, 1974).

GB   'Remarks on Frazer's "The Golden Bough" ', ed. R. Rhees, *Synthese*, 17 (1967), 233–53; references are to the version in PO.

BB   *The Blue and Brown Books* [1933–5] (Oxford: Blackwell, 1958).

EPB   *Eine philosophische Betrachtung* [1936], ed. R. Rhees, *Schriften* 5 (Frankfurt am Main: Suhrkamp, 1970) 117–237.

LPE   'Wittgenstein's Notes for Lectures on "Private Experience" and "Sense Data" ' [1936], ed. R. Rhees, *Philosophical Review*, 77 (1968), 275–320.

CE   'Cause and Effect: Intuitive Awareness', ed. R. Rhees, tr. P. Winch, *Philosophia*, 6 (1976), 392–430; references are to the version in PO.

RFM   *Remarks on the Foundations of Mathematics* [1937–44], ed. G. H. von Wright, R. Rhees and G. E. M. Anscombe, tr. G. E. M. Anscombe, rev. edn (Oxford: Blackwell, 1978).

PI   *Philosophical Investigations* [German–English parallel text], ed. G. E. M. Anscombe and R. Rhees (Oxford: Blackwell, 1967; 1st edn 1953). References are to sections of Part I (except for footnotes) and to sections and pages of Part II.

RPP I   *Remarks on the Philosophy of Psychology* [1945–7, German–English parallel text], Volume I, ed. G. E. M. Anscombe and G. H. von Wright, tr. G. E. M. Anscombe (Oxford: Blackwell, 1980).

RPP II   *Remarks on the Philosophy of Psychology* [1948, German–English parallel text], Volume II, ed. G. H. von Wright and H. Nyman, tr. C. G. Luckhardt and M. A. E. Aue (Oxford: Blackwell, 1980).

Z   *Zettel* [1945–8, German–English parallel text], ed. G. E. M. Anscombe and G. H. von Wright, tr. G. E. M. Anscombe (Oxford: Blackwell, 1967).

LW I   *Last Writings on the Philosophy of Psychology* [1948–9, German–English parallel text], Volume I, ed. G. H. von Wright and H. Nyman, tr. C. G. Luckhardt and M. A. E. Aue (Oxford: Blackwell, 1982).

LW II   *Last Writings on the Philosophy of Psychology* [1949–51, German–English parallel text], Volume II, ed. G. H. von Wright and H. Nyman, tr. C. G. Luckhardt and M. A. E. Aue (Oxford: Blackwell, 1992).

ROC   *Remarks on Colour* [1951, German–English parallel text], ed. G. E. M. Anscombe, tr. L. L. McAlister and Margarete Schättle (Oxford: Blackwell, 1980; 1st edn 1977).

OC   *On Certainty* [1951, German–English parallel text], ed. G. E. M. Anscombe and G. H. von Wright, tr. D. Paul and G. E. M. Anscombe (Oxford: Blackwell, 1969).

PO   *Philosophical Occasions* [German–English parallel texts where appropriate], ed. J. Klagge and A. Nordmann (Indianapolis: Hackett, 1993).

2. Lectures and Conversations

WVC   *Wittgenstein and the Vienna Circle* [1929–32], shorthand notes recorded by F. Waismann, ed. B. F. McGuinness (Oxford: Blackwell, 1979).

LE   'A Lecture on Ethics' [1929], *Philosophical Review*, 74 (1965), 3–12.

MWL   'Wittgenstein's Lectures in 1930–33', in G. E. Moore, *Philosophical Papers* (London: Allen and Unwin, 1959). References are to the reprinted version in PO.

AWL   *Wittgenstein's Lectures, Cambridge 1932–35*, from the notes of A. Ambrose and M. MacDonald, ed. A. Ambrose (Oxford: Blackwell, 1979).

LC   *Lectures and Conversations on Aesthetics, Psychology and Religious Belief* [1938–46], ed. C. Barrett (Oxford: Blackwell, 1966).

LFM   *Wittgenstein's Lectures on the Foundations of Mathematics, Cambridge 1939*, from the notes of R. G. Bosanquet, N. Malcolm, R. Rhees and Y. Smythies, ed. C. Diamond (Chicago: University of Chicago Press, 1976).

LPP   *Wittgenstein's Lecture on Philosophy of Psychology 1946–7*, notes by P. T. Geach, K. J. Shah and A. C. Jackson, ed. P. T. Geach (Hemel Hempstead: Harvester Press, 1988).

3. Nachlass

All references to unpublished material follow von Wright's catalogue (G. H. von Wright, 'The Wittgenstein Papers', in his *Wittgenstein* (Oxford: Blackwell, 1982), 35–62; expanded version in PO, 480–506.

The full *Nachlass* on CD-ROM has been published by Oxford University Press, edited by the Wittgenstein Archives at the University of Bergen: *Wittgenstein's Nachlass: The Bergen Electronic Edition* (Oxford: Oxford University Press, 2000).

The early parts of the *Nachlass* are currently being published as the *Wiener Ausgabe/Vienna Edition*, ed. M. Nedo (Vienna and New York: Springer, 1994–).

MS   Manuscripts from the *Nachlass*. References are by MS number (101–82) followed by page number.

TS   Typescript from the *Nachlass*. References are by TS number (201–45) followed by page number.

Wittgenstein's Knight Move: Hacker on Wittgenstein's Influence on Analytic Philosophy

AVISHAI MARGALIT

1. Elucidation and Explanation

My title is based on the knight's move in chess, a metaphor that Victor Shklovsky, the illustrious literary scholar, made famous. Philosophical influence moves the way the knight moves in chess, partly forward and partly sideways. Wittgenstein's influence in philosophy is rarely straightforward—hence my title. In my essay, I would like to reflect on the notion of philosophical influence by viewing and reviewing Peter Hacker's account of Wittgenstein's influence on twentieth-century analytic philosophy. My suspicion is that Wittgenstein had more presence in philosophy than influence on philosophy. There are those who put Wittgenstein in the Pantheon, and those who put him in the Pandemonium. But he leaves no one indifferent: all find him impressive. Yet being impressive is not the same as having influence.

Peter Hacker served successfully as apprentice to the master-craftsman Wittgenstein, as attested by his book *Insight and Illusion*. He then spent many years as a journeyman, at the end of which he submitted to the guild a masterpiece in four volumes dedicated to the work of the master. For Hacker, Wittgenstein is the Hans Sachs of the philosophical guild who discovered, when he was about to join the great masters, that not much of the guild was left from the golden days at Oxford. To commemorate the guild and its great master from Cambridge, Hacker wrote a book that sings the praises of the great guild and highlights the great role his master played in shaping it.

The book is called *Wittgenstein's Place in Twentieth-Century Analytic Philosophy*. It comprises two elements: a comparison of Wittgenstein's philosophy to other analytic philosophies of the twentieth century, and an account of Wittgenstein's influence on analytic philosophy. In comparing, one is committed to presenting the 'true' Wittgenstein, while in tracing influence one must be concerned with how Wittgenstein was perceived by others, be it the true Wittgenstein or a false one. It is not easy to keep these two elements apart. After all, if Hacker believes that someone gets Wittgenstein very wrong, how can he tell that it was Wittgenstein who influenced that thinker rather than a Wittgenstein–dummy?

There is, however, a much deeper tension between the two elements: a tension between causal explanation (influence) on the one hand and elucidation (comparison) on the other. Indeed, this very tension is at the heart of Wittgenstein's own philosophy. It is central to his effort to keep philosophy from turning into an ideology of science, namely scientism. He calls for a sharp division of labor: science is the realm of explanation and causality, whereas philosophy is the realm of elucidation and understanding. The conflation of the two is bad for science. It may be good for scientism, but then scientism is no good.

However, when it comes to the history of ideas we need both elements: causal explanation and conceptual elucidation. Influence is a causal concept, whereas comparison of ideas, based on similarities and differences, is elucidation. Explanation and elucidation yield two different methodologies in history: interpretative history, which has to do with understanding the meaning of human actions in history, and scientific history, which concentrates on the causal effects of historical actions. I believe that the history of ideas should include both explanation and elucidation. For a good history of ideas, one has to understand both the content of the ideas and their influence.

2. The History of Analytic Philosophy

The recent outpouring of literature devoted to the history of analytic philosophy is a puzzling phenomenon. For many years, analytic philosophy was perceived as a school (or schools) of thought that viewed itself not in historical terms, but as perennial philosophy. True, some analytic philosophers, especially at Oxford, were keenly interested in the history of philosophy. The number of books written by analytic philosophers on philosophers of the past is considerable. What is new in the recent trend is that analytic philosophy itself is viewed as a proper subject for historical investigation. This new tendency might be regarded as a sign of decay, along the lines of Hegel's famous dictum: 'The owl of Minerva takes its flight only when the shades of night are gathering.'[1]

Historical accounts come at dusk, not at dawn. Hacker is very troubled by what he believes is the decline of analytic philosophy. His lamentation appears as the last chapter in the book. For him the decline is due to failure of nerve and not because of anything wrong in analytic philosophy properly conducted, namely, conducted under the tutelage of Wittgenstein.

My role here is neither to praise analytic philosophy nor to bury it. My interest is in Hacker's account of Wittgenstein's influence on analytic philosophy. My suspicion is that Wittgenstein's influence, like the presence of air, is everywhere, but not in our grasp.

Hacker, however, tries to get Wittgenstein in his grasp. His picture of Wittgenstein's influence is not atmospheric, but hydraulic:

The influence of individual thinkers upon the stream of philosophy may be likened to that of tributaries that pour into it. Some may flow quietly into the running waters, adding their volume and creating eddies in the persistent flow. Others may burst into the mainstream as a great fall erupts into the river, moving the very riverbed, shifting the sandbanks, creating powerful new currents and undercurrents, and sweeping away familiar landmarks along the banks by their torrent and turbulence. It is then only many miles downstream that the waters of the river subside and flow calmly again. By then it may be barely possible, and perhaps of little interest, to determine which water originated in which tributary.[2]

This is a refreshing simile. But it is not clear whether Hacker abides by his river picture, for he believes that he is standing miles downstream and yet he still finds it possible and important to determine the source of the river—and the source is Wittgenstein. Hacker's rivers are the Cam and the Isis, metonymies for the Cambridge of Russell, Moore, and Wittgenstein and for the Oxford of Ryle, Austin, and Strawson. There are no true

---

[1] Hegel, G.W., *Philosophy of Right*, trans. S.W. Dyde (Kitchener, Ontario: Batoche Books, 2001), 20.
[2] Hacker, P.M.S., *Wittgenstein's Place in Twentieth-Century Analytic Philosophy* (Oxford: Blackwell, 1996), 3. Unattributed references in what follows are to this book.

waterfalls in these two rather placid rivers. Yet it is clear that, for Hacker, Wittgenstein is a waterfall of Niagara proportions, and so Hacker turns to another river: 'The stream of philosophy that flowed from Cambridge does not compare in volume with the torrent of the Vienna Circle' (p. 87).

Hacker's idea is that Wittgenstein's early philosophy, the philosophy of the *Tractatus*, exerted tremendous influence on logical positivism, a leading trend of thought in the twentieth century that had its origin in the Vienna Circle, and that Wittgenstein's later philosophy exerted immense influence first in Cambridge, among his disciples, and then in Oxford. The influence in Oxford was exerted via the samizdat lecture notes as well as the semi-authorized *Blue and Brown Books*, later followed by the *Philosophical Investigations*. I believe, however, that the Wittgenstein who had an influence on analytic philosophy, in its 'golden age', is neither the early Wittgenstein of the *Tractatus* nor the late Wittgenstein of the *Investigations* but the intermediary Wittgenstein of *The Blue and Brown Books*.

One sobering way to evaluate Wittgenstein's alleged influence is to take a central figure in each philosophical trend, say Rudolf Carnap of the Vienna Circle and Peter Strawson of Oxford, and to see in what sense if any Wittgenstein influenced them. The choice is not accidental, for both claimed that Wittgenstein had influenced them and both are major philosophers in their own right. In later sections of this essay, I shall try to see whether it is true or, rather, in what sense it is true that Wittgenstein influenced them.

There are of course philosophers on whom Wittgenstein's influence is straightforward. Elizabeth Anscombe is a case in point. Her 1957 book *Intention* is a clear example of Wittgenstein's influence in the sense that it could have passed as Wittgenstein's own piece of writing. Anscombe was a pupil in Wittgenstein's studio in Cambridge just as Ferdinand Bol was a pupil in Rembrandt's studio; and Anscombe's book could have passed, perhaps with minor modifications (such as omitting references to Aristotle or for that matter to Wittgenstein), as Wittgenstein's—as Bol's portrait of Elizabeth Bas passed for many years as Rembrandt's. This is not to say that Anscombe's ideas in her truly important book are not hers, any more than Bol's portrait is not very much his: but in both cases, the influence is clear.

Hacker's choice of analytic philosophers—Carnap, Ryle, Strawson, Quine, and Austin—is a good selection. But it is a good selection for comparison with Wittgenstein, and not a terribly good selection to attest to Wittgenstein's influence. The exception is Gilbert Ryle, who is a good candidate for exemplifying both comparison and influence. But then I remember Peter Hacker telling me that Ryle was once asked if he was influenced by Wittgenstein, and his reply was: 'Influenced never, but I learned a great deal from him.' This is an important distinction. To learn a great deal from someone does not automatically mean being influenced by him or her. This is quite evident in learning a skill, such as logic. Yet learning a certain style of exercising a skill may manifest influence.

If Ryle can serve equally as an object of comparison and as a subject to the influence of Wittgenstein, Quine can serve only as object of comparison. Hacker's comparison of Wittgenstein and Quine is skilful, except that he gives all the good shots to Wittgenstein. Hacker recognizes the radical element in Quine's philosophy—and calls it 'apostasy'. Indeed, Quine contested all the dichotomies cherished by Carnap and Wittgenstein, much as Hegel contested all the dichotomies cherished by Kant.

Wittgenstein and Quine both share a deep suspicion of the concept of meaning, as it is employed in philosophy. Their attack on the concept of meaning is like the economists' attack on viewing the value of paper money as essentially dependent on the value of gold. The latter attack is anchored in the claim that the value of paper money lies not in any metal behind it, but in the fact that it gains currency through its use in transactions. Because paper money is accepted it has value—and, similarly, because words are used they have meaning. What is required is to reverse the order of explanation.

Quine's doctrine of the indeterminacy of translation is an attack on the illusory notion of meaning. He finds an elective affinity between his stand and Wittgenstein's—an affinity, not an influence. He writes, 'Perhaps the doctrine of indeterminacy of translation will have little air of paradox for readers familiar with Wittgenstein's latter-day remarks on meaning'.[3] I believe that Quine is right. Yet, I also believe that the deep connections between Wittgenstein's 'rules paradox' and Quine's 'indeterminacy of translations', as well as Goodman's 'grue paradox' (understood as a problem of meaning rather than as a problem of induction), were exposed by Kripke in *Wittgenstein on Rules and Private Language*. But Hacker will have

---

[3] Quine, W.V.O., *Word and Object* (Cambridge, Mass.: MIT Press, 1960), 77.

none of it. He believes that Kripke's account has little to do with the true Wittgenstein, and that even this little is wrong. Hacker and I once quarreled about Kripke's account and I am in no mood to pick this fight all over again, for the sole reason that my concern in this essay is with Hacker's claims about influence and not with his elucidatory comparison. We both agree that Quine is a good object of comparison with Wittgenstein and not a good example of Wittgenstein's influence.

Hacker makes an explicit comparison between Wittgenstein's influence on philosophy and Picasso's influence on art. I am very sympathetic to analogies between the history of art and the history of philosophy. The history of art is more like the history of philosophy than like the history of science: for one thing, there is no cumulative knowledge in philosophy and art, but in science there is. Influence in art is felt in the way of doing things (technique) and in the way of seeing things. Caravaggio and Picasso were most influential on both counts. Hacker would have us believe that Wittgenstein is the Picasso of philosophy. I am not convinced. But then again I am not convinced of the opposite.

I divide the sequel into two parts: the sections of the first part deal with Wittgenstein's influence. The second part deals with Wittgenstein's own attitude to influence.

3. Senses of Influence

Naked power is for anyone to see. Influence is not. It works its wonders in ways not readily observable. Influence is inferred from its effects. This is a major reason for the elusive nature of influence.

Influence does not require an intention to influence on the part of influencer. Nor, for that matter, is an intention to be influenced required from the one who is influenced. Influence does not require knowledge or awareness: one can be influenced without knowing it. Moreover, one may be more prone to being influenced, the less one is aware of the possibility of being influenced.

In general, correct attribution of influence is neither a necessary nor a sufficient condition for influence. One may be under the illusion of being influenced by the great minds, whereas in fact only minor ones influenced him. Minor philosophers are neither foxes that see many little things, nor hedgehogs that see one big thing. They are woodpeckers that see one little thing—but what they see they may see clearly.

Since influence is known by its effects, it is easier to deal with influence from the perspective of the influenced than from the perspective of the influencer. 'Being influenced' is a generic term that takes many forms: one can be 'shaped' by Wittgenstein or be 'molded', 'transformed', 'inspired', 'triggered', 'enchanted', or 'towered over' by him. Each of these terms suggests a different subtle nuance.

Hacker refers to Wittgenstein's 'impact' in addition to his 'influence'. 'Impact', unlike 'influence', conveys a sense of directness. 'Impact' can be used to suggest a direct and strong influence, but it can also suggest a direct and strong impression. Strong impression in turn may end up suggesting admiration, or even veneration, but it does not necessarily mean influence in the cognitive sense of affecting content or method.

One important nuance taps into the difference between being impressed and being influenced. Peter Strawson was immensely impressed by Wittgenstein but hardly, I believe, influenced by him. Strawson was influenced by Kant and Hume as well as by Austin and Grice. He responded polemically to Carnap, Russell, and Quine, but he was not influenced by Wittgenstein in any straightforward sense. True, Strawson wrote an early review of Wittgenstein's *Investigations*, a review that for a while set the tone for the way in which the book was received. But writing an influential review is not a sign of being influenced.

Hacker purports to attest to the influence of Wittgenstein on Ryle and his peers by quoting the following passage from Ryle: 'It comes natural to us now—as it did not thirty years ago—to differentiate logic from science much as Wittgenstein did; it comes natural to us not to class philosophers as scientists or *a fortiori* as super-scientists' (p. 139). Yet Ryle is not attributing his and his peers' attitude to science and philosophy to Wittgenstein's influence. He is only saying that the author of the *Philosophical Investigations* 'has his finger on the pulse of philosophical activity'.

The philosophers of the 'golden age' at Oxford had very little training in science, and did not view themselves as scientists or for that matter as super-scientists; many however were well trained in classical philology. They were experts in the art of 'reading slowly', to use Nietzsche's apt description, and attuned to fine distinctions among words. The attentiveness to the use of language did not come to Austin, Grice, or Ryle from Wittgenstein, but from glossing Greek texts. Even Ayer, the village logical positivist, was hardly a fanatic science worshiper, nor one to promote scientism in philosophy. Ayer felt more at ease with Hume's induction than with Goedel's numbers or Einstein's simultaneity.

Hacker, to his credit, is very tentative in describing Wittgenstein's influence on Strawson. 'Where, if at all, can one discern a Wittgenstein influence or, if not influence, then a convergence of view?' he asks (p. 176). My answer is that Strawson was impressed and inspired by Wittgenstein, rather than influenced by him. Influence has to do with content or with method, whereas being impressed and inspired does not. The question is, does the influence of Wittgenstein on Strawson manifest itself in method rather than in content? Was Strawson's method of 'connective analysis' influenced by Wittgenstein's method of *Übersicht*, namely, scanning various uses of relevant words and presenting them in perspicuous presentation? I doubt it and I shall air my doubt later.

Can one be influenced without being impressed? This is tricky. It is possible to be impressed by a thought without being impressed by the originator of the thought. Great philosophers have on occasion been influenced by minor philosophers without being impressed by them. Moreover, it is this situation of the great mind being influenced by a thought of an unimpressive minor mind that makes it hard for the former to admit the influence of the latter. 'Influence' seems to retain, in a metaphorical way, its astrological etymology of emanation from the stars. In astrology, stars influence living creatures, whereas living creatures do not have an effect on the stars. Yet the astrological picture of influence as emanation from the stars, when applied to the history of philosophy, is misleading, for it conveys the idea that only stellar philosophers exert influence.

Being impressed, unlike being influenced, has a passive quality to it. One may be impressed without being moved to act. In contrast, being influenced has an active quality: one is moved to act, either physically or mentally. Being inspired, too, unlike being impressed, is not a passive attitude: it fills one with a high level of enthusiasm and readiness to act. Being inspired may bring new ideas to mind, but not necessarily ideas connected to those that inspired them. Inspiration may for example lead one to 'think big', to be bold and free, without the inspirer and the inspired having any thoughts in common.

Wittgenstein, the tormented genius, captured the imagination of many who aspired 'to do philosophy'. However, inspiration should not be conflated with influence. I repeat: influence in the realm of ideas requires some relation of content, or method, or both, between the ideas of the influencer and the ideas of the influenced. Inspiration is an indication of strong presence, but not necessarily of strong influence.

The expression 'Wittgenstein's inspiration' is of course ambiguous as to whether he inspired others or was inspired by others. Regarding the latter, Wittgenstein left a strong impression that he was inspired by divine agency. Even someone as coolheaded as Carnap talks about Wittgenstein 'as if insight came to him as through a divine inspiration, so that we could not help feeling that any sober rational comment or analysis of it would be a profanation'.[4] I think that this impression that Wittgenstein conveyed, of having access to 'revealed philosophy', contributed greatly to his presence but not necessarily to his influence. It is not clear how to grapple with revealed philosophy. I shall come back to Wittgenstein's inspiration at the end, when I address his role as an esoteric teacher. But let me stay longer with Carnap's account of Wittgenstein's influence on him—influence rather than inspiration.

4. Carnap's Testimony

Rudolf Carnap writes that he always found Wittgenstein's ideas stimulating, and I believe Carnap meant 'stimulating' in the serious sense of provoking further thought and not in the polite, noncommittal sense conveyed by 'thank you for your stimulating talk', addressed to an indifferent lecturer. Carnap mentions Wittgenstein, along with Frege and Russell, as the philosophers who influenced him most. This, if true, is very important testimony. It helps assess Wittgenstein's influence on analytic philosophy, since Carnap's own influence on logical positivism needs no documentation. I do not assume that, as a rule, influence is a transitive relation. But it can be assumed in this particular case. Yet, when Carnap describes the influence of Wittgenstein on his thought in detail, this influence does not

⁴ Carnap, R., 'Autobiography', in P. A. Schilpp (ed.), *The Philosophy of Rudolf Carnap*, The Library of Living Philosophers, Volume 11 (La Salle: Open Court, 1963), 26.

amount to much, at least not in terms of doctrine. He writes, reverently, about Wittgenstein's influential insight 'that many philosophical sentences, and especially in traditional metaphysics, are pseudo-sentences, devoid of cognitive content'.[5] Then he adds, 'I found Wittgenstein's view on this point close to the one I had previously developed under the influence of anti-metaphysical scientists and philosophers.'

So we might say that Wittgenstein's influence on Carnap was in strengthening and radicalizing his anti-metaphysical views. But even this is far from clear, since Carnap did not find Wittgenstein's anti-metaphysical attitude radical and consistent enough. He writes, 'When Schlick, on another occasion, made a critical remark about a metaphysical statement by a classical philosopher (I think it was Schopenhauer), Wittgenstein surprisingly turned against Schlick and defended the philosopher and his work.'[6] Carnap has an elaborate account of the inner tension and ambivalence in Wittgenstein's attitude to metaphysics, in contrast to Schlick and his attitude, which spares 'no love for metaphysics or metaphysical theology'.

My conclusion is that Carnap and his friends did not need Wittgenstein for their anti-metaphysical attitude, nor did they need him for enhancing its intensity. If Wittgenstein had an influence in that regard it should be located not in his anti-metaphysical attitude but in his theory of the sources of metaphysical illusions (what Kant dubs 'dialectics'), and in his principle of verification according to which metaphysical statements are nonsense.

On Carnap's account, metaphysical illusions are a product of 'the material mode of speech', which is a particular 'transposed mode of speech' (where, in order to assert something about A, something corresponding is asserted about B, which stands in a certain specified relation to A). Metaphors or analogies that are recognized as such are examples of the transposed mode of speech. 'The origin of a transposed mode of speech can sometimes be explained psychologically by the fact that the conception of the substituted object b is for some reason more vivid and striking, stronger in feeling and tone, than the conception of the original object a.'[7] In the material mode of speech, the use of universal words can 'very easily lead to pseudo-problems'.[8] Universal words are words such as 'number' and 'space'. They lead us to ask whether numbers are real or whether space is real.

[5] Carnap, 'Autobiography', 25.   [6] Carnap, 'Autobiography', 26-7.
[7] Carnap, R., *The Logical Syntax of Language* (Paterson, NJ: Littlefield, Adams, & Co., 1959), 309.
[8] Carnap, *The Logical Syntax of Language*, 310.

I consider what Gustav Bergmann called 'the linguistic turn'[9] in analytic philosophy to have arisen from the belief that metaphysical illusions are by-products of the use of language. On my understanding, the linguistic turn is mainly due to a negative doctrine, according to which metaphysical illusions are essential by-products of the use of language, and to a lesser extent to the positive doctrine of turning to language to account for what thoughts are. The linguistic turn is perhaps the most characteristic feature of analytic philosophy.

In the history of philosophy, we can discern two types of theories of errors: motivational and cognitive. Descartes' account of error is clearly motivational: our will—our wishful thinking—stands in the way of our cognitive 'natural light' to grasp the truth. Kant's account is clearly cognitive: metaphysical errors are an essential by-product of the structure of our ability to know, in the same way as optical illusions are a by-product of our very ability to see. On Wittgenstein's account, our metaphysical illusions are a by-product both of the surface structure of language (early Wittgenstein) and of its use (later Wittgenstein). This means that our errors are cognitive, but the remedy is motivational. We can avoid being under a metaphysical illusion only by exercising our will. Detecting an error cognitively is not enough.

Wittgenstein had an influence on the linguistic turn because he diagnosed the disease, and because he found in language the cure for the metaphysical malaise. On Carnap's testimony, Wittgenstein influenced the anti-metaphysical move by introducing what he calls 'Wittgenstein's principle of verifiability'. This principle was adopted by the Vienna Circle as a tool for disqualifying metaphysical sentences as 'meaningless' in not being verifiable in principle. Verification is what gives a sentence its meaning.

The truth is that Wittgenstein had little patience with the Vienna Circle's 'boastfulness' about its 'renunciation of metaphysics'. There was nothing new in that, he claimed. There is no question that William James and John Dewey prefigured the use of the verification principle as a criterion for meaningfulness and as a weapon against a certain kind of metaphysics. But it is most likely that rather than James and Dewey it was Wittgenstein—passing through Friedrich Waismann—who influenced the Circle. In any case, Wittgenstein's anti-metaphysical influence was influence

---

[9] Bergmann, G., *Realism* (Madison: The University of Wisconsin Press, 1962).

with respect to method (the verification principle) rather than with respect to doctrine.

Nietzsche, in his *Twilight of the Idols, or How to Philosophize with a Hammer*, suggests two methods for dealing with metaphysical illusions (for which he borrows Francis Bacon's term 'idols'): a crude method he calls a 'hammer', and a refined method he calls a 'tuning fork'. Wittgenstein also suggested a hammer (the verification method) and a tuning fork (*Übersicht*, or a fine-tuned description of the uses of relevant philosophical words). My contention is that while Wittgenstein's hammer was influential, his tuning fork was not.

Carnap mentions another one of Wittgenstein's influences on him: 'The most important insight I gained from his work was the conception that the truth of logical statements is based only on their logical structure and on the meaning of the terms. Logical statements are true under all conceivable circumstances: thus, their truth is independent of the contingent facts of the world. On the other hand, it follows that these statements do not say anything about the world and thus have no factual content.'[10]

Hacker quite rightly points out that the idea of logical truths, which are based on the meaning of logical operators as defined by truth tables, is far from Wittgenstein's idea of using T/F notation to eliminate logical connectives. He thinks that Carnap 'arguably' created a catastrophic modification of Wittgenstein's position. Catastrophic or not, it is not clear what the influence of Wittgenstein on Carnap's conception of logic amounts to.

On top of all of this, Wittgenstein and Carnap had such utterly different philosophical temperaments (Carnap, the man of the enlightenment, versus Wittgenstein, the man of the counter-enlightenment) that even when their positions look the same, they are quite different. One good example of their phony similarity is the ways in which the two handled the issue of color exclusion.

Hacker has made, in the past, a powerful case for the claim that Wittgenstein abandoned his early philosophy of the *Tractatus*, mostly because of his inability to handle the issue of color exclusion. Color exclusion posed an intractable difficulty to Wittgenstein's view that the only kind of defensible notion of necessity is logical necessity. The question was how to analyze within the frame of the *Tractatus* frame the proposition

---

[10] Carnap, R. 'Autobiography', 25.

'A is red and A is blue' as incompatibility, so as to exclude from any state of affairs the possibility of including two independent elementary propositions: 'A is red' and 'A is blue'. This seems to be a minor technical problem but Hacker is right in writing, 'Just as a great scientific theory may in *special circumstances* be confirmed or falsified by one single crucial kind of observation (e.g. relativity theory and the precession of the perihelion of Mercury) so Wittgenstein's first philosophy collapsed over its inability to solve one problem—color exclusion.'[11]

Carnap faced a structurally very similar problem. His semantics, based on state-descriptions, is composed of conjunctions and negations of elementary statements. The sole notion of necessity in his semantics was that of L-true, true in all state descriptions. But then, Yehoshua Bar-Hill and John Kemeny, independently, raised the difficulty that color exclusion poses for Carnap's account of state descriptions: color terms cannot appear as primitive predicates in elementary propositions, for a state of affairs in which A is red is, by necessity, incompatible with 'A is blue'. Yet the incompatibility is quite clearly due to the descriptive meaning of the color terms ('blue' and 'red') and not to the logical connectives ('and', 'or', and 'not').

Necessity as L-true is an idea that Carnap 'developed' from Wittgenstein's *Tractatus*.[12] Carnap, unlike Wittgenstein, was unruffled by the color exclusion problem and treated it as a mere technical problem to be solved by adding meaning postulates to his system, postulates such as 'If A is blue then A is not red'. A state description that includes 'A is both red and blue' violates that meaning postulate and should be ruled out. Wittgenstein's late philosophy has no 'meaning' rules but it has something equivalent, namely rules of grammar that guide, among other things, the use of color terms whereby 'A cannot be both red and blue' is a rule that governs the use of both 'red' and 'blue'. In short, the problem of color exclusion and its solution looks very similar in the philosophies of Wittgenstein and Carnap. Nevertheless, the attitude of the two to the problem of color exclusion is radically different: what Carnap regards as a mere technical problem that calls for mere technical amendment strikes Wittgenstein as a difficulty that calls for a radical change in his whole philosophy.

[11] Hacker, P.M.S., *Insight and Illusion* (Oxford: Oxford University Press, 1972), 86.
[12] Carnap, R., *The Logical Foundations of Probability* (Chicago and London: The University of Chicago Press, 1962; originally published in 1950), 83.

Pascal refers to the fact that the most famous dictum in philosophy, 'cogito ergo sum', occurred in Augustine long before it was made famous by Descartes. Yet he comments that someone who made this dictum the cornerstone of his philosophy cannot be compared with someone for whom it was a passing remark. Something similar could be said about Wittgenstein and Carnap in their attitude to color exclusion.

5. Influence: Agenda and Method

Another clear sense of influence is that of setting the philosophical agenda. Philosophers exert an influence if they have the power to make their philosophical concern the concern of others. This does not necessarily mean that the others accept the position of the agenda setter, but it does mean that they think about and wrestle with what the agenda setters made them think about.

It seems that a glaring example of Wittgenstein's influence as an agenda setter is his concern with the possibility of a private language and of a private rule, namely, with a language and a rule that in principle cannot be shared with others. It seems to be a good example, given that Wittgenstein's topic of private language came to dominate the philosophical scene. The possibility, or rather impossibility, of such a language became, as we all know, a keen concern for many philosophers. But even in this purportedly clear case, we are left with a historical query: was the saddling of philosophy with the issue of private language due to Wittgenstein's direct influence, or was it to a large extent due to the famous intervention of Saul Kripke? The debate about private language predates Kripke's lecture, but the debate was almost all about the right interpretation to Wittgenstein. It did not stand as a topic on its own right.

Put metaphorically, was the setting of the philosophical agenda with the private language argument a rook move or was it, as I suspect, a knight move? Whatever it is, I think that, on the whole, the most promising place to look for Wittgenstein's influence is in his setting of the agenda. Still, we also have to try to detect his influence on doctrine and on method.

Let me return to influence on method, namely, on the systematic way of doing philosophy. I have already mentioned 'Wittgenstein's principle of verification' as a case of influence on method. A related notion of Wittgenstein's from the intermediary period between the *Tractatus* and the *Investigations* is the notion of criterion: the requirement for a special kind of evidence to settle a dispute over the question whether something satisfies a concept. A prominent example is the issue of other minds: do creatures other than me satisfy the concept of having a mind? The issue is understood by Wittgenstein as a matter of criterion and not as a matter to be settled like an empirical hypothesis. In any case, Wittgenstein's notion of criterion looms large in such disputes.

I have already said that if one wants to locate a real influence of Wittgenstein on method, one should look at the Wittgenstein of the intermediary period: the Wittgenstein who advanced the methods of verification and criteria. One reason is that verification and criteria are clear methods, relative to the method of the logical atomistic analysis of the *Tractatus*, and to the *Übersicht* method of the *Investigations*. We may say that these are crude methods ('hammers' in Nietzsche's language), but crudity is no argument against influence. Crude, or 'vulgar', Marxism is the Marxism that had true influence, while refined Marxism, with all its clever epicycles and calculated hedges, had but little influence.

Abraham Kaplan introduced the idea of 'the law of the instrument'. He formulated it thus: 'Give a small boy a hammer and he will find that everything he encounters needs pounding'.[13] Criterion and verification can be useful tools. Wittgenstein, I believe, believed it when he said that there is no one method in philosophy, but methods, in the plural (PI, 133). Each, I would add, has a limited scope and a limited use. But Wittgenstein was often understood in the light of the law of the hammer: every problem is a philosophical nail only to be pounded by the hammer. Wittgenstein's notion of criterion was taken as such a hammer.

Good bureaucrats work with criteria. Criteria serve as a social institution with limited use such as enrollments in universities, entitlements for subsidies, and certified drugs. The idea that every concept has criteria for settling its applicability is an analogical overextension of the bureaucratic use. It may serve on occasion as a suggestive way to look at language, but believing that almost every use of a word has criteria (with the exception of avowals and a few other cases) strikes me as a case of using analogy

[13] Kaplan, A., *Conduct of Inquiry* (San Francisco: Chandler, 1964), 28.

without recognizing that it is nothing but analogy. It is exactly the danger Wittgenstein constantly warns us against.

The bureaucratic picture of language is not the only picture of language that Wittgenstein helped entrench. He also formed a schoolmasterly picture of language. It is a picture that suggests that in acquiring language we are guided by special kinds of explanations, which he calls 'meaning explanations'. Indeed, he thinks that by scanning such explanations we can glean criteria for the use of words and reveal the grammatical rules that guide their use. This picture, I believe, is fine for chess and misleading for language.

There is a story about the great chess master Raul Capablanca. According to the story, no one ever taught Raul the rules of the game. He figured them out by observing others playing the game. The child Raul could not glean from what he observed a distinction between bad moves in chess and illegitimate moves. It is quite possible that by watching adults playing, he never observed an illegitimate move in his life.

This way of learning the game, if it ever happened, is very unusual. But it is the commonest way in which humans acquire language. The only exception perhaps is the way middle-class kids in the West acquire their language by explicit explanations from ambitious and anxious parents and schoolmasters. These kids are taught language in a way not unlike the way most of us were taught chess.

What I just described holds true, not only for language acquisition, but also for language criticism. Throughout life we are rebuked for what we say in such an undifferentiated manner that the belief that we can systematically sort out a grammatical ground for criticism—in Wittgenstein's eccentric sense of grammatical—strikes me as odd. Yet, I find it very odd to be told that it is a grammatical mistake to say 'The dog believes that his master will return in a week', whereas it is grammatically correct and factually false to say of a one-year-old baby that she believes that her mother will return in a week. But then, I also find it odd to be told that ascribing the belief to the one-year-old baby is ruled out by grammar: facts and grammar are inextricable.

There are of course activities for which we have well-defined rules of representation, such as rules for drawing the equator and other auxiliary lines on a globe. To try to find an auxiliary line on the ground is to conflate the model with the modeled. To take a broom in order to mop the equator, as in Erich Kaestner's *Thirty-Fifth of May*, is to misunderstand what the equator is due to a conflation of the rules of representation and reality. But to expand the analogy of rules of representation to language as a whole, expecting to be able to sort out among the uses of language what is truly descriptive and what is part of the representation, is, I believe, to expand the analogy beyond belief.

'Criteria', 'rules', 'games', and 'grammar', in Wittgenstein's extended use, are analogies; when not recognized as such they are misleading pictures. We are left with dogmas and not with methods of doing philosophy. Wittgenstein was rather tentative about his methods. He stressed, for example, the constant fluctuations between criteria and symptoms. This means that there is no workable second-order criterion to decide when we face a criterion and when we face a symptom.

Wittgenstein had an influence on methods that are used in analytic philosophy. Not all of it has been good influence, because some of the methods adopted from Wittgenstein are more in the service of dogmatism than in the service of illumination. On my understanding of the 'true' Wittgenstein, who is very tentative in his attitude to method, this should not have happened, but it did.

6. Connective Analysis

Peter Hacker writes, 'Under the influence of Wittgenstein in Cambridge (and later of his posthumous publications), analytic philosophy became more syncretic, and entered yet another phase. Reductive and constructive analyses were repudiated. Connective analysis, exemplified in various forms in Oxford after the Second World War, emerged, and with it, therapeutic analysis' (p. 4). Hacker means by analytic philosophy 'mainstream Anglophone, and for a while Viennese, philosophy in this century' (p. 4).

I shall characterize analytic philosopher recursively: an analytic philosopher is a disciple of an analytic philosopher. The recursion goes back to the first analytic philosophers who are postulated as such: Frege, Russell, and Moore. (Bernard Bolzano on my account should be viewed as a proto-analytic philosopher, for he had no immediate followers.) Analytic philosophy is what analytic philosophers produce qua philosophers.

Hacker accepts Strawson's distinction between reductive analysis (decomposing concepts to their elementary constituents) and connective analysis (elucidating concepts by their relations to other concepts, which are not more elementary). Carnap's *Aufbau* is a glaring example of reductive analysis. Concepts are constructed out of total moments of basic experience, the *Elementarerlebnisse*. Defining knowledge as justified true belief is an example of connective analysis: 'justification', 'belief', and 'truth' are not more elementary than 'knowledge'.

Strawson's notion of connective analysis does not do justice to an important distinction between two types of connective analysis: formal and informal. Wittgenstein had no influence on formal connective analysis; the question is whether he had an influence on informal connective analysis.

Tarski's analysis of truth is a good example of formal connective analysis. Truth, on Tarski's account, is not analyzed in terms that are better understood or have better status in the explicatory order of things. Reference and satisfaction are no better than truth. What Tarski succeeded in doing was giving a rich structure to the notion of truth through its connective relations to notions such as satisfaction. Carnap's notion of explication is close to the idea of formal connective analysis. When he mentions some forerunners of his notion of explication he mentions Husserl, Langford (explicating Moore), and Kant; but he does not mention Wittgenstein.

It is clear that Wittgenstein had no influence on the method of formal connective analysis. It is less clear but nevertheless true that he had little influence on informal connective analysis at Oxford. Here is what Strawson had to say about it at the end of his chapter 'Reduction or Connection' in his *Analysis and Metaphysics*.

In the course of my first chapter I contrasted the positive conception of analysis, illustrated by the analogy of grammar, with the negative or anti-theoretical conception, favoured by the extreme adherents—if there are any—of the analogy of therapy. Evidently, the latter can be expected to look with a fairly cold eye on the project of bringing to the light underlying conceptual structure. For the message is: don't look for anything underlying. Look at concepts which puzzle you actually in use in various human concerns ('forms of life' in Wittgenstein's phrase), which give them their whole significance. Get a clear view of *that*—admittedly not an easy thing to do—and then you will be free. Don't try for a general theory. That is the message.[14]

Strawson does not regard Wittgenstein as being engaged in connective analysis. Instead, he thinks that Wittgenstein is suggesting a competing idea: therapeutic treatment. He doubts that anyone seriously subscribed to the therapeutic view of philosophy. Well, Wisdom (at Cambridge) and Waismann (for a while at Oxford) took an oath of loyalty to Wittgenstein's therapeutic analogy. But I think that only Gordon Baker recognized the full sway of the therapeutic method. For one thing, the therapeutic method is directed at a particular individual who suffers from philosophical anxiety. A philosophical problem is not an outcome of an impersonal use of common language. It is the outcome of the use and the misuse of a particular idiolect, the idiolect of the philosophical patient.

Whatever we think of Baker's understanding of the therapeutic method as an account of the true Wittgenstein, one thing is clear: this method was not shared by anyone except Baker, and even he adopted it only toward the end of his life.

7. Wittgenstein on Influence

In 1929 Wittgenstein congratulates himself: 'It's a good thing I don't allow myself to be influenced!' (CV, 1e). In 1931 he laments: 'I don't believe I have ever *invented* a line of thinking, I have always taken one over from someone else. I have simply straightaway seized on it with enthusiasm for my work of clarification. That is how Boltzmann, Herz, Schopenhauer, Frege, Russell, Kraus, Loos, Weininger, Spengler, Sraffa have influenced me. Can one take the case of Breuer and Freud as an example of Jewish reproductivness?—What I invent are new *similes*' (CV, 19e). Properly understood, there is no real contradiction between the self-congratulation and the lamentation. Wittgenstein is not influenced in his project of philosophical clarification. Clarification is clarification of old lines of thinking, and no new line of thinking is added by making

---

[14] Strawson, P., *Analysis and Metaphysics: An Introduction to Philosophy* (Oxford: Oxford University Press, 1992), 27.

old thoughts clear. Clarity may inspire new thoughts but it does not add new ones.

Wittgenstein upholds the nonsense about the parasitic nature of the Jewish mind. He imputes to himself the parasitic Jewish mind, a mind capable of understanding someone else's work better than that someone understands it himself. Yet the parasitic mind is incapable of producing anything original, not 'even the tiniest of flowers'. Instead of creating a flower it draws a flower 'that grows in another's mind and puts it in a comprehensive picture' (CV, 19e).

Wittgenstein makes the distinction between the productive mind and the reproductive mind, between creation and clarification, in a telling episode from his own life. At the time when he was working as an architect on his sister's house in Vienna, he took up sculpting and visited the studio of his friend the sculptor Michael Drobil. Once Wittgenstein criticized a work of Drobil, and, to make his point, he modeled the bust of a young girl. Referring to this incident he writes: 'At the time I modeled the head for Drobil too the stimulus was essentially a work of Drobil's and my contribution once again was really clarification. What I do think essential is carrying out the work of clarification with *courage*: otherwise it becomes just a clever game' (CV, 19e).

Even though he and Drobil were seemingly engaged in producing a sculpture, their intentions were very different: Wittgenstein's bust was a commentary on Drobil's work, a clarifying comment. One cannot detect the point of the work by merely looking at it. The point of Drobil was to create an object of original art. The point of Wittgenstein was to criticize Drobil's art. The distinction between creative work and clarificatory work lies in the intention of the artist and in the use of the work, and not in the object.

Wittgenstein's conception of philosophy as a 'Jewish' project of clarification (as in drawing a flower rather than creating a flower) is an expression of a picture—the picture of a parasite living off the creation of others. This wretched picture of the Jews as parasites was accompanied by the idea that Jews are only capable of artificial civilization but not of organic culture: Jews are cultural peddlers in the same way as they have the role of middlemen in economic life. It is tragically ironic that Wittgenstein, whose business was to free us from the grip of misleading pictures fostering prejudice, was himself in the grip of a most pernicious picture. What is wrong in this picture is not only what it tells us about Jews, but also what it tells us about the mind, namely, that there is a natural division of labor between creation and clarification.

The self-abasing nature of Wittgenstein's confession of his Jewish reproductive mind (CV, 19e) is misleading. It should be read in a passive-aggressive tone of voice: we 'Jews of the mind' are not creative (passive tone), but we understand what you creative thinkers are doing better than you yourselves do (aggressive tone). This double tone can be harmless, unless the passive one believes that she is entitled to tell the creators what they should create. My pronoun 'she' in the last sentence is not meant to be understood in the polite, politically correct use of the language. The use of 'she' here is substantial. The Jewish mind in Wittgenstein's thought is a female mind. It has the creativity of the soil, in contrast to the creativity of the seed (CV, 36e). This dreadful nonsense is a variation on Otto Weininger's contrast between the passive nature of the female and the creative, productive nature of the male. On this picture, the Jew is made out of feminine substance. Like a woman, the Jew can only be a matchmaker who finds the right connections among things, but never a masculine genius who can create things.

8. Bourgeois Philosophy and Radical Philosophy

In addition to the Jewish parasitic thinker, Wittgenstein constructed another type of thinker: the bourgeois thinker.

Ramsey was a bourgeois thinker. i.e., he thought with the aim of clearing up his affairs of some particular community. He did not reflect on the essence of the state—or at least he did not like doing so—but on how *this* state might reasonably be organized. The idea that this state might not be the only possible one in part disquieted him and in part bored him. He wanted to get down as quickly as possible to reflecting on the foundations—of *this* state. This was what he was good at and what really interested him; whereas real philosophical reflection disturbed him until he put its result (if it had one) to one side and declared it trivial. (CV, 17e)

The irony is that when Hacker spells out Wittgenstein's philosophical project, the most convincing account is the one based on Ramsey's philosophical maxim. Ramsey's idea is that when there is a dispute in philosophy that goes on forever, and the positions upheld in the dispute are 'extremely unsatisfactory to anyone with real curiosity about such a fundamental question . . . it is a heuristic maxim that the truth lies not in one of the two disputed views but in some third possibility which has not yet been thought of, which we can only discover by rejecting something assumed as obvious by both the disputants.'[15]

Hacker in turn writes, 'I do not know whether Wittgenstein ever read this remark, but his practice in philosophy conforms with striking fidelity to Ramsey's maxim' (p. 100). Hacker demonstrates Wittgenstein's fidelity to Ramsey's practice by the following example: in the dispute about the relation between language and reality, all sides to the dispute agreed that words represent reality. The dispute is about the nature of the connection between the two. Wittgenstein, according to Hacker, denies what the two sides to the dispute agree on, namely that '*in the relevant sense invoked*, words are not *connected* with the world at all'. Hacker sums it up by saying: 'Given this disposition to reject the shared presuppositions of the traditional debates on the central questions of philosophy, it is no wonder that Wittgenstein's philosophical stance on these central questions of philosophy has so often been misunderstood.'

I believe, with Hacker, that Wittgenstein indeed followed the radical maxim of the bourgeois Ramsey, but unlike Hacker, I do not believe that he followed it with fidelity: in denying a shared presupposition, he did not opt for a 'third possibility'. Wittgenstein regards a shared, uncontested presupposition underlying an unending dispute as a symptom that the disputants are in the grip of a picture. A strong indication that one is in the grip of a picture is one's feeling that the presupposition must be right, for 'how else can things be?'.

The denial of a shared presupposition is not meant to force us to adopt its negation, but rather to indicate that there is nothing compelling in the 'how else'. There are other possibilities. Wittgenstein does not necessarily side with those other possibilities, for the alternative possibilities do not necessarily suggest a better picture. But viewing alternatives might weaken the grip of a picture: what Wittgenstein denies is not so much the shared presupposition, but its necessity and its air of obviousness.

---

[15] Ramsey, F.P., *The Foundations of Metaphysics* (Paterson, NJ: Littlefield, Adams & Co., 1960), 115–16.

Had Wittgenstein clung to Ramsey's maxim, as Hacker claims he did, he would not have been so misunderstood. What makes the maxim in the hands of Wittgenstein so confusing is that Wittgenstein does not subscribe to any position in the dispute, not even to the one expressed by the denial of a shared presupposition.

9. Wittgenstein's Esotericism

Esotericism is based on the idea that certain knowledge and certain practices should be confined to the initiated. They are the only ones attuned to the message and capable of understanding its deep significance. Esotericism is based on a crucial divide between a deep and concealed meaning of the teaching and an overt and shallow understanding of it. What makes the deep meaning deep, in the life of those who can understand it, is its redemptive force for those who can understand it.

Moshe Halbertal, in his new book *Concealment and Revelation* on esotericism in the Jewish tradition, insightfully writes, 'We might say that what is common to all types of esotericists is the metaphor of the "key". Esotericists do not understand, interpret, and explain; rather, they open, decipher, liberate, or expose.'[16] In the aftermath of the fallout between Wittgenstein and two of his disciples, Ayer and Wisdom, Hacker mentions a telling remark by Wittgenstein: 'Some philosophers make much of the keys they have stolen (Ayer and Wisdom), but it does not matter: they cannot open any lock with them' (p. 306, footnote 24). Elsewhere Wittgenstein writes, 'Yes, a key can lie forever in the place where the locksmith left it, and never be used to open the lock the master forged for it' (CV, 54e). There is nothing new, then, in the rift between a paranoid master and his disciples, suspected of revealing esoteric teachings to the public.

On the face of it, Wittgenstein's late philosophy seems to be a negation of esotericism. Philosophy puts everything before us; it has no interest whatsoever in what is hidden: 'For what is hidden, for example, is of no interest for us' (PI, 126). But this is misleading: 'The aspects of things that are most important for us are hidden because of their simplicity and familiarity'

---

[16] Halbertal, M., *Concealment and Revelation*, trans. Jacki Feldman (Princeton: Princeton University Press, 2007), 2.

(PI, 129). The two elements of esotericism are present in Wittgenstein's account: the important and the hidden. But the twist is that the important is hidden not deep down but on the surface. We do not see the hidden, much as the fish does not see the water. This idea is not new. Shklovsky advocated an artistic method of estrangement, presenting the familiar in an unfamiliar way so as to let us notice the familiar and recognize its great significance.[17] Wittgenstein severed the relation between the deep and the hidden and also between the deep and the important. But he did not give up on the important as hidden.

In tractate *Hagiga* of the Mishna (the first written codification of the Jewish oral law, from the first and second centuries), there is an effort to regulate the study of esoteric knowledge. It proscribes that the highest esoteric teaching should be taught one on one. Esoteric knowledge is limited to a sage who alone can understand it, by his own light. The esoteric teacher does not teach something unknown to the student. Teaching is nothing but identifying an elective affinity between teacher and student; both have the same, or similar, thoughts. Compare this to Wittgenstein's *Tractatus*: 'Perhaps this book will be understood only by someone who has already had the thoughts that are expressed in it—or at least similar thoughts.—So it is not a textbook.—Its purpose would be achieved if it gave pleasure to one person who read and understood it' (TLP, p. 3). The joy of esoteric teaching is not in transmitting knowledge, but in recognizing others as sharing the same unusual thoughts and experiences.

An esoteric sect, like a war cabinet, is terrified of leaks. The fear of leaks is in many instances a primary reason for publishing oral esoteric knowledge in written form: it drives out of circulation 'bad versions' of the esoteric knowledge and practice. Thus Wittgenstein: 'Up to a short time ago I had really given up the idea of publishing my work in my lifetime; it used, indeed, to be revived from time to time: mainly because I was obliged to learn that my results (which I had communicated in lectures, typescripts, and discussion), variously misunderstood, more or less mangled or watered down, were in circulation' (Preface to PI, p. ix). But then of course there is also the fear that Wittgenstein expresses in his preparatory notes for the preface of the *Philosophical Investigations* that the book will fall into the wrong hands: 'It is not without reluctance that I deliver this book

---

[17] Shklovsky, V., *Theory of Prose*, trans. B. Sher (Elmwood Park, Ill: Dalkey Archive, 1990).

to the public. It will fall into hands which are not for the most part those in which I like to imagine it' (CV, 66e). The anxiety Wittgenstein indicates is not the anxiety of being influential but the anxiety of having the wrong sort of influence, such as the influence of watered-down versions of his thoughts.

Wittgenstein was a meddler in the lives of his friends and disciples, telling them what they should do and learn, sometimes with tragic consequences. But Wittgenstein's principled position, in his esoteric and therapeutic teaching, was against the idea of having influence on philosophy. The philosopher is a Socratic midwife: he can help to deliver what is already there. Helping is not influencing.

A teacher may get good, even astounding, results from his pupils while he is teaching them and yet not be a good teacher; because it may be that, while his pupils are directly under his influence, he raises them to a height which is not natural to them, without fostering their capacities for work at this level, so that they immediately decline again as soon as the teacher leaves the classroom. Perhaps this is how it is with me: I have sometimes thought so. (When Mahler himself conducted his students in training sessions he obtained excellent performances; the orchestra seemed to deteriorate at once when he was not conducting it himself.) (CV, 38e)

Was Wittgenstein a Picasso or a Mahler? For me this is still an open question.

Wittgenstein and Frege's *Logical Investigations*

WOLFGANG KÜNNE

Jeder von uns, meine ich, hat vom Andern empfangen im geistigen Verkehr. (Each of us, I believe, has drawn from the other in intellectual exchange.)

Gottlob Frege, letter to Ludwig Wittgenstein, 9 April 1918

1. Introduction: Biographical Facts and Conjectures

During the three years preceding the First World War, Wittgenstein paid several visits to Frege. They met in Jena, where Frege worked as a decidedly unpopular *ordentlicher Honorarprofessor* of mathematics, and in Brunshaupten, a small town on the Baltic Sea coast, where Frege used to spend his holidays.[1] It is remarkable that Wittgenstein sought Frege's acquaintance, for at that time Frege was still little known, and the few who knew him tended to regard him, to use Husserl's shamefully ungrateful turn of phrase, as 'an oddball, shrewd, but not fruitful either as a mathematician or as a philosopher'.[2] Who or what had made Wittgenstein aware of Frege's intellectual stature? Nobody knows for sure. Maybe he had read Appendix

---

[1] See Norbert Wiener's letter (summer 1914) in *The Autobiography of Bertrand Russell*, Vol. II (London: George Allen and Unwin, 1968), 41.

[2] '[E]in scharfsinniger, aber weder als Mathematiker noch als Philosoph fruchtbringender Sonderling': quoted in Gottlob Frege, *Wissenschaftlicher Briefwechsel* (henceforth WB) (Hamburg: Meiner, 1976), 92; trans. as *Philosophical and Mathematical Correspondence* (PMC) (Oxford: Blackwell, 1980), 61. In this essay I shall use the following abbreviations for the titles of Frege's writings: BS for *Begriffsschrift* (Halle: Nebert, 1879); GL for *Die Grundlagen der Arithmetik* (Breslau: Kober, 1884); GG for *Grundgesetze der Arithmetik* (Jena: Kober, Vol. I: 1893, Vol. II: 1903); KS for *Kleine Schriften* (Hildesheim: Olms, 1967), and CP for the translation: *Collected Papers on Mathematics, Logic, and Philosophy* (Oxford: Blackwell, 1984); LI for *Logical Investigations* (Oxford: Blackwell, 1977), including T for 'Thoughts' ('Der Gedanke'), N for 'Negation' ('Die Verneinung') and CT for 'Compound Thoughts' ('Gedankengefüge'); NS for *Nachgelassene Schriften* (Hamburg: Meiner, 1969), and PW for the translation: *Posthumous Writings* (Oxford: Blackwell, 1979). Page numbers cited are always those of the original publication. Responsibility for translations from Frege's and Wittgenstein's German is mine.

A of Russell's *The Principles of Mathematics* (1903). Perhaps the philosopher Samuel Alexander gave him a hint when he studied at Manchester in 1908.[3] And there is also the possibility of an earlier Austrian connection that seems not to have been noticed in the literature. Wittgenstein once mentioned Frege and Ludwig Boltzmann, among others, as thinkers who had an impact on him.[4] Now the *Festschrift* for the Viennese physicist, published in Leipzig in 1904, contains Frege's paper 'What is a Function?'[5] Wittgenstein owned Boltzmann's collection *Populäre Schriften,* which was published by the same press in 1905.[6] According to his own account, he had originally wanted to study physics with Boltzmann.[7] Perhaps he also took an interest in the *Festschrift,* and if he did he may have been struck by Frege's lucidity even before he enrolled at the Technische Hochschule in Berlin in 1907. He certainly knew Frege's contribution to the Boltzmann *Festschrift,*[8] but of course that may have been due to the fact that Frege had given him an offprint.

Wittgenstein visited Frege for the first time in 1911, probably during the summer.[9] Thirty-five years later he told Geach of this visit, and here is what Geach remembers of this report:[10]

I wrote to Frege, putting forward some objections to his theories, and waited anxiously for a reply. To my great pleasure, Frege wrote and asked me to come and see him. [...] I was shown into Frege's study. Frege was a small, neat man with a pointed beard, who bounced around the room as he talked. He absolutely wiped the floor with me, and I felt very depressed; but at the end he said, 'You must come again', so I cheered up. I had several discussions with him after that.

---

[3] Brian McGuinness, *Wittgenstein: A Life. Young Ludwig 1889–1921* (London: Duckworth, 1988), 75 f. The only witness for the Alexander story is R. L. Goodstein ('Wittgenstein's Philosophy of Mathematics', in A. Ambrose and M. Lazerowitz (eds.), *Ludwig Wittgenstein: Philosophy and Language* (London: Allen & Unwin, 1972), 271 ff.), and he is very unreliable. Wittgenstein told him in the early 1930s, Goodstein claims, that after their second meeting Frege never again talked philosophy with him. This contention is clearly falsified by Frege's letter to Jourdain of 28 Jan. 1914 (see below). When Wittgenstein invited Frege to Vienna during the war and when he planned to visit him in December 1919 (see below), he certainly wanted to talk philosophy with him. For further reservations as regards Goodstein's reliability see LPP, Geach's Preface, p. xiii; McGuinness, *Life,* 75 n. 5, 83 n. 21, 191.

[4] CV, 19 (1931).   [5] In KS (CP).

[6] See M. Nedo and M. Ranchetti (eds.), *Ludwig Wittgenstein: Sein Leben in Bildern und Texten* (Frankfurt am Main: Suhrkamp, 1983), no. 74.

[7] McGuinness, *Life,* 39, 54.   [8] Peter Geach, Preface to Frege, *LI* (henceforth Preface).

[9] McGuinness, *Life,* 73 f.

[10] Peter Geach, 'Frege', in E. Anscombe and P. Geach, *Three Philosophers* (Oxford: Blackwell, 1967), 130. Cf. Drury's reminiscences in Rush Rhees (ed.), *Ludwig Wittgenstein: Personal Recollections* (Oxford: Oxford University Press, 1981), 125, and the report by Wittgenstein's sister Hermine in McGuinness, *Life,* 73 f.

Frege would never talk about anything but logic and mathematics; if I started on some other subject, he would say something polite and then plunge back into logic and mathematics. He once showed me an obituary of a colleague, who, it was said, never used a word without knowing what it meant; he expressed astonishment that a man should be *praised* for this.

Frege, who was by forty-one years Wittgenstein's elder, soon became rather fond of the young man from Vienna: none of his extant letters show as much affection as the postcards and letters he sent to Wittgenstein.[11] On Frege's advice Wittgenstein went in autumn 1911 to Cambridge to study with the man who had shattered his advisor's logicist project. Late in 1912 Wittgenstein saw Frege again, for in December of that year he told Russell: 'I had a long discussion with Frege about our Theory of Symbolism, of which, I think, he roughly understood the general outline. He said he would think the matter over.'[12] Perhaps that is what Frege did when he wrote down '4 pages of notes . . . on the Wittgensteinian point of view as conveyed in discussion'.[13] In 1912 Russell's friend Philip Jourdain published a paper on Frege's logical and mathematical doctrines, together with Frege's notes on his 1910 manuscript.[14] From a letter he wrote to Frege on 29 March 1913 we know that Jourdain and Wittgenstein discussed Frege's *Grundgesetze* in Cambridge. On 22 October Wittgenstein asked Frege for permission to visit him again [22 October 1913]. In a letter he presented what Scholz calls 'important arguments against Frege's theory of truth, especially against the stipulation of *Bedeutung* for function[-expression]s' [28 November 1913].[15] As Russell had done long before, he rejected

---

[11] These letters were discovered in the store room of a real-estate broker in Vienna in 1988 (Reinhard Merkel reported on this in *Die Zeit*, 28 Apr. 1989, 'Dossier', 13–16), and they were edited by A. Janik and C. P. Berger as 'G. Frege, Briefe an Ludwig Wittgenstein', *Grazer philosophische Studien*, 33–4 (1989), 5–33. The letters are cited here by date. A translation by Burton Dreben and Juliet Floyd is to appear in Enzo De Pellegrin (ed.), *Successor and Friend: Georg Henrik von Wright and Ludwig Wittgenstein* (Berlin and New York, forthcoming). Floyd has supplemented the edition with a very useful 'Chronology of the Known Frege–Wittgenstein Correspondence' and a (not so useful) paper entitled 'The Frege–Wittgenstein Correspondence: Some Interpretive Themes': she takes the correspondence as 'an emblem or lesson for us about the difficulty of reaching agreement about what "clarity" in one's thought and expression requires' (§II) and is silent on all first-order philosophical issues.

[12] Ludwig Wittgenstein, *Briefwechsel mit B. Russell, G. E. Moore, J. M. Keynes, F. P. Ramsey, W. Eccles, P. Engelmann und L. von Ficker*, ed. B. F. McGuiness and G. H. von Wright (Frankfurt: 234).

[13] WB, 265.

[14] Reprinted in WB, 275–301. Jourdain first wrote to Frege in 1902, and they corresponded fairly regularly thereafter.

[15] Only the catalogue of Wittgenstein's letters to Frege, compiled by Heinrich Scholz, seems to have survived bombing during the Second World War. References to dates in *square brackets* are based on

Frege's conception of truth-values as objects and of assertoric sentences as names of those objects.[16] (There is a very brief passage in the *Tractatus* from which one can glean what the criticism in that letter may have consisted of: see Section 4.3 below.) Some time before Christmas 1913 Wittgenstein and Frege again had 'lengthy conversations'.[17] When Jourdain asked Frege in January 1914 for permission to publish a translation of parts of *Grundgesetze*, he added: 'Wittgenstein has kindly offered to revise the translation'.[18] Frege gladly gave his permission. The translation was eventually published in three instalments in 1915–17, and it was rather bad.[19] But Wittgenstein did not have much time to look at it (if he did so at all), for in August 1914 he volunteered for army service and was sent to Cracow.

Throughout the war Frege and Wittgenstein kept in contact. Twice Wittgenstein asked Frege to visit him in Vienna when he was on leave from the front,[20] but for all we know, after December 1913 they never met again. In the second year of the war, Wittgenstein apparently reported for the first time in his exchange with Frege on the *Abhandlung*, which was to become the *Tractatus* [25 August 1915]. In spring 1918 Frege was taken very much by surprise when Wittgenstein talked of his 'great debt of gratitude' to him and asked him for permission to send him a cheque. Frege was deeply moved and gratefully accepted the gift [9 April 1918]. It may have been this that allowed him to buy a house in Bad Kleinen in Mecklenburg, where he was to spend the last years of his life. In reply to a letter in which Wittgenstein had reported on progress with his *Abhandlung* (not in Scholz's catalogue), Frege wrote:

I am especially pleased about what you write of your work . . . If you could send me a copy you would make me very happy. I think that shortly a little piece of mine will appear [i.e. 'Der Gedanke', or T] which I can send you as a return gift. There is perhaps little new in it; but perhaps said in a new way and therefore more intelligible to some. I hope that I will have the pleasure of

Scholz's catalogue, as reproduced in WB, 265–8. Since functions do not *have* a *Bedeutung* (unless the post-BS Frege regards functors themselves as functions, which is extremely doubtful), I have taken the liberty of interfering with Scholz's annotation.

[16] Bertrand Russell to Frege, 12 Dec. 1902, 20 Feb. 1903, and Russell, *Principles of Mathematics* (2nd edn, London: Allen & Unwin, 1937; 1st edn 1903), 504. Cf. NL, 97, 98.

[17] Frege to Philip Jourdain, 28 Jan 1914, WB, 129 (PMC, 81). See also WB, 266, nos. XLV/4–5.

[18] Jourdain to Frege, 15 Jan. 1914, in WB, 126 (PMC, 78).

[19] Gottlob Frege, *The Fundamental Laws of Arithmetic* (Vol. 1, Preface, Introduction, §§1–7), trans. Philip Jourdain and Johann Stachelroth in *The Monist*, 25–7 (1915–17).

[20] See Frege to Wittgenstein, 21 Apr. 1916 and 30 June 1917.

learning about your views more thoroughly in conversation than is possible via the printed word. I still have fond memories of our walks in Jena and Brunshaupten. [12 September 1918]

The 'little piece' was the first instalment of a series of papers called *Logische Untersuchungen* through which Frege planned, as he put it, to 'bring in the harvest of [his] life'.[21] A month later Wittgenstein told Frege that he had just completed his *Abhandlung* [12 October 1918]. Frege replied:

I congratulate you on the conclusion of your work and admire you for having finished it during these times and under such conditions. May you see the work in print, and may I read it! I hope to be able to send you soon something I wrote [i.e. T]. You will probably not agree with it entirely; but then there will be even more of an edge to our talks about it if we will be given a chance to see each other healthy again, in friendlier and more peaceful times. I have already finished a draft of a second small treatise on negation [i.e. N] that I am thinking of publishing as soon as can be arranged. I conceive of it as a continuation of the first. I am grateful for your good memory; I will always think of you too in friendship. [15 October 1918]

Incidentally, as one can conclude from the date of this letter and as one can see on the cover of the original printing, 'Die Verneinung' did not come out in 1918, *pace* the best bibliographies and the secondary literature, but in the following year.[22] From the prisoner-of-war camp in Monte Cassino, where Wittgenstein is reported to have recited long passages from the Preface to *Grundgesetze der Arithmetik* by heart,[23] he arranged for Frege to be sent a typescript copy of the *Abhandlung*. For quite a while he was kept in suspense. He sent Frege three postcards, at least one of them with a 'request for judgement of his work' [23 February, 10 April and 9 June 1919]. After one of his fellow-prisoners read his work and gave voice to his enthusiasm, Wittgenstein replied, 'If only Frege would receive the *Tractatus* thus!'[24] And then it turned out that Frege had already got stuck at the very beginning of the book, lamenting over methodological and conceptual unclarities in the exposition of the ontology of states of affairs and facts

---

[21] Frege to Hugo Dingler, 17 Nov. 1918, WB, 45 (PMC, 30).
[22] *Beiträge zur Philosophie des Deutschen Idealismus*, 1/3–4 (1918–19), published in Erfurt, 1919.
[23] McGuinness, *Life*, 270.
[24] GT, 154 n. (Presumably, Wittgenstein said *Abhandlung*—he seems never to have used the Spinozistic title that was suggested by Moore.)

(28 June 1919).[25] (I shall return to this in Section 2.) When this letter had finally reached him in the Campo Concentramento, as he called it,[26] Wittgenstein complained to Russell: 'I also sent my MS to Frege. He wrote to me a week ago. And I gather that he doesn't understand a word of it at all' (19 August 1919).[27] In his reply to Frege [3 August 1919] he tried to explain, among other things, the purpose of his work. But Frege frowned at the image of the reader whom Wittgenstein took himself to be addressing:[28]

What you write to me about the purpose of the book strikes me as strange. According to you, that purpose can only be achieved if others have already thought the thoughts expressed in it ... Thereby the book becomes an artistic rather than a scientific achievement: what is said therein moves into the background of how it is said. I had supposed in my remarks that you wanted to communicate a new content. And then the greatest perspicuity would indeed be the greatest beauty. [16 September 1919]

(In his final remark Frege quotes a master of German prose, G. E. Lessing, whom Wittgenstein also admired: 'Die größte Deutlichkeit war mir immer die größte Schönheit', from the dialogue 'Das Testament Johannis' of 1777.[29])

Wittgenstein had returned to Vienna when, on the very day when Frege wrote this, he acknowledged receipt of an offprint of 'Der Gedanke' which

---

[25] The 'tedious business affairs' Frege alludes to in this letter are not an apologetic invention. In the unlikely event that you want to know more about this, see Lothar Kreiser, *Gottlob Frege: Leben, Werk, Zeit* (Hamburg: Meiner, 2001), 504–6, 510–12.

[26] To be on the safe side, his sister had sent copies of Frege's letter to Monte Cassino from two different places: Hermine Wittgenstein to Wittgenstein, 18 July 1919, in *Ludwig Wittgenstein: Familienbriefe*, ed. B. McGuinness *et al.* (Vienna: Hölder-Pichler-Tempsky, 1996), 61 ff.

[27] Wittgenstein, *Briefwechsel*, 252; *Ludwig Wittgenstein: Cambridge Letters*, ed. Brian McGuinness and G. H. von Wright (Oxford: Blackwell, 1995), 124. Cf. Wittgenstein to Hermine Wittgenstein, Aug. 1919, in *Familienbriefe*, 65.

[28] Cf. TLP, Preface, first sentence.

[29] In: *G. E. Lessing, Werke und Briefe*, Vol. VIII, ed. A. Schilson (Frankfurt am Main: Suhrkamp, 1989), 447–54, at 449. I took pride in having discovered this, until I read that Wolfgang Kienzler had already identified the quotation (see Floyd, 'Some Interpretive Themes', final footnote). Lessing's dialogue was available to Frege in any of the following editions of Lessing's works: Karl Lachmann (ed.), 1838–40, 1853–57 (co-ed. W. v. Maltzahn) and 1886–1924 (co-ed. F. Muncker), here in vol. 13, pp. 9–17. Frege's father was a theologian, so Lessing's works may have been on his shelves in Wismar. Stylistically, Lessing's brilliant polemics against the pastor Goeze at St Katharinen in Hamburg may well have set the example for Frege's no less brilliant polemics against a professor at the Johanneum in Hamburg ('Ueber die Zahlen des Herrn H. Schubert', 1899, KS (CP)). On the former see Wittgenstein to Russell, 1922, *Cambridge Letters*, 178–9; on the latter Frank Ramsey to Wittgenstein, 11 Nov. 1923, *Cambridge Letters*, 190–1.

had in the meantime appeared in *Beiträge zur Philosophie des Deutschen Idealismus*,[30] made 'critical remarks on it' and asked Frege for his help in getting his *Abhandlung* published in that journal [16 September 1919]. The editorial advice he thereupon received from Frege [30 September 1919] cannot have been to his liking. This time Wittgenstein complained to Russell in German: 'Er versteht kein Wort von meiner Arbeit und ich bin ganz erschöpft vor lauter Erklärungen' ('Frege doesn't understand a word of my work, and I am quite exhausted by explaining again and again') [6 October 1919].[31] To Wittgenstein's dismay it later became apparent that he might as well use the pronoun 'he' in this sentence to refer to Russell. Scholz's notes on the letters that Frege received from his Jena colleague Bruno Bauch [31 October 1919] and from Arthur Hoffmann, the editor of *Beiträge* [23 January 1920], show that Frege did approach the journal on Wittgenstein's behalf. But he seems to have communicated to the editor of *Beiträge* his own suggestions for making the *Tractatus* more digestible, for Wittgenstein reported to Ludwig von Ficker, the fourth publisher he approached: 'The editor [of *Beiträge*] told me he would publish my work provided I were prepared to mutilate it from beginning to end.'[32] When Wittgenstein met Russell in The Hague he wrote to Frege [third week of December 1919] 'announcing a visit on the way home to Austria. The visit, however, had to be cancelled because Wittgenstein's companion on the journey to Holland... had fallen seriously ill.'[33] Back in Vienna Wittgenstein told Frege in a letter about the meeting in The Hague and expressed the hope that Russell might see to it that the *Abhandlung* would be printed in England as a book [29 December 1919].

   In what apparently was his last letter to Frege [19 March 1920] (not listed in Scholz's catalogue), Wittgenstein returned to his criticism of 'Der Gedanke', hoping that Frege would not take offence at his frankness. From Frege's reply in his last (extant) letter to Wittgenstein we can see what this criticism of 'Der Gedanke' was concerned with, and from a remark towards the end we can conclude that it at least partially

---

[30] '*Beiträge*..., 1/2 (1918–19), published in 1918.
[31] Wittgenstein, *Briefwechsel*, 93; *Cambridge Letters*, 131.
[32] Wittgenstein to Ludwig von Ficker (Oct. 1919), *Briefwechsel*, 95.
[33] G. H. von Wright, *Wittgenstein* (Oxford: Blackwell, and Minneapolis: University of Minnesota Press, 1982), 88.

coincided with an objection Wittgenstein had put forward already [16 September 1919]:

Of course I do not take offence at your frankness. But I would like to know what the deep reasons for idealism [*tiefe Gründe des Idealismus*] are that I am supposed not to have grasped. If I understood you correctly you yourself do not take epistemological idealism to be true. Thereby you acknowledge, I think, that there simply are no deeper reasons for this idealism. The reasons for it can only be apparent, not logical ... Would you please go through my paper on 'Der Gedanke' until you hit upon the first sentence you disagree with and then write to me which sentence it is and why you disagree. This will presumably be the best way for me to find out what you have in mind. Perhaps I did not intend to combat idealism in the sense you mean it. I did not use the expression 'idealism' at all, I think. Take my sentences just as they stand, without imputing to me an intention that may have been foreign to me ...

I just notice from an earlier letter of yours that you acknowledge a deep and true core in idealism, an important emotion [*Gefühl*] that is satisfied in the wrong way, so presumably a legitimate need. What kind of need is this? I would be glad if you would help me to understand the results of your thinking by answering my questions. In abiding friendship ...   [3 April 1920]

For all we know, Wittgenstein never answered Frege's questions. So after nine years the exchange between the two men ended with mutual disappointment: Frege was disappointed with Wittgenstein as author, and Wittgenstein was disappointed with Frege as reader.

The *Tractatus* appeared first as an article, 'Logisch-philosophische Abhandlung', not in *Beiträge* but in *Annalen der Naturphilosophie* (which ceased publication immediately after publishing the work), and only after that as a book, published in London with German–English parallel text. The Preface contained a statement with an unmistakable evaluative nuance, and Frege knew this statement when he harshly criticized the first moves in the book: 'I am indebted to Frege's great works and to the writings of my friend Mr Bertrand Russell for much of the stimulation of my thought.' Even as a teacher at elementary schools in remote villages in Lower Austria, Wittgenstein liked to have a copy of *Grundgesetze* with him.[34] In 1923 Frank Ramsey visited him in one of these places; back in

---

[34] Wittgenstein to Paul Engelmann, 31 Oct. 1920, *Briefwechsel*, 118.

Cambridge he wrote to him, 'I do agree that Frege is wonderful'.[35] In the late twenties and the thirties Wittgenstein continued to reflect on the criticism of formal arithmetic in the second volume of *Grundgesetze*.[36] In his Cambridge lectures in 1939 he referred to Frege as 'a great thinker'.[37] When in 1949 he visited his former student Norman Malcolm in the USA he planned to read with him and his colleagues Frege's 'Über Sinn und Bedeutung'.[38] He still disliked 'Der Gedanke', and for the very same reason as in 1919. When his former students Max Black and Peter Geach were preparing the first fairly comprehensive collection of Frege's writings, *Translations from the Philosophical Writings of Gottlob Frege* (which appeared one year after Wittgenstein's death),[39] Wittgenstein gave advice 'on points of translation'[40] as well as on the selection. He advised them, Geach recalls,

to translate 'Die Verneinung' but not 'Der Gedanke': that, he considered, was an inferior work—it attacked idealism on its weak side, whereas a worthwhile criticism of idealism would attack it just where it was strongest. Wittgenstein told me that he made this point to Frege in correspondence [presumably two letters already mentioned above [16 September 1919, 19 March 1920]; see above]: Frege could not understand—for him, idealism was the enemy he had long fought, and of course you attack your enemy on his weak side. (Preface)

Two weeks before his death Wittgenstein observed, 'Frege's style of writing is sometimes *great*'.[41] When Geach met him for the last time, they were 'discussing "On Concept and Object"; he ... read for a while in silence, and then said, "How I envy Frege! I wish I could have written like that".'[42]

---

[35]   Ramsey to Wittgenstein, 11 Nov. 1923, *Cambridge Letters*, 190.
[36]   WVC, 103–5, 150–1; PG, 289–95; BB, 4.   [37]   LFM, 144.
[38]   Cf. Erich Reck, 'Wittgenstein's "Great Debt" to Frege', in Reck (ed.), *From Frege to Wittgenstein* (New York: Oxford University Press, 2002), 3–38, at 26 and n. 53.
[39]   In the Preface we are told that 'Professor Ryle and Lord Russell have been most helpful by lending works of Frege that were otherwise almost unobtainable.' Wittgenstein's help and support are not mentioned, perhaps because he could no longer be asked for his permission. A quarter of a century later, Geach made good the omission, in the Preface to his and Stoothoff's complete translation of LI. Russell owned a collection of Frege's writings, bound in hard cover, and 'Wittgenstein knew that Russell had preserved in this form some articles not easily found elsewhere. On Wittgenstein's advice', Geach recalls, 'I wrote to Russell, mentioning the source of my information. Russell generously sent the volume round to my house at once. Both men retained a reverence for Frege to the end of their lives' (LPP, Editor's Preface, p. xiv).
[40]   LPP, Editor's Preface, pp. xiii–xiv.   [41]   VB, 87 (1951).   [42]   LPP, Editor's Preface, p. xiv.

2. The Philosophical Content of the Frege–Wittgenstein Correspondence

Does it *have* any such content? When Heinrich Scholz asked Wittgenstein in 1936 whether he possessed any letters from Frege and, if so, whether he would be prepared to leave them to the Frege Archive at Münster University, Wittgenstein refused to cooperate: 'I do possess a few cards & letters of Frege's, but their contents are purely personal and not philosophical.'[43] This is true of all postcards, but it is definitely not true of Frege's last four letters.[44]

Did Frege really 'not understand a word' of the *Tractatus*? I cannot believe this, because even I understand one or two sentences in this enigmatic book. In the *correspondence* Frege engaged with only the first page of the book,[45] and he raised at least one serious objection:

The part [*Teil*] of a part is part of the whole. If a thing is a constituent [*Bestandteil*] of a fact [*Tatsache*] and every fact is part of the world, then the thing is also part of the world... [If] Vesuvius is a constituent of a state of affairs [*Sachverhalt*] [t]hen it seems that constituents of Vesuvius must also be constituents of that fact. Hence the fact will also consist of solidified lava. That does not seem right to me. [28 June 1919]

Obviously 'that' cannot seem right to the author of 'Der Gedanke', since he identifies facts with true thoughts, takes thoughts to consist of nothing but senses, and regards senses as immaterial. In Frege's discussion with Russell in 1904, the snowfields of Mont Blanc had prefigured the lava of Vesuvius.[46] In 1914 the argument moved on to Italian soil: in a draft of a letter to Jourdain that was written shortly after 'lengthy conversations' with Wittgenstein, Frege rejects as absurd the idea that pieces of solidified lava of Etna might be parts of a thought about that mountain.[47] To be sure, Frege's objection in our excerpt does not pay heed to the distinction between facts (*Tatsachen*) and states of affairs (*Sachverhalte*) in the *Tractatus*, but since

---

[43] WB, 265.

[44] Floyd, 'Some Interpretive Themes', §I speculates extensively about Wittgenstein's motives.

[45] Section 3 below explains why I use italics in this sentence.

[46] Frege to Russell, 13 Nov. 1904; Russell to Frege, 12 Dec. 1904.

[47] Frege to Jourdain, Jan. 1914, WB, 127 (PMC, 79).

Wittgenstein's account of this distinction is notoriously unstable,[48] this is only a venial sin, and in any case, it does not invalidate the objection. If objects are constituents (*Bestandteile*) of states of affairs and (obtaining) states of affairs are in turn constituents of facts, as we are told in the *Tractatus*,[49] then objects are bound to be constituents of facts, and every constituent of an object has to be a constituent of every fact about that object. Since Wittgenstein gives us no reason to believe that being a *Bestandteil* (constituent) does not entail being a *Teil* (part), Frege's argument from the transitivity of the relation designated by the rude four-letter word 'part' goes through.[50] And, as Frege noticed, it makes for a problem for *Tractatus*, 1.1, 'The world is the totality of facts, not of things': if facts are composed of things then the world cannot consist of facts without consisting of things.

Wittgenstein's belated reply to this (dated June 1931) is not an attempt at refining the notion of being a constituent or at explaining the difference between facts and states of affairs that was intended in the *Tractatus,* but an endorsement of Frege's objection:

To say that a red circle is composed of redness and circularity, or is a complex with these constituents [*Bestandteile*], is a misuse of these words and is misleading. (Frege knew this and told me.) In the same way it is misleading to say that the fact that this circle is red (that I am tired) is a complex whose constituents are this circle and redness (myself and tiredness). . . . The part [*Teil*] is smaller than the whole: applied to fact and constituent, that would yield an absurdity.   (PG, 200–1 = PR, 302–3; cf. BB, 31)

'Wittgenstein told me', Geach recalls, 'how he had reacted to Frege's criticism of the Russellian doctrine of facts—a doctrine still presupposed in the *Tractatus* . . . Frege asked Wittgenstein if a fact was *bigger* than what it was a fact about. Wittgenstein told me this eventually led him to regard the Russellian view as radically confused, though at the time he thought the criticism silly.'[51]

Let us now look into the other side of the correspondence. Wittgenstein's early criticism of 'Der Gedanke', repeated to Geach in the last months of

---

[48] Cf. Hans-Johann Glock, *A Wittgenstein Dictionary* (Oxford: Blackwell, 1996), 116–17.
[49] TLP, 2, 2.01, 4.2211.
[50] 'the rude . . .' is Geach's phrase. From the quotation it is clear that Frege takes *Bestandteil* and *Teil* to be stylistic variants of each other. Unlike 'constituent' the German word does not sound technical at all.
[51] Geach, Preface. Cf. McGuinness, *Life*, 164.

his life, is concerned only with the epistemological part of Frege's essay, which takes up a fifth of the text (T, 69–74). Frege's aside is correct: he did not use the word 'idealism' in his essay, although he did not hesitate to employ it in a similar context both in the Preface to *Grundgesetze* and in his 'Logic' manuscript of 1897, which is a precursor of the essay.[52] But in the passage that Wittgenstein must have in mind Frege is rather attacking the *sceptical* hypothesis that for all I know there may be nothing but my own ideas (*Vorstellungen*), or, in more high-flown language, he tries to undermine the assumption that subjective idealism (there is no external world) and solipsism (there are no other minds) are epistemically possible. Frege does not claim to have shown that this sceptical hypothesis is false but rather, (1), that it is very improbable and, (2), that we are prudentially justified in taking a minimal epistemic risk. His arguments for (1) are untypically weak, but apparently Wittgenstein did not directly confront them in his letters to Frege.[53] As to the allegedly deep reasons *for* idealism, Wittgenstein presumably took himself to have shown in the *Tractatus* passage on solipsism (5.6–5.641) what they are. Unfortunately these reasons are only 'opaquely sketched',[54] so I hope to be forgiven for not giving them here.

In his second letter on the *Tractatus* Frege is pleased to have found a passage in Wittgenstein's first response to his criticisms [3 August 1919] that he takes to be in complete harmony with his own views:

It is the sentence: 'The sense [*Sinn*] of those two sentences is one and the same, but not the ideas [*Vorstellungen*] which I associated [*verbinden*] with them when I wrote them.' Here I fully agree with your distinguishing the sentence from its sense, leaving open the possibility that two sentences have the same sense and yet[55] differ as regards the ideas that are associated with them. In the aforementioned essay [i.e. T] I have treated the matter on p. 63[–p. 64]. You underline the word 'I'. In this too I see a sign of agreement. The real sense of the sentence is the same for everyone; however, the ideas someone associates with the sentences belong

[52] NS, 141, 155–6 (PW, 130, 143–4). Cf. NS, 250 (PW, 232), in a manuscript of 1914.

[53] Peter Hacker did so on Wittgenstein's behalf: see his 'Frege and the Private Language Argument', *Idealistic Studies*, 2 (1972), 265–87, at 281–4.

[54] Peter Hacker, 'Frege and the Early Wittgenstein', in his *Wittgenstein: Connections and Controversies* (Oxford: Clarendon Press, 2001), 191–218, at 193. His attempt at illuminating TLP, 5.6 ff. is still second to none: see his *Insight and Illusion* (Oxford: Clarendon Press, 1972), Ch. 3 (Ch. 4 in the 1986 edn).

[55] I suggest replacing the editors' *und dann noch* with *und dennoch*, which makes far better sense.

to him alone; he is their bearer. No one can have the ideas of someone else. [16 September 1919][56]

Let us put aside for a while Frege's implicit assumption that by 'sense' his Viennese friend means Jena sense. Whatever Wittgenstein may have meant in his lost letter, Frege's comment is rather strange. In 'Der Gedanke' (T, 67–8) and at many other places he does indeed uphold the thesis expressed in the final sentence of the excerpt above: an idea that x has can be identical with an idea that y has only if x is identical with y. But on the page to which he wants to draw Wittgenstein's attention he is talking about utterances that express the same thought though 'illuminating' or 'colouring' it in different ways. Here Frege fortunately (*gottlob*) does not commit himself to the claim that the colouration lent to a thought by an utterance is an idea the speaker has while making the utterance. The difference in content between utterances of 'Some people own a dog' and 'Some people own a cat' is as objective as that between utterances of 'Some people own a dog' and 'Some people own a cat'.

In the second part of 'Der Gedanke' the term 'idea' is used as a term of art stipulated to cover all sorts of mental events, acts, states and capacities. In particular, it is meant to cover visual impressions and pains. Thus, when Frege says, 'Nobody else has my pain' ('Kein Anderer hat meinen Schmerz') (T, 68), he regards this as a special case of ideas being owner-individuated: 'Any idea somebody else has is, just as such, different from mine' (T, 67). Now the late Wittgenstein paid special attention to the special case. In his *Philosophische Untersuchungen* he begins his attack on Frege's individuation claim with a near-quote from 'Der Gedanke': ' "Another person cannot have my pains." —Which pains are *mine*? What serves here as a criterion of identity? . . .' (' "Der Andre kann nicht meine Schmerzen haben." —Welches sind meine Schmerzen? Was gilt hier als Kriterium der Identität? . . .') (PI, 253).

I do not think that Wittgenstein's reflections in this section and the next really succeed in undermining Frege's contention (and that of Strawson and many other philosophers) that pains are individual accidents of those who

---

[56] Here the Dreben–Floyd translation is deficient: *Sinn* is first rendered as 'sense' and then as 'meaning', *Vorstellungen* is translated by 'images', which does not fit the use of the word in T at all, and *sich unterscheiden* ('differ') is confused with *unterschieden werden* ('be distinguished').

suffer them. To be sure, we say such things as 'Ann and I have the same pain, a throbbing headache in the temples', but if this were a true identity statement to the effect that Ann's pain is my pain (rather than to the effect that the kind of pain Ann has is the kind of pain I have), then her pain could not have begun before mine, it could not get worse without mine getting worse, and an executioner could remove her headache by beheading me.[57] Which throbbing headache is *mine*? Well, the one that prevents me from falling asleep, the one I can reasonably expect to be removed by my taking an aspirin, etc. There are various criteria for deciding whether my pain is the same *kind* of pain she has. In declaring pains to be owner-individuated one does not make the bizarre claim that the person who suffers is a property of the pain she has: surely, I do not declare the Earth to be a property of its axis (or Socrates to be a property of his death) by saying that the axis of the Earth (the death of Socrates) is, just as such, different from that of any other heavenly body (from that of any other human being). Wittgenstein might have done better to compare pain talk with talk about axes and deaths, rather than with talk about chairs.[58]

PI, 253–4 is not the only place where the late Wittgenstein engages with the philosophy of mind in 'Der Gedanke'. Suppose that pains are, *pace* the late Wittgenstein, owner-individuated. This does not imply that Ann's pain and mine cannot be compared. The axis of the Earth can very well be compared with the axis of the Moon, notwithstanding their being owner-individuated. But Frege notoriously went on to say, using sense-impressions as paradigmatic 'ideas', that 'it is impossible to compare my sense-impression with someone else's' (T, 67).[59] He notices that this incomparability claim has a semantic consequence: 'when the word "red" is not used to specify a property of things but to characterize sense-impressions

---

[57] Cf. T, 73. In BB, 54–5 Wittgenstein declares that 'it would be no argument to say [this]', which is not much of a counterargument.

[58] If you find this criticism less than convincing, you have Hacker on your side: see his *Wittgenstein: Meaning and Mind* (Oxford: Blackwell, 1993), Pt. I, 19–25 and Pt. II, 46–52.

[59] As early as GL, §26; NS, 4 (PW, 3 f.); 'Über Sinn und Bedeutung' (1892), 30, KS (CP); GG, Preface, p. xviii; 'Review of E. Husserl, *Philosophie der Arithmetik*' (1894), KS (CP), 317 (according to Geach, Preface, Wittgenstein knew this review). The incomparability claim was also embraced in the Vienna Circle: see Moritz Schlick, 'Leben, Erkennen, Metaphysik' (1926), in *Gesammelte Aufsätze* (Vienna: Gerold & Co., 1938), 2–17, at 2–3, 5, and Rudolf Carnap, *Der logische Aufbau der Welt* (Vienna: Artur Wolf Verlag 1928), §66.

belonging to my consciousness, it is only applicable within the realm of my consciousness' (T, 67, 68). A few pages later in PI, Wittgenstein alludes to this very passage, I take it, when he asks: 'Now what about the word "red"? Am I to say that it designates "something that stands vis-à-vis us all", . . . and in addition, for each person, something known only to him? . . .' ('Wie ist es nun mit dem Worte "rot"—soll ich sagen, dies bezeichne etwas "uns allen Gegenüberstehendes", . . . und für Jeden, außerdem, etwas nur ihm Bekanntes? . . .') (PI, 273).

Actually, there is a further respect in which this is a quasi-quotation. The locution in quotation marks can be found almost *verbatim* not only on p. xviii of the Preface of *Grundgesetze* which Wittgenstein knew so well,[60] but also in 'Der Gedanke' (p. 66) and 'Die Verneinung' (p. 147).[61] In Frege's metaphorical use it applies to everything that is not subjective, not a mental event, act, state or ability. (The locution is not a play on the German word *Gegenstand* ('object'), as has been suggested,[62] for a sense-impression, a pain, etc. is something that can be referred to by a singular term, hence by Frege's lights it *is* a *Gegenstand*. Let us leave the allusion where it belongs: with Heidegger and his ilk.) Now if Frege were right in assuming a subjective–objective split in the use of colour-words, there would be at most one person who could know whether the conditions for applying the predicate 'is red', or rather (since sense-impressions aren't coloured) the predicate 'is an impression as of a red object', to one of my visual impressions are satisfied. So a part of my vocabulary would in principle be comprehensible only to me. If Wittgenstein succeeded in showing that there cannot be such a vocabulary, then he refuted the incomparability claim via refuting its semantic consequence. Actually, Frege himself comes close to refuting it in the passage about the two doctors who discuss the question of what might have caused the patient's pain (T, 73). In any case, Geach seems to understate the case that can be made here when he writes, 'In spite of Wittgenstein's unfavourable view of "Der Gedanke", his own later thought may have been influenced by it' (Preface).

[60] This reference was registered in Hacker, 'Frege and the Private Language Argument', 277 and *Meaning and Mind*, Pt. II, 84.

[61] Also in NS, 138, 145, 160, 214 (PW, 127, 133, 148, 198).

[62] Montgomery Furth in his translation of parts of GG (*The Basic Laws of Arithmetic* (Berkeley and Los Angeles: University of California Press, 1964)); Hacker, *Meaning and Mind*, Pt. II, 84.

3. Frege on the Tractarian Philosophy of Logic

The discussions with Wittgenstein that Frege had enjoyed so much had mostly concerned topics in the philosophy of logic. That makes it very unlikely, I think, that after his vain attempt at fathoming the ontological pronouncements at the beginning of the *Tractatus* he never bothered to look at the central sections, in which Wittgenstein presents his philosophy of logic. We do not know why Frege's third Logical Investigation, the essay 'Gedankengefüge' (Compounds of Thoughts') that was to be his last publication, appeared only four years after the second.[63] Maybe he waited for the publication of the *Tractatus* as a book, which Wittgenstein had announced to him in a letter [29 December 1919] (see Section 1). Be that as it may, I shall try to show in this section that Frege's essay engages with the questions that are most likely to have come up in his discussions with Wittgenstein and that reappeared in the *Tractatus*.

Geach reports: 'Wittgenstein never mentioned "Gedankengefüge" to me, and very likely never knew of its existence' (Preface). I take his word for it: after all, they seem to have talked a lot about Frege, and I know of no trace of a reading of that essay in Wittgenstein's œuvre. So in this section I shall look only for Frege's reactions in 'Gedankengefüge' to some part or other of the Tractarian philosophy of logic.

3.1. On Understanding New Sentences

In autumn 1913 Wittgenstein said in his *Notes on Logic*: 'We must be able to understand propositions which we have never heard before' (NL, 98), and this observation was to recur in the *Tractatus*.[64] In winter 1913 he had 'lengthy conversations' with Frege. In January 1914 Frege composed the draft of a letter to Jourdain in which he mentioned those conversations and said:[65] 'Our ability to understand sentences we have never heard obviously depends upon our building up the sense of the sentence from parts that correspond to the words.' This can be described as an attempt to explain the Wittgensteinian datum by means of the *Grundgesetze* principle of sense-compositionality (GG I, §32). In summer 1914 Frege repeated this move in

---

[63] Beiträge..., 3/1 (1923–6), published in 1923. Since Frege regards every thought as compound, that is, according to my dictionary, as something made up of two or more combined parts, 'Compounds of Thoughts' would have been not only a more literal but also a more appropriate translation of the title.

[64] TLP, 4.02, 4.026, 4.027, 4.03.   [65] WB, 127 (PMC, 79).

the manuscript for his lecture 'Logic in Mathematics',[66] and he did so once again in the introduction of 'Gedankengefüge', which is the most often quoted passage of that essay.

3.2. On Negation

According to 'Der Gedanke' and 'Gedankengefüge' the following sentences express one and the same thought:[67]

(a) Socrates is wise.
(b) It is true that Socrates is wise.
(c) It is not the case that Socrates is not wise.
(d) Socrates is wise, and Socrates is wise.
(e) Socrates is wise, or Socrates is wise.

The truth prologue in (b) does have a sense, but this sense is said to have a truly remarkable property:[68] 'The word "true" has a sense that contributes nothing to the sense of the whole sentence in which it occurs as a predicate.' '(Das Wort "wahr" hat einen Sinn, der zum Sinne des ganzen Satzes, in dem es als Prädikat vorkommt, nichts beiträgt.)' The formulation is a bit careless: firstly, because the word 'true' isn't a predicate but a general term, and secondly, because Frege's propositional redundancy claim can at best hold of the unary connective 'It is true that'. Frege had upheld this claim as early as 1892, and Wittgenstein endorsed it (or a close relative of it) in NB [6 October 1914].[69]

As to the pair (a/c), Frege apparently changed his mind between the second and the third Logical Investigations.[70] In 'Die Verneinung' he refers to the thought that p and the thought that not-not p as 'two thoughts', and he says that in the latter thought the former is 'wrapped in double negation' (N, 156–7).[71] By 'double negation' he means the *sense* of 'It is not the case that . . . not . . .'. If somebody who is already wearing a coat now puts on another coat (Frege's simile) the performance doesn't look like a striptease.

---

[66] NS, 243 (PW, 225).

[67] For (a/b) see T 61–2 (as early as 1892 in 'Über Sinn und Bedeutung', 34; 1897 or later in NS, 153 (PW, 141)). For (a/c) see CT, 44; for (a/d) CT, 39 n., 49; and for (a/e) CT, 49.

[68] NS (manuscript of 1915), 272 (PW, 252).   [69] Cf. NM, 113; PG, 123 f.; PI, 136; RFM, 117.

[70] There is a similar change of mind as regards pairs instantiating '$p \to q$' and '$\sim q \to \sim p$': cf. N, 146 and CT, 48.

[71] What he had written about 'Christ is not immortal'/'Christ is mortal' in N, 150 suggested an identification of the thought that p and the thought that not-not p.

But the non-identity claim is not in accord with Frege's presupposition, in 'Die Verneinung' and elsewhere, that for each thought there is exactly one negation.[72] The predicate '...is the negation of...' designates, he maintains, 'a symmetrical relation' (*eine umkehrbare Beziehung*).[73] But the thought that p can only be *the* negation of the thought that not p if the former is identical with the thought that not-not p. It looks as though every thought would have infinitely many negations if the thought that not p were not identical with the thought that not not-not p, and so on for any odd number of repetitions. If they were different, how could one of them lay claim to being *the* negation of the thought that p? In 'Gedankengefüge' Frege makes the identification that is required for the uniqueness of the negation of a thought (CT, 44, 49). Wittgenstein had done the same in his *Notes on Logic* (1913).[74]

Frege's identifications as regards (a/b), (a/d) and (a/e) are also required for upholding that uniqueness. If the thought that it is true that not p, the thought that (not p *and* not p) and the thought that (not p *or* not p), as well as their iterations, were not the same as the thought that not p, there would still appear to be infinitely many negations of the thought that p in the offing, for if they were different, how could one justify singling out one of them as *the* negation of the thought that p? Wittgenstein makes essentially the same point on 20 October 1914 in one of his 'Notebooks':[75]

What negates in '$\sim p$' is not the '$\sim$' in front of the 'p', but is what is common to all the signs that have the same meaning as [*sind gleichbedeutend mit*] '$\sim p$'; so what is common in

$\sim p$

$\sim \sim \sim p$

$\sim p \vee \sim p$

$\sim p \mathbin{\&} \sim p$

etc. etc.

If every thought were to contain the sense of the negation operator twice, and hence n-times for each even number n, every thought would be

---

[72] N, 146, 153; CT, 44, 50. 'Every sentence has only one negative' (NB, 6 May 1915; PT, 5.3132; TLP, 5.513).

[73] NS, 161 (PW, 149), in a manuscript of 1897 or later. Cf. NB, 18 Apr. 1915.

[74] NL, 93, 100, 102; NB, 17 Nov. 1914 and 4 Dec. 1914; TLP, 5.43.

[75] In PT, 5.313 = TLP, 5.512 the message is rephrased so as to avoid ascription of *Bedeutung* to sentences.

infinitely fat, as it were. So presumably the thought that $\sim \sim p$ does not contain the sense of the negation operator at all: like the truth-prologue, the operator '$\sim \sim$' has a sense that contributes nothing to the thought expressed by the whole sentence of which it is a part.[76] If this is Frege's view then he can applaud Wittgenstein's remark: 'The occurrence of negation in a proposition [*Satz*] is not yet a feature of its sense ($\sim \sim p = p$)'.[77] As we shall see in Section 3.3, in assenting to this dictum Frege would not assert exactly what Wittgenstein wants to assert, but at this point this is not yet important. If one wants to apply the idea of self-effacing senses also to (d) and (e), one should say something like this: for any sentence *s*, the sense of the expression which consists of an 'and' ('or') followed by *s* annihilates itself when this expression is appended to *s*.

'That from a single fact *p* an infinity of *others*, not-not *p* etc., follow is hardly credible' (NL, 100; TLP, 5.43). Frege couldn't agree more: a fact is a true thought, and the thought that *p* is the same as the thought that not-not *p* (etc. *ad nauseam*).[78] It is quite another matter, he would presumably add, that from one *sentence* expressing that thought infinitely many other sentences are derivable. Wittgenstein, on the other hand, takes this to be a 'reason for thinking the old notation wrong' (NL, 93). (Did this lead Frege, in a draft of a letter [probably of 9 November 1913], to reprove Wittgenstein for 'attaching too much value to signs'?[79]) Apparently the early Wittgenstein's proposals for a perfect logical notation were to a large extent motivated by his reflections on pairs like (a/c). 'If... an affirmation can be generated by double negation, is negation in such a case—in some sense—contained in affirmation? Does "$\sim \sim p$" negate $\sim p$, or does it affirm *p*, or both?' (TLP, 5.44; cf. NL, 103; PT, 5.231.)

---

[76] No wonder Donald Davidson once nicknamed the redundancy theory of truth 'the double-negation theory of truth' (*Inquiries into Truth and Interpretation* (Oxford: Oxford University Press, 1984), 38). (Frege should not be classified as an adherent of such a theory of truth. See Section 4.3.)

[77] PT, 4.0922 = TLP, 4.0621. Within quotations I follow, with little enthusiasm, the standard practice of rendering *Satz* in NB, PT and TLP as 'proposition'.

[78] Wittgenstein seems to suggest that it is generally incredible that from a single fact an infinity of others follow. Is that correct? It is a fact that in 1880 Jena had 10,337 inhabitants (according to Werner Stelzner, *Gottlob Frege: Jena und die Geburt der modernen Logik* (Stadtroda: Verein zur Regionalförderung von Forschung, Innovation und Technologie für die Strukturentwicklung e.V, 1996), 32). Doesn't an infinity of other facts follow from this one: that in 1880 Jena had fewer than 10,338 inhabitants, etc.? There is only a one-way entailment, so one cannot plead for identification. To be sure, most of the facts in this series are not worth stating, but that is irrelevant.

[79] WB, 265.

His answer is: 'In regard to notation, it is important to note that not every feature of a symbol symbolizes . . . In "not-not-p", "not-p" does not occur; for "not-not-p" is the same as "p", and therefore, if "not-p" occurred in "not-not-p", it would occur in "p" ' (NL, 99). Transposed into a Fregean key, this is the contention that sometimes a significant part of a sentence does not contribute its sense to the thought expressed by the sentence. So far Frege agrees. In a more adequate logical notation, Wittgenstein maintains, a sentence and its double negation should be rendered by one and the same symbol: 'If $p = $ not-not p etc., this shows that the traditional method of symbolism is wrong, since it allows a plurality of symbols with the same sense' (NL, 102). In his reformed symbolism 'p', '$\sim \sim p$', '$\sim \sim \sim \sim p$', etc. are all rendered by '(TF) (p)', and '$\sim (p \,\&\, \sim q)$', '$p \to q$', '$\sim p \lor q$' and their logically equivalents are represented by '(TFTT) (p, q)'.

Long before he met Wittgenstein, Frege had toyed in a letter to Husserl with the idea that in a logically perfect language, we would need for each set of sentences that express the same thought only one sentence in normal form (*Normalsatz*). If one then goes on to claim that logically equivalent sentences express the same thought (a temptation to which Frege yielded in the same letter), then the *Normalsatz* for such a set of sentences could be formulated in Wittgenstein's reformed symbolism, provided the logical complexity of the sentences belonging to the set is wholly due to truth-functional connectives.[80] 'How should a notation be constructed which will make every tautology recognizable as a tautology *in one and the same way*?' This was 'the great question' that Wittgenstein posed in a letter he wrote to Russell in Norway in November or early December 1913, shortly before he visited Frege on his way back to Vienna.[81] His host could bring him close to the answer if he aired the *Normalsatz* conception in their 'long conversations'.

3.3. On Sense and Senselessness

In his *Notes on Logic* (1913) Wittgenstein made a remark that is repeated in the *Tractatus* and that goes very much against Frege's grain: 'We must be able to understand a proposition without knowing if it is true or false' (NL, 98).[82] Is this really *always* the case (under a non-idiosyncratic reading of

---

[80] Frege to Edmund Husserl, 30 Oct. 1906, WB, 102 (PMC, 67 f.).
[81] *Cambridge Letters*, 58.
[82] Cf. NM (Apr. 1914), 112; TLP, 4.024.

'[i.e. Behauptungs]*Satz*')? Consider 'A year is longer than a minute' and 'If the Earth moves then the Earth moves'. Whoever fully understands these sentences, Frege would say, cannot fail to realize that they express truths, so both have a sense. The machinery of the *Tractatus* does not apply to the first example, but Wittgenstein would declare the second example to be senseless: 'All tautologies say the same thing. (Namely nothing.)'[83] Or consider 'A year is shorter than a minute' and 'The Earth moves just in case it doesn't'. Whoever fully understands these sentences, Frege would say, *eo ipso* recognizes that they express falsehoods, so both have a sense. And again Wittgenstein would maintain that the second example lacks sense. Now as regards understanding, Frege and Wittgenstein cannot both be right. As regards sense, the disagreement is more apparent than real, for they do not mean the same thing by 'sense'. A sentence lacks Tractarian sense if it does not tell us (correctly or incorrectly) how things contingently stand. Wittgenstein thereby cuts the tie between 'understanding' and 'sense': the Fregean sense of an expression is what one grasps when one fully understands that expression, whereas its Tractarian sense is not, for surely we understand tautologies and contradictions despite their lack of Tractarian sense.

According to the *Tractatus* two sentences have the same sense if and only if they entail each other, and two sentences entail each other just in case their biconditional is a tautology.[84] If a consistent sentence S entails another sentence T, but not *vice versa*, then S has *more* Tractarian sense than T in that the truth of S would restrict the way things may stand more than the truth of T would do.[85] Thus (1) 'Cathérine loves Jules' has *more* sense than (2) 'Cathérine loves Jules or Jim'. From Frege's point of view, things are rather the other way round: the sense of (1) is a proper part of the sense of (2).

---

[83] NB, 10 June 1915; TLP, 5.43. Strictly speaking, by Tractarian lights (cf. TLP, 4.06 and 4.461) a string of signs is not even a *Satz* unless it provides us with (mis)information about how matters contingently stand, so my two examples are sentences only by courtesy. Most of the time Wittgenstein himself is not that strict (cf., for example, TLP, 4.46).

[84] Wittgenstein puts the first point by saying that propositions that entail each other are identical (TLP, 5.141), and his second point has the consequence that all tautologies entail each other, hence Sheffer's dictum: 'There is but one Tautology and Wittgenstein is its prophet' (Norman Malcolm, *Ludwig Wittgenstein: A Memoir* (Oxford: Oxford University Press, 1984), 86).

[85] For first traces of this conception of 'quantity of sense' see NB, 3 June 1915, 10 June 1915; then TLP, 5.122, 5.14; WVC, 85 (5 Jan. 1930); AWL (1934–5), 137.

By Wittgenstein's lights 'one could append "and" and some tautology to any proposition without altering its sense' (NB, 25 May 1915).[86] He compares that operation with adding zero to a number.[87] Obviously, Tractarian senselessness is not an infectious disease, whereas lack of Fregean sense is: 'if one of the sentences that are parts [of a compound sentence] [is] senseless, then the whole [is] senseless' (N, 146).[88]

Fregean sense is far more fine-grained than Tractarian sense. From a manuscript of 1906 one can extract the definition of a relation between sentences which Frege, somewhat misleadingly, calls equipollence and which I prefer to call *cognitive equivalence*:[89] two sentences are cognitively equivalent if and only if nobody who fully understands both can assent to one of them without immediately being ready to assent to the other as well. Frege regards cognitive equivalence as a necessary condition for identity of sense. Two sentences that have the same Tractarian sense need not be cognitively equivalent, which is another symptom of its not being what is grasped when one fully understands a sentence.[90]

If cognitive equivalence were also to guarantee identity of thought, Frege would have to swallow some consequences that are certainly not acceptable to him. The sentences 'If the Earth moves then the Earth moves' and 'Nothing is larger than itself' are cognitively equivalent, since the content of either sentence is such that (to use Frege's own words) 'it would have to be immediately accepted as true by anyone who had grasped it properly'.[91] Hence if cognitive equivalence were a sufficient condition of sameness of thought, then our two sentences would express the same thought. *All* sentences the contents of which simply defy disbelief

---

[86] Cf. NB, 3 Oct. 1914, 12 Dec. 1914; TLP, 4.465, 5.513c.   [87] AWL (1934–5), 137.

[88] In Frege's usage *sinnlos* ('senseless') and *unsinnig* ('nonsensical') are stylistic variants (cf. N, 145, 146; CT, 42, 45–6). Contrast TLP, 4.461c, 4.4611.

[89] 'Two sentences A and B can stand in such a relation that anyone who accepts the content of A as true must straightaway accept the content of B as true, and conversely, that anyone who accepts the content of B as true must immediately accept that of A as true (equipollence). It is here being assumed that there is no difficulty in grasping the content of A and B . . .' (NS, 213 (PW, 197)). 'Equipollence' is traditionally used in the sense of 'logical equivalence', and that is clearly not the sense in which Frege takes it here.

[90] Michael Dummett pointed this out a long time ago (*Frege: Philosophy of Language* (London: Duckworth, 1973), 633–4, 679–80; 'The Social Character of Meaning' [1974], repr. in his *Truth and Other Enigmas* (London: Duckworth, 1978), 420–2, and I followed suit (*Abstrakte Gegenständ* (Frankfurt am Main: Suhrkamp, 1983), Ch. 6, §4).

[91] NS, 213 (PW, 197).

would express one and the same thought. In other words, there would be only one thought that is 'self-evident' (*unmittelbar einleuchtend*).[92] Surely Frege's conception of a basic law does not allow him to accept this result. Furthermore, any conjunction one conjunct of which expresses a self-evident truth would express the same thought as the other conjunct by itself. But doesn't the Fregean sense of 'Caesar was murdered, and if the Earth moves then the Earth moves' contain the sense of the predicate '*x* moves', whereas the sense of the first conjunct does not?

As a matter of fact, Frege takes cognitive equivalence only to be a *necessary* condition for identity of thought. In the very same manuscript from which I culled the concept of *cognitive equivalence* we can find what he regards as a *sufficient identity condition*:[93] two sentences express the same thought *if* [i] they are cognitively equivalent, *and* [ii] neither of them is, or contains a part which is, such that one cannot fully understand it without immediately being ready to assent to it—or without immediately being ready to dissent from it.

By adding condition [ii], up to '−', Frege forestalls the unpalatable consequences of taking cognitive equivalence to guarantee identity of sense. Now he would hardly want to say of each disjunction, one disjunct of which expresses a thought that self-evidently lacks truth ('The Earth moves iff it does not'), that it expresses the same thought as the other disjunct by itself. So I took the liberty of adding the dissent clause in [ii]. Once again, Wittgenstein would maintain that one can append 'or' followed by some contradiction to any sentence without altering its sense, and under the Tractarian reading of 'sense' this is clearly correct. (According to Frege, a thought expressed in a logically non-purified language may lack truth without being *false*. So he should allow for cases in which a thought self-evidently lacks truth although it isn't false. The thought that the natural number between 5 and 6 is greater than 4, and the thought that the round square on this blackboard is white, fit this bill. Consequently, we must allow for cases of dissent that do not amount to imputations of falsity.)

---

[92] NS, 242 (PW, 224).

[93] '. . . I assume that there is nothing in the content of either of the two equipollent sentences . . . that would have to be at once immediately accepted as true by anyone who had grasped it properly . . . [The thought expressed] is the same in equipollent sentences *of the kind given above*' (NS, 213–14 [PW, 197–8], my italics).

It is most likely that we hear echoes of questions that Frege had been asked by Wittgenstein, when we read in 'Gedankengefüge': 'In such a case [i.e. in the case of a sentence of the form "If *p* then *p*"] the following questions suggest themselves: "Does this sentence express a thought? Doesn't it lack content? Do we learn anything new upon hearing it?" [. . .]' (CT, 50). Here is Frege's answer: '[. . .] Well, before hearing this sentence someone may not have known [*kennen*] and hence not have acknowledged [*anerkennen*] this truth at all. To that extent one can, under certain circumstances, learn something new upon hearing it' (CT, 50). When hearing an utterance of the sentence 'If the Earth moves then the Earth moves', one might for the first time entertain the thought that if the Earth moves the Earth moves, and thereupon immediately acknowledge its truth. In this way one can come to recognize (*erkennen*) a truth one did not recognize before. That this particular truth isn't exactly electrifying is correct, but irrelevant. (The same holds, *mutatis mutandis*, for the sentence 'The Morning Star is the Morning Star'.) Now if one has recognized that *p* one *knows* that *p*, no matter whether '*p*' is replaced by a 'picture of reality' or by a tautology. So at this point Frege flatly contradicts Wittgenstein's contention that 'if I know that this rose is red or not red, I know nothing' (NL, 104; cf. NB, 21 September 1914). We should think of the first occurrence of 'know' in this remark as surrounded by scare-quotes so as to shield off the threat of inconsistency. Now it is conceded on all sides that I do not know which colour the rose is if I know only that it is red or not red, but that does not show that in having this alleged knowledge I do not know *anything*.[94] In this respect, the famous dictum in the *Tractatus* is more circumspect: 'I know nothing about the weather, if I know that either it is raining or it is not' (TLP, 4.461). But now one wonders whether any bite is left.

In the manuscript that is nowadays known as *Proto-Tractatus* (1917–18), Wittgenstein contends that the result of completing 'Ann knows that . . .' with a tautology is itself 'tautologous' (PT, 5.04441). Now it is hard to see, to put it mildly, how any ascription of knowledge could be a tautology under the technical Tractarian reading of this term. (Certainly no knowledge ascription is a substitution-instance of a universally valid schema in the sentential calculus.) Presumably that's why in the *Tractatus*

[94] Cf. G. E. Moore, 'Wittgenstein's Lectures in 1930–3', in his *Philosophical Papers* (London: Allen & Unwin, 1959), 253–324, at 272.

the adjective 'tautologous' is replaced here by 'senseless' (TLP, 5.1362). But this is not very helpful either because officially 'senseless' in the *Tractatus* is coextensive with 'either tautologous or contradictory'. The contention seems to be that we are not told how things contingently stand with Ann if we are told that she knows that either it is raining or it is not. But is this correct? Let us change the example. Suppose we insert into the frame 'Ann knows that . . .' the tautology 'a tachyon is constrained to the space-like portion of the energy-momentum graph just in case a tachyon is constrained to the space-like portion of the energy-momentum graph': is the resulting knowledge ascription true? It is not if this particle talk is all Greek to Ann. Perhaps she was never exposed to utterances in the language of modern particle physics, so she never acquired the concepts expressed in the content clause of that knowledge ascription. (She might know that a sentence 'p' that is largely incomprehensible to her is a tautology, but that does not make her a person who knows that p.) Now it is as contingent a fact that Ann acquired the concept of rain as it is a contingent fact that she lacks the concepts of modern particle physics, and the truth of our original knowledge ascription depends on that contingency. If this is correct, then it is grist to Frege's mill.

4. The Early Wittgenstein on Frege's Philosophy of Logic

The early Wittgenstein seems to have understood 'the writings of [his] friend Mr. Bertrand Russell' far better than 'Frege's great works'. At any rate, some of his comments on Frege's philosophy of logic definitely misrepresent it. In this final section of my essay I shall try to justify this verdict by scrutinizing Wittgenstein's critical remarks on the appeal to self-evidence, on the prefix '⊢' and on the True and the False.

4.1. On Self-Evidence

The thought that the Earth moves if the Earth moves is one of those truths Frege calls 'self-evident' (*unmittelbar einleuchtend* or *selbstverständlich*).[95] Since

---

[95] NS, 242 (PW, 224). Frege uses the bracketed German expressions interchangeably (cf., for example, CT, 40–1 and 50). Robin Jeshion's claim to the contrary is partly based on what is presented

it is self-evident, it is not *in need* of proof, but one can prove it by deriving
it from a 'basic law of logic' (*logisches Grundgesetz*),[96] namely

(A) ⊢ ∀p (p → p)

(Originally Wittgenstein, too, classified general statements like the one in
(A), and *not* the tautological substitution-instances of the open sentence
after the quantifier, as 'propositions of logic'.[97]) One of the earliest entries
in Wittgenstein's 'Notebooks' is a dismissive remark about appeals to 'that
extremely dubious "self-evidence [*Einleuchten*]" ' in the philosophy of logic
(3 September 1914), and the verbal noun in the German text leaves no
doubt that he has not only Russell but also Frege in mind. If the role
of the notion of self-evidence was one of the topics in the debates they
had before the war, Frege was unmoved by Wittgenstein's objections,
for he repeats in 'Gedankengefüge' that basic logical laws like the one
asserted in (A) are self-evident truths: '[T]he truth of a [basic] logical law
is immediately evident from itself, from the sense of its expression' ('Die
Wahrheit eines logischen [Grund-]Gesetzes leuchtet unmittelbar aus ihm
selbst, aus dem Sinne seines Ausdrucks ein') (CT, 50). Now not only do
basic laws not require proof, they are also not *capable* of proof. An axiom
that is worthy of that ancient title[98] is always a basic law, though not
necessarily a basic *logical* law. (Recall Frege's conservative attitude towards
Euclidean geometry.) Even a basic law may figure in a theory as a theorem,
but if it does, its derivation from the axioms of that theory is not a *proof*.
Thus the basic law

(B) ⊢ ∀x (x = x)

as a fine point about German: 'the term *selbstverstandlich* [sic] translates, literally, as 'self-standing' (in
her instructive paper 'Frege's Notion of Self-Evidence', *Mind*, 110 (2001), 937–76, at 948). Either she
looked up the wrong word (i.e. *selbständig*) in her dictionary, or she should throw her dictionary away.
(If I may make a suggestion: why not occasionally ask a native speaker, preferably a non-philosopher?)

[96] GG I, §18, no. (I). I do not use Frege's notation for the connectives and the quantifiers.
[97] Wittgenstein to Russell, Nov. or Dec. 1913, *Cambridge Letters*, 56; cf. NL, 94, 104. Contrast
TLP, 6.1231.
[98] Here, too, Frege might have quoted Lessing: 'Wer weiß nicht, dass Axiomata Sätze sind, deren
Worte man nur gehörig verstehen darf, um an ihrer Wahrheit nicht zu zweifeln?' ('Who doesn't know
that axioms are sentences which are such that one does not doubt their truth as soon as one properly
understands their words?') ('Axiomata, wenn es deren in dergleichen Dingen gibt', 1778.). By the end
of the nineteenth century this was no longer a rhetorical question. 'Unfortunately,' one can hear Frege
answer, 'Hilbert doesn't know this.' (What Lessing calls axioms Frege prefers to call sentences that
express axioms, for he takes axioms to be thoughts.) See G. E. Lessing, *Werke und Briefe*, Vol. IX, ed.
K. Bohnen and A. Schilson (Frankfurt am Main: Suhrkamp, 1993), 53–89, at 55.

is an axiom in *Begriffsschrift*, but a theorem in *Grundgesetze*,[99] and the same holds for the law of the identity of indiscernibles:[100]

(C) $\vdash \forall\varphi x \forall y\, ((\varphi x \leftrightarrow \varphi y) \to x = y)$

So, unlike being a basic law, being an axiom is a property that a truth has only relative to some system or other.

Each of (A–C) is formulated in a topic-neutral vocabulary, and each is a quantification over all objects.[101] (C) also involves quantification over all concepts (in Frege's acceptation of this term). By assigning to the sentential variables in (A) truth-values as semantic values, Frege is not yet committed to regarding sentences as 'proper names' of truth-values. (Somebody who assigns to predicates extensions as semantic values need not, and should not, take predicates to be 'proper names' of extensions, and certainly Frege is as far as can be from regarding monadic predicates as 'proper names' of concepts.) Frege advocates what has been aptly called a *universalist* conception of logic,[102] for he regards every logical law as a truth about all objects and/or all functions (including concepts and relations of various orders) and he takes everything to be either an object or a function. The *Tractatus* breaks with this universalist view, but it is more than doubtful that its conception of logic is superior, for the decision procedure envisaged by Wittgenstein is provably not sufficient to encompass all of classical first-order logic.[103]

Even so one might share Wittgenstein's aversion against the appeal to self-evidence. What does Frege mean by 'self-evident'?[104] In 'Gedankengefüge'

---

[99] BS, §21, no. (54); GG I, §50, no. (IIIe).   [100] BS, §20, no. (52); GG I, §50, no. (IIIa).

[101] Thus (A), as understood by Frege, is not a 'generalization about propositions (judgements or thoughts)', as Hacker, 'Frege and the Early Wittgenstein', 215 assumes.

[102] Warren Goldfarb, 'Frege's Conception of Logic', in Juliet Floyd and Sanford Shieh (eds.), *Future Pasts* (Oxford: Oxford University Press, 2001), 25–41.

[103] Simons has Church's result, among others, in mind when he (rightly) complains: 'Wittgenstein's disdainful attitude to the results of mathematical logic in PI §124 ... is unfortunately endorsed by Gordon Baker, for whom the undecidability of first-order predicate logic is supposed to have *nothing* to do with Wittgenstein's *philosophical* motivation for his logical reforms, as if philosophical motivations could not include the idea that there should be a method for showing all logical truths to be tautologies' (Peter Simons, 'Frege and Wittgenstein, Truth and Negation', in *Wittgenstein: Eine Neubewertung* (Vienna: hpt, 1990), 125). The reference is to Gordon Baker, *Frege and the Vienna Circle* (Oxford: Blackwell, 1988), 73.

[104] The most enlightening study on the topic of this section is Tyler Burge, 'Frege on Knowing the Foundation', *Mind*, 107 (1998), 305–47, reprinted in his collection *Truth, Thought, Reason: Essays on Frege* (Oxford: Oxford University Press, 2005), 317–55. Nobody has done more than Burge to uncover the Leibnizian features of Frege's philosophy.

he says twice: 'Whether the falsity of a thought can be seen with greater or less difficulty is irrelevant from a logical point of view, for the difference is a psychological one' (CT, 46; cf. 42). So hermeneutical charity demands that we do not take the difference between self-evident truths and others, which Frege invokes in the same essay, to be a psychological difference. I think the dominant conception of self-evidence in Frege's writings is this: a thought x is objectively self-evident if and only if in clearly grasping x one realizes that x is true. The subjectivist counterpart to this notion is this: a thought x is subjectively self-evident to a thinker y just in case x seems to y to be objectively self-evident. If a thought is subjectively self-evident to me then I have not a conclusive but a *prima facie* good reason for believing it to be objectively so. Only *subjective* self-evidence, obviousness, is a matter of degree.[105] It is one of the lessons of the history of mathematics, Frege thinks (GL, §1), that what is subjectively self-evident may not be objectively so; it may even be false. In the case of aspirants to the title of a basic logical law, too, we are not immune to the risk of error:

If anyone should find anything defective, he must be able to state exactly where the defect, according to him, is located: in the basic laws [*Grundgesetze*], in the definitions, in the rules or in their application at a certain point.   (GG, Preface, p. vii)

I could only accept something as refutation if someone were to show, by deed, that a better, more durable edifice can be erected on different basic convictions [*Grundüberzeugungen*], or if someone were to prove to me that my principles [*Grundsätze*] lead to obviously false conclusions.   (GG, Preface, p. xxvi)

As regards the ill-starred 'basic law (V)' Frege had never been certain that it is objectively self-evident.[106] But it seemed to him to be so, for otherwise his maxim that one should not assert anything in a theory without a proof unless it is self-evident (GG II, §60) would have obliged him to try to prove it. Apparently his conviction was that he had not yet clearly grasped its content but only apprehended it 'through a glass darkly'.[107] The road to clarity in this area is deductive systematization: 'the whole of Part II ["Proof of the Basic Laws of Number"] is really a test of my logical convictions' (GG, Preface, p. xxvi). By going through these proofs one obtains further

---

[105] GG II, App., 253 and NS, 198 (PW, 182): 'not as self-evident as'.
[106] Cf. GG, Pref., p. vii; GG II, App., 253; NS, 198 (PW, 182).
[107] Cf. the mist metaphor in NS, 228, 234 (PW, 211, 217).

reasons for *holding* the so-called basic law (V) *true*. These reasons are not grounds for its *being true*, for if a thought really is a basic law there are no such grounds.

The notion of objective self-evidence certainly needs critical scrutiny, but Wittgenstein's criticism misses its target:[108]

If the truth of a proposition does not *follow* from its being self-evident to us [*daraus daß ein Satz uns einleuchtet*], then this self-evidence [*das Einleuchten*] does not justify our belief in its truth.   (TLP, 5.1363, Wittgenstein's italics).

It is strange that a thinker as rigorous as Frege appealed to the degree of self-evidence [*Grad des Einleuchtens*] as the criterion of a logical proposition. (TLP, 6.1271)[109]

Why does something that justifies belief in the truth of P have to *guarantee* its truth? Frege does not take the fact that P is 'self-evident to us' to entail that P is true, but he regards it as a *prima facie* good reason for accepting P as true. Being (objectively) self-evident is not a sufficient condition for being a 'logical proposition', since the truth that it is not always Tuesday has the former property without having the latter, and if Frege is (were) right about Euclidean geometry then objective self-evidence is (would be) a property of some geometrical propositions. Being (objectively) self-evident is not a necessary condition for being a 'logical proposition' either, since logical laws that are not basic lack this property.

4.2. On the Judgement Stroke

In autumn 1913 Wittgenstein declared: 'Assertion is psychological' (NL, 95). 'The assertion-sign is logically quite without significance. It only shows, in Frege and Whitehead and Russell, that these authors hold the propositions so indicated to be true' (NL, 103). 'Assertion-sign' (or *Behauptungszeichen* in PI) is *Russell's* title for the sign '⊢'.[110] The question whether this sign really lacks 'logical significance' may very well have been a topic in the 'long conversations' between Frege and Wittgenstein

---

[108] To a large extent, I agree here with Jeshion, 'Frege's Notion of Self-Evidence', 972–3.

[109] 'What is the criterion for a proposition being a proposition of logic? One claimed criterion is self-evidence . . .', Wittgenstein is reported to have said in a lecture in 1934–5, and the next paragraph is explicitly about Frege (AWL, 135).

[110] For a concise characterization of Russell's use of this symbol and a thorough discussion of Frege's use see Markus Stepanians, *Frege und Hussel über Denken und Urteilen* (Paderborn: Schöningh, 1998), 11–202, on Russell pp. 18–21.

later that year. In the same letter of 15 January 1914 in which Jourdain told Frege of Wittgenstein's readiness to revise the translation of excerpts from *Grundgesetze* he asked him: 'tell me...whether you now regard assertion (⊢) as merely psychological'. (A strange question: what made Jourdain think that Frege *changed his mind* about assertion? Did Wittgenstein convey this impression to him?) In his draft for a reply Frege tried to explain his negative answer. In 'Der Gedanke' he carefully set the stage for introducing the judgement stroke. An assertoric sentence of a natural language like English has no part or feature X of which one could rightly say: if a sentence that has X is correctly used, then it serves to make an assertion. The syntactical form in virtue of which a string of English words is an assertoric sentence is *not* such a feature, for a sentence of that form is not misused when it occurs unasserted as antecedent or consequent in a conditional, say. In a 'logically perfect language (ideography)'[111] some inscriptions have a part—i.e. the judgement stroke—that complies with the condition we have put on X. One can approximately reproduce this characteristic of Frege's ideography in a variant of English. Suppose we could not make an assertion except by uttering a yes/no interrogative followed by 'yes'. Then the final word in a sequence of utterances like 'Is the moon round? Yes' is the counterpart to the judgement stroke.[112]

Why is it good to have such a sign in one's language? The raison d'être for an ideography is to serve as a medium for writing down gapless *proofs*. If one proves something one's premises are truths that one takes to be truths. Something that is essential to a proof would not be represented if the representation of a proof in an ideography would not mark premises

---

[111] 'Über Sinn und Bedeutung', 41. Jonathan Barnes has shown that Jourdain's translation of the term *Begriffsschrift* is optimal: 'What is a *Begriffsschrift*?', *Dialectica*, 56 (2002), 65–80.

[112] If you want to ask a yes/no question in this variant of English, you have to take a deeper breath and say something like 'Is the moon round? Decide this!' In his attack on Frege's conception of assertion Hacker claims: 'The idea that there might be a form of words that can be said to...express a true thought and yet cannot be used to make an assertion is not coherent' ('Frege and the Early Wittgenstein', 211). Frege explains in T, 62 and N, 143–7 that a yes/no interrogative in our language is a form of words that can express a truth although it cannot be used to assert it. So he seems to have refuted Hacker's claim *avant la lettre*. 'Nor is the idea [coherent] that there might be a symbol that can be used to make an assertion, but cannot be used without making an assertion' ('Frege and the Early Wittgenstein', 211). If we insert between 'cannot' and 'be' the adverb 'correctly', the incoherence evaporates. An instantiation of '⊢ p' is correctly used only if used to assert that p: after all, Frege sets the rules for the use of his symbols, and they are such that you misuse that sequence of signs if you employ it in an embedded position or (a very different matter, of course) in writing fiction.

and conclusions as put forward as true. If Frege ever tried to explain this to Wittgenstein (as he did to Jourdain) his explanation was lost on him, for in the *Tractatus* the earlier claim is repeated:

Frege's judgement stroke '⊢' is logically altogether meaningless; in Frege (and Russell) it only shows that these authors hold as true the propositions marked this way. (Frege's 'Urteilstrich' '⊢' ist logisch ganz bedeutungslos; er zeigt bei Frege (und bei Russell) nur an, daß diese Autoren die so bezeichneten Sätze für wahr halten.)   (TLP, 4.442)

Wittgenstein misapplies the Fregean term he mentions: what Frege calls *Urteilsstrich* is only one of the two strokes combined in the prefix, namely the vertical.[113] (Since the prefix is not one of the 'primitive signs' (*Urzeichen*) of his ideography, Frege did not bother to label it.) Of course, neither the prefix nor the vertical has a Fregean *Bedeutung*, and Frege never said anything to the contrary. But presumably, what Wittgenstein wants to say of the prefix when he calls it logically altogether *bedeutungslos* is rather that it is logically pointless, that it has no logical significance (see the penultimate excerpt). But the vertical does have a logical point: it serves to mark candidates for the role of premise or conclusion in the articulation of a proof. Admittedly, 'we can *draw conclusions* from a false proposition' (NB, 20 October 1914; TLP, 4.023), and we can also draw conclusions from what we do not accept as true, but it would be extremely uncharitable to take this to be a refutation of Frege's two-pronged claim: 'We cannot infer anything from a false thought' (N, 145); and 'before acknowledging its truth, one cannot use a thought as premise of an inference' (CT, 47). Frege does not regard the derivation of a conclusion as an 'inference' (*Schluss*) unless it is a proof of the conclusion.

[113] In 'The Early Wittgenstein on Assertion' Ian Proops remarks in passing that in BS Frege did not yet call the vertical *Urteilsstrich*, and he implies that Wittgenstein misspelt this word (*Philosophical Topics*, 25 (1997), 121–44, at 123 and 144 n. 53). As to the first point, I suggest a look at BS, pp. ix, 2. As to the second, in GG, and only there, *Urteilsstrich* has indeed lost one S. (But there *is* a misspelling in the quotation: in PT, 4.4311 Wittgenstein still gets the German genitive of 'Frege' (i.e. 'Freges') right, but in TLP he is already under the spell of British punctuation. Cf. also the German text of PT, 4.4221 with that of TLP, 4.431. Who cares? Well, being an admirer of Karl Kraus, Wittgenstein might care.) Just for the record, because I cannot go into this here, I agree with Proops's main thesis that 'much of the obscurity in [the *Tractatus*'s discussion of assertion] is owed to Wittgenstein's having read into . . . the Frege of *Grundgesetze* . . . certain ideas and conceptions that stem from Russell's work in the period 1900–5' ('The Early Wittgenstein on Assertion', 122).

Since every *Begriffsschriftsatz* ('ideographic sentence') begins with the vertical, no ideographic sentence is a name.[114] So Wittgenstein's complaint that 'Frege said "propositions are names"' (NL, 97) has to be carefully hedged: Frege says this of the string of signs that follows the judgement stroke (and as regards our 'ideographic' variant of English, he would say it of the string of words that precede the 'yes'). Of course, this may be bad enough . . .

4.3. On the Horizontal and the True

At no point does Wittgenstein acknowledge that for the author of *Grundgesetze* (though not for Russell) the sign '⊢' is not atomic. I suspect that this vitiates some of his comments on the account Frege gives of his ideography in GG. (Whether those comments, or some of them, are more to the point if applied to the account Frege gave in 1879 is an interesting question, but I shall not pursue it here, for surely Wittgenstein takes himself to be attacking Frege's mature doctrines.)

Like many other commentators I find the following remark rather bewildering—and for more than one reason: 'The verb of a proposition cannot be "is true" or "is false"—as Frege thought—but whatever "is true" must already contain the verb' (TLP, 4.063).[115] First of all, this is a hyperbolic pronouncement, for what is the 'verb' in the sentence 'The witness's statement is true (false)' if not 'is true (false)'? *Ab esse ad posse valet consequentia.* To be sure, the witness can hardly have made her statement without using a verb, but that does not justify Wittgenstein's 'cannot'. So let us assume that the exaggeration is somehow removed. Secondly, Frege never ever thought that 'is false' is 'the verb of a proposition'. So let us imagine this disjunct deleted. Is then anything left for Frege to disagree with? Nothing at all—as far as natural languages are concerned. In 'Der Gedanke' he writes: 'In the form of an assertoric sentence [*in der Form des Behauptungssatzes*] we express acknowledgement of truth [*Anerkennung der Wahrheit*]. We do not need the word "true" for this' (T, 53). And of

---

[114] 'Function and Concept' (in KS (CP)), 22 n.; GG I, §§2, 5.

[115] The precursor of this in NL, 93 is still without the Frege parenthesis (and without the confusing final pair of quotation marks); not so in PT, 4.094.

course, it isn't needed either when we want to express a thought without committing ourselves as to its truth-value.

Things look different, though, when we turn to Frege's ideography. Every *Begriffsschriftsatz* begins with the prefix. It follows from Frege's explanation of the horizontal stroke that it can be read as the predicate 'is identical with the True'.[116] Now an ideographic sentence like

(1) ⊢ The Earth moves

cannot correctly be rendered (in the 'ideographic' variant of English briefly employed in the last sub-section) as

(*) Is the Earth moves identical with the True? Yes.

What precedes the counterpart to the judgement stroke in (*) is grammatically garbled, so it cannot express what '—The Earth moves' in (1) expresses (unless the latter formulation is also garbled). Some kind of nominalization is required. But we cannot simply place the complementizer 'that' in front of 'the Earth moves', for the result of this operation, Frege would say, designates a thought, and no thought, not even a true one, is identical with the True. (Otherwise there would be only one true thought.) Actually, Frege himself has shown what is to be done: we must embed the Copernican sentence in 'The truth-value of the thought that . . .'.[117] Thus we arrive at

(2) Is the truth-value of the thought that the Earth moves identical with the True? Yes.

as a reading of the *Begriffsschriftsatz* (1). Since the horizontal is a predicate that is present in every ideographic sentence, Frege could rightly say of the horizontal: 'what distinguishes it from all other predicates is that predicating it is always included in predicating anything'.[118] So something like the view that Wittgenstein imputes to Frege in TLP, 4.063 can correctly be ascribed to him. But the omnipresent predicate is not 'is true' (which applies to

---

[116] 'Function and Concept', 21; GG I, §5 and n. 3. Hacker's pen slips when he writes, 'the horizontal function . . . is the concept of *being a truth-value*' ('Frege and the Early Wittgenstein', 210, his italics, 211). If that were correct, '—snow is black' would express a truth.

[117] In GG I, §§12–13 Frege uses locutions such as 'the truth-value thereof that 2 is prime'.

[118] NS, 140 (PW, 129). Here the Oxford translation gets it exactly right: *aussagen* in Frege does not mean what it often means in colloquial German, to assert, but rather: to predicate. Predications need not have assertoric force.

many thoughts), but 'is identical with the True' (which does not apply to any thought). The singular term that saturates this predicate in (2) is a nominalization of a sentence that 'already contains a verb'. (It wouldn't be a sentence if it didn't.) But this is not to say that what the horizontal applies to already contains a predicate, for a truth-value is hardly the sort of thing, one gathers, that can contain a predicate. Now does any of this show that Frege is wrong in what he says about ideographic sentences? I cannot see that it does.

Let us now turn to the passage that apparently contains the upshot of 'important arguments against Frege's theory of truth, especially against the stipulation of *Bedeutung* for function[-expression]s' that Wittgenstein raised in a lost letter to Frege (see Section 1 above): 'Only Frege's explanation of the truth-concept is mistaken: if "the True" and "the False" were really objects and were the arguments in $\sim p$ etc., then Frege's determination would not determine the sense of "$\sim p$" at all' (TLP, 4.431).[119] One might protest against an implication of the first statement: Frege always denied that the truth-concept can be explained.[120] So let us not press Wittgenstein's wording at this point: what he objects to is Frege's conception of truth. Suppose the logical connectives designate functions, and truth-values are objects that are arguments of those functions: then Frege's attempts at specifying the sense of those connectives fail, or so we are told. Unfortunately we are not told why. *Perhaps* the reason Wittgenstein has in mind is this:[121] if truth-values are objects among others, then Frege's 'specification' of the *Bedeutung* of the negation operator, for example, leaves undetermined what the value of the negation function allegedly designated by that operator is for objects that are not truth-values, hence the *Sinn* of the operator is also left undetermined. *If* that is the reason (not spelt out in the *Tractatus* but apparently mentioned in the letter [28 November 1913]),

[119] In PT, 4.4221 the word 'determination' (*Bestimmung*) is helpfully flanked by scare-quotes.
[120] Cf. NS, 189 (PW, 174), earlier than 1883, I think; NS, 140 (PW, 129), 1897 or later; T, 60.
[121] The reader is urged to consult the (widely divergent) interpretations of our passage in Elizabeth Anscombe, *An Introduction to Wittgenstein's Tractatus* (London: Hutchinson, 1959), 107; Simons, 'Frege and Wittgenstein, Truth and Negation', 122–5; Hacker, 'Frege and the Early Wittgenstein', 213; and H.-J. Glock, 'Sense and Meaning in Frege and the *Tractatus*', in G. Oliveri (ed.), *From the Tractatus to the Tractactus, Wittgenstein Studies*, 1 (2000), 53–68, §4. My interpretation follows that in Proops, 'The Early Wittgenstein on Assertion', 129. The wide divergence is at least partly due to the regrettable fact that Wittgenstein does not bother to spell out the argument. As Frege said, 'the sense would become clearer with more detailed justification' (Janik and Berger (eds.), 'G. Frege: Briefe', 28 June 1919).

the objection crumbles, since the horizontal takes care of those allegedly fatal cases: the value of the function designated by '—ξ' for the argument Jena, say, and for every other object that isn't identical with the True, is the False, the negation operator applies to something that is preceded by the horizontal, and according to Frege's attempt at specifying its *Bedeutung* (GG I, §6), the value of the negation function for the argument Jena, far from being left undetermined, is the True. How could Wittgenstein overlook this? Maybe because Russell misled him into regarding Frege's prefix as atomic.

But this reply presupposes that we know which objects the True and the False are. Only at one place in his publications did Frege try to equip us with the required knowledge: 'By the truth-value of a sentence I understand the circumstance [*Umstand*] that it is true or that it is false. There are no further truth-values. For brevity I call the one the True [*das Wahre*], the other the False [*das Falsche*].[122] With a minor emendation, this gives us: for all sentences *s*, the truth-value of *s*, if it has any, is either identical with the circumstance that *s* (expresses a thought that) is true or with the circumstance that *s* (expresses a thought that) is false. If this is to help, Frege must rely on our ordinary understanding of 'circumstance'. But that lets us down here, as Hacker has pointed out.[123] The circumstance that the sentence 'The Earth moves' expresses a thought that is true is *not* identical with the circumstance that 'Socrates is wise' expresses a truth, but under Frege's (and anybody else's) reading of the term 'truth-value' these two sentences, like all others that express true thoughts, have the *same* truth-value.

Did the author of the *Logical Investigations* still regard truth-values as objects? Did he still think that what the judgement stroke is prefixed to stands to a truth-value in the same semantical relation as that in which the name 'Socrates' stands to the man Socrates? If the term 'truth-value' were to occur only in contexts of the following two types:

(a) *s* has a truth-value

(b) s_1 and s_2 have the same truth-value

then such formulations might just serve as handy abbreviations of

---

[122] 'Über Sinn und Bedeutung', 34; cf. NS, 211 (PW, 194), dated 10 Aug. 1906.
[123] Hacker, 'Frege and the Early Wittgenstein', 196.

(A) *s* expresses a true thought, or *s* expresses a false thought

(B) s_1 and s_2 both express truths, or they both express falsehoods.

But then no objects that are not referred to, or quantified over, in (A) or (B) are referred to, or quantified over, in (a) or (b). Now the only contexts in which 'truth-value' occurs in Frege's LI are of type (b): see T, 66, N, 157 and CT, 51. (It is a sheer accident that it does not occur in a context of type (a): whenever Frege says in LI that *s* expresses a thought that 'belongs to fiction' (*gehört der Dichtung an*), he might as well have said, and he would have done better to say, that *s* (or the thought expressed by *s*) has no truth-value.) So this is evidence for the thesis that the late Frege no longer commits himself to truth-values as objects.[124]

But there is also evidence that points in the opposite direction. In 'Der Gedanke' Frege observes that prefixing the truth-prologue to a declarative sentence does not enrich the content of that sentence. He takes this to be a reason for doubting that 'true' is used to ascribe a property:

May we not be dealing here with something that is not a property in the ordinary sense at all? In spite of this doubt I shall *for the time being* express myself in accordance with ordinary usage, as if truth were a property, until something more appropriate [*etwas Zutreffenderes*] is found.   (T, 62, my italics)

In 'Die Verneinung' and 'Gedankengefüge' Frege does not keep the promise made at the end of this passage, nor does he do so in the fragment of a fourth instalment.[125] But the project of the *Logical Investigations* was not yet completed when he died in 1925, and he had developed in 'Über Sinn und Bedeutung' and *Grundgesetze* a conception of truth that in 1918 he may still have deemed 'more appropriate'. In spring 1914 he argued that we should 'count a truth-value as an object',[126] and this was *after* the last of his 'long conversations' with a stern critic of this conception. If substitution-instances of 'the truth-value of *x*' are what they appear to be, namely *bona fide* singular terms, then truth-values are objects (in the Fregean acceptation of this term). But by 'counting them as objects' one is not committed to underwriting the *Grundgesetze* claim that what follows the

---

[124] See Hacker, 'Frege and the Early Wittgenstein', 192 n. As the final paragraph will show, I am afraid that at this point I may have misled my first and best friend in Oxford, to whom I hereby, somewhat discreetly, dedicate this essay with affection and with gratitude for his friendship over several decades.

[125] NS, 278–81 (CP, 258–62).   [126] NS, 263 (CP, 244).

judgement-stroke in an ideographic sentence is a singular term designating such an object. There is no evidence that the late Frege continued to endorse this claim. He may have come round to accepting Wittgenstein's point that 'sentences are not names'.[127] If he did, this would confirm one half of the remark that I have used as the epigraph for this essay: 'Each of us, I believe, has drawn from the other in intellectual exchange.'

---

[127] But recall that Frege himself emphasized that *ideographic* sentences are not names (see above, end of §4.2).

'Moses': Wittgenstein on Names

JOACHIM SCHULTE

In the first volume of their commentary on Wittgenstein's *Philosophical Investigations* Gordon Baker and Peter Hacker give ample space to discussions of Wittgenstein's views on names. In various parts of their commentary they review a number of manuscript passages foreshadowing, or contrasting with, Wittgenstein's later remarks on this topic as printed in the *Investigations*. Clearly, the most important and, perhaps, most controversial of these remarks is PI, 79, which centres on the biblical name 'Moses'. In this essay I shall rely on the same sort of manuscript material to tell part of the story of Wittgenstein's 'Moses' remark in my own way—often in agreement with Baker's and Hacker's findings, but sometimes emphasizing different aspects of Wittgenstein's thought. There is one point, however, regarding which Baker and Hacker take issue with Wittgenstein's account of the matter where I for my part feel that Wittgenstein's approach can be seen in a more favourable light. Baker and Hacker write as follows:

Wittgenstein seems to be committed to a similarly implausible view [as Frege], since on his account each John Smith will have a name with a different fluctuating and indeterminate meaning. [. . .] It is not necessary to assume that names have meanings that determine their reference. Traditional accounts of their meaning have unwelcome consequences. So we can now jettison the three dogmas [. . .] that names have meaning (in the preferred sense), that explaining who N is, is explaining the meaning of 'N', and therefore that names are typically polysemic. If we jettison the assumption that names have meanings that identify their bearer, then there can be no such thing as explaining their meaning.[1]

---

[1] G. P. Baker and P. M. S. Hacker, *Wittgenstein: Understanding and Meaning, Volume 1 of an Analytical Commentary on the Philosophical Investigations, Part I—The Essays*, 2nd edn, extensively revised (Oxford: Blackwell, 2005), 'Proper names', 245–6, 247. (*Part 2—The Exegesis* will be referred to as 'Exegesis'.) Cf. Strawson's remark in his 'Critical Notice' of PI: 'If we speak at all of the meaning of proper names, it is only in quite *specialised* ways [. . .]. This is not an accident of usage, but reflects a radical difference between proper names and other names. But here, as elsewhere, Wittgenstein neglects the use of "meaning"' (*Mind*, 63 (1954), 75).

The following is, among other things, an attempt at pointing out a reason why Wittgenstein may have found it natural to speak freely of the meaning of names. In trying to characterize this reason, I shall at the same time try to throw light on one particular passage of *Philosophical Investigations*—the celebrated 'Moses' remark (§79). This way of proceeding will involve ignoring a number of relevant passages like PI, 37 ff., which discuss names chiefly in the context of atomism. Instead of examining the *Investigations* context of the 'Moses' remark, I shall look backward and forward, as it were: partly in the spirit of Hacker's own practice, I shall consider the manuscript context in which the 'Moses' remark originated. That will be the first step. The second step will consist in connecting some elements of Wittgenstein's discussion with a characteristic thought developed in his later work. Both steps will be taken to make it easier to understand Wittgenstein's talk about the meaning of names. The second step, in particular, may serve to show that a certain way of conceiving the meaning of names can have repercussions for our understanding of the notion of meaning in general.

I

The 'Moses' remark, which is one of the longest remarks in the book, is also one of the oldest. Most of it was written down in November 1931. A striking point about these manuscript pages is that large parts of three further remarks of its immediate PI context (§§81, 83, 87) were drafted on the same or the next day (see MS 112, 185–93).[2] This material and many further observations belonging to that context were included in section 58 of the so-called 'Big Typescript' (1933).[3] If one looks at earlier manuscript pages, one will soon notice that the topic of names crops up again and again, often without any explicit distinction between proper names of persons and other kinds of names, especially colour names. Most readers

---

[2] Page references to manuscripts 110–12 correspond to the pagination given in the relevant volumes of the *Wiener Ausgabe* (Vienna: Springer, 1993–). English translations of manuscript passages are my own.

[3] This section bears the somewhat baroque title 'The Strict Grammatical Rules of a Game and the Fluctuating Use of Language. Logic as Normative. To What Extent do we Talk about Ideal Cases, and Ideal Language? ("The Logic of a Vacuum.")'. Cf. BT, 195.

of these passages will find it difficult to discern a clear train of thought connecting these scattered observations. Indeed, it is sometimes difficult to judge whether Wittgenstein is moving backward or forward: occasionally, one may well wonder whether what one is reading is a continuation or a criticism of certain *Tractatus* ideas.

Whatever one may eventually conclude about the import of these remarks, it is clear that their interpretation has a bearing on the image we shall form of continuities and discontinuities in Wittgenstein's philosophy. This is a topic I shall say little about, though it is clear that my choice of thematic orientation involves implicit judgements about the development of Wittgenstein's thought. What is of especial importance to my remarks is the idea that Wittgenstein's late views on meaning as informed by his considerations of meaning–experiences and the imaginary case of meaning-blindness can be seen as more or less naturally growing out of earlier reflections expressed in the context of discussing names and their meanings. Of course, this perspective on the development of Wittgenstein's thought is incompatible with interpretations attempting to foreground questions of a systematic conception or theory of meaning. But I can live with this incompatibility, as I do not believe that such questions are liable to play a helpful role in trying to understand Wittgenstein's observations.

Here, my suggestion is that it will be helpful to see Wittgenstein's remarks in the light of one central notion and three prominent contrasts. (Readers unfamiliar with the relevant manuscripts may be surprised to learn that this is an extremely *selective* approach.) The central notion is that of *Vertretung*, or *Stellvertretung*. This obviously harks back to the *Tractatus*, where it is used to formulate certain particularly important ideas. There, Wittgenstein writes for example that 'In a picture the elements of the picture are the representatives of objects' (TLP, 2.131). And 'the fundamental idea' of the book is expressed by saying 'that the "logical constants" are not representatives; that there can be no representatives of the *logic* of facts' (TLP, 4.0312). The three contrasts I want to mention and to some extent exploit in the sequel are the following: (1) primary vs. secondary signs, (2) sample vs. word, (3) explanation vs. description.

   (1) The relevant distinction between primary and secondary signs is not the only contrast Wittgenstein tries to articulate in these terms in his writings of the time around 1930. The contrast we are concerned

with here is basically that between ostensive gestures and verbal language.

(2) The distinction between sample and word is closely connected with the first distinction. Ostension serves to explain words and their uses, their meanings. It can do so by employing samples rather than words. So one may use drawings or photographs, specimens or models, and proceed to teach the use of a certain expression 'X' by way of pointing and saying 'This is X' (or 'This is called "X" '). Similarly in the case of pointing at elements of real-life situations or at people: here one accompanies the pointing gestures with words like 'This is a fashion show' or 'This is George Clooney', hoping that the other person will correctly identify the intended feature or object and thus be enabled to use the relevant expression in appropriate ways. In this kind of teaching situation the feature or object indicated is a sample, not a word (even if it looks or sounds like a word).[4] To put it in a different way: whatever plays an essential role in the use of primary signs, i.e. in the context of ostensive explanations, is, not a word, but a sample or a part of one.

(3) The contrast between explanation and description is familiar from later remarks like PI, 109. In fairly early passages as for instance MS 110, 284 (4 July 1931), we find Wittgenstein discussing a situation of looking for and expecting to find a flower of a certain colour. He says that in describing this situation we have taken up a perspective remote from any kind of explanation: 'We can only give a description, since causal connections—that is, the actual sequence of events—don't interest us (for, as far as they are concerned, we are prepared to believe anything). And the connections which will then be left over are formal ones; these cannot be described but will express themselves in grammar.' In other words, as regards philosophical considerations causal explanations are pointless. A mere description, however, of certain uses of words may help to bring out formal, or grammatical, connections. But these in their turn *cannot* be

---

[4] Wittgenstein explicitly says that (in certain types of situation, at any rate) a word in quotation marks is a sample—and not a word (MS 112, 171). The contrast between what Wittgenstein calls 'samples' and 'words' is one between different functions of verbal or non-verbal objects. According to Wittgenstein's remarks from this period, verbal objects (like 'red') can be, or function as, samples while non-verbal objects (like coloured slips of paper) can be, or function as, words: 'If [colour] specimens don't function as samples, they just function as words' (MS 112, 168).

described, let alone explained. (Naturally, one is tempted to continue by saying that 'they can only be shown'.) The idea of description that Wittgenstein has in mind here is not easy to grasp, however. Shortly after an early remark on meaning and use ('Understanding the meaning of a word amounts to knowing, understanding, its use', MS 111, 12), Wittgenstein proceeds to say about words like 'here' and 'now' that 'of course, I can only do what I do in other cases too, namely describe their use. The description, however, must be general, i.e. [given] in advance, prior to every use' (MS 111, 28; 16 July 1931). One difficulty about this and other passages mentioning a priori descriptions of uses of words is that it is not clear how to reconcile them with remarks like the one previously quoted about the impossibility of describing grammatical relations.[5]

To give anything resembling a full account of the ideas and distinctions sketched above would require dozens of pages and is hence out of the question in the present context. Yet it is important to have some conception of the flavour and tendency of Wittgenstein's remarks about names considered in the light of those ideas and distinctions as they developed in his manuscripts of 1931. Let us first look at an early passage (3 July 1931) discussing the concept of *Vertretung* (i.e. being a representative, going proxy, standing in for somebody, deputizing) and the way in which gesture languages work (MS 110, 270–1). To begin with, Wittgenstein tries to articulate the idea of two different domains facing each other: a sign system, on the one hand, and a realm of objects, events, etc. to be

---

[5] It is very difficult to decide whether and to what extent Wittgenstein succeeded in relieving the tension between these two claims. In his later writings there is, as I suggest below, a clear tendency towards playing down, or losing sight of, the idea of grammar as a network of rules governing the whole of language and its uses. On the other hand, even in his later writings Wittgenstein's notion of description sometimes seems to involve a peculiarly strong, *Tractatus*-like, idea of grammar. It does seem to involve this in the sense that the descriptions of language use appealed to could be seen as meant to be revelatory of features that go way beyond what is open to view. To the extent that this inclination towards finding out about some kind of a priori data survives, it is, and remains, irreconcilable with the specific form of anti-dogmatism spelled out and endorsed in WVC, 182 ff. A succinct formulation of Wittgenstein's brand of anti-dogmatism can also be found in a letter to Schlick (20 Nov. 1931) where he writes that he has 'recognized that the analysis of a proposition does not consist in discovering hidden things but in tabulating, giving a surveyable account of, grammar, i.e. of the grammatical use of words. Thus, all the dogmatic statements I used to make [. . .] fall away.' But the notion of grammar appealed to in this and other passages is not a sufficiently humdrum one to rid the kind of description ('surveyable account') involved of its supposed capacity to capture intrinsic, as it were transcendental, features of language-use: the tension mentioned above continues to characterize (and mar) some of Wittgenstein's remarks on grammar and description.

described by means of the sign system, on the other. He wonders whether it is merely an accident that we have to abandon the domain of signs and their system if we want to explain these signs. Does that not mean that we shall have to enter that other domain to which those objects and occurrences belong that we describe by means of our signs? But if we really have to step outside the sign system and enter the described world, it may appear strange that our signs are any use at all. From this perspective it looks as if our signs were merely proxies of what goes on in reality; and now it will be important to understand how this kind of representation is possible. What is clear is that the kind of going proxy for something we are interested in is not just a matter of doing one thing instead of another: if I drink water rather than milk it does not help to add that the water is going proxy for the milk (MS 110, 271). On the other hand, it *is* quite appropriate to say that the definiendum can work as a representative of the definiens. And here the right image to use is this: that 'the latter stands behind the former as the electorate stands behind their deputy' (MS 110, 271). This is the sense in which we can say that the sign explained through an ostensive definition can function as a representative of this ostension, for the sign can simply be introduced into the gesture language and there do the work formerly done by gestures. But then we are talking about two different *languages*, not about two different kinds of domain. 'Und das ist vielleicht der Succus dieser Betrachtung' (MS 110, 271).[6]

But still, there are various problems here that continue to worry Witt-genstein. He often wonders about strange kinds of explanations of signs, that is, explanations that do not seem 'natural' to us. One problematic sort of explanation involves tables and similar diagrams and our ways of reading them. We find it natural to move from left to right, following a straight line. But as Wittgenstein indicates in PI, 86 and earlier remarks to the same effect, there is no deep reason why such tables should not be read in all kinds of other ways. In a similar fashion, he wonders whether we could not introduce colour names by way of an antecedent convention stipulating that the colour meant is the colour complementary to the one indicated. Analogously, in the context of discussing personal proper names he raises the question whether we could introduce names by pointing, not to the person meant (who may be absent), but to

---

[6] 'And that is perhaps the quintessence of our considerations.'

somebody else exhibiting certain features suggestive of the person really intended.

A particularly instructive example is that of a catalogue containing coloured slips to illustrate which colours are to be referred to by certain names or numbers. Here, a moment's reflection will reveal that there is no profound reason why a green slip should not go proxy for a red one. This could work just as well as using the word 'green' to characterize red things. But if we do so, Wittgenstein explains, we are using the green slip not as a sample but *as a word*. It is not used in its primary role as a sample, but in its secondary role as a word. One way of bringing out the difference is by reminding ourselves of the fact that the idea of producing an exact copy of something makes sense in the case of true samples but not in situations where we use a green slip to represent red—to represent it in the way we use words to go proxy for things or features of things. Confusion of the roles of sample and word is engendered by the idea that in either case we apply a method of projection, only a less familiar one in cases like the one where a green slip is used to function as a proxy for red (MS 112, 168–9). One can try to avoid thinking along these lines by continuing to insist on a radical conceptual distinction between samples and words. But in that case there remains the residual worry whether in case we start from such a distinction words can be said to be defined in terms of anything but words; that is, whether successful definitions of words are not bound to proceed by way of words: 'Isn't it inescapable that everything used to define a word ipso facto *is* a word, operates as a word, even if it is a coloured slip and could hence work in a different way too?' (MS 112, 169, emphasis added; cf. MS 112, 210, 215).

One of the points that interest Wittgenstein, and one which is of great importance to our discussion, is whether it is right to say that the definiendum is the *name* of the definiens (MS 112, 205). Wittgenstein's suggestion is that it is *not* right to say so: the definiendum is a true *Vertreter* of the definiens; it can assume the latter's office (to use Wittgenstein's expression) and fulfil its duties. But whenever the original holder of the office (the definiens) returns from its holiday, it can take over again and do the job in the meantime managed by its deputy.

This image, Wittgenstein says, does not really fit names and their role. There are cases where it does seem to work: name-cards placed at a dinner table where guests will later sit on the chairs indicated by the cards are mentioned as one example, even if as a slightly cumbersome one—and perhaps as a joke (MS 112, 205): while the names (cards) function as placeholders for the guests, the guests can also be seen as replacing the names (cards). But while in most cases it is possible to say that in a sense names stand for their bearers, it is only rarely appropriate to say that they can stand in for them: only seldom can the bearers of names do the jobs of their names, and their names will equally rarely be able to discharge the duties of their bearers.

Differences between names (which can typically be introduced by means of ostensive definitions) and those kinds of words which are typically introduced by means of verbal definitions are the topic of a number of remarks composed by Wittgenstein in November 1931. Some of these remarks have cautionary implications. At one point Wittgenstein writes:

Both definition and naming assign a sign to a thing (in the former case, a sign to a sign).—A *name*, however, is given to the thing to enable me to speak of it.—This sounds as if the name were like a telescope and the previous sentence analogous to this sentence: I am given a telescope to enable me to see him[7]. But 'speaking of him' only consists in this: that first 'he → is called "N"' is uttered and then the name 'N' is used in the language and in transitions from language to actions, etc.—Surely to speak of N is different from an operation performed by means of N. Indeed, it is also different from operating by means of an object which is represented (*vertreten*) by N but in whose stead N could be used.[8]—But suppose I want to see, for example, where in this room it would be most convenient to place a table and for this purpose push around a box of roughly the same size: cannot I say that in this case I *speak* of the table, *mean* the table, and that the box means the table?   (MS 112, 210–11)

Evidently we are supposed to answer 'Yes, I can say that': it is a nice example of functioning as a representative but it does not seem to be an example of using a name. Wittgenstein does imagine all kinds of unusual situations where non-linguistic objects can be employed as names. In this way one can for example imagine that an object N serves as the name of its name 'N'. And if the sign 'N' is used instead of the quoted sign

---

[7] Here Wittgenstein switches from 'it' to 'him'.

[8] Perhaps the import of these last two sentences is not clear. One might even suspect that Wittgenstein forgot to put quotation marks around 'N'. I take these two sentences to express certain scruples arising from the thought that there is a deep divide between the worlds of language and action. The ensuing remark on the box as going proxy for the table is a response to this and goes in the opposite direction by pointing out that non-verbal gestures can be interpreted as a kind of speech.

' "N" ', the new use of 'N' will be entirely different from its old use (MS 112, 212). At any rate, the difference between expressions introduced by verbal definitions, on the one hand, and names, which can be introduced by ostensive definitions, on the other, is forcefully summed up by saying that 'definition is like transferring an office from one sign to another. A name and its bearer, however, do not hold the same office without further ado. To bestow the office of name is not the same as giving a name to a name' (MS 112, 212).

In Wittgenstein's view, signs can only be explained by means of other signs (MS 112, 210; cf. 215). For this reason he is committed to drawing a radical conclusion: As ostensive definitions of the kind 'This → is N' are signs, the bearer of 'N'—that is, the object pointed to—is to be regarded as part of a sign. Its role, however, is different from that played by verbal and other more conventional types of sign. Wittgenstein compares it to the role of samples. Associating a name with a sample and declaring that two expressions are equivalent (in the sense of having the same meaning) are fundamentally different activities. Wittgenstein illustrates this by means of the example '1 + 1'. My accepting that 1 + 1 = 2 simply allows me to use '2' in the place of '1 + 1', which amounts to saying that the rules governing the use of one expression are the same as those governing the use of the other. But if I use the sign '2' as a *name* of '1 + 1', no licence is given to use '2' in accordance with the rules we follow in using '1 + 1' (MS 112, 216).

II

The points mentioned so far are by no means sufficient to draw a complete picture of the ideas entertained by Wittgenstein around 1930 about names, their introduction by means of ostensive definitions, and the notion of being a representative of somebody or something. They may, however, allow us to take our second step by using them as an instructive context in terms of which the 'Moses' remark can be considered fruitfully. In the manuscript version this remark is introduced by the following series of considerations:

That the bearer of a name is dead is a fact which we describe by means of this name (which hence has meaning in this case). But suppose we say that the bearer has never lived!

The meaning of a name consists in what it can make sense for us to assert (truly or falsely) of the [hypothetical] bearer.[9]

Is the bearer's hypothetical existence involved in defining the name by pointing to the bearer and saying 'This is N'?

It is all a matter of my being able to say 'Moses does not exist' ('did not exist') but not 'This man (I am pointing to) does not exist'.

[. . .]

That is, for the time being I play the game with nothing but the name, without the bearer. And in doing so I don't miss the bearer.   (MS 112, 184)

Here it is of course important to remember that a distinction between the bearer and the meaning of a name had been drawn in earlier manuscripts (MS 110, 276; MS 111, 115–17; cf. PI, 40–4).[10] The most prominent ideas expressed in this sequence of considerations are (1) that language-games with names can be played quite independently of whether these names have, or had, bearers; (2) that names can have a meaning (*Bedeutung*) even if they lack a bearer; and (3) that the meaning of a name depends on what it makes sense to assert of the hypothetical or intended bearer.

The fact that language-games involving names can be played irrespective of whether or not these names have bearers plays an important role in the context of Wittgenstein's examination of logical atomism. What is of greater interest to us now is the claim that names can be said to have a meaning even if they have no bearer and never had one. A point that plays a great role in Wittgenstein's considerations is the difference between names commonly introduced by ostensive means and those that do not admit of ostensive explanations. The biblical name 'Moses' is clearly a name of the latter kind and can therefore be the target of questions like 'Did Moses really exist?'. In his manuscript (as in PI, 79) Wittgenstein points out that questioning Moses' existence can amount to various things: Has there ever been a man bearing that name who performed all or most of the actions ascribed to him by the tradition? Has there been such a man who, however, was not called 'Moses'? Etc. As Wittgenstein continues to point out, such questions can be phrased by using, and modifying, Russell's

---

[9] This rendering of the second paragraph is very much an interpretation. The German original runs as follows: 'Die Bedeutung des Namens liegt darin, was wir von ihm mit Sinn (wahr oder falsch) aussagen können.' I take it that 'ihm' refers back to 'Träger' in the first paragraph.

[10] In view of Wittgenstein's subsequent reflections as summarized above it may be a little confusing to find him stating the distinction as follows: 'It's true—names can be representatives of things; but they are not representatives of their meanings [. . .]' (MS 111, 115).

idea of analysing the meaning of 'Moses' by way of spelling out various descriptions of the supposed bearer of the name.

Some readers of PI, 79 have made much of the fact that the first two paragraphs of this remark can be read as if Wittgenstein were giving an account of how *other* people, and in particular Russell, proposed to deal with the question how names signify.[11] These readers think that accordingly the first two paragraphs do not commit Wittgenstein to buying into any of those Russellian ideas involving disguised descriptions—ideas whose allegedly Wittgensteinian version inspired other readers to formulate a 'cluster' theory of names.[12] But even if one admits that PI, 79 can be read this way, the manuscript version does not appear to be amenable to such an interpretation.[13] Besides other clues that speak in favour of describing Wittgenstein's attitude towards the description account as amounting to countenancing some version of it, the manuscript version of the 'Moses' remark uses the fairly explicit phrase 'I surely want to say what Russell expresses by saying that the name Moses can be defined through various descriptions [. . .]' (MS 112, 185).

So, if one accepts the view that Wittgenstein holds that there is a peculiar way in which our use of 'Moses' is connected with, or perhaps dependent on, our countenancing certain descriptions as to some degree constitutive of what one understands when one understands a number of uses of that name, then this may be regarded as a first reason for attributing meanings to names of that sort. After all, if we can be said to understand an expression and can also be said to be able to indicate under which circumstances we are inclined to regard a use of that expression as justifiable or not, it is prima facie natural to speak of a meaning of that expression and to say that what one understands if one understands the use of a name is its meaning. However, apart from the fact that an opponent of the view that names have meanings could easily indicate a number of disanalogies between uncontroversially meaningful expressions and names, this whole line of

---

[11] See, for example, James Cappio, 'Wittgenstein on Proper Names', *Philosophical Studies*, 39 (1981), 93.

[12] See John Searle, 'Proper Names', *Mind*, 67 (1958), 166–73. Cf. Saul Kripke's discussion in *Naming and Necessity* (Cambridge, Mass.: Harvard University Press, 1980); Baker and Hacker, *Wittgenstein: Understanding and Meaning*, 'Proper Names', section 3: 'Cluster theories of proper names'.

[13] Here I am not suggesting that this is sufficient evidence for refuting those readers who insist that in the *Investigations*, as opposed to the early manuscripts, Wittgenstein does not commit himself to a disguised-description account.

argument does not fit Wittgenstein's way of thinking. He does not argue for the claim that names have meaning; he simply employs the notion of meaning in connection with names. What we have to find out, if we can, is the point (or *a* point) of his using this notion in this way.

First it should be noted that in 1931 the 'Moses' case sits very uncomfortably with various other ideas Wittgenstein is inclined to hold at that time. On the one hand, he claims not to be worried by the circumstance that 'in a certain sense we use the name N without a fixed meaning, that is to say: that we are prepared to change the rules of the game according to our needs' (MS 112, 186–7). On the other hand, he not only insists that the possibility of a lack of bearer 'must be part of the [name's] meaning'; he also suggests that the meaning is to be explained in terms of rules and that indeterminacy of meaning is to be understood, not so much in terms of vagueness, but rather in terms of oscillating between several meanings (MS 112, 190–1). That is, the indeterminacy is not so much true fuzziness but more like absence of a clear choice between several well-circumscribed options. One idea which is likely to lie behind this is a rigid notion of grammar, according to which meaning is to be understood as a kind of resultant of a number of rules: the rules of the game delimit the possible positions of a piece, and a sufficient number of rules and their applications will pinpoint its position, or its degrees of freedom, exactly. It is in this sense that Wittgenstein says that the meaning of a name is its position or function in a game, explaining that a correct grasp of the word 'bearer' will help to fix the meaning of a name except for one residual specification (MS 112, 198). This residual specification, I take it, can be supplied by means of ostension—a means which evidently is not available in the case of names like 'Moses'.[14]

This tension between an awareness of many forms of indeterminacy and a tendency to see indeterminacy in terms of, and as reconcilable with, a system of more or less rigid rules is characteristic of Wittgenstein's writings of the early 1930s. Interpretations of his later work vary a great deal according to whether and to what extent they regard this tension

---

[14] In various papers I have argued that this rigid notion of grammar was dropped after a while. Cf. my 'Phenomenology and Grammar', in Rosa M. Calcaterra (ed.), *Le ragioni del conoscere e dell'agire: Scritti in onore di Rosaria Egidi* (Milan: Franco Angeli, 2006), 228–40; 'Wittgenstein's "Method"', in R. Haller and K. Puhl (eds.), *Wittgenstein and the Future of Philosophy: A Reassessment after 50 Years* (Vienna: öbv & hpt, 2002), 399–410.

as lessened in these later writings. The direction of the development of Wittgenstein's thought (and what may be looked on as one way of mitigating that tension) is revealed by two major additions to the original 'Moses' remark. In the *Investigations*, but not in his earlier manuscripts, Wittgenstein uses two related images: he speaks of the familiar descriptions of Moses given in the Old Testament as 'a whole series of props in readiness'; and he emphasizes the usefulness of words (names) without a *fixed* meaning by comparing them to tables that owing to their having, not three, but four legs sometimes wobble. Both images suggest that the support on which our use of names rests is more than sufficient; and the second metaphor implies that, indeed, it is this abundance which is to some extent responsible for the lack of stability or determinacy typical of our use of names like 'Moses'. Neither image indicates that the indeterminacy noted needs to be understood, or can be remedied, in terms of grammatical rules.

In 1931 the 'Moses' case is, as was pointed out above, more of a problem for Wittgenstein than part of a convincing solution. The way in which the case worries him can be illustrated by reference to his central notion of *Vertretung* or, as he calls it at one point (MS 112, 207), 'the muddle' of the word *stellvertreten*. One part of the muddle is connected with the fact pointed out by Wittgenstein that names should not be said to be representatives of something because normally they and their bearers cannot take each other's place. At the same time, he is clearly keen on elucidating the function of names by means of the idea of *Vertretung*. He explicitly says that names can be representatives of things (MS 111, 115) and that names are 'appointed' representatives of things in the same way in which one person is appointed representative of another (MS 112, 201). And in the passage where he speaks of 'the muddle' of the word *stellvertreten* he at the same time claims that 'in one sense' names *are* representatives. This sense, I gather, is not the one illustrated by the idea of one person's standing in for another but by another image alluded to in an earlier quotation (see p. 68, above?). Here Wittgenstein says that the definiens backs ('stands behind') the definiendum in the same way in which a deputy is backed by his voters (MS 110, 271). Similarly, the analogy of account books used by Wittgenstein (MS 112, 207) suggests an economic or financial sense of 'backing' which can help to illuminate relevant notions of *Vertretung*. The first sense of *Vertretung* brings in the idea of intersubstitutability: I can be your representative (stand in for you) because and to the extent you could be mine. The second sense *excludes* intersubstitutability: in his role as deputy a man cannot back his voters (in the same sense) as they back him; and the machines in my factory can back or bear out what is written down in my account books in a way in which these books cannot back those machines. It is this sort of asymmetry which may contribute to throwing some light on the comparison between names and representatives as well as on the idea of attributing meaning to names.[15]

In Wittgenstein's writings of the early 1930s names are called 'primary' signs or symbols, and this characterization is apt to the extent they stand out against other symbols. In some ways they resemble samples and stand out in similar respects. Thus, they can play a role independently of additional linguistic context. In the case of samples this is clear, as many objects figuring as samples when employed in the context of ostensive explanation can do so precisely because they do independent jobs: a pen can serve as a sample to explain 'pen' because it can be used to write letters and other things; a chair can serve as a sample to explain 'chair' because I can sit in it and thus demonstrate its purpose. And so on. Analogously, names can be used without linguistic context to *call* people (cf. PI, 27). Another relevant use is the use of names as *labels* (cf. PI, 15, 26): again, attaching a label to a thing to signify that this bottle contains gin or that this monument represents Bismarck can succeed without linguistic embedding.[16] Another obvious function that does not require a verbal context is that of ostensive explanation. While it is true that other kinds of words are also explained ostensively, the case of names seems special in so far as disambiguation seems rarely required as long as it is understood that the word to be explained is, or functions as, a name.

It may well be in virtue of their standing out through this kind of independence that names lend themselves to all kinds of peculiar uses that are not paralleled by other sorts of word. Thus, the weird use of 'this' described in the last lines of PI, 38 could more easily be imagined to

---

[15] Part of this idea—that the meaning of a name depends on a complicated kind of backing afforded by a mixture of convention, consensus and standard practice—is captured by the typical statement 'The meaning of a name is its position (I mean, its function) in a game' (MS 112, 198).

[16] Of course, names are not the only words or symbols that can function without additional linguistic context. But still, they are perhaps the only *sort* of linguistic symbol where such context-free uses are common practice.

take place if a name were employed instead of 'this': to *address* an object by its name or by the name of what it goes proxy for is a fairly natural form of human behaviour. Wittgenstein's remarks that were inspired by his reading of Frazer's *Golden Bough* form a particularly suggestive context for discussions of such uses of names.[17] There, Wittgenstein compares burning in effigy with kissing the picture of one's beloved. He emphasizes that such procedures are *not* based on beliefs regarding the causal efficacy of behaving in these ways. They are not based on anything inasmuch as they constitute completely natural, instinctive ways of acting. As Wittgenstein points out, not only kissing the picture of one's beloved is an activity of this kind but also kissing her *name*. And in this case, he says, the name's functioning as a *Stellvertreter* is clear (MS 110, 182; 20 June 1931; PO, 123): the name is a representative of the beloved, and it is in this capacity that I can kiss it. Such kinds of representation are characteristic of magical forms of thinking and acting. But as Wittgenstein underlines, it is not magical thinking which induces us to treat language, and in particular names, in this way but the principles of symbolism and language that manifest themselves in magic (ibid.; PO, 125). Names in particular can play outstanding roles: they may even be regarded as sacred in virtue of being both important *instruments* (recall the function of summoning somebody by his name) and *ornaments*—a kind of gift presented to us at birth (MS 110, 184; PO, 125).

The fact that names can be regarded as sacred is connected with another peculiarity emphasized by Wittgenstein. This is the possibility of identification of name and bearer: my name can be so valuable to me that an attack on it will be felt as an attack on my person. Perhaps I conceive of my name as part, or an extension, of myself. And if I can feel this in my own case, it should be possible to regard other people and their names in a similar way. At one point (MS 131, 141; RPP I, 326) Wittgenstein alludes to a passage in Goethe's autobiographical *Dichtung und Wahrheit* where the author describes how much he was hurt by a pun on his name: '[. . .] a man's name is not like a mantle, which merely hangs about him, and which, perchance may be safely twitched and pulled, but is a perfectly fitting garment which has grown over and over him like his very skin, at

---

[17] For Wittgenstein's remarks on Frazer, see Hacker, 'Developmental Hypotheses and Perspicuous Representations: Wittgenstein on Frazer's *Golden Bough*', reprinted in his *Wittgenstein: Connections and Controversies* (Oxford: Clarendon Press, 2001), 74–97.

which one cannot scratch and scrape without wounding the man himself.'[18] If it is natural to regard one's name as part of one's own person and to identify with it to the extent of perceiving an assault on one's name as an assault on oneself, it becomes even more plausible to construe names as in some respects similar to samples: pointing to a face or displaying a portrait are ways of presenting people with samples, and mentioning a name can be understood as a similar gesture. Identification, one may say, is an essential feature of our use of language. It is a mechanism which is so natural that it will defy explanation, but careful description of individual cases may help to throw light on how it works.[19]

Representation (i.e. 'being a representative'), identification and person-ification in the sense just alluded to are, as it were, intrinsic features of language. There is nothing to criticize here, for language would not get off the ground without these possibilities. What is important is to identify these features and find out where we are tempted to construe different uses of linguistic expressions after the model of those paradigmatic uses of names. One of the most critical points in our use of names is the way in which we associate characteristics of the bearer of a name with this name. This does not refer to associated images that happen to be evoked in the minds of individual speakers through the use of names but to descriptions mostly or collectively held true of the (supposed) bearer of a name. The characteristics attributed to Moses in PI, 79 are a case in point. Wittgenstein mentions a number of further examples, some of which will be discussed presently. What these examples seem to have in common is this: to the extent that it appears to be advisable to speak of the meaning of a name, the descriptions associated with a name strike us as the only items one might mention in an attempt at explaining the meaning of a name.

---

[18] Tr. S. Oxenford, quoted in Baker and Hacker, Exegesis of §171. A striking example from Victor Hugo is quoted in their essay 'Proper Names', p. 239n. Cf. Schulte, *Experience and Expression* (Oxford: Clarendon Press, 1993), 68–9.

[19] I think one may say that cases of identification do not explain but help to show how names manage to 'stick' to their bearers. For the idea of identification, see RPP I, 336: 'Goethe's signature intimates something Goethian to me. To that extent it is like a face, for I might say the same of his face. | It is like a *mirroring*. Does this phenomenon belong with this other one: "I have been in this situation before"? | Or do I *'identify'* the signature with the person in that, e.g. I love to look at the signature of a beloved human being, or I frame the signature of someone I admire and put it on my desk? (Magic that is done with pictures, hair etc.)'. At one point (RPP I, 853) the relevance of the naturalness of this type of association is put in question.

III

The way in which descriptions of the bearers of names are associated with these names is the topic of a number of reflections to be found in Wittgenstein's later writings. And in reading these remarks it is helpful to bear in mind what we have tried to capture by speaking of 'being a representative', 'identification' and 'personification'. In a remark from the *Investigations* Wittgenstein speaks of *unity* and *fusion*: '[...] the faces of famous men and the sound of their names are fused together. This name strikes me as the only right one for this face' (PI, 171).[20] In a remark written in 1946 (MS 131, 29) Wittgenstein speaks of the impression we get that the names of famous writers and composers seem to have 'absorbed' or 'soaked up' a particular meaning—and 'meaning' is surely to be understood as referring to the specific character of these people's works and what is seen as corresponding to this character in their lives, portraits and other documents.[21] In another remark where he discusses the way in which a person's name, his picture and his works seem to be inseparably fused he uses the graphic expression that Schubert's name has 'grown together' or 'merged' with features of his works and his face: the 'shades' or 'spirits' of his music and his physiognomy 'hover around' his name (MS 169, 4v).[22] A well-known passage where Wittgenstein tries to capture this peculiar form of association characteristic of our use of names can be found in the so-called 'second part' of the *Investigations*. There he writes:

[20] A fuller version of this remark can be found in Wittgenstein's German revision of the *Brown Book* (*Eine philosophische Betrachtung*, p. 184), quoted in Baker and Hacker, Exegesis of §171.

[21] Here one may want to point out that Wittgenstein's use of 'meaning' in his late manuscripts is extremely different from the way he uses the word in his manuscripts from the time around 1931. That is true—but it is true only up to a point: even in his earlier writings the meaning of names is not exhausted by descriptions relevant to identifying bearers of names. Many of the Frazer remarks written at that time involve a much broader notion of meaning. What also bears on this issue are Wittgenstein's largely contemporaneous remarks on the idea of 'the life' of signs and 'the soul' of a sentence, cf. my article ' "The Life of the Sign": Wittgenstein on Reading a Poem', in John Gibson and Wolfgang Huemer (eds.), *The Literary Wittgenstein* (London and New York: Routledge, 2004), 146–64. What I want to make plausible, even though I cannot fully argue this here, is that Wittgenstein's late—and obviously broad and complex—notion of meaning can fruitfully be seen as growing out of various aspects of earlier things he says about names. Taking these aspects as well as certain features of the development of Wittgenstein's thought into account may then render his ways of speaking of 'the meaning' of proper names intelligible, and perhaps even helpful.

[22] 'Der Name Schubert, umschwebt von den Geistern seines Gesichts, seiner Werke.' Unaccountably, the text given in LW II, 4, has '...umschattet von den Gesten...'. Accordingly, the translation runs 'The name Schubert, shadowed around by the gestures of his face, of his works'.

Closely associated things, things which we *have* associated, seem to fit one another. But what is this seeming to fit? How is their seeming to fit manifested? Perhaps like this: we cannot imagine the man who had this name, this face, this handwriting, not to have produced *these* works, but perhaps quite different ones instead (those of another great man).   (PI, p. 183)

It is due to the closeness of this type of association that we find the idea of a painting showing Goethe in the process of writing the Ninth Symphony 'embarrassing and ridiculous' (PI, p. 183).

Wittgenstein's writings, and in particular the manuscripts written between 1946 and 1949, contain many further remarks describing the peculiar ways in which we feel that names and features of what they (are supposed to) stand for fit each other or are fused together. But surely the quotations and hints given above are sufficient to get an impression of what he is driving at. And I hope that they are also sufficient to indicate that these later remarks can be seen as rooted in ideas Wittgenstein developed when reflecting on primitive aspects of symbolism. The central notion bringing his Frazer-inspired remarks into focus was that of *Vertretung*, and some of its quasi-magical features are clearly related to the type of association discussed in Wittgenstein's later manuscripts on the philosophy of psychology. I also hope that the material I have brought together is sufficient to lend plausibility to my claim that Wittgenstein not only found it natural to speak of the meaning of names but also had a good philosophical reason for doing so.

This reason is connected with Wittgenstein's refusal to put up with a restricted concept of meaning of the kind beloved by many philosophers working in the tradition of Frege. One way in which this refusal finds expression is Wittgenstein's abiding interest in word-feelings (e.g. 'if-feeling') and related phenomena, in particular in the area of music. This interest is clearly one in certain aspects of what Wittgenstein regarded as meaning. This becomes obvious when he invents the figure of a 'meaning-blind' person who would not be able to perceive certain shades of meaning. This inability is revealed by his failing to understand and produce sentences about the flavour of words or about what reading a certain word felt like.[23] More generally speaking, such a person would not be able to

---

[23] In MS 135, 54r–v, Wittgenstein refers to the following passage from Grillparzer: 'I cannot describe the dreadful impression which the *h* in the English word *ghost* makes on me. When the

experience the meanings of words or phrases. This notion of experiencing the meaning of an expression is central to Wittgenstein's remarks on the philosophy of psychology and is one point that, in his own judgement, gives his reflections on aspect-seeing and aspect-blindness their importance (see PI, p. 214).

There is no doubt that the phenomena I have illustrated under the headings 'being a representative', 'identification', 'personification' and 'close association' are paradigm examples of what a meaning-blind person would find it extremely difficult or impossible to make sense of. And if we grant that this person's difficulty is one which concerns the *meaning* of words, phrases and all kinds of symbols, then we have no reason to withhold the word 'meaning' in other contexts of talking about names and what they signify. Once we admit that 'Schubert' has a meaning that you and I can understand and experience whereas the ignorant and the meaning-blind would (for different reasons) be unable to understand or experience it, we shall be obliged to concede that 'Moses' and similar names can also be said to have meanings. Of course, no one is forced to accept this way of talking. But if you share Wittgenstein's interest in the phenomena and expressions discussed in this essay, you will be hard put to avoid it.

In conclusion I want to remark on the central notion and the three contrasts I mentioned towards the beginning of this essay. What has become clear, I think, is that there is a way of seeing Wittgenstein's later reflections on names and how they can be regarded as meaningful as having roots in the ideas of *Vertretung*, the primary use of certain symbols and the role of samples. To be sure, of the original framework which gave these ideas whatever sense can be attributed to them very little was still in place when Wittgenstein inserted the 'Moses' remark into the earliest version of what became *Philosophical Investigations*; but still, his early reflections in terms of these ideas can be seen as having contributed to his later ideas. What about our third contrast, that is, 'description vs. explanation'? Here, I think, the situation is somewhat different. The slogan 'Away with explanation, description is the only game in town' survives into Wittgenstein's later writings but it is used with different expectations in mind. In the early

word is spoken it does not sound particularly solemn, but whenever I see it written it does not fail to have its effect on me; I believe I am seeing a spectre before me.' Quoted in Schulte, *Experience and Expression*, 69.

1930s description was believed to be capable of revealing the logical or grammatical structure of language. Later, however, the idea that there is such a structure to be revealed faded away: of course, description is still expected to contribute to our understanding of the workings of language, but the dream of a full and uniform account of these workings has been abandoned.

Analytic Truths and Grammatical Propositions

SEVERIN SCHROEDER

I

There is a well-known view that analytic statements are true simply in virtue of the meanings of the ingredient words. They are typically used as linguistic explanations. Instead of

(1) The word 'cygnet' means: young swan.

one can also, and more idiomatically, say:

(2) A cygnet is a young swan.

The two sentences have the same use, fulfil the same function in language, and hence have the same meaning. A statement of (1) is true because the word 'cygnet' *does* mean a young swan. That is to say, (1) is true in virtue of the meaning of the word 'cygnet'. But as (1) functions in the same way as the corresponding analytic statement (2), the same can be said about (2). This too can be verified simply by looking up the meaning of the word 'cygnet' in a dictionary. Of course the truth of (1) and (2) is dependent not only on the meaning of the word 'cygnet', but also on the meanings of their other words. If, for example, the word 'young' meant: black, the statements would be false. So just like (1), (2) is true in virtue of the meaning of the whole sentence.

However, this account of analyticity is widely regarded as untenable owing to a number of objections. I shall consider them in turn.

1. Quine's Attack on the Analytic/Synthetic Distinction

The analytic/synthetic distinction was famously attacked by Quine in his article 'Two Dogmas of Empiricism' (1953).[1] Quine observed that the notion of analyticity could not be defined 'extensionally', that is, in terms of 'truth' or 'reference', but only in terms of a cluster of other 'intensional' words (such as 'synonymous', 'self-contradiction', or 'necessity'), that is, words that, again, cannot be defined in terms of 'truth' or 'reference' alone. He regarded such definitions as viciously circular and dismissed the analytic/synthetic distinction as ill-founded. The weakness of this line of argument has been well exposed by Paul Grice and P.F. Strawson,[2] and further by H.-J. Glock,[3] who concluded that:

Quine's circularity-charge comes down to the rather odd complaint that 'analytic' can be explained only via notions with which it is synonymous, and not via notions with which it is not synonymous. . . . The idea that legitimate concepts must be translatable into a purely extensional language presupposes that intensional notions have been discredited, which is what the circularity-charge set out to do.[4]

Another line of argument in Quine's paper is based on his *holism*, the view that our statements do not admit of confirmation or disconfirmation individually, but face the tribunal of experience only as a whole.[5] Thus, when a scientific prediction turns out false, it is really the whole web of our beliefs, including mathematics and logic, that is in conflict with experience. We could resolve the conflict in numerous ways, even by abandoning some of our logical or mathematical statements. Hence no statement is *a priori* and immune from revision in the light of new experience, not even the axioms of logic and mathematics.[6] Apart from the fact that this holistic picture appears to exaggerate the extent to which our beliefs are logically interrelated, it seems hard to imagine how we might possibly give up our ordinary logical thinking without undermining the whole idea of

---

[1] W. van O. Quine, 'Two Dogmas of Empiricism', in his *From a Logical Point of View* (Cambridge, Mass.: Harvard University Press, 1953).

[2] Paul Grice and P.F. Strawson, 'In Defence of a Dogma' (1956), in P.F. Grice, *Studies in the Way of Words* (Cambridge, Mass.: Harvard University Press. 1989).

[3] Hans-Johann Glock, 'Necessity and Normativity', in H. Sluga and D.G. Stern (eds.), *The Cambridge Companion to Wittgenstein* (Cambridge: Cambridge University Press, 1996); §1; *Quine and Davidson on Language, Thought and Reality* (Cambridge: Cambridge University Press, 2003); ch. 3.

[4] Glock, *Quine and Davidson*, 75.   [5] Quine, 'Two Dogmas', 41.

[6] Quine, 'Two Dogmas', 42 f.

a web of interrelated beliefs and, indeed, the very idea of confirmation or disconfirmation by experience. But the most telling weakness in Quine's argument is this: The fact that any sentence, even '2 + 3 = 5' or '∼(p.∼p)', may in future be rejected as false, does not show that they do not *now* express an *a priori* (mathematical, logical or analytic) truth. Rather, if future generations decide that '2 + 3 = 5' is false, we know that at least one of these signs must have *changed its meaning*.[7] For the current meaning of those signs is such that '2 + 3 = 5' *is* an *a priori* truth, a norm of representation which we do not regard as subject to empirical confirmation or disconfirmation.

Although it is widely acknowledged that Quine's attack on the analytic/synthetic distinction was unsuccessful, many philosophers have misgivings about the idea that some statements are true in virtue of meanings or conventions. Another radical attack on the traditional account of analyticity is:

2. Williamson's Denial of Conceptual Truth

Timothy Williamson disputes that there are any analytic or conceptual truths 'in the epistemological sense', i.e. statements that one cannot fully understand without knowing that they are true.[8]

Note, first of all, that Williamson does not distinguish between analytic truths and trivially analytic truths.[9] A proponent of the view that analytic truths are true in virtue of meaning is not committed to the claim (which Williamson is trying to attack) that their truth is self-evident to anybody who understands their meaning. It may require some calculations or reasoning to work out that a given statement is indeed analytically true, calculations in which one may easily make a mistake that would not betoken linguistic incompetence. Just as one can easily get an arithmetical calculation wrong without any misunderstanding of the mathematical symbols involved. Anyway, this can be set aside, as the standard examples of analytic truths are indeed claimed to be self-evident.

Williamson argues as follows:

Consider the proposition

---

[7] Cf. Grice and Strawson, 'In Defence', 211; Glock, 'Necessity', 211 f.

[8] Timothy Williamson, 'Conceptual Truth', *Aristotelian Society Supplementary Volume*, 80 (2006), 1–41.

[9] Cf. Wolfgang Künne, *Abstrakte Gegenstände: Semantik und Ontologie* (Frankfurt am Main: Suhrkamp, 1983); 221 ff.

(3) *Every vixen is a vixen.*

Peter and Stephen both understand the meaning of (3). However, Peter takes universal quantification (in English) to be existentially committing and he believes that in fact there are no vixens.[10] *Stephen believes that there are some borderline cases for 'vixen': and 'for such an animal as the value of "x", "x is a vixen" is neither true nor false, so the conditional "x is a vixen → x is a vixen" is also neither true nor false'. Hence, Stephen argues, (3) is also neither true nor false.*[11] *Thus, both Peter and Stephen, although they understand (3), do not accept it as true. Williamson takes this to show that there are no analytic truths 'in the epistemological sense'.*[12]

The first of these alleged counterexamples can be dismissed fairly quickly. Peter takes (3) to have *empirical* content. On his understanding, it has the logical form:

(3a) $(\exists x)Fx . (\forall x)(Fx \rightarrow Fx)$.

By contrast, those who take (3) as an example of an analytic truth, construe it as:

(3b) $(\forall x)(Fx \rightarrow Fx)$.

Perhaps both readings are possible. Then, (3) is ambiguous. Similarly, someone might reject the statement:

(4) All bachelors are unmarried.

on the grounds that, in fact, some bachelors *of arts* are married. But, obviously, this would have no tendency to show that on another, more natural, reading, (4) is a self-evident analytic truth. In both cases, rejection of the analytic statement betokens a divergent understanding.

Williamson seems to think that Peter is actually mistaken in his belief that (3) has existential implications.[13] Be that as it may, we can certainly agree that Williamson's second example ('Stephen') is of somebody who is mistaken. An empirical statement of the form 'Every *F* is *G*' may be threatened by a borderline case *F* that is not *G*: for allowing the borderline case would make the statement false. Not so in this case (of 'Every *F* is *F*'): Since it is logically impossible for anything to satisfy the antecedent

---

[10] Williamson, 'Conceptual Truth', 9 f.   [11] Williamson, 'Conceptual Truth', 10 f.
[12] Williamson, 'Conceptual Truth', 39.   [13] Williamson, 'Conceptual Truth', 11, 26.

predicate, but not the consequent predicate, the possibility of borderline cases becomes patently irrelevant. Stephen's view that (3) implies that there are no borderline cases for the predicate 'vixen' is mistaken. By asserting (3) I do not make (or commit myself to) any such empirical claim. But then Stephen's misguided construal of (3), as having empirical import, fails to be the counterexample it is meant to be. The claim at issue is that one cannot *understand* a trivially analytic statement without *ipso facto* understanding it to be true. Stephen can obviously not provide a counterexample to that claim if he *mis*understands the statement in question. Williamson, however, tries to resist the diagnosis that Stephen and Peter (assuming that Peter too is mistaken about (3)) have a deviant *understanding of the meaning* of the sentence. Though, why he should resist it, is not so easy to make out.

First he notes that Peter's and Stephen's deviant views make 'little difference in practice'.[14] That may be true, but is patently irrelevant. Some semantic misunderstandings are big, some are small and hardly ever noticeable. Still, Williamson labours the point: Peter and Stephen defend their misconceptions fluently; they have even published articles in English;[15] their English is better than that of young children or foreigners still learning the language.[16] As if in order to make a semantic mistake one needed to be semi-inarticulate!

Secondly, Williamson notes that Peter and Stephen are emphatic that they intend their words 'to be understood as words of our common language, with their standard English senses'.[17] *Of course* they do. Otherwise, if they intentionally flouted linguistic conventions, it wouldn't be a misunderstanding.[18]

Thirdly, and perhaps most importantly, Williamson claims that the understanding which Peter and Stephen lack 'is logical, is not semantic'.[19] What they disagree with us about is not the meaning of an expression, it is the 'logical facts about "every"'.[20] Now, where do those 'logical facts' about specific words spring from? Supposing that it is a 'logical fact about

---

[14] Williamson, 'Conceptual Truth', 11.   [15] Williamson, 'Conceptual Truth', 12.
[16] Williamson, 'Conceptual Truth', 13.   [17] Williamson, 'Conceptual Truth', 12.
[18] Williamson becomes curiously indignant at the idea that we might find it necessary to correct Peter's or Stephen's understanding of English words ('gratuitously patronising' (pp. 13 f.)), or insist against their misconstrual of (3) that what they meant would be more correctly expressed by different words: that would be: 'to treat them less than fully seriously as human beings, like patients in need of old-fashioned psychiatric treatment' (p. 25). This, I suppose, is what one calls an *argumentum ad misericordiam*.
[19] Williamson, 'Conceptual Truth', 14.   [20] Williamson, 'Conceptual Truth', 13.

"every" ' that a proposition of the form 'Every F is F' has *no* existential import: that its logical form is (3b), rather than (3a), this is evidently a *conventional* fact. After all, we can easily imagine, or even create, a language in which the corresponding word (the word used to make a claim about everything of a certain kind) does have an existential implication. Indeed, we may *change the meaning* of 'every' in English, or at least a dialect of English, so that from now on it is a 'logical fact about "every" ' that propositions of the form 'Every F is F' have the logical form (3a) (or that they are to be understood to carry the implication that there are no borderline cases of F). Consider some real examples. Is it a logical fact about the negation sign that two negation signs in succession cancel each other out? That depends on the language, and thus on the meaning of the words used as negation signs. Sometimes they do, sometimes they don't. Many languages, or dialects, allow for double negation to be used as a straightforward or emphatic negation. Again, consider the English sentence:

(5) She must not come.

and its word-by-word translation into German:

(6) *Sie muß nicht kommen.*

In fact the latter means: 'She need not come'. The 'logical facts' about the English words 'must' and 'not' are slightly different from the 'logical facts' about their German counterparts. 'Logical facts' about words are conventional semantic facts.

It is of course true that there are logical mistakes that are not semantic mistakes. For instance, the fallacy of denying the antecedent is not a semantic error: it does not normally betoken a misunderstanding of the meaning of any words. Is it plausible to regard Peter's and Stephen's deviations as defects in their 'deductive competence', as Williamson seems to suggest,[21] rather than semantic errors?—No. For this diagnosis to be plausible it is not enough that their deductions lead to the wrong result, since that, of course, also happens when one is wrong about the meaning of words. For example, someone under the impression that 'if' means 'if and only if', will accept the argument: 'If p then q; not p; therefore not

---

[21] Williamson, 'Conceptual Truth', 22.

q'—not because of any deductive incompetence, but simply because of a semantic misunderstanding. In order to make out that it *was* deductive incompetence, we would have to establish first that both premises were correctly understood: that there was agreement as to when the conditional is to be regarded as true and when it is to be regarded as false. If the disagreement about an argument can be traced back to a disagreement about the truth conditions of one of its premises, a simple conditional, it is obviously a *semantic* disagreement, and not distinctively logical. Similarly in the case of our disagreements with Peter and Stephen: it is not just (and not primarily) the results of deductive arguments that they get wrong (indeed, no deductive arguments figure in Williamson's example). It is simply that in a given situation (viz., when there are no vixens, or when there are borderline cases of vixens, respectively) they regard proposition (3) as false, thus contradicting the conventionally accepted understanding of this kind of proposition. Deductive competence doesn't come into it.

Note, incidentally, that Williamson's example (3) is, anyway, slightly out of focus. Obviously, it is not a typical analytic statement in that it is a logical truth (an instance of a theorem of the predicate calculus). Later on in his paper Williamson moves on to a related analytic truth that is not a logical truth, namely:

(7) Every vixen is a female fox.

—arguing that his conclusions about (3) hold for (7) as well. It is worth noting, however, that (7) is not idiomatic English, but a philosophers' translation of:

(8) A vixen is a female fox.

The expression '*every* vixen' (rather than '*a* vixen') is naturally used for *empirical* generalisations about vixens, and, hence, misleading when—as is typically the point of analytic statements—the explanation of a word is at issue.

The philosophers' misleading assimilation of analytic statements to empirical generalisations is driven by a commitment to a system of formal logic that lacks the resources to distinguish between empirical generalisations and statements such as (8). It is worth noting that Williamson's argument is not only unconvincing, but based entirely on complications that arise from this problematic assimilation.

Finally, let us briefly consider Williamson's alternative picture. If, as he has tried to argue, the understanding of the meaning of a trivially analytic statement does not bring with it an understanding of its truth, the question arises of how else we are to know that it is true. How, according to Williamson, do we know that all vixens are vixens? Or do we? 'What strike us today as the best candidates for analytic or conceptual truth some innovative thinker may call into question tomorrow for intelligible reasons.'[22] This sounds as if Williamson doesn't take himself to know for certain that vixens are vixens!

Williamson's opinion is that *one can have a 'minimal understanding' of a word without yet grasping the concept in question. Thus, for example, one can understand the words 'furze' and 'gorse' without knowing that furze is gorse. A shared understanding of a word doesn't require a shared stock of platitudes; rather, what holds a linguistic practice together is that different uses of the same word are causally related, together with the fact that individual speakers allow the references of their words to be fixed by its use over the whole community.*[23]

The first claim is true if 'minimal understanding' is taken to mean: partial understanding. You can know that 'furze' and 'gorse' are names of plants—even that they both name some yellow-flowered shrubs—without being aware that they are synonymous. It is of course true that of a huge number of words in our language we only have such a 'minimal understanding': we can only vaguely classify them as denoting, say, a flower, a mineral or some part of a combustion engine.[24] And it is also true that in many conversational contexts such a 'minimal understanding' is quite enough to get by. However, if you don't know *which* kind of yellow-flowered shrub is called 'gorse': if you are unable to identify gorse and tell it apart from other yellow-flowered shrubs, you can hardly be credited with a *full* understanding of the word. Just as a full understanding of the word 'magenta' requires more than the knowledge that it is a colour word; or even that it denotes a shade of red. To know what exactly 'magenta' means you need to be able to tell that colour apart from other shades of red.

Now, that somebody with only a 'minimal', or partial understanding of the meaning of a word may fail to recognise the truth of an analytic

[22] Williamson, 'Conceptual Truth', 37.   [23] Williamson, 'Conceptual Truth', 34–40.
[24] But note also that the most common words are not like that.

statement involving that word is small wonder, and in no way at odds with the traditional account of analyticity. Again, that there are causal relations between different speakers' uses of the same word where some of those speakers have only a partial understanding of the word's meaning and defer to the experts' account of what exactly it means is perfectly true—but quite irrelevant to the question of analyticity. Where Williamson goes wrong is in setting up this picture of a 'division of linguistic labour' as an alternative to the view that 'a shared understanding of a word requires a shared stock of platitudes'.[25] In fact, what characterises such cases of 'division of linguistic labour' is exactly that the understanding of a word is not fully shared. When the man at the garage says to me: 'I'm afraid we'll have to replace the dog flange', then (although he and I can up to a point communicate: I can tell him to go ahead and do so) it is quite evident that I don't fully share his understanding of that technical term. To the extent that the understanding of a word is *shared*, so is the knowledge of trivial analytic truths that constitutes this understanding. Consider:

(9) What has been refuted is false.

For those who use the verb 'to refute' in its standard sense, this is an analytic truth. Yet a considerable number, perhaps the majority, of English speakers today would not accept (9) as true, because they have a different understanding of the word 'refute' (as meaning merely: to deny). Disagreement over an analytic truth indicates a misunderstanding. (Note the difference between this case and a case of 'division of linguistic labour', which should never lead to an actual disagreement. If all I know about furze and gorse is that they are yellow-flowered shrubs, I am in no position to know that furze *is* gorse, but neither can I have reason to deny it. If somebody were to deny the analytic truth that furze is gorse, he would thereby betoken a misunderstanding of at least one of the terms, not just an only partial understanding.)

More common than the radical denials of analyticity discussed so far is the view that analyticity, although an undeniable phenomenon, cannot be explained as truth in virtue of meaning.

---

[25] Williamson, 'Conceptual Truth', 35 f.

3. *Argument from the Use/Mention Distinction*

(1) cannot be synonymous with (2), for the word 'cygnet' is used in (2), but only mentioned in (1). Therefore an understanding of (2) requires an understanding of the word 'cygnet', whereas one can fully understand (1) even if one doesn't know that word.

It is a curiously widespread prejudice among analytic philosophers that when a linguistic expression is mentioned (presented in inverted commas) it cannot at the same time be used. The truth is that mentioning, or quoting, a word or sentence is one—quite common—way of using that expression. I can utter the words:

> (10) As Macbeth puts it: 'If it were done when 'tis done, then 'twere well it were done quickly.'

mentioning a well-known sentence from *Macbeth*, in order to admonish somebody to act without delay. Again, the response:

> (11) This is what in court is called 'a leading question'.

mentions an expression while at the same time applying it.

Anyway, it is a mistake to think that one can generally fully understand a statement without understanding any of the expressions it contains in inverted commas. It is of course true in the case where what is presented in inverted commas is not a meaningful expression: where there is nothing to understand. For instance:

> (12) 'srxx' is not a word.
> (13) My neighbour's owl goes: 'Oohoo.'

But consider:

> (14) My neighbour's wife often says: 'Jöögd hett keen Döögd.'
> (15) The word 'подросток' is difficult to translate into English.

Who would seriously maintain that these two statements are fully understandable without any knowledge of foreign languages? (Note that (14) conveys information not only about the *noises* made by the speaker's neighbour's wife, but about what she *says*.)

It is of course true that somebody as yet unfamiliar with the word 'cygnet' will understand:

(1) The word 'cygnet' means: young swan.

as an explanation of that word. But clearly, the same is true of:

(2) A cygnet is a young swan.

Just as the sentences:

(16) This colour is sepia.
(17) This colour is called 'sepia'.

are both equally suitable for an ostensive explanation of the term 'sepia'.

4. Argument from the Contingency of Meaning

Analytic propositions are necessary propositions. But to suppose an analytic statement to be a statement about linguistic meaning amounts to saying that it is not a necessary truth. The negation of a true statement about linguistic meaning is contingently false, whereas the negation of an analytic statement is self-contradictory, i.e., arguably, not false, but nonsensical.

First of all, it is worth noting that in ordinary conversation the negation of an analytic statement would not in fact be regarded as self-contradictory. Rather, it would be treated as a linguistic error: as false. Somebody who said:

(18) A cygnet is not a swan, it's a farming tool with a semicircular blade.

would not be taken as contradicting himself, as making an illogical claim. Rather, we would take the speaker as having confused two different words. What he means is obviously a sickle. We would not take him to express a self-contradictory belief, but a false linguistic claim (a false association of sound and meaning).

However, it is of course true that, disregarding linguistic error and insisting on the correct meanings of the words, (18) is inconsistent (for it implies that a swan of a certain description is not a swan). But the same inconsistency can be found in a negation of (1):

(19) The word 'cygnet' does not mean: young swan.

Here it is important to remember that a word is not just a sound or a sequence of letters. A word is essentially a word of a language: it is a sound or a sequence of letters *that has been given a certain meaning*. Thus, 'nguxä' is not a word; and the English 'also' is a different word from the German 'also' (which means: therefore). That is to say, *the meaning is part of the word*: it makes it the word it is.[26] It follows that:

(1) The word 'cygnet' means: young swan.

is just as much a necessary truth as the corresponding analytic statement (2). The *English word* 'cygnet'—that is, 'cygnet' with its current meaning in English (viz., young swan)—has its current meaning in English (viz., young swan). That could not possibly be otherwise, for a word with a different meaning would be a different word—not the English word 'cygnet'. A word with a different meaning could at most be a homonym: a different word with the same spelling. That is to say, (1) must not be confused with:

(20) The sequence of letters 'cygnet' is used in English to denote a young swan.

This is a contingent statement. The same *sequence of letters* might have been given a different meaning (and still be the same sequence of letters). By contrast, the correct statement that a given *word* (partly defined by its meaning) has a certain meaning is as much a necessary truth as the claim that a bachelor is an unmarried man.[27]

Does that imply that the meaning of a word cannot change? No, our criteria of diachronic identity are not as pedantic as that. A word may change slightly in meaning and still remain, recognisably, the same word; just as a word may change slightly in spelling (e.g. from 'chace' to 'chase') or pronunciation (e.g. from/kneɪv/to/neɪv/) and still be called the same word. On the other hand, a *radical* semantic change produces a new word. The Middle English word 'nice', for example, meaning: stupid, silly (from Latin *nescius*: ignorant), can hardly be regarded as the same word as its modern descendant.[28]

It is of course true that at the bottom of the necessity of an analytic truth is nothing more than a contingent socio-linguistic fact. There are

---

[26] A homonym is 'a word of the same spelling or sound as another but of different meaning' (*Oxford Concise English Dictionary*). In other words, a different (and unrelated) meaning makes a different word. However, one may prefer to say that some words have more than one meaning. That does not affect the point I am stressing: that a word is not just a sequence of letters or sounds, but to be identified also by what it means.

[27] In *Tractatus* terminology: a word is a symbol, not just a sign (TLP, 3.32).

[28] Or should we say 'descendants'? A nice question.

two perspectives: an internal one, from inside the practice, where the norms are taken for granted, and an external one, from the outside, where other norms are equally conceivable. Inside the game of chess, it is not negotiable that the white queen's bishop moves only on black squares: it is a necessary truth, as opposed to the contingent truth that in a given game its first move is to b2 (and not, say, to d2). We can explain this necessity by citing the rules of chess (the form of the chessboard, the way the pieces are set up, the way they are allowed to move). Thus, given that we want to play *chess*, it is a necessity that the white queen's bishop moves only on black squares. Different rules would make a different game. But then of course, (moving now to the external perspective) we *could* have invented and played a different game (or a variant of the same game).[29] The invention and subsequent popularity of the game of chess is a historical contingency. Similarly, the establishment of certain linguistic norms is a historical contingency. Still, when we speak a language (taking up the internal perspective) we accept its norms, and what they prescribe is accepted as not negotiable.

5. *Argument from the Apparent Difference in Subject Matter*

(1) says something about a word, whereas (2) says something about a certain kind of animal; so evidently, they do not mean the same.

That is what one is inclined to say when considering only the formulation and not the use. It is at the heart of Wittgenstein's philosophy that that is a recipe for error or confusion. Frequently, similar formulations hide crucial differences in use; and occasionally different formulations disguise striking similarities in use.

First, consider the pair:

(21) He kicked the bucket.
(22) He popped off.

They too might appear to have different subject matters. But in fact, (21) is merely an idiomatic variant of (22). Again, metaphors are idiomatically

---

[29] *Slightly* different rules would more naturally be said to make a variant of the same game, rather than a different game, and if the deviation from the rules of an established game was unintended, the result might still be regarded as the same game although played incorrectly. Likewise, there are different variants of English and there is faulty English.

succinct ways of drawing comparisons, while on the face of it, taken *au pied de la lettre,* they usually appear to say something absurd or pointless.[30]

Secondly, can one really make sense of the suggestion that analytic statements are *not* about words or concepts? On the face of it (2) seems to say something about a certain kind of animal: but *what* does it say about that kind of animal? That it is the kind of animal it is. Remember, 'cygnet' and 'young swan' are synonymous expressions. Their meaning is exactly the same. So what (2) tells us about cygnets cannot be different from what the following tells us:

(23) A young swan is a young swan.

—namely nothing.[31]

Some philosophers would protest that (23) is not empty as it ascribes to young swans the quality of self-identity. But what quality is that? Quine says that it is 'an obvious trait of everything'.[32] Gilbert Harman calls the fact that everything is self-identical 'a general feature of the way the world is'.[33] Here language has evidently gone on holiday.[34] Of course nothing can prevent a philosopher from defining a predicate (be it 'entity', or 'self-identical') to apply to everything. But then to call it a 'quality', 'feature' or 'trait' of things that this predicate applies to them is, arguably, a misuse of those words, which in ordinary English are used for *distinctive* attributes. Anyway, call self-identity a 'quality' or a 'trait' if you like, the fact remains that by ascribing such a Pickwickian 'quality' to something—you haven't really said anything. The problem with the attempt to construe analytic statements as statements about objects (such as cygnets), rather than words or concepts, is that it would make them entirely vacuous and pointless. It fails to account for the fact that, unlike (23), an analytic statement such as (2) can be *informative* and *useful*. It can be used to explain the meaning of words. So it is plausible to construe it as a statement about words.

---

[30] Cf. Severin Schroeder, 'Why Juliet is the Sun', in M. Siebel and M. Textor (eds), *Semantik und Ontologic* (Frankfurt: Ontos Verlag, 2004).

[31] Of course one can say that (2) tells us what a cygnet is; but so does (1). In general, the explanation of a word '*F*' (in a dictionary, for example) tells us what (an) *F* is.

[32] W. van O. Quine, 'Carnap and Logical Truth' (1963), in his *The Ways of Paradox* (Cambridge, Mass.: Harvard University Press, 1979), 113.

[33] Gilbert Harman, 'Quine on Meaning and Existence I', *Review of Metaphysics*, 21 (1968), 128.

[34] Cf. PI §216.

Consider also the following analytic statement in German:

(24) *Sonnabend ist Samstag.*

It is impossible to translate it into English. Is that, as Heidegger might have suggested, because the German language is closer to the pulse of being than other languages (with the possible exception of ancient Greek), so that certain profound metaphysical insights cannot possibly be rendered in English? No, it is simply because German has two words for 'Saturday', English (as far as I know) only one. So, following a dictionary, the only possible translation of (24) is:

(25) Saturday is Saturday.

But obviously, (24) and (25) differ in meaning: (25) is utterly trivial, of the form '*A* is *A*', whereas (24), of the form '*A* is *B*', might well be news to some people (especially in the south of Germany). And what could that news possibly be if not that *Sonnabend* is another word for the day called *Samstag*?—By the same token, (2) and (23) differ in meaning, even though the one can be derived from the other by the substitution of synonymous expressions. That is exactly because (although phrased in material mode, without inverted commas) those statements are in effect *about the expressions* in question. Hence the difference between those two expressions matters even if it is not a difference in meaning. (2) and (23) differ in meaning just as the potentially informative ' "*A*" is synonymous with "*B*" ' differs in meaning from the trivial ' "*A*" is synonymous with "*A*" '—even if '*A*' *is* synonymous with '*B*'.

6. Argument from Translation

The two analytic statements

(26) *Red is a colour.*

and

(26D) Rot ist eine Farbe.

have the same meaning, which would not be the case if (26) was a statement about an English word, while (26D) was a statement about a German word.

The claim that analytic statements are about words seems to be contradicted by the fact that usually (although, as just shown, not always) they can be translated into another language. But the contradiction is only apparent. As noted above, a word is not just a sequence of letters; an essential part of a word is its meaning. And two words of different languages can have the same meaning, for instance: 'red' and *rot*. Indeed, of the two aspects of a word—the sequence of letters and the meaning—the latter (the semantic aspect) is clearly the one that matters. The former (the graphic/phonetic aspect) is just a tag or marker, which by being used in a certain way acquires a certain meaning. The tag is necessary, no doubt (you can't have the meaning without a bearer), but essentially replaceable. Any other combination of letters could have fulfilled the job just as well.

According to these two aspects of a word, there are two kinds of statements one might make about a word: One can comment on its spelling (or pronunciation) or one can comment on its meaning. Now it should be evident that where what we say about a word concerns its meaning (and not its spelling) it applies equally to any other word with exactly the same meaning. Thus, what we say about the meaning of the English word 'red' can also be said about the meaning of the synonymous German word *rot*. And what we say *in English* about the one word, we can say *in German* about the other one. Thus:

(27) 'Red' is a colour word.

is correctly translated into German as:

(27D) *'Rot' ist ein Farbwort.*

Both statements make the same semantic claim about a word with the same semantic characteristics. Therefore, (27D) is (in most contexts) a correct translation of (27), and vice versa. If (27D) occurred in a German novel—say, in a primary school classroom scene—it would have to be rendered into English as (27). Even though, to be sure, the two sentences are not identical in meaning: (27) is about an English word, (27D) is about a German word. The alternative English translation of (27D):

(28) *Rot* is a colour word.

would (in most contexts) be unacceptable. For (28) is about a *foreign* word, whereas both (27) and (27D) are about a word in their respective languages; and that is something a good translation (for most purposes) needs to preserve.

Now it should be clear where the objection under discussion goes wrong. The two statements (26) and (26D) do *not* have exactly the same meaning. They are indeed about different words. The reason why they *appear* to have the same meaning and are indeed adequate translations of each other is that they make the same semantic claim about two words that have the same meaning, that take up exactly the same position in their respective languages' 'grammatical space' (BT, 30).

Of course we are strongly inclined to believe that (26) and (26D) *must* have the same meaning since they are constructed in the same way out of words with the same meaning. But the analogous pair of sentences shows that this reason is not conclusive: (27) and (27D) are constructed in the same way out of words with the same meaning, and yet differ in meaning. And what I have been arguing is that (26) and (26D) should be seen as variants of the other pair.

This point is also relevant to another standard objection:

7. Argument from Analytic Truth's Apparent Independence of a Given Language

What is expressed by, say,

(8) A vixen is a female fox.

cannot be true in virtue of the meaning of the English word 'vixen', because it would still have been true if English had never existed.

This objection, too, is based on the—not entirely correct—assumption that analytic truths are synonymous with their translations into other languages. The meaning that (8) and its translations share is then thought to be a truth that exists independently of any language. However, as argued above, (8) and its equivalent in another language are not strictly synonymous, but only semantically analogous. (8) expresses a logical relation among the three English predicates 'vixen', 'female' and 'fox', and the same relation can be said to hold among the three corresponding French predicates *renarde, femelle* and *renard*. Hence, although it is not true that (8) is used in English as an expression of a language-independent and timeless truth, it may be said that such a language-independent, timeless truth can be derived from (8), which might be put like this:

(8*) The concept of a vixen is identical with the conjunction of the concept of a female and the concept of a fox.

In short, although English analytic statements are about English words, implicit in them are truths about the concepts expressed by those words, concepts that could obviously also be expressed by words of other languages. Nonetheless it is important to bear in mind that analytic statements are not only about those concepts, but about specific words in our language expressing them. It is true that we are interested in the *meanings* of certain words, the concepts they express (which are independent of our language), but at the same time we are interested in the meanings *of certain words* (which are not).

8. The Lewis–Lewy Objection[35]

Another standard objection to the traditional account of analyticity can be traced back to C.I. Lewis,[36] but was also put forward by Casimir Lewy[37] and more recently by P. Boghossian:

> What could it possibly mean to say that the truth of a statement is fixed exclusively by its meaning and not by the facts? Isn't it in general true—indeed, isn't it in general a truism—that for any statement S,
>
> S is true iff for some p, S means that p and p?
>
> How could the mere fact that S means that p make it the case that S is true?[38]

Or, as Glock puts it in plain English, 'all that linguistic conventions do is to determine what a sentence *says*; whether what it says is true is another question, to which linguistic conventions are irrelevant'.[39] Glock notes afterwards that that is not strictly true: conventions are obviously not irrelevant to the truth or falsity of statements *about* conventions. But, he urges, truths *about* conventions—e.g.:

(29) In 1795 France adopted the metric system.

—are not true *by* convention.[40]

That, however, is too quick. Statements about conventions need not be reports of historic events, such as the introduction of a standard of

[35] This label is taken from H.-J. Glock, 'The Linguistic Doctrine Revisited', *Grazer philosophische Studien*, 66 (2003), 159.

[36] C.I. Lewis, *An Analysis of Knowledge and Valuation* (La Salle, Ill.: Open Court, 1946).

[37] Casimir Lewy, *Meaning and Modality* (Cambridge: Cambridge University Press, 1976).

[38] Paul Boghossian, 'Analyticity', in B. Hale and C. Wright (eds.), *A Companion to the Philosophy of Language* (Oxford: Blackwell, 1997), 335.

[39] Glock, 'Linguistic Doctrine', 158.   [40] Glock, 'Linguistic Doctrine', 159.

measurement, they can also be reports or explications of what those conventionally agreed standards are. Thus,

(30) One metre is 100 centimetres.

—is also a truth about a convention (or at any rate, a true report of a conventional fact). Yet unlike the historic statement (29), (30) *is* true by convention. It is true because what it reports to be the case is indeed what has been conventionally agreed to be the case.

Analytic statements express (the contents of) a linguistic convention about a word by using the word according to that convention, i.e., in a way that is true by linguistic convention. For instance, the linguistic convention that the word 'cygnet' is applicable to a young swan makes it true to say:

(31) This is a cygnet [pointing at a young swan].

Hence, naturally, it makes it also true to say:

(2) A cygnet is a young swan.

Both (31) and (2) are correct applications of the word 'cygnet'. The difference is that whereas (31) *happens* to be true (as the object referred to happens to be a young swan), the truth of (2) is not in such a way dependent on the circumstances. (2) makes explicit what qualities an object must have to count as a 'cygnet', according to the meaning of that word. It is an explanation of meaning, and it is true because the word does have that meaning.

So, 'how could the mere fact that S means that p make it the case that S is true?' Well, evidently, in order to explain how truth can be due to meaning alone, something more needs to be said about the meaning of a given statement than that the statement 'means that p'—i.e., that it has the meaning it has. As long as we content ourselves with staring at some sentence letters, Boghossian's question may indeed seem puzzling. But as soon as we say a little more about an analytic statement's meaning, the puzzle can be dissolved. For instance, whenever in a statement of the form 'An F is a G', the expressions 'F' and 'G' are synonymous, the statement (typically used to convey that synonymy) is regarded as true—owing to the meaning of the terms involved ('is', 'an F', 'a G') and the way they are meaningfully combined. That is the type of explanation that answers Boghossian's question.

II

Wittgenstein, in his later philosophy, does not use the expression 'analytic truth'. Instead, he introduces the term 'grammatical statement' (or 'statement of grammar', or 'grammatical proposition') for 'a statement which no experience will refute' (AWL, 16) and which can be used to 'explain the meaning of its terms' (AWL, 31). He also says that grammatical propositions are rules about the use of words (AWL, 105). Is 'grammatical proposition' just another name for 'analytic truth'? That is emphatically denied by G.P. Baker and P.M.S. Hacker in their magisterial essay 'Grammar and Necessity',[41] which offers by far the most detailed and illuminating account of Wittgenstein's concept of a grammatical proposition. Baker and Hacker argue that there are three significant differences between analytic truths and grammatical propositions:

[First:] The analytic/synthetic distinction is framed in terms of the forms and constituents of type-sentences, whereas whether an utterance expresses a grammatical proposition depends not only on its form, but on its roles on occasions of utterance.[42]

[Secondly:] Many of the propositions which [Wittgenstein] calls propositions of grammar have no place in anybody's catalogue of analytic truths.[43]

Thirdly, whereas analytic truths are said to *follow* from the meanings (definitions) of their constituents, grammatical propositions are rules that partly *constitute* the meanings of their constituents.[44]

These points are persuasive vis-à-vis the logical positivist account of analyticity which was grounded in a concept of meaning that Wittgenstein came to criticise as far too narrow. I am, however, going to argue that when we adopt Wittgenstein's own construal of meaning as use, those three points can be answered. To be sure, there remain differences between the concept of an analytic truth and that of a grammatical proposition, but there is a substantial overlap: typical examples of analytic truths can also be described as grammatical statements, and vice versa. I shall now consider the three points in turn.

---

[41] G.P. Baker and P.M.S. Hacker, 'Grammar and Necessity', in their *Wittgenstein: Rules, Grammar, and Necessity, Volume 2 of an Analytical Commentary on the Philosophical Investigations* (Oxford and Cambridge, Mass.: Blackwell, 1985).

[42] Baker and Hacker, 'Grammar', 268.   [43] Baker and Hacker, 'Grammar', 268.

[44] Baker and Hacker, 'Grammar', 268; 312 ff.

First: Analyticity is defined in terms of truth, so that only bearers of truth can be called analytic. That, to my mind, makes it rather implausible to classify type-sentences as analytic or synthetic, especially if type-sentences are construed in such a way that they can be ambiguous. For instance, the sentence:

(32) Ladies don't swear.

may be used as a (dubious) empirical generalisation based on the speaker's experience, or it may be used to make an analytic statement, partly explaining a certain concept of a lady (as a woman with refined manners). Again, the ambiguous sentence:

(33) A lime is a tree with heart-shaped leaves.

—can be used to express an analytic truth, and yet in another context an utterance of the same sentence might be dismissed as false: when the word 'lime' is taken to mean *Citrus aurantifolia* (rather than *Tilia europaea*). Hence, the analytic truth at issue is not the type-sentence (33). Admittedly, this conclusion can be avoided by construing ambiguous sentences as two different sentences, just as 'lime' may be regarded as two different words (different in meaning, though identical in spelling).[45] But even if type-sentences are in this way individuated by form *and* unambiguous meaning, many of them containing indexical elements can obviously be neither true nor false. At most one could say that such a sentence is true or false when uttered on a given occasion, in which case the bearer of truth would appear to be a token-sentence. I find it more natural, however, to say that the statement made, or the proposition expressed, with that sentence is true or false. Hence, in this respect, analytic truths are plausibly construed just like grammatical propositions: as statements in a suitable context, rather than type-sentences.

One might perhaps suggest that since grammatical propositions are characterised as rules, they are identified by their purpose (teaching, correcting, justifying), unlike analytic truths. Therefore, when used for different purposes (or uttered without any purpose) an analytic truth would not count as a grammatical proposition. Thus,

(34) What I have written I have written.

[45] Cf. Section I.4 above.

would be an analytic truth, but not a grammatical statement. It is of course possible to construe the concept of a grammatical statement in this way, but it is not clear that following Wittgenstein's characterisation we have to. For it is not true that rules are expressed only for didactic or justificatory purposes. I may, for example, cite a rule of chess ('Knights can also move backwards'), not because my addressee isn't fully conversant with the rules, but as a hint of a good move.

However, even if a rule can be expressed without any didactic or justificatory purpose, it would hardly be called a rule if it *could* not also be used to explain, correct or justify. Hence there is a difference between rules and the logical consequences of rules unsuitable for any such purpose. For example, it may be called a rule of chess that the white queen's bishop is placed on a black square, but one hesitates to call it a rule that the white queen's bishop can never move to b8. And one would certainly not call it a rule of chess that in the position White: Kc3, Qa8, Be4; Black: Ka1, Ba2, White can mate in three moves. And yet as these statements are true in virtue of the meanings of their terms (defined by the rules of chess), they qualify as analytic. So the concept of an analytic truth is wider than that of a grammatical proposition.

Baker and Hacker claim, on the contrary, that the concept of a grammatical proposition or rule is more inclusive (their second point). Examples of grammatical propositions that one may perhaps hesitate to call analytic are:

(35) Nothing can be red all over and green all over simultaneously.
(36) Black is darker than white.

It is true that none of these propositions is what one might call 'Frege-analytic': it is not possible by substituting synonyms for synonyms to transform any of them into a logical truth. But if we follow Wittgenstein in taking the meaning of a word to be its use in the language (PI §43), and if we note further that knowledge of the use of a word cannot be identified with knowledge of a synonymous expression[46]—we should not expect analyticity to boil down to Frege-analyticity. In other words, if meaning comprises more than can be captured by paraphrase, we should not expect truth in virtue of meaning always to be susceptible of a formal proof by

[46] See Severin Schroeder, *Wittgenstein: The Way Out of the Fly-Bottle* (Cambridge: Polity, 2006); ch. 4.4.

paraphrase. It characterises the meaning of primary colour words that—like different values on a scale—their applications are mutually incompatible: when a surface is correctly described as 'red' it cannot also be called 'green'. This aspect of the use of these words makes (35) true—analytically true. Again, knowledge of the correct use of the words 'black', 'white' and 'darker than' is enough to make out that (36) is true.

In some 1950–1 manuscripts (*Remarks on Colour*), Wittgenstein suggests that the following propositions are conceptual truths:

(37) There is no reddish green.

(38) There is no transparent white.

If Wittgenstein is right, they may well be regarded as analytic. Indeed, he himself calls them the results of 'conceptual analysis' (ROC II §16). He does not call them 'grammatical rules', and rightly so.[47] Far from being (suitable as) didactic instruments,[48] these truths have to be *discovered*. (They are perhaps comparable to the discovery that in a certain chess position one can mate in three moves.) The logic of our colour concepts is far more complicated than it seems (ROC III §106), and thus we can find 'internal properties' of colours of which we had not thought before (ROC III §63).

Finally, let us consider ostensive explanations, of which Wittgenstein suggested in the 1930s that they could be regarded as grammatical rules (PG, 88; BB, 12), e.g.:

(39) This is black [pointing at a sample: ■].

Such an explanation is not an analytic statement, for its truth depends not only on the meanings of its words but also on the colour of the sample. (The empirical element is more obvious when the sample cannot be presented in print, e.g.: 'This is an elm tree ☞ . . .') But then (39) should not be regarded as a grammatical rule either. Roughly for the same reason: the sample (unlike a canonical sample, such as the metre bar in Paris) only *happens* to instantiate the predicate. It is not a linguistic convention, but an empirical fact that the particular coloured patch I point to is black. Of course, as a means to teach someone the meaning of the word 'black' it will

---

[47] In one passage he speaks of a 'rule of spatial interpretation of our visual experience', but this to be a 'rule for a painter', rather than a linguistic rule (ROC III §173).

[48] Cf. BT, 241.

do, but this is teaching by exemplification, rather than teaching by giving a rule. An everyday ostensive explanation, such as (39), is an exemplification in two respects: Not only do we point out a suitable object, say, a blot of ink (or an elm tree), as an example of something black (or of an elm tree); our utterance itself is also an example: an example of the correct application of the predicate 'black' (or 'elm tree'). As Wittgenstein remarked in 1931, an explanation such as (39) is 'the paradigm of the transition . . . which is made by an empirical statement'.[49]

Baker and Hacker's diagnosis of the third point of difference between analytic truths and grammatical propositions appears to be based mainly on the following passage from notes of Wittgenstein's lectures in 1932–3:

> Are the rules, for example, $\sim\sim p = p$ for negation, responsible to the meaning of a word? No. The rules constitute the meaning, and are not responsible to it. . . . Rules are arbitrary in the sense that they are not responsible to some meaning the word already has. If someone says the rules of negation are not arbitrary because negation could not be such that $\sim\sim p = \sim p$, all that could be meant is that the latter rule would not correspond to the English word 'negation'. The objection that the rules are not arbitrary comes from the feeling that they are responsible to the meaning. But how is the meaning of 'negation' defined, if not by the rules? $\sim\sim p = p$ does not follow from the meaning of 'not' but constitutes it. (AWL, 4; cf. PG, 52 f.; 184; LFM, 282; RFM, 106)

What Wittgenstein is concerned to undermine is the idea of the meaning of a word as 'something over and above the use of the word'; some abstract or psychological entity 'attaching to the word itself' (RFM, 42), from which the rules for its use could be derived and against which they could be checked. To use a chess analogy: one may be tempted to think that each piece has an inner nature that determines its possible moves, and that the rules of chess have to be derived from, and must be in accord with. The truth is, of course, that the rules of the game were not derived from anything, but are arbitrary stipulations; and the rôle of a piece in the game is determined, or constituted, by the rules.

---

[49] MS 112, 152. For a more detailed discussion of the concept of an ostensive explanation, see Severin Schroeder, 'Elucidation and Ostensive Explanation', in G. Oliveri (ed.), *From the 'Tractatus' to the 'Tractatus'* (Frankfurt am Main: Peter Lang, 2001).

However, there is no need for the concept of analyticity, as truth in virtue of meaning, to commit itself to the implausible account of meaning rightly criticised by Wittgenstein. Rather, we should understand an analytic statement as one that is true in virtue of the *use* of its constituent words, in particular of the expression it is meant to explain. Now, is it plausible to object that a would-be analytic statement, such as:

(2) A cygnet is a young swan.

should not be seen as true in virtue of the established use of the word 'cygnet', because it is a rule, partly constituting the correct use of that word? I don't think we need to choose between these two views. Consider a rule of chess:

(40) The bishop moves only diagonally.

This rule can indeed be said to *constitute* the way the bishop moves (rather than being derived from the alleged 'inner nature' of that piece). However, at the same time it is *true* that the bishop moves only diagonally: it is true because the bishop has indeed been defined to be the piece that moves only diagonally. Thus (40) can be said to be true in virtue of the rules of chess; one of which it correctly reports.

Against this, one may want to object that although the sentence (40) can indeed be used either normatively, as a rule, or descriptively, as a report that something is a valid norm, it cannot be used in both ways at the same time. I disagree. An utterance of (40), as part of an explanation of how to play chess, is both descriptive and normative. It provides a rule according to which a bishop's move can be assessed as correct or incorrect, but at the same time this is implicitly claimed to be a valid rule of chess. After all the learner asked me to teach him the game of *chess*, and not some other game of my own invention (where I would be free to stipulate a rule). Most linguistic explanations—whether spoken or printed in a dictionary—have the same double character: they tell us how to use words *by* describing how those words are used in the language. The normative aspect owes its authority to the descriptive aspect: 'That is the way you should speak because that is the way one speaks.' Even where there is no explicit reference to common usage, the expression of a linguistic rule can be criticised as *false* if it deviates from common usage. Wittgenstein appears to acknowledge this amalgamation of description and normativity when he speaks indiscriminately of grammatical *statements* and grammatical *rules*. 'Grammar is a description of the language *ex post*' (MS 109, 110), yet grammar is essentially normative.[50]

[50] I am grateful to Hans-Johann Glock, John Hyman, John Preston and Daniel Whiting for helpful comments on earlier drafts of this essay.

Back to the Rough Ground: Wittgenstein and Ordinary Language

JOHN V. CANFIELD

This essay is a contribution to the work of Wittgenstein exegesis, a task Peter Hacker has so insightfully pursued. My topic is ordinary language. While it goes without saying that the later Wittgenstein's remarks are often directed at our day-to-day speech, several points of his relation to it need clarification. Thus my aim: to discuss a number of aspects of the connection between Wittgenstein's later philosophy and the talk of Everyman.

1. Repugnance

I begin with a nod toward some comments by Russell concerning philosophical elucidation. He wondered why he was being asked to care about niceties of ordinary usage.[1] One can sympathize. Indeed, philosophical appeals to the speech habits of *hoi polloi* might well arouse disinterest if not distaste. There are weighty issues to be settled, and to concern ourselves with what ordinary people say in ordinary situations seems quite beside the point. I remember my own feeling as a graduate student during the heyday of ordinary language philosophy, that surely there must be more to this enterprise than wondering about our mundane employment of words.

Wittgenstein was aware of such an attitude:

What is it that is repulsive in the idea that we study the use of a word, point to mistakes in the description of this use and so on? First and foremost one asks oneself: How could *that* be so important to us? It depends on whether what one calls a wrong description is a description that does not accord with established

---

[1] Bertrand Russell, 'Mr. Strawson on Referring', *Mind*, 66 (1957), 385–9.

usage or one which does not accord with the practice of the person giving the description. Only in the second case does a philosophical conflict arise. (RPP I, 548)

The descriptions that have gone wrong would of course include those that are the target of Wittgenstein's own corrective remarks, such as, 'It is right for me to speak of knowing I am in pain, but not acceptable to say I can know whether another is.' By his lights this claim has it backwards: it is incorrect for me to speak of knowing I am in pain, and equally wrong to say I cannot know whether another person is.[2] Or again the description, 'My announcements of my own intentions concern mental entities and their causal consequences.' In these instances we might have, as proffered in RPP I, 548, a description of use, a pointing out of an error in that description, and two ways for the incorrect description to count as wrong. The first is that the description violates rules our established usage (*sanktionierten Sprachgebrauch*) is subject to, and the second, that the description is not in accord with the practice of the one who made the description.

On the first way of taking such allegations of incorrectness, the mistake concerns words not deeds. In the realm of words certain combinations are ruled out, just as proper syntax rejects the utterance 'Me intend to go.' Similarly, it might be held, 'I know that I am in pain' is ruled out: that alignment of the sounds of speech could be seen as going against established regulations. The reasoning behind the claim that 'I know I am in pain' conflicts with rules governing word-combinations might go as follows. Claiming to know requires the possibility of error, but a sentence saying I can err about whether I am in pain conflicts with proper usage. There is an implicit rule that says I cannot sensibly speak of my being wrong about whether I am in pain. However, as long as the describer stays within the realm of words, it could be argued that there is no real conflict with what a philosopher would want to say about knowing one is in pain. For if the point in question just concerns a matter of words and their allowed combinations we can always sidestep the prohibited sentence, or so it seems. We might grant that 'I know I am in pain' is disallowed, but, on the other hand, we could introduce a new word, 'know*', which is to be employed in speaking of one's indubitable epistemic access to, or immediate awareness

---

[2] See PI, 246.

of, the inner object *pain*. So, while 'I know I am in pain' (supposedly) violates the norms governing legitimate word combination, 'I know* I am in pain' does not. The latter carries the import we wanted from the start. That it is possible to rewrite the offending descriptions, in the case where we deal only in the realm of words, underlines the philosophically trivial nature of those descriptions.

It might be objected that my remarks illegitimately assume we can understand the rogue sentence 'I can know* I am in pain.' The reply would be: you know very well what it means. There is this *thing*, pain, and to say I know* it (if you insist on driving me to that odd way of speaking) simply means that I am directly acquainted with it. Thus the choice between, for example, 'know' and 'know*' is, as far as metaphysics goes, trivial, and hence we may feel repugnance at the idea of concerning ourselves with it when we discuss the matter in the context of philosophical inquiry. The general feeling would be that such concern can be no more philosophically significant than the parallel correction of simple grammatical mistakes such as 'He run fast.' Its no big deal, we might say, whether 'I know I am in pain' violates those rules, because, really, we know what the wrongly expressed sentence is getting at, just as we know what someone means who says 'The men runs fast.'

But as far as philosophical significance goes, do things fare any better with the second way of going wrong, where the description 'does not accord with the practice of the person giving the description'? As a first step toward answering that question we should get clear on what a corrective description showing the original one to be wrong would look like. To discuss this I shall consider the more easily accessible case of intention-talk. As suggested above, for Wittgenstein it would be wrong to say something like, 'Intentions are mental entities; to state an intention is to refer to such an object.' Against this, how shall we correctly describe what it is to speak of our intentions? As the second option in RPP I, 548 would have it, this description will concern the speaker's practice. We can get a line on the assumed notion of 'practice' by considering how a child might learn to speak its intentions. First and foremost what is required is a certain hard-wired mode of human interaction: we are creatures who want to know what our fellows are up to; we take a great interest in one another's projects. We can often tell by looking what another is after or is attempting. And we react to what we see, by joining in, or hindering, and so on. Against such a background of natural interest in and response to what others are up to, a child might develop gestures to indicate where it is going. The child's nod or glance might communicate to another its immediate goal. Later, certain words from the community's language might be spontaneously uttered by the child, replacing the earlier gestures. These new intention statements stand in for the gestures and do the same job. It is that job, that function, that is characteristic of intention-statements. The crucial point is that the development of a language of intention-talk requires a context of human interaction. Our words operate within such a context. In speaking of intention-talk we are speaking of a network of doings of a certain kind.

The view of language underlying this approach treats speech as custom-constrained interaction. Language is custom; custom involves action; such action constitutes a language-game. To describe a language-game is to depict one of the ways people move through space and time. We get to attack the wrong description by contrasting the philosopher's picture of what occurs with an account of the interactions that constitute his engaging in this or that language-game.

What happens if we attempt to apply here the strategy employed above with regard to 'know' and 'know*'? Even if we could somehow rule out talk like 'My intention is a mental object', we might seek another way of speaking that gets us what we want, namely to be responsive to the intuition that an intention is something, and obviously not something outer, therefore something inner that we are aware of. But when we test that intuition about intentions by contrasting it with an account of our actual practice, as regards speaking of what we are up to, we see that the intuition totally misses the mark. That is, the idea that an intention is a mental object conflicts not just with some imagined rules of syntax or semantics, but with how the word 'intention' works or functions in our day-to-day life. In talking of our intentions we in fact do not concern ourselves with what is going on in the speaker's mind. Rather we speak of projects we are engaged in, and the hearers take it that we will be carrying out those projects. Such concern with action or practice is an essential feature of intention-talk, whether spoken by Russell or his char-lady, or anyone else.

In cases like that of knowing the metaphysician can reply to his oppon-ents: 'Fine, I'll give you the word "know"; giving it up doesn't bother me, because I can find another way of describing how things are here. And how things are is the crucial thing.' But a parallel response will not do for the case where one describes the related language-games. One can give up the words 'know' or 'intend' but not the corresponding interactions. Given such and such a description of, say, the language-game of intention-talk, it is clear that the mentalist picture of intentions cannot stand. It is one thing to be in conflict with an established form of words, but another for our descriptions to be in conflict with how it is we live.

A second source of repugnance at the idea of Wittgenstein as, in John Cook's phrases, a 'champion of the vernacular' or 'patron of ordinary language', is much more easily dealt with. Cook quotes an old criticism of Wittgenstein by Maurice Cornforth, one that can still attract those who think that appeals to ordinary language are in some deep and unwelcome way conservative. Cornforth writes, as quoted by Cook:

When Wittgenstein set up the actual use of language as a standard, that was equivalent to accepting a certain set up of culture and belief as a standard. ... It is lucky no such philosophy was thought of until recently or we should still be under the sway of witch doctors. ...[3]

Cornforth's error is to infer from Wittgenstein's concern with examining details of ordinary use to the supposition that he takes that use to be frozen in time. But of course Wittgenstein recognizes that usage changes, as do the cultural surrounds that support language.[4]

2. 'Logic'

The second aspect of Wittgenstein's relation to ordinary language that I wish to consider holds—surprisingly enough—that he sometimes, and wrongly, writes in opposition to it. Consider this list of assertions:

(1) One cannot say that the standard meter in Paris is one meter long.
(2) '2 + 3 = 5' is not true.
(3) 'I' (in 'I think it will rain') does not stand for anything.

---

[3] Maurice Cornforth, *Marxism and the Linguistic Philosophy* (New York: International Publishers, 1965), 163. Quoted by John Cook, 'Did Wittgenstein Speak with the Vulgar or Think with the Learned? Or Did he Do Both?', *Philosophy*, 2 (2007), 213.

[4] See William James DeAngelis's discussion of Wittgenstein and Spengler in *Ludwig Wittgenstein: A Cultural Point of View* (Burlington, Vt.: Ashgate, 2007).

These claims all seem false; if we were to put them to some randomly selected, competent English speaker, they would be enthusiastically rejected. Of course, Everyman says, the standard meter is a meter long; of course '2 + 3 = 5' is true; of course the 'I' of 'I am thinking' stands for something. And yet, it seems plausible to say, the later Wittgenstein would defend each of (1)–(3).[5] How can the champion of ordinary language not join in with the common person here?

But first it should be established textually that Wittgenstein really does assert the claims in question. With regard to the standard meter his position is, apparently, clear: 'There is *one* thing of which one can say neither that it is one meter long, nor that it is not one meter long, and that is the standard meter in Paris...' (PI, 50). Our proposition (1) of course follows immediately from the first sentence of this quotation. In discussing PI, 50 Saul Kripke writes: 'This seems to be a very extraordinary property, actually, for any stick to have. I think he must be wrong. If the stick is a stick, for example, 39.7 inches long...why isn't it one meter long?'[6] We could read this as making an implicit appeal to ordinary language, or alternatively as one to intuition. I discuss intuition later in this essay; for the nonce I will treat Kripke's remarks as a striking example of an appeal to ordinary language of the type I am presently examining. It is quite plausible to think that an ordinary speaker would agree that it would be extraordinary, and plain wrong, to say the meter rod in Paris is not correctly describable as one meter long. Nonetheless Wittgenstein makes this claim.

I jump now to statement (3). That Wittgenstein believes the 'I' of 'I think it will rain', or 'I have pain' is not a referring expression is clear from his remarks in the *Blue Book*. He writes, for example: 'To say I have pain is no more a statement *about* a particular person than moaning is' (BB, 67). He then speaks in the voice of his interlocutor: 'But surely the word "I" in the mouth of a man refers to the man who says it...' and goes on to deny that there is reference in this case. Similar remarks can be found in the *Investigations*, paragraph 404, for instance.[7]

[5] See Danièle Moyal-Sharrock, *On Understanding Wittgenstein's On Certainty* (New York: Palgrave, 2004).
[6] *Naming and Necessity* (Oxford: Blackwell, 1972), 274.
[7] See Danièle Moyal-Sharrock, 'Words as Deeds', *Philosophical Psychology*, 13 (2000), 355–72.

The matter of (2) is not so clear cut. The question of whether Wittgenstein held it is tied to the issue of his treatment of the term 'proposition'. For instance, concerning arithmetical statements, Moyal-Sharrock quotes Moore as reporting on Wittgenstein's lectures as follows: '... [H]e sometimes said that they [arithmetical statements like '2 + 3 = 5'] are not propositions at all (MWL, 60)'.[8] Rather, he treats them like rules—'grammatical' rules—and these, he will go on to say, are neither true nor false: 'There must be something wrong in our idea of the truth and falsity of our arithmetical propositions' (RFM, 90).[9] (There is a seeming contradiction between these two quotations; first it is said that the mathematical statements are not propositions at all, and then in the next quotation, that there is something wrong with attributing truth or falsity to such propositions. Here 'proposition' in the second remark is the translation of the German *Sätze*, so the claim would be better understood as denying truth or falsity to arithmetical statements; and that would remove the apparent contradiction.)

It appears that Wittgenstein would hold to (2) since he would deny that '2 + 3 = 5' is a proposition, and if it is not a proposition it can hardly be counted true. So Wittgenstein would defend all our three statements. The question is, how could he do so plausibly? Let us begin with (2).

Someone familiar with elementary arithmetic and with a mastery of the use of 'true' might be asked whether '2 + 3 = 5' is true. There are two contexts in which the question could be put and answered. The first concerns what Everyman would say. I believe that virtually everyone with a command of the ground level use of 'true' will say that, as the term is used in everyday speech, '2 + 3 = 5' is true. Why? Well, it appears overwhelmingly obvious that it is. We might speak here of the 'duh' response. The answer to the question about the arithmetical sentence would be, 'Why ask, when the answer is so obvious?' The same response holds for the other instances. Does the 'I' of 'I believe it will rain' stand for someone? Is the standard meter one meter long? All would get the '... of course! Why even ask!' reply and hence would be counted as true. The response in question is the same, whether the respondent is the common

[8] Quoted by Moyal-Sharrock, *Understanding Wittgenstein's On Certainty*, 37.
[9] Quoted by Moyal-Sharrock, *Understanding Wittgenstein's On Certainty*, 38.

man or the philosopher speaking in the role of the common man. Thus when Hacker writes, 'Surely it is *true* that $2 + 3 = 5$? Indeed it is; that is what is called a true proposition of arithmetic'[10] he speaks in concert with Everyman. In the context of inquiry in question, then, the question being asked amounts to this: 'Give me your gut response: is it true, for example, that the standard meter is one meter long?'

In the second context of inquiry the spotlight shifts from Everyman or his philosophical double to the Wittgensteinian logician. We are now no longer interested in those commonplace answers. Rather we see these matters in the light of the later philosophy.

Thus consider (1). The sentence quoted from PI, 50 reads, again: 'There is *one* thing of which one can say neither that it is one meter long, nor that it is not one meter long, and that is the standard meter in Paris.' Wittgenstein here is speaking as a 'logician'. As he goes on to say, to affirm the above sentence is to 'mark its [the standard meter's] peculiar role in the language-game of measuring with a meter rule.' Equally clearly, the sentence in question is not to be understood as a claim about what people (or philosophers) would naturally say if asked 'Is the standard meter one meter long?' Rather Wittgenstein wants to draw our attention to the fact that a paradigm sample like that of the standard meter, or, in an imagined example of his, a standard color patch for the use of 'sepia', is 'not something that is represented but is a means of representation' (PI, 50). We represent the length of the table or its color by utilizing the standard samples, or copies thereof. The samples provide a means of representation, in that we could compare the table's length with the standard meter, and its color with the standard sepia. 'This is one meter', as said of the standard meter, doesn't tell us about the results of measurements, but rather sets up a standard utilized in the language-game of measuring. That we cannot *say* of the standard meter that it is one meter long means only that 'The standard meter is one meter long' is not made within the language-game, but rather lays down how, in part, the game is to be played. Since Wittgenstein is not concerned here to report on what people would say if they were questioned about the length of the standard meter, Kripke's dismissive response to the statement in PI, 50 is beside the point. He has failed to

---

[10] Hacker *Insight and Illusion*, 207 n.; quoted by Moyal-Sharrock, *Understanding Wittgenstein's On Certainty*, 41.

distinguish different contexts within which the sentence in question might be uttered.

Kripke offers an argument for his claim that the standard meter is one meter long, and it should be examined. It goes, as already quoted: if the stick is a stick, for example, 39.7 inches long…why isn't it one meter long?[11] The original question is, why can't one say within the language-game that the stick is one meter long? And the answer is: because it is a means of representation and not something represented. It is such within that particular language-game. Kripke's argument implicitly brings in a second language-game. We measure in inches, and then convert the result to meters using the formula 'One meter equals 39.7 inches.' 'This stick (which is in fact the standard for the meter language-game) is one meter long' is said in the inches language-game, where it no longer has the status of a standard. So the response to Kripke is: the fact that we can say the stick is one meter long within the inches language-game does not imply that one can say that within the meter language-game.

Next consider the question whether 'I' (in 'I think it will rain') is a referring expression. Both Everyman and the philosopher who seeks to rely on or to echo the intuitive, meta-level judgments made by Everyman will say 'I' refers; that it does is as it were the default position. It does refer if we are to judge by what anyone would naturally say if asked. In saying it does not refer Wittgenstein speaks from within the context of establishing the nature of the language-game with 'I'. In particular he is prompting us to see the employment of the word 'I' here as analogous to that of the 'it' of 'It is raining', and as different from subject terms like 'Jones' or 'she'. The difference is that the speaker does not first pick out a referent from among a possible array of items. Another, related difference is that the speaker cannot make a mistake about who is doing the thinking. Given these features it is a logical truth that in the cases in question 'I' does not refer, meaning that its use does not conform to those central, paradigmatic cases of referring.

John Cook, in an article cited earlier, holds that Wittgenstein's '"I" is not a referring expression' conflicts with and therefore is refuted by Everyman's judgment that 'I' does indeed stand for something, namely the speaker. He imagines a diary entry that runs: 'I heard distant thunder this

---

[11] Kripke, *Naming and Necessity*, 274.

afternoon . . . .' and writes, 'Having come across this entry wouldn't I say that I had found a[n] . . . occasion on which Hal had spoken of himself? Of course I would.'[12] (This example ignores the fact that Wittgenstein held his '"I" does not refer' only with regard to *present* tense psychological utterances.) This and similar instances that he offers are supposed to refute Wittgenstein's view that when I say 'I am in pain' I am 'not making statements *about* a particular person'.[13] In giving this argument Cook conflates the two positions I have distinguished. That the naive speaker of ordinary language might say, if asked, that the uses of 'I' in question do refer, does not conflict with Wittgenstein's grammatical assertion that it does not. It is one thing to do depth grammar and another to appeal to naive meta-level judgments of the kind in question.

As for (2) its role in a Wittgensteinian logic is connected with the use of the term 'proposition'. '"$2 + 3 = 5$" is not true' will be rejected in the 'duh' context of inquiry but admitted as a statement of 'logic' (as discussed further in the following section). In general, what we say about (1)–(3) hangs on which context of inquiry is in question. Understood rightly Wittgenstein's affirmation of them is justified.

3. Bipolarity

There is an exegetical controversy that touches on my treatment of (2). The issue concerns bipolarity—the idea that for a given statement to be meaningful it must be possible for it to be true and possible for it to be false. Bipolarity was an essential thesis of the *Tractatus*. The question is, did Wittgenstein continue to hold it in his later work? The arithmetical statement in (2) is central to the controversy. The principle of bipolarity would dictate that '$2 + 3 = 5$' is not a proposition (and hence not true), for it is not possible for it to be false. Similarly for statements like 'Red is a color.'

Professors Hacker and Glock deny that for the later Wittgenstein statements count as propositions only if they are bipolar. Instead, they say, 'proposition' in the later philosophy is a family resemblance concept. Hacker writes: '[Wittgenstein's] later philosophy cut . . . free from the

---

12 Cook, 'Did Wittgenstein Speak with the Vulgar . . .', 228.
13 Cook, 'Did Wittgenstein Speak with the Vulgar . . .', 228.

dogmatism of . . . bipolarity as the essence of the proposition . . .'.[14] Rather he adopted the view that 'proposition' is a family resemblance concept. Bringing these two points together, he writes: 'Wittgenstein was later to relinquish the thesis of bipolarity, arguing instead that the concept of a proposition is a family resemblance concept.'[15] Moyal-Sharrock opposes that account. She presents an array of quotations meant to support the claim that throughout his work, Wittgenstein maintained that what he sometimes called 'grammatical' truths, like '2 + 3 = 5' or 'Red is a color', do not count as propositions, nor as being true or false, the reason being that they fail the test of bipolarity. Thus she writes: 'In his specialized use of the term . . . ["proposition"] Wittgenstein . . . is from first to last unequivocal about whether a proposition is bipolar.'[16]

On the other hand the idea that 'proposition' is a family resemblance concept, and one that includes statements lacking a possible negation, seems eminently plausible. After all Wittgenstein does often stress that propositions come in an enormous variety. Why shouldn't '2 + 3 = 5', which seems so obviously true, be counted among that wide and variegated class?

How to settle this dispute? There can of course be no quarrel over whether Wittgenstein ever held the thesis of bipolarity; it was as noted a central feature of the *Tractatus* and was certainly appealed to in his work in the early 1930s. The question is when, if ever, he gave it up. The issue concerns the texts and what we are to make of them. But before going into those matters I want to examine two arguments. These are not advanced by Hacker or Glock, but they might be appealed to by a disinterested third party as settling the issue in their favor.

Someone might proffer an argument built on the following plausible-seeming proof, where 'BP' stands for the thesis of bipolarity:

(a) BP *entails* '2 + 3 = 5' is not true.
(b) '2 + 3 = 5' is true.
(c) *Therefore* not-BP.

[14] *Wittgenstein's Place in Twentieth-Century Analytic Philosophy* (Oxford and Cambridge, Mass.: Blackwell, and Cambridge, Mass., 1996), 35.
[15] Hacker, *Wittgenstein's Place*, 279. H.-J Glock also holds that for the later Wittgenstein, 'proposition' is a family resemblance concept. See his *A Wittgenstein Dictionary* (Oxford: Blackwell, 1996), 65.
[16] *On Understanding Wittgenstein's On Certainty*, 34.

The idea would be that in one's attempts to understand the later Wittgenstein a principle of charity should hold. (b) is obviously true, so not wanting to stick Wittgenstein with an unpalatable claim we should say that he would accept (b), and if he does then he cannot support bipolarity. But the proof is not sound. The allegedly entailed sentence in (b)—that ' "2 + 3 = 5" is not true'—could be said in either of the two contexts of inquiry I spoke of in the previous section. When we are dealing with the first of these the thesis of bipolarity does not entail that the sentence '2 + 3 = 5' is not true. The sentence '2 + 3 = 5' can be true in the sense that Everyman will affirm it, even though, in the second context of inquiry, it gets assigned to the class of timeless or logical sentences, and for that reason gets counted as neither true nor false. My point may be clearer if we build into the sentences in question markers indicating which context of inquiry obtains. The context in which someone who agrees with Hacker concerning bipolarity would wish to defend the truth of '2 + 3 = 5' is that where Everyman's intuitive response rules. The question about whether '2 + 3 = 5' is true comes down to asking what Everyman would affirm concerning it. Thus premise (b) could be written: ' "2 + 3 = 5" is true [Con 1].' For the argument to hold, then, premise (a) would need to be rendered as: BP entails ' "2 + 3 = 5" is not true [Con 1].' But that entailment does not hold. A Wittgensteinian logical remark may flout the naive judgments of the man in the street. Otherwise put, the principle of bipolarity does not imply anything about what the ordinary man will say in a context where we count something as true in virtue of our naive meta-level judgments.

A second argument that might be advanced to show that the later Wittgenstein rejected bipolarity is that he came to believe instead in the notion of family resemblance. 'Something is a proposition only if it is bipolar' gets replaced by ' "Proposition" is a family resemblance concept.' Hacker gives a list of many different sorts of statements that would be included in the family resemblance idea of a proposition:

...The members of the family include such diverse cousins as propositions of arithmetic, theorems of geometry, ethical and aesthetic propositions, scientific generalizations, laws of nature, empirical descriptions, historical propositions, avowals of experience, fictional propositions, theological propositions, propositions of the 'world picture', etc.[17]

---

[17] *Wittgenstein's Place*, 279.

We could add to the variety by looking inside the different classes; for example, empirical propositions are governed by a large number of different criteria. There is no doubt that 'proposition' is a many faceted thing. But that Wittgenstein adopted the idea of family resemblance counts against bipolarity only if non-bipolar statements are included in the family resemblance class of propositions. So how is it to be established that all the items on Hacker's list are truly to count as propositions, on that family resemblance understanding of the term? We can imagine the following exchange:

'What are you doing?'
'I'm thinking about the proposition that you can't trisect an angle with ruler and
   compass.'
'That's no proposition!'
'Of course it is!'

The same exchange might occur for any of the statements on Hacker's list. They all count as propositions, on the assumption that the test will be what the naive informant, or his philosophical counterpart, says.

It does not follow that Wittgenstein would count them all as such. The family resemblance view of concepts says only that, as with the notion 'game', there are no necessary and sufficient conditions circumscribing the class 'proposition'. That fact does not rule out Wittgenstein's making a cut within the things Everyman might be willing to call a proposition, and reserving the term for those that do not count as timeless. In saying that the members of that subset are not propositions Wittgenstein would be using 'proposition' as a term of art. 'Proposition' would now function as a specialized tool used by Wittgenstein in his philosophical investig- ations. On that mandated sense 'proposition' applies only to contingent statements.[18]

In the later philosophy 'proposition' is not alone in being assigned a special use. There is a group of terms from everyday speech that Wittgenstein uses in a special way, in his efforts to draw the contours of the language-games he discusses. In addition to 'proposition' they include 'picture', 'utterance', 'true', and 'say'.[19] He is not consistent in his use of these terms. Pictures are sometimes just plain pictures; utterances merely

---

[18] See Moyal-Sharrock's discussion of this point: *On Understanding Wittgenstein's On Certainty*, 49 ff.
[19] Concerning 'say' see Moyal-Sharrock, *On Understanding Wittgenstein's On Certainty*, 43 ff.

utterances, and so on. But sometimes pictures are false analogies that befuddle us, and utterances certain spontaneous voicings of an inner state like pain. For example 'utterance' (*Äusserung*) is used at RPP II, 620 in an innocent, non-logical way, and at RPP II, 486 as a term of art. In any given case Wittgenstein leaves it to us to sort the matter out. Similarly we must decide whether a given report about propositions—including the question of whether something is or is not one—occurs within the language-game, as part of a Wittgensteinian description of it, or as a naive meta-level remark of Everyman's.

In the attack on bipolarity that I have been addressing the underlying error is to think the naive meta-level remark that ' "2 + 3 = 5" is a proposition' trumps the corresponding 'logical' denial that it is, whereas the statement ' "2 + 3 = 5" is a proposition' and what (misleadingly) appears to surface grammar as its negation can co-exist, rather in the way that 'Parallel lines never meet' can be true in one system of geometry and false in another.

Here it can be objected that if by fiat 'proposition' is reserved for contingent statements, then ' "2 + 3 = 5" is no proposition' reduces to the claim that '2 + 3 = 5' is not contingent. That's hardly news, it will be felt. What would Wittgenstein be doing in affirming such a seemingly obvious truth? The answer is that to speak of something's not being a proposition, in that special sense, is not merely to say it is contingent. It is in addition to remind us that the equation belongs to that key class of statements that lack a sensible negation. Behind that placement is the fundamental Wittgensteinian distinction between the class of 'logical' truths and those that are not 'logical'. The extension of each class cannot profitably be given in terms of some abstract characterization such as 'logical' or 'contingent'. It can be so given only by citing a range of examples on each side of the division. Thus ' "2 + 3 = 5" is not a proposition' says that the equation belongs together with 'Red is a color', 'There are objects', ' "I" is not a referring expression', and so on. Wittgenstein counts the failure to honor that distinction as a major source of philosophical confusion, a point I will return to below.

But now what do the texts have to say? First we should be clear about what we are looking for. We would know that Wittgenstein held to bipolarity at time t in two circumstances. One is that at t he affirms the principle, as in the quote below from the *Big Typescript*; the other is that at *t* he denies that something is a proposition on the ground that it cannot be false. With those guidelines in place let us look at the texts. While Hacker and Glock, as far as I can see, do not cite textual evidence for their position, Moyal-Sharrock gives a number of quotations in her favor. Obviously bipolarity is in place in the *Tractatus* and in Wittgenstein's manuscripts and lectures in the early 1930s. By citing lecture notes by Moore (1930–3) and others by Ambrose (1932, 1933), Moyal-Sharrock shows that Wittgenstein maintained bipolarity in the early 1930s. In addition, there is the following remark in the *Big Typescript*: 'When one says that a proposition is everything that can be true or false, that means *the same as*: a proposition is everything that can be denied' (BT, 61). This shows that Wittgenstein held to bipolarity at least as late as 1932. But that point is not at issue. The question is, how much further along in time did he assume bipolarity? Moyal-Sharrock's quotations from the *Philosophical Grammar* (PG, 123, 376) bring us up to 1933 and very early 1934. Is there a smoking gun, a citation from later than, say, the first months of 1934, which plainly shows his sticking to bipolarity? Moyal-Sharrock gives some citations from after 1934 but not all of them are definitive. For example one is from the *Notes for Lectures on 'Private Experience' and 'Sense Data'* written in late 1934 or early 1935 and completed in 1936: 'Examine the sentence: "There is something there", referring to the visual sensation I am now having. Aren't we inclined to think that this is a statement making sense and being true: and on the other hand, isn't it a pseudo-statement?'[20] It is not clear whether the statement rejected here as a pseudo-statement is dismissed on the ground that it fails the test of bipolarity, or because it is an unavailing attempt to describe the immediately given. Another of Moyal-Sharrock's quotations is from *Zettel*, and therefore presumably from well into the later philosophy; it runs as follows: ' "I have consciousness"—that is a statement about which no doubt is possible.' Why should that not say the same as: ' "I have consciousness" is not a proposition'?[21] But to accept this as evidence for Wittgenstein's continued embrace of bipolarity one must enlarge the principle. In addition to saying 'Something is a proposition if and only if it can be true and it can be false', one must add, 'and only if doubt is not possible concerning it. There are grounds for the

---

[20] LPE, 271; quoted by Moyal-Sharrock, *On Understanding Wittgenstein's On Certainty*, 38.
[21] Z, section 401, quoted by Moyal-Sharrock, *On Understanding Wittgenstein's On Certainty*, 43.

impossibility of doubting the statement other than its not being able to be false.'

Moyal-Sharrock also cites the *Remarks on the Foundations of Mathematics*, where Wittgenstein writes: '—And in that case there must be something wrong in our idea of the truth and falsity of arithmetical propositions' (RFM, 90)[22] This counts as a late occurrence of bipolarity only if the case in question concerns the impossibility of being false. But as I read the passage the case referred to is rather the 'queer possibility' of our having 'always gone wrong up to now in multiplying 12 × 12'.

However, I believe one other of her quoted instances does settle the issue; the following quotation from *On Certainty*, part of which she cites, seems to me decisive.

§36. 'A is a physical object' is a piece of instruction which we give only to someone who doesn't yet understand either what 'A' means, or what 'physical object' means. Thus it is instruction about the use of words, and 'physical object' is a logical concept. (Like color, quantity . . . .) And that is why no such proposition as: 'There are physical objects' can be formulated. . . .[23]

Here we have the denial that a certain utterance—'There are physical objects' is a proposition. To complete the proof of Wittgenstein's late adherence to bipolarity it needs to be established that the ground for the denial is that the utterance cannot be false. The route to establishing that goes through the utterance 'A is a physical object'. That this cannot be false implies that 'There are physical objects' cannot be false. For example if it cannot be false that the stove is a physical object, then it cannot be false that there are physical objects. The statement about the stove cannot be false because 'physical object' is a logical property; that is, it is an internal property of the stove. It is of the essence of being a stove that it be a physical object, just as it is of the essence of red that it be a color. When Wittgenstein writes, 'and that is why no such proposition as: "There are physical objects" can be formulated . . .', the 'that' refers to the fact that 'A is a physical object', and all such similar remarks, involving as they do a logical property of the things in question, are necessary truths, and as such cannot be false.

[22] Quoted by Moyal-Sharrock, *On Understanding Wittgenstein's On Certainty*, 38.
[23] Quoted in part by Moyal-Sharrock, *On Understanding Wittgenstein's On Certainty*, 43.

It cannot be false; it expresses a rule; it cites an essential property: for all these more or less equivalent reasons it is, in Wittgenstein's terminology, no proposition. In this reasoning we see the principle of bipolarity at work: If it cannot be false it is no proposition. But perhaps one clear example from Wittgenstein's very latest writings is not sufficient to show that he held to bipolarity to the end. Perhaps the quoted remark is an aberration. That is for the reader to judge. To my ear the statement from *On Certainty* is *echt* Wittgenstein. It is a clear echo of another *Tractatus* passage that Moyal-Sharrock quotes: 'So one cannot say, for example, "There are objects", as one might say, "There are books"' (TLP, 4.1272). However, we should pause to be clear on what it is we have, or have not, proven. There are two ways of understanding 'Wittgenstein keeps to bipolarity throughout his later thought'. (1) Wittgenstein, in his later philosophy, sometimes uses 'proposition' as bound by bipolarity. (2) 'Whenever Wittgenstein uses "proposition" he treats it as bound by bipolarity.' (2) is obviously false, and (1) perhaps less controversial than one might have supposed.

It remains to say something about what might have been Wittgenstein's motive in holding to bipolarity, in so far as he did. Why does he, by assuming a special use of 'proposition', emphasize the contrast between the logical or timeless and the contingent or temporal? It is because he believes that philosophical perspicuity requires being clear on the difference. For example, a metaphysician might say that her pain is private to herself; only she can have *this* pain sensation. Here 'Pain is private' gets treated as an obvious truth about the world, whereas Wittgenstein thinks that the speaker has confused a grammatical remark with a contingent one. And so, for example, his statement, 'The proposition "Sensations are private" is comparable to "One plays patience by oneself"' (PI, 248).

4. Beyond Ordinary Language

Appeals to ordinary language of the kind found in the late 1950s and early 1960s are long out of fashion. In some instances philosophical theory-building supported by intuition has taken their place. Kripke's book *Naming and Necessity* provides an influential example of such theorizing. We can better understand several facets of Wittgenstein's thought—including some concerning ordinary language—by contrasting it with the position Kripke defends. To carry out that project I begin with a critical survey of some main themes in *Naming and Necessity*. There Kripke writes:

...Some philosophers think that something's having intuitive content is very inconclusive evidence in favor of it. I think it is very heavy evidence in favor of anything, myself. I really don't know [...] what more conclusive evidence one can have about anything, ultimately speaking. But in any event people who think the notion of accidental property unintuitive have intuition reversed, I think.[24]

Of course one can have evidence stronger than that intuition provides—what we see or hear, for example. Kripke must mean to confine his claim to the realm of philosophy. There, the assertion would be, intuition can provide the highest possible conclusive evidence (if there can be degrees of conclusiveness). Or, to be done with superlatives, it can at least provide conclusive evidence.

The term 'intuition' and its variants are not prominent in Kripke's subsequent theorizing in *Naming and Necessity*, although they do occur. He writes, for example, of his central idea: 'One of the intuitive theses I will maintain in these talks is that *names* are rigid designators.'[25] The use of 'intuitive' here indicates that the thesis in question is backed by intuition, as are the other views he advances, such as those concerning kind terms. And although 'intuition' appears only rarely (as well as 'intuitively' and 'intuitive content'), other terms take their place and convey the same idea. Among the words that go proxy for 'intuition' are references to what he or we *would say* in certain counterfactual situations, and '*what seems to me*'. Here are some examples:

If there were a substance...which had a...different atomic structure from that of water, but resembled water in these respects [i.e. '*feel, appearance and perhaps taste*'] would we say that some water wasn't H_2O? I think not.[26]

Again:

Cats are in fact animals. ...Consider the counterfactual situation in which in place of these...animals...we have in fact little demons. ...Should we describe this as a situation in which cats were demons? It seems to me that these demons would not be cats. ...[27]

---

[24] Kripke, *Naming and Necessity*, 265, 266.   [25] Kripke, *Naming and Necessity*, 270.
[26] Kripke, *Naming and Necessity*, 323.   [27] Kripke, *Naming and Necessity*, 321.

There are related remarks bunched around the idea of intuition: 'We would say', 'I think we would say', 'It seems to me'.[28] These and similar comments relate what intuition will tell the inquiring philosopher about various counterfactual situations.

The role of intuition and its variants in Kripke's book is, again, to serve as evidence. We can understand that role better if we take note of two facts. The first is that his questions about what to say, or what intuition is to tell us, arise only in certain imagined outré instances. In many circumstances that actually occur in real life, appeals to intuition will have no place. Lost in the desert I see what looks like water ahead. 'Is that water or a mirage?' The reply, 'Well, what does intuition tell you?' has no use here. Forget intuition—let's take a look! Similarly, when we arrive at the oasis, and drink greedily, the question 'Is this stuff water?' has no role to play, the answer being too obvious. The Kripkean questions about intuition get a grip only when in thought we abandon normal circumstances. Again, if we are standing on the shore of a lake in cottage country the question 'Is that [pointing] water?' seems absurd. Kripke's questions aren't posed in such normal circumstances but rather in imagined situations beyond the scope of ordinary language. Standing before the lake we ask, 'Suppose this stuff had a different molecular make-up, even though it retained all the usual characteristics of water—it quenches one's thirst, provides a home for fish, looks like so, runs down hill, pours, and so on. Would it be water?' What does intuition say? In general, the salient feature of such questions as this, where Kripke in answering appeals to intuition, is that the normal criteria governing the central terms in the questions do not apply. For example the age-old criteria for whether something is water are not taken as governing the question, 'Is this stuff water, given that it is not H_2O but XYZ?' A new criterion governs here, namely what 'intuition' dictates.

The second fact of note about Kripkean intuition is that it is not backed up by what we might call hard evidence, meaning by that what we would normally cite as evidence. In a familiar example, to test Einstein's general theory of relativity scientists filmed an eclipse of the sun. That the result was as Einstein had predicted counted as evidence in favor of his theory. If someone had said, 'Intuition tells me that this theory is true', there was the possibility of testing it against facts as yet undiscovered or not considered. Similarly, the detective's intuition that the butler did it can be tested against the facts. New evidence may convict or exonerate him. But in the instance of the philosopher's appeal to intuition there are no facts, no independent evidence, to come upon which would support or count against an intuition. There is no evidence of the kind science relies on. The sole test is what we are inclined to say—what it seems to us must be said. To see how strange this is, imagine theoretical physics done on the basis solely of people's intuitions.

In the picture operative hereabouts, 'intuition' is being treated as evidence. It is as if in addition to sights and sounds and feels that count as evidence for empirical matters there is a kind of inner feeling, analogous to a perception, that informs us of how things are. I see, by consulting my intuition, that this imagined stuff is not water. But in fact there is no such inner state to appeal to.

To recap, what is the status of Kripke's appeal to intuition in instances like, 'Is it water given that it is not H_2O?' First, such questions cannot be decided on the basis of the criteria that govern our day-to-day use of the terms in question. The examples we are asked to consider outstrip those familiar criteria. Ordinary language—our normal use of 'water' for example—doesn't come equipped with a standard governing answers to Kripke's questions. Secondly, there is no hope of further discoveries that will settle the question. Intuition must stand on its own, as the sole arbiter of 'Is it water?', 'Is it gold, given that it does not have the atomic number 79', and so on. Given these two points, Kripke's report on what he would say, or what his intuition is, in those outré instances, comes to no more than an implicit fiat on how he will use the terms 'water', 'cat', 'tiger', 'gold', and so on in those imagined counterfactual instances.

But to say in these cases that reliance on intuition is really a disguised adoption of a stipulation may seem dogmatic. How can it be justified? It will help us get an answer if we consider one further feature of philosophical intuitions like those Kripke appeals to. There are two approaches to them, one dogmatic and the other open. On the former alternative one says: Well, people might disagree with my intuitions, but I am right and they are wrong. This is Kripke's attitude. On the other hand one might say that while reasonable people may disagree, I favor this intuition not that, and so in my investigations I shall assume it holds, and address certain problems that arise on that assumption. In the latter case one encounters phrases like

'Friends of *externalism* maintain . . .'. The question of truth is put off in favor of what is explicitly said to be, for the moment at least, mere preference; the task is to explore the ramifications of adopting this rather than that stance.

Now, whether a given intuition is treated dogmatically or liberally, the point remains that there are alternatives to be considered. Kripke's intuition tells him that this XYZ stuff is not water; another person's intuition may speak differently, saying it is indeed water, but that there are two kinds of water, that is, two different types of water as determined by molecular structure. In all the cases Kripke cites there are, naturally enough, alternatives to what his intuition claims. He says, again, that this stuff, lacking atomic number 79 but meeting the everyday criteria governing 'gold', is not gold. Someone might say, with the same justification or lack thereof, that it is gold, and that gold comes in two forms. That decision about what to say can have friends too.

Which choice of how to speak is correct? Since our mastery of the use of 'water' will not dictate an answer, and there are no facts to appeal to—nothing like what science will count as evidence pro or con—the defender of this or that intuition is left high and dry; there is nothing that speaks for him but his bare unadorned intuition. All we know concerning the reliability of the intuition is that he has it. His sticking to it, or at least, on the liberal alternative, his holding to it as one possible preference, amounts to no more that his holding to an implicit fiat.

I cannot claim to have demonstrated that intuition, in the Kripke cases, cashes out as implicit stipulation. But when his intuition-guided judgments are seen to lack justification in terms of ordinary criteria or by appeal to fact, it is hard to imagine what else they could be. If not stipulations they must amount only to bare statements of preference—and the practical difference between fiat and mere acknowledged preference seems non-existent.

Here it may be objected that Kripke has more than bare intuition in his favor. He also has an argument, which goes something like this. Kind terms are like proper names in being rigid designators. We fix the referent of the word 'cat', say, as standing for these creatures we meet in everyday life. It has been discovered, if that is the right word, that cats are animals (and not demons). So when we imagine certain counterfactual claims about this cat we are speaking of a certain referent that comes with all its cardinal properties—in particular its status as an animal. 'Suppose this cat had not got underfoot,' someone might say, 'then you would not have tripped and awakened Aunt Constance.' In saying this, the person delineates a possible world in which this cat does not trip you and in which Aunt Constance is not awakened, and so on. But the creature in the possible world is that very cat referred to when it was said 'Suppose this cat had not got underfoot.' That creature, in being transported to a possible world via supposition, retains all its essential properties. But how do we know that being an animal is an essential feature of cats? That is something science has established, as it has determined that water is H_2O. In this argument a thesis about one kind term—that these (demon) creatures are not cats or that this stuff is not water—is buttressed by an account that applies to and seemingly legitimizes a whole class of entities. But the general account no less than any particular one relies on an implicit appeal to 'intuition'. Or to put it differently: the general account can have no more validity than each particular one. And the latter rely on intuition. For example there is the intuition that when I speak of this water—in order to make a counterfactual supposition—I am speaking of a stuff that is essentially H_2O.

If you collect all those particular intuitions, implicit stipulations, or bare preferences, you can produce a theory, or at least a 'picture', of the nature of kind terms. If science discovers that the essence of water is to be H_2O, then it is a necessary truth that water is H_2O, and similarly for 'gold', 'tiger', 'cat', and so on. Here the philosopher seems to copy the scientist's method. The latter collects evidence and shapes theories to accommodate it; the former does the same, but with 'intuitions' taking the place of hard evidence. One might grant the difference between intuitions that can be cashed out in terms of hard evidence and those that cannot—those caught forever in the realm of what-we-would-say—while yet affirming that in this case the philosopher still has worthwhile work to do, and is not merely a scientist manqué. The scientist discovers that water is H_2O; the philosopher discovers—or maybe establishes—that 'Water is H_2O' is a necessary truth. One goes in the direction of an analysis of what this substance is; the other collects the analyses in the proper intellectual grouping, namely the class of necessary truths. The scientist allows us to know better what the nature of water is; the philosopher allows us to place statements of that knowledge ('Water is H_2O', etc.) in the proper modal category. We now understand the statements better.

But do we? It is an open question whether applying the term 'necessary' to the statement 'Water is H_2O' tells us something about the statement, or about how we will use the term 'necessary'. Have we discovered that the class of necessary truths is larger than we thought, or changed by implicit stipulation what is to count as necessary? Do we understand the examples better by collecting them under the idea of necessary truth, or do we now understand the concept of necessary truth in terms of those examples? For Wittgenstein, who always seeks elucidation through examples, the answer will be plain. Or again: let 'necessary' equal 'true in all possible worlds'. Then the question of whether 'Gold has atomic weight 79' is necessary depends on whether, in the circumstances Kripke imagines, we would still call this gold, even though it does not have the usual atomic weight. Which brings us back to intuition and its vicissitudes.

5. Philosophical Anthropology

No one would count Kripke as an ordinary language philosopher. Instead, riding the Zeitgeist, he has gone on to develop the theory-oriented accounts based on intuition that we have been examining. Many philosophers have followed the same line; theory-related appeals to intuition—of both the dogmatic and the liberal variety—are commonplace in contemporary Anglo-American philosophy.

Wittgenstein would reject this shift towards theory building. The major intended result of the previous exposition of Kripke's stance is to indicate what exactly, in this instance, Wittgenstein would reject. We get to understand the later philosophy a little better by setting out clearly one thing it is not.

The main negative point is this: He would not treat the fruits of intuition as evidence but as grist for the mill of his critical investigations. He is suspicious of intuition. One reason for suspicion is that by his lights one's mastery of a concept does not justify one in applying it, in the Kripkean manner, beyond its limits. This attitude is apparent in the following quote from the *Big Typescript*, for example:

Let's think of a game, say tennis, whose rules say nothing about the maximum height for a ball's trajectory. And now imagine that someone were to say: This game isn't regulated at all, for if someone throws the ball so high that it doesn't return to earth...then we don't know whether this ball is to count as 'out' or 'in'. We'd answer him—I believe—that if such a case were to come about we'd set up rules for it, but that for now it isn't necessary.   (BT, 196)

In this remark the focus is on instances where one of our concepts has no clear application. The rules embodied in the language-game in question do not reach out to cover the imagined instance. In such a case Kripke might appeal to intuition. Wittgenstein's opposing attitude is that we needn't worry in advance or torment ourselves with wondering what to say, or what intuition might dictate about such imagined instances. When the time comes, if it does, we can adjust the rules. Wittgenstein takes natural language as it is, merely noting that it is designed to work in normal conditions, and that its not covering the abnormal ones is no defect.

In contrast to Kripke's drive to construct a philosophical theory or 'picture' by employing evidence intuition provides, Wittgenstein is suspicious of intuition and does not rely on it. Rather his aim is in part to examine critically what intuition claims to tell us. When faced with a philosophical intuition Wittgenstein's response would be to investigate the everyday use of the terms that figure therein. The aim is not to construct a theory but to map the customs or language-games governing those words. Intuition—for example my intuition that an intention is a causally effective mental something or other—still has a role to play, but only, in a case like this, as marking places where the philosopher looks at his own language and radically misunderstands it. Here is where the Wittgensteinian philosophical anthropologist returns to the rough ground. Back to ordinary language, but not via naive meta-level judgments about what we would say, nor by reliance on what intuition, whether of the dogmatic or liberal variety, would dictate.[29]

---

[29] Thanks to Jack Sidnell and Danièle Moyal-Sharrock for helpful comments on an earlier draft.

The Private Language Argument

BEDE RUNDLE

Wittgenstein disowned any concern to advance theories, his avowed aim being to describe rather than to explain or justify. His readers have not always been convinced. Some of his observations on mathematics have seemed counter-intuitive, to both mathematicians and non-mathematicians; certainly not to be mere rearrangements of what we have always known (PI, 109). His understanding of religion has struck many as idiosyncratic, and his account of dreaming appears to be at odds with common belief. In the philosophy of psychology more generally we find observations which, being distinctly verificationist in character, go beyond this limited descriptive task. Thus, when treating of what we might call the 'laws of evidence' of the mental, he maintains that psychological ascriptions to others are grounded in behaviour, to such a point that evidence for a psychological state is always evidence for a further 'outer' condition, never for something somehow 'behind' what we observe. Wittgenstein is not a behaviourist, in that he allows that our mental lives may, on a given occasion, be in no way apparent to others, but there is nothing that may not in principle enter the public domain, which means, in this context, nothing which cannot be manifested in behaviour, verbal or non-verbal. We may well have an opposing picture whereby a person's mental state could be unfathomable to others, that there should be no behaviour that might clinch a hypothesis concerning that state, but without prejudice to the fact that he himself should know all along how things stood. For Wittgenstein, however, where we might say that he alone knows, the inconclusiveness of the behavioural evidence means no more than that there is an indeterminacy in the language game.[1]

I do not wish to suggest that Wittgenstein is wrong in his analysis, only to query whether his description of what he is doing applies in this instance.

---

[1] See P.M.S. Hacker, *Wittgenstein: Meaning and Mind, Volume 3 of an Analytical Commentary on the Philosophical Investigations* (Oxford and Cambridge, Mass: Blackwell, 1990), 281–6.

That description is in doubt given the elements of justification, explanation, and possible departure from our ordinary beliefs that his penetrating analyses involve. One of Peter Hacker's most important achievements has been to point the way to an understanding of Wittgenstein which has brought with it an appreciation of his writings as subtle and profound where we might otherwise have found little more than a questionable conflict with common sense. The issue just broached is of interest in that it leads on to another topic where we may harbour similar uncertainties about what Wittgenstein is actually doing, namely, the argument for the impossibility of a private language. Uncertainties here relate both to how that argument proceeds, and to the extent to which it is simply making articulate conceptual connexions which we implicitly recognize, and not contradicting views which stem from generally held beliefs. The observations that follow are no more than a footnote to Peter Hacker's comprehensive and illuminating exegesis and commentary in chapter 1 of *Wittgenstein: Meaning and Mind*, but a footnote which may be of interest to those who have shared my puzzlement.

I

Consider the following (true) autobiographical observations. I once suffered from unpleasant feelings in the head which did not compare closely to anything I had ever experienced. It is not that I could say nothing about them—as I say, they were in my head, and they were decidedly unpleasant (though not painful)—but I could not say anything that pinned them down in any more informative way. I knew nothing of their causation, nor of any other circumstance through which they might be identified. But if a doctor had asked me to keep a record of the occurrences of this sensation, might I not sensibly have made this task easier by appropriating a name 'S' for the sensation? Surely my introduction of 'S' would have been of equal intelligibility to the doctor's instruction?

Such a procedure might be embarked upon in all innocence, but there is at least a case for it to answer from the perspective of Wittgenstein's private language argument, and the considerations which lie at the heart of that argument appear to be irresistible. So, we are asked to imagine a person ostensibly referring to his immediate sensations in a language which cannot be understood by another. Its words for sensations are not tied up with any natural expressions thereof—as would indeed make for the possibility of understanding—but the person is simply to associate a name, 'S', with a certain sensation. However, far from establishing a connexion between sign and sensation, Wittgenstein contends, the person's production of the former in the presence of the latter is nothing more than an idle ceremony. Since no connexion has been established, there is no question of getting the connexion *right* with a subsequent use of 'S', no sense to the idea of a correct use of 'S'. It is this observation that is at the heart of the argument:

A definition surely serves to establish the meaning of a sign.—Well, that is done precisely by the concentration of my attention; for in this way I impress on myself the connexion between the sign and the sensation.—But 'I impress it on myself' can only mean: this process brings it about that I remember the connexion *right* in the future. But in the present case I have no criterion of correctness. One would like to say: whatever is going to seem right to me is right. And that only means that here we can't talk about 'right'.   (PI, 258)

The problem is not that we cannot draw a distinction between seeming to have S and actually having S. There is no such distinction with pains either. What is at issue is whether 'S' is being used correctly, whether it is the right word for the sensation the person is having, and as yet it simply has not been laid down how that is to be determined. Contrast the use of 'S' with that of a word for a sensation in the public language, such as 'pain'. How do I know that the experience I am having is the one we call 'pain'? I know that, because my spontaneous behaviour in certain situations is what is called the expression of pain (RPP I, 304). However, as already intimated, it is not unnatural to feel that something we might find ourselves drawn to saying is being denied us, and it is the point in the argument at which this is likely to be felt that I shall focus upon.

While public circumstances may serve to identify a sensation as one of pain, the same cannot be said for my head trouble. Relevant behaviour on my part, both voluntary and involuntary, may substantiate my characterization of the sensation as unpleasant, but that is all. So, I may display involuntary reactions associated with a sensation of that nature, as with recoiling or grimacing, and if I find a means to rid myself of the sensation or to avoid the occasions on which it arises, I shall doubtless act accordingly. However, such behaviour is not sufficient to narrow down the sensation within the broader category of the unpleasant, a category which subsumes pains—which this sensation certainly was not. For pains, a plausible differentia brings in their causation. We may learn the term 'pain' in connexion with cuts, burns, grazes, and other such injuries, pains with unknown causes being adjudged pains on the strength of their likeness to what is experienced in these cases. Moreover, causation is of importance when there is no regular connexion with behaviour, as with the many minor sensations, neither agreeable nor disagreeable, that we experience. While public criteria of a causal kind are there to invoke with feelings of this variety, the problem met with in the present instance is that the causation of the unpleasant sensations was quite unknown to me.

The problem posed by the paucity of links between my sensation and public criteria is worth pursuing further. As an alternative to the view that a simple association is all that connects the sign with the sensation, Wittgenstein draws attention to the expressive role which the relevant language may enjoy. At PI, 244 he asks how words relate to sensations. Here I use 'relate' in translating *sich beziehen*, which is rendered in the Anscombe translation as 'refer to'. I should have thought that the more general 'relate' was a better choice, the suggestion that words 'refer to' sensations being one of the possible *answers* to Wittgenstein's question—and not necessarily one which he would give, natural though it may strike us. A point in favour of my rendering is that 'relate', like *sich beziehen* but unlike 'refer', is symmetric: we can ask how sensations relate to words just as readily as we may ask how words relate to sensations; the question is: how are words and sensations related to one another? At all events, Wittgenstein then goes on to ask how we learn the meaning of names of sensations, of 'pain', for instance. His answer:

Here is one possibility: words are connected with the primitive, the natural, expressions of the sensation and used in their place. A child has hurt himself and he cries; and then adults talk to him and teach him exclamations and, later, sentences. They teach the child new pain-behaviour.   (PI, 244)

It is noteworthy that, while this is put forward as just one possibility, no others are mentioned, yet pain is not typical of sensations. Its intensely disagreeable character makes for a conceptual link with behaviour—it is not a contingent matter that we tend to avoid what we dislike—but we experience all manner of milder sensations, as of temperature or pressure, which in general provoke no response from us. Moreover, even 'I am in pain' is likely to differ from something as close to a groan or a cry as is 'ouch!' While it may be prompted by a sudden pain, 'ouch!', unlike 'I am in pain', is not appropriate to the case where an enduring pain is being reported. And reported to *someone*. The words typically enjoy a communicative role, parallel to that of 'I am no longer in pain', whereas the exclamation 'ouch!' may well come from a solitary sufferer, an involuntary cry detached from any intention. We move even further away from an expressive use when qualifications as of a temporal or locational character are introduced—'I'm still in pain', 'I've got a pain in my back'. The attraction of the expressive account is that it aligns verbal behaviour with other behaviour criterial of sensations, thereby breaking the grip of a picture of avowals of sensations as reports of introspectively gained privileged knowledge, claims which invite a check but which defy corroboration. However, it may be that this conception has to be corrected while accepting our reports of sensations at their face value.

Application of the notion of an expression is less forced in other areas. So, exclamations such as 'aha!', 'wow!', and 'ugh!' often just *are* surprised, delighted, or disgusted reactions. And, in a very different way, the notion is of service with respect to an elucidation of belief and intention. If I say, 'I'll show you the way out', I am expressing an intention, but an intention that may well take shape *with* the announcement, rather than an intention harboured before that point. The latter would be suggested by 'I intend to show you the way out', a form which, as geared to the *reporting* of an intention, would be very much out of place if a spontaneous offer were being made. Similarly, on reading an advertisement I may say 'There is a job going at the post office', thereby giving voice to a belief, but 'I believe there's a job going at the post office' is suited to reporting a more long-standing belief, a belief which antedates the announcement rather than a declaration which simply relays what I have just learned.

But, returning to the question how words and my odd sensation are related, do we as yet have even the semblance of a private language? Despite its novelty, the sensation could have been identified readily enough in plain English: as, say, 'the sensation which I first experienced at noon on Boxing Day, 1980'. Or I might speak of the sensation which led me to complain to my wife or to see a doctor at that time. I also have the concept, acquired through learning the common language, of 'same sensation'. Any moves taken to comply with the doctor's instruction could proceed within that language, so without reliance on 'S'—unless 'S' is simply taken as a harmless abbreviation of something like the given identification. However, we should like to know just what is involved in the concept of *same sensation*, seemingly drawn from actual usage, which we may find ourselves invoking here. We shall now address this query, making use of an analogy with names of colours.

II

It may be thought that, by concentrating one's attention on a green expanse and uttering 'green', one could come by a concept of green—the empiricist's picture of concept formation. However, such a performance does not determine how we are to respond when presented with any of the other numerous shades which fall under that concept. We can call such a shade green or not as we please, either decision being equally consistent with our initial christening. But if it is thus indeterminate what is to count as green, we cannot suppose that we are dealing with a well-defined concept. When first using the word we stand, as it were, at a point from which many paths lead, paths corresponding to the different decisions possible as to what is to count as green. It is not until we have a well-trodden path, not until the decisions have been taken over a larger range of cases, that a definite concept has taken shape. Likewise with the sensation in my head. Even though I may use familiar language in referring to that sensation, it remains indeterminate what is to count as a recurrence thereof.

On the other hand, what are we to make of the following consideration? Suppose we see an object of a colour which we have not previously encountered. Might we not subsequently come across another object which, we are inclined to say, is of *exactly* the same colour? Granted, what will count as the same has not yet been laid down once we depart from exact sameness, but that would not deter us from pronouncing judgement in these terms. After all, if we are dealing with a uniformly coloured expanse, then thinking of it as divided in two will perforce be thinking of it as comprising two identically coloured halves. Equally, there can be cases where we should not hesitate to say that two unfamiliar colours, or sensations, were noticeably different.

It is commonly recognized that the private language argument is not to be represented as a form of scepticism about memory. Since it is an illusion to suppose that 'S' has had a meaning conferred upon it, there is no question of remembering or misremembering what one meant by 'S' on an earlier occasion. The question is, accordingly, not so much whether we can repose any confidence in a seeming memory of our experience, but, to repeat, how we can know that we are using 'S' correctly. However, while the reliability of memory is not the issue, it is useful to consider a case where memory plays no part, since this brings home forcibly the inclination to speak of sameness. So, imagine that while a novel sensation is being felt in one arm, it suddenly makes an appearance in the other. We should not hesitate to make the identification given here with 'a novel sensation' and 'it'. No doubt there could be cases in which we were uncertain whether to speak of sameness, but in the limiting case, where we simply cannot distinguish the two occurrences in anything but location, we shall see nothing amiss in speaking of identity. And this limiting case need not be exceptional. In theory, the area of indeterminacy may be large, but in practice it may be that the only candidate sensations tend to be more or less indistinguishable. I should be hard pressed to differentiate in any way the sensations I have had of the kind one gets when one knocks one's 'funny bone'. Or again, we often say such things as 'What is that smell? I noticed it last time I was here.' We may be unable to put a name to the smell, yet be in no doubt that we have encountered it before. Is our strange sensation significantly different?

Wittgenstein's observations on identity or sameness do not appear to bear upon this form, but what concerns him is more the kind of sameness that we get with a phrase like 'same colour' taken more broadly, as it might extend to all the shades of green, for instance. We may well feel that such sameness 'comes from the language', to use a phrase of Rhees's,[2] in that we can readily imagine that speakers of other languages should find alternative groupings of colours more natural. Likewise when the question is raised whether someone following a rule is going on in the same way as before. Here, too, possibilities of choice may arise to a degree that is not met with when the sameness is explicable as indistinguishability.

[2] Rush Rees, *Discussions of Wittgenstein* (Bristol: Thoemmes Press, 1996), 59.

And yet sameness of this latter variety has some claim to be regarded as basic in many contexts. Consider tastes. Writers of detective stories tell us that prussic acid has the same taste as bitter almonds. Here priority is given to the kind of comparison which may issue in the verdict 'indistinguishable', rather than simply leaving it to the bearer of the taste to define its identity. I mean, we do not say that, bitter almonds being clearly different from prussic acid, the taste of bitter almonds is ipso facto a different taste from that of prussic acid. Moreover, the sameness which indistinguishability can secure would appear sufficient for other moves we might naturally go on to make. Do we not from time to time experience sensations which occur detached from public criteria, which strike us as being just like earlier instances and which prompt our doctor to ask such questions as: When did you last have this feeling? For how long did it last? Did it vary in intensity? and so forth. That language game must be played in surgeries all over the globe. Furthermore, merely to suppose that in time the causation of my head sensations may come to light assumes that my identifications of this sensation are intelligible—as I say 'yes' or 'no' to such questions as 'Do you feel it now?' Indeed, to grant, as we must, that 'the sensation which I first experienced at noon on Boxing Day, 1980' is intelligible surely is just to grant the possibility of these variant forms of reference; not merely that, but the logic of 'sensation' is such that sensations are repeatable, so if the circumstances are such that the only form which repeatability might take is as with an indistinguishable recurrence, then again this is provided for in the public language. Contrast an attempt to ground talk of sameness in some brute-factual act of 'primary recognition'. We are not saying that there is some positive but ineffable condition which we just take in. The negative character of our characterization is something we can happily acknowledge. Note too that, without being able to specify the respect in which they differ, we can say that x and y are barely distinguishable or almost indistinguishable.

It was suggested that the term 'S' might bear the meaning 'the sensation which I first experienced at noon on Boxing Day, 1980', but the private linguist presumably wishes to cling to 'S' as having a more specific sense. To invoke again the analogy of colour, we have taken 'the colour of grass' as our model for 'S' when it is really 'green' that comes closer to his thought. Let us suppose that, whatever x may be, x is green if and only if x is the colour of grass. None the less, these two phrases give very different identifications of the colour—one via a particular bearer, the other directly—and it is natural to suppose that one cannot make use of the former to convey the sense of the latter. Likewise, while my rendering of 'S' leaves it in the public domain, when it is taken as corresponding to 'green' its salient feature is its incapacity to convey the precise character of S to another, even though—at least as far as the private linguist is concerned—it may serve to capture that character for the person who introduced it. And, the private linguist might argue, this character is surely what figures in my judgements of sameness. Do I not judge my current sensation to be like the original S in virtue of its specific character as a sensation—what sets it apart from pains, tickles, and other feelings? I need make no use of the original identification; indeed, I may well have forgotten the identifying information which that incorporated.

Compare tastes. Suppose we are presented with a range of different wines to sample. It may well be that we notice considerable differences between them, but without having any vocabulary in which to describe these differences. Of course, we may come by the necessary words, but in a way this is secondary, these words being of use only in so far as there is a perceived character for them to latch on to. Taste is a guide to grape variety as much as grape variety is a guide to taste. Again, the problem of bringing to mind tastes for which one has no name is not significantly different from that of bringing to mind tastes which one can categorize, and even when a public name is provided, it may be that all it does is facilitate communication rather than identification. A given wine has been presented to us as being the most expensive of the samples. This label offers no direct clue as to the character of the wine, but we have to make use of our ability to discriminate and identify independently of anything which the information as to expense might offer. Note, too, that a smell or taste currently experienced may change, and be appreciated as changing, even though we have no descriptions to hand with which to register the phases of the change. A very old wine is sampled immediately after the cork is drawn, and it is found after only a few minutes to have taken on quite a different taste, though perhaps only the experts can put a name to any of the stages through which it passes.

III

If a case can be made out for 'S' as equating neither to the initial identification, as 'the experience which I first experienced at noon on Boxing Day, 1980', nor to any other phrase which draws upon a connexion with behaviour or other public conditions, then the private linguist will have achieved a notable victory. In reality, however, he has added nothing new to what we have already allowed him. First, it would be wrong to think that 'S' as the private linguist would represent the name is superior to the suggested use in the way he claims. A person who is capable of identifying green objects as being 'of the colour of grass', yet is without 'green' or an equivalent in his vocabulary, is not somehow missing out on the specific character of such objects, as though, 'green' being the exact word for the colour, its use went with a more exact knowledge of the character of that colour. Consider the example of smells, where the 'indirect' identification is the rule—the smell of burning rubber, of coffee, of dead fish. It is true that direct and indirect forms will differ in meaning, but so long as a person is able to identify the smell, colour, or whatever directly—i.e., without having to proceed via an identification of its source or bearer—he shows himself to have the same recognitional capacities whichever form he uses.

Second, while it is true that the private linguist is not tied to the exact terms of the initial identification, 'the sensation which...', he must none the less make implicit reference to the sensation to which this identification and its variants relate, since the only content we can attach to his identifications of sensations as 'S' is that they compare closely with the earlier sensation, however that might be picked out. He is said to judge his current sensation to be like the original in virtue of its specific character as a sensation—what sets it apart from pains and the rest—but there appears to be no reason to suppose him to be doing anything other than proclaim the indistinguishability of the two as initially proposed, when he will simply be relying on his grasp of 'same sensation', a phrase in the public language. Similarly with tastes. It is enormously tempting to say, as implied above, that words which we use in their regard are no more than labels for various tastes that we have identified in advance of acquiring their names, but all that we have in advance is what we express by speaking of one taste as indistinguishable—to us—from another.

Third, the appeal to indistinguishability does nothing to confirm the meaningfulness of the private linguist's name, 'S', let alone *confer* a meaning upon it. We are saying that in those cases where we cannot tell the difference between *x* and *y*, then if we call *x* 'S' we shall be right to call *y* 'S', but this holds *whatever* the meaning of 'S'. It is just a general truth about the way we use words for sensations, when sameness is understood in terms of indistinguishability.

The (ostensible) knowledge which I have of my head sensations is, in a sense, knowledge I can share with others: from what I say you may learn that the sensation I am now experiencing is comparable with the sensation which I first had on Boxing Day, 1980. It is just that you do not know what that is like, in the sense that you would not know that that was what you were having if you had it. Contrast this identification with, say, 'the taste of dandelion wine'. The meaning of the latter is not in the least problematic, but I have no idea what the taste in question is like. On the other hand, while this phrase offers a means of identifying the taste which anyone might make use of, the identification which I give of my sensation is simply unavailable for others to exploit.

We say that we don't know what the private linguist is experiencing, but does he? Is not his peculiar position distinguished, not in terms of knowledge, but simply in that there is something he *has* which, as far as we know, no one else does? This touches on one of the seemingly counter-intuitive aspects of Wittgenstein's approach. Think how much there is in our experience that we find ourselves unable to put into words. How can we possibly get across the subtle differences in taste of different kinds of fish or fruit, the differences in peoples' voices, the different scents of flowers, and so on endlessly? And yet our lack of an adequate vocabulary in no way detracts from our recognitional capacities.

Some caution is needed here in putting the case for unverbalized knowledge. If someone despairs of conveying to another the taste of pineapple, say, it is in place to point out that he is not without words for that taste; rather, he may be without words *further* than 'the taste of pineapple'. But it is doubtless true that we often cannot come up with *any* description of what we experience that is not hopelessly vague or general. Whether or not one has the requisite vocabulary, there are difficulties in speaking of knowledge with respect to one's sensations, but, as just intimated, in the case of tastes and so forth it might be said that the subject knows what a particular taste, as of pineapple, say, is *like*. This has two readings. Either—the more literal interpretation—he can make a comparison with other tastes (to the point of specifying them), or—less demandingly—he is capable of recognizing the taste, can identify it correctly when he comes across it. So does the diarist know what his novel sensation is like? Well, by hypothesis he cannot *say* what it is like in any useful way, but he can recognize it, tell when he has it rather than something else.

Or so he says. Our preparedness to accept this depends on whether we grant sense to his claim that what he is now experiencing is more or less indistinguishable from what he experienced on the earlier occasion. Certainly, in playing down the importance of the initial identification, both in the taste example and with 'the sensation which I first experienced at noon on Boxing Day, 1980', we are shifting the weight, not onto an as yet undefined term, 'S', which need not figure in this discussion at all, but on to the notion of indistinguishability. And is this not simply our notion, or one of our notions, of sameness already there in the public language for us to exploit?

I say that my deeming the current sensation to be the same as the sensation I first experienced on a certain date is to be understood negatively: a matter of not being able to distinguish the one from the other. Of course, if I cannot even recall the earlier sensation, then, clearly, I shall not be able to distinguish what I am now feeling from it, but this is, equally clearly, *too* negative to be of use. I must have at least some memory of the earlier sensation if there is going to be any question of a re-identification. Two observations concerning memory are of interest at this point, one which the private linguist will welcome, the other which is of no assistance to him. First the latter. While we may compare different wines, say, in respect of taste, what is remembered about an earlier wine is how it tasted—it had a flavour of ripe spiced bramble, a hint of black cherries, or a crisp green-apple freshness, as one says. A conceptualization may form the basis of our comparison, rather than an olfactory analogue of a visual image, and this is clearly unavailable with respect to the private linguist's sensation. Second, and more in his favour, is the consideration that, even in the normal case we may not pronounce our present sensation to be such and such on the basis of a likeness to anything we actually recall. My attention may have an exclusively present focus when I characterize a smell as one of cigar smoke, petrol, or bacon cooking. I do not, as it were, carry around memories of smells I have experienced, having them available for comparison with any other smells that turn up. Rather, it generally takes a recurrence of a smell to bring earlier exemplars to mind. And even that may be lacking, the only impression being one of familiarity. Likewise with my strange sensations in the head. Here, too, there is no exercise of memory on my part, in the sense of casting my mind back to previous occasions, bringing the sensation to mind at will. When it assails me the memory of earlier occurrences may flood back, but again nothing more specific than the thought 'I've had that before' may occur to me.

With the example of smells just given, one's being right or wrong is readily enough ascertained, but the problem posed by my odd sensation is to some extent repeated if we should wonder whether strawberries, say, taste the same today as they did in our youth, since now it is not just the simple matter of establishing that one has got it right in one's identification of a taste as that of a strawberry. This is the kind of case which Wittgenstein's argument appears to cast doubt upon. That is, identification of a current taste as the taste of strawberries takes us from the 'sensation' to the public defining conditions, but the latter appear to fall out of the picture when we ask whether the taste of strawberries may not have changed over time. We may, of course, get general agreement that this is in fact so, but this is a matter of summing individual impressions rather than appealing to public criteria. Clearly, an impression must individually count for something if there is to be probative significance in such a sum.

If I say that a wine tastes just like the one we had yesterday, I run the risk of being contradicted by others, and to the extent that it is possible to protect a wine from change over such a period of time, it is possible to judge where the truth lies. If my claim is the more modest one—that this wine tastes *to me* just as did yesterday's—then production of yesterday's wine may lead me to revise my judgement, but it may also be that I stand by that judgement in the face of a differing verdict from others. The difficulty arises when there is nothing filling the role of the wine, nothing *having* a taste, smell, or whatever, that might be sampled anew. And that is how it is both with the sensation envisaged in the private language argument and with my head sensations. It certainly *seems* to me that this sensation is like one I've had before. Is this as much as can be said? Can even this much be said? Do I not have to know what it would be for it to *be* just like for it to *seem* just like? Given that there is nothing analogous to having the bearer of a property persist into the present, it would appear that all we can appeal to is an irredeemably hypothetical supposition: if the present sensation had followed immediately on the earlier, I should not have detected a difference. But what would have entitled me to say in that situation that the second sensation was *this* sensation, the one I am having now? The knowledge sought is essentially what we set out to determine—that my present sensation is the same as the one experienced at the earlier time. Or again, 'If I had this sensation a year ago, . . .' is acceptable, its meaning clear, only if the same can be said of 'I had this sensation a year ago'. How can we find 'If I had . . .' unproblematic if there are doubts about 'I had . . .'? They, along with 'I might have had this sensation a year ago', stand or fall together.

The problem presented by the supposed relocation of a present sensation in the past can be brought out in the following way. Consider the seemingly uncontentious observation, with respect to either the first or the second sensation, namely, 'I might have had that sensation ten minutes earlier'. Can I say this if I do not know what would have counted as that, i.e., the same, sensation? All that 'that' identifies is the sensation as it occurred at a particular time in a particular part of my body. Time and place being the only individuating conditions which mark out the sensation, we are still in the dark as to what would have counted as the same sensation when those individuating conditions do not apply.

We introduced a case where the comparison of sensations appears to be unproblematic: a novel sensation in one arm is matched by an indistinguishable sensation in the other. It is the difference which comes when the sensations are separated in time that makes for our problem: we experience an unusual sensation, detached from behaviour and any known cause, and, at a later time, we have a sensation which, we are inclined to say, is just like the earlier one. But there are no memory claims which can be considered infallible, and, however strong our conviction that the current sensation is identical with the earlier, we have still to clarify what this means.

If this is correct, then, modest though it appears, even 'My earlier sensation may not have been as I remember it' is a concession that may be questioned, since, in the circumstances, there is no way of ascertaining, even in principle, how my sensation was. The considerations which oblige me to stop short of saying that my current sensation is indistinguishable from the sensation as earlier experienced put paid to affirming this as a possibility as much as an actuality. Or, at least, this is how matters stand if memory is not allowed to decide the matter. Since the sacrifice of even this bare possibility is one of the costs of discounting memory, we must consider further whether we have an alternative.

IV

Let us go back to the claim which, I have suggested, is at the heart of Wittgenstein's argument, namely: '. . . in the present case I have no criterion of correctness. One would like to say: whatever is going to seem right to me is right. And that only means that here we can't talk about "right".' But suppose we do not take the step from 'seeming right' to 'right'. That is, we still stand by 'it seems to me to be just the same as the earlier sensation', but we are prepared to add: I may be right, I may be wrong. Can we explain being right and being wrong? If it is a matter of a sensation which occurs in each of my arms at the same time, then we can apply our notion of indistinguishability; and if the one sensation, whether in arm or head, follows immediately on the other sensation, leaving no room for a failure of memory, I could judge the matter of sameness. If it struck me as just a continuation of the first sensation, then we have sameness; otherwise not.

It seems that if we are to make any progress towards clarifying the identity claim, something must come to light by way of a known replicable condition with which the sensation is associated—as might be given by its typical causation, for instance. And why does the problem which comes with a lapse of time, the problem of judging our current sensation to be the same as an earlier, not recur with respect to an associated physical or behavioural condition? It is not because we have with the latter resolved a problem of memory which defeated us with the former, but because we are dealing with a condition for which there is a distinction between being and seeming, the key consideration in Wittgenstein's argument. Our beliefs can be confirmed, our errors brought home to us, whether by observations and investigations of others or of ourselves. The phrase 'the sensation which I first experienced at noon on Boxing Day, 1980' may serve to identify a sensation unambiguously, but for all that be by itself incapable of providing an identification of the earlier sensation in terms of which sameness, in the relevant respect, may be understood.

Something along the above lines may take us to the right conclusion, but it is not entirely satisfactory in that we do not appear to have done justice to the certainty we have that we are experiencing a sensation we have had before, uncheckable though this may be. This dissatisfaction also relates to an earlier point: sameness of sensations need not require a corresponding sameness of public criteria.

Our difficulties have stemmed from the problem met with in seeking to compare a past and a present sensation, but consider the case where I seemingly bring to mind a past smell. It is, I say, the smell that greeted me when I last opened the cupboard. An identity is affirmed, but not one involving a comparison of two smells, or even of a memory of a smell with a smell now experienced. There is accordingly not a problem generated by the lack of a criterion for judging two items to be the same. It is a matter of whether it is *that* smell, where time and place of occurrence do provide an adequate identification. Of course, it is likely, at least in my case, that I seemingly remember the past smell only when my memory is prompted by a present smell, but I still need not be resting anything on a comparison. If my memory is deceiving me, it will be because I am not bringing to mind the smell as identified by the time and place given. But I do claim that it is a particular smell I am recalling, so is not a criterion required for the correctness of that claim?

Acceptance of this requirement appears to leave us where we were before, but consider the following case of memory, also problematic. Suppose you are asked what thoughts passed through your head on awakening this morning. You may unhesitatingly give your answer, yet be quite at a loss for anything useful to say if asked to substantiate your claim. You spoke to no one of your thoughts, nor did you commit them to paper. Your confidence will not be one wit diminished in the face of a clear and vivid recollection, but how could that be justified if there is nothing you might offer by way of proof? We note, first, that it is memory itself that generally puts an end to queries about events which have taken place in the recent past and which are within the competence of the subject to judge, so it should be said, not that there is no proof, but that there is no *further* proof.

A memory qualifies as *direct* knowledge by comparison with mere signs of past happenings, so may well be accorded the title. Thus, what makes for directness of a report such as 'There is a crack in the wall' is retained with a transposition to the past-tense memory report: 'There was, as I recall, a crack in the wall.' Moreover, even if we should look in vain for independent support, that is not to say that our seeming memory may not receive backing in more general terms. With many memory claims we can establish that we were right, since the evidence for this lies in the present, as when a person claims to remember where something is to be found. It is such cases as these that establish one's dependability, a dependability that is still there to draw upon when, as in the present instance, circumstances preclude such confirmation. In the light of a general backing, the full confidence which we place in our judgement is not misplaced, is not without reason. Our unblemished track record is enough to see us through when we are denied further support of a more direct character.

Our memory report, with respect to both our past thoughts and a past sensation, thus has the standing of a presumptive truth. It is this notion that fills the gap left by the possibility of a final verification. Is this to say that, when verification is logically excluded, we have to interpret rightness and wrongness—if they make any sense at all—exclusively in the light of what holds now; in other words, that we are committing ourselves to a form of anti-realism about the past? But it is standing only as a *presumptive* truth that is being claimed. It is not that present findings can put the matter beyond doubt, to such an extent that there is no logical space for alternative hypotheses about how things were. The matter is not closed, but there is room for further considerations to be adduced, both for and against the truth of our memory claim. No conclusive proof, but for all that, we can, in the appropriate circumstances, repose full confidence in such a claim. With respect to our odd sensation, there is not the indeterminacy met with when we seek to compare two instances of what we are inclined to reckon the same sensation, so it is not an objection that sameness is not defined.

V

So have we done anything to rehabilitate the concept of a private language? We suggested that the term 'S' could bear the meaning 'the sensation which I first experienced at noon on Boxing Day, 1980', or that of some other identifying phrase, and we have not advanced beyond this point, not reinstated the view that 'S' could have a meaning grasped only by the person experiencing S. Not only have we not committed ourselves to such a possibility, but we leave it open that some associated condition should come to light in terms of which a public criterion for occurrence of the sensation might be defined. We leave it open, in the sense that we do not make the character of the sensation logically incommunicable, as the private linguist would have it.

Suppose I find that the sensation which I am disposed to identify in the same terms is found to occur when my spine comes under pressure at a certain point. To establish that this is suited to playing the part of a public criterion for the sensation, we should have to ascertain that when I was able to judge sameness unproblematically, so when the sensations to be compared were not separated by a significant time, that same physical condition held. Any physical condition has to answer to such a test if it is to match our experientially based judgements of identity, so in this respect the latter are fundamental, as we saw in the way a judgement of sameness of tastes might override salient physical differences in what is tasted. Indeed, since we are not defending a claim to be able to make sense of an identity of a present sensation with a past one, we do not run up against the private language argument. What we have defended is, essentially: if I have experienced a totally unfamiliar sensation, then I can meaningfully speak of remembering that sensation, even if I cannot put a name to it, where name is as like 'itch' or 'tickle' in implying a comparison with other sensations, rather than just an identifying phrase of the kind suggested for 'S'.

To sum up, I experience a sensation which does not compare closely with any sensation I have had before. This raises two questions. First, can I, at a later date, speak of experiencing the same sensation? Second, can I, at a later date, bring to mind the earlier sensation? Both questions involve a matter of identity. With the first, it is a question of what counts as the same sensation, a question which, on the private language argument, cannot be satisfactorily answered in the circumstances envisaged. With the second, the question is whether I am bringing to mind the sensation I claim to be recalling, and for that I do not have to decide whether another sensation I might experience counts as the same. True, we have to disallow the possibility of final proof and settle for more general considerations which support the memory report as a presumptive truth, but the claim for sameness is then as good as my claim to dependability as this is established in cases where a check is possible. What I purport to remember is the sensation as felt on such and such an occasion, a pinning down of the sensation in purely temporal or spatio-temporal terms which does not rely on the availability of a categorization of the sensation. This does justice to our initial impression that we could bring to mind the earlier sensation, but it also seemed apparent that we could proceed to a comparison of a current sensation with the one recalled, and it may still be felt that the two impressions are difficult to keep apart. After all, I can say I remember how the sensation felt, even if I cannot answer the question 'And how is that?' But if I can remember how it felt, can I not say that it felt just like what I am experiencing now, where 'just like' is explicable in terms of indistinguishability? As intimated at the outset, Wittgenstein's attack on privacy is sometimes felt to be at odds with everyday beliefs, beliefs which come naturally to us, without any philosophical motivation. If the suggested comparison can be coherently made, it would appear not only that there is such a conflict, but that the understandable misgivings which his critique provokes may not be misplaced.

Language-Games and Language: Rules, Normality Conditions and Conversation

STEPHEN MULHALL

The analogy between speaking and playing a game, embedded in Wittgenstein's pervasive talk of language-games, has always been central to Peter Hacker's deservedly influential interpretations of Wittgenstein's later philosophy. Here is how he summarizes the matter in the second edition of the first volume of the commentary he began writing with Gordon Baker thirty years ago, at the conclusion of his essay 'The Language-Game Method':[1]

A primary factor that made the idea of a language-game appealing is its stark contrast with the calculus model that dominated the *Tractatus*. It provided a powerful analogy which offered a normative (i.e. rule-governed) activity to compare with language and its use, but without the falsification that is involved in the idea of a calculus governed by rigid and closed rules. Moreover, the game analogy encourages us to abandon a preoccupation with the geometry of calculi and to focus instead upon the activities into which our symbolism of language is woven. It can therefore be used, as Wittgenstein used it, to emphasize the logical diversity and multiplicity of our speech activities. It highlights the ways in which the variety of speech-acts which we perform by the use of sentences are part of the tapestry of our lives, conditioned in many different ways by the world around us and by our perceptual abilities, our powers of recall and of surveying data, our natural interests and shared responses. For the language-games we play are moulded by the nature of the world we live in and by our nature, and they are partly constitutive of our forms of life.   (Hacker, WUM I, 64)

As I understand this passage, it suggests three inter-related ways in which the analogy between language and games might be illuminating. First, it

---

[1] *Wittgenstein: Understanding and Meaning, Volume 1 of an Analytical Commentary on the Philosophical Investigations, Part I—the Essays* and *Part II—the Exegesis*, 2nd edn, extensively revised (Oxford: Blackwell, 2005), hereafter WUM I and II.

reminds us that thinking of our use of words as rule-governed does not necessitate thinking of those rules as rigid and closed; second, it highlights that fact that saying is a kind of doing, that using words is a matter of performing speech-acts; and third, it underlines the relation between speech and the various general facts of nature (including human nature) that condition it. It is against this background of thought that Hacker earlier in the same essay draws the following philosophical moral: 'Games, like languages, are creations of human beings in their social inter-actions. They are not answerable to reality for correctness'.[2] The tapestry of our lives in the world may mould the language-games we play in various ways, but it can neither falsify nor justify the rules that make up those games—in part because rules are not descriptions of any kind, in part because rules constitutive of the meanings of the words we employ in descriptions of reality can hardly be falsified by such descriptions. This is Hacker's interpretation of Wittgenstein's idea of the autonomy of grammar, and so of the autonomy of grammatical investigation—of what gives such investigations their power, and of what renders certain kinds of objection to the authority of their findings utterly powerless.

But of course, an analogy is not an identity; and any analogy, if taken the wrong way, can cause more harm than good. Accordingly, in his essay, Hacker is careful to point out a number of important disanalogies between language and games. He stresses, for example, that speaking a language is not playing a game, any more than making a move in a game is a kind of speech-act; and he also points out that, while one game is not interwoven with another, the various language-games we play *are* systematically interconnected—they are all parts of the larger whole of our language and speech. Nevertheless, at the conclusion of this list of differences, Hacker declares: 'None of this detracts from the power or illumination of Wittgenstein's analogy. It merely indicates the need for care.'[3]

In this essay, I want to consider in more detail the specific analogies and disanalogies to which Hacker here draws our attention, which will mean exploring further the conception of language as a normative activity that underlies or is supported by it. For that conception was one of the central lessons I have drawn from Peter Hacker's teaching and writing over the

---

[2] Hacker, WUM I, 52.   [3] Hacker, WUM I, 54.

years, beginning with my first undergraduate tutorials with him more than twenty-five years ago—tutorials without which I simply could not imagine having retained any interest in philosophy as it is presently configured in Anglo-American circles, let alone discovering a specific trajectory within it that I could think of as my own. But when, in the course of following out that trajectory in recent years, I attempted to find points of connection between Peter's work on Wittgenstein and that of philosophers such as Stanley Cavell and Rush Rhees, I found myself engaged in a project that seemed unwelcome to both parties. Cavell's and Rhees's ways of inheriting Wittgenstein's words and examples have always appealed far more to me than they have to Peter, whose writing rarely even refers to them. At the same time, I have regularly been severely criticized by other philosophers inclined to take Cavell and Rhees seriously for thinking that Hacker's conception of language as normative can survive a proper acknowledgement of the aspects of Wittgenstein's philosophy to which Cavell and Rhees invite sustained attention.

It is my aim in this essay to think further about both lines of criticism, whose opposing directions nevertheless seem to lead to a single conclusion. For me, this is essentially an attempt to discover whether the aspects of Wittgenstein's work highlighted by Cavell and Rhees can be seen as, if not exactly following from Peter's work on that work, then accessible from it—that is, as forming part of a way of going on from it rather than going against it. If so, then a conception of Wittgenstein, and so of philosophy, that has room for such interests can be thought of as part of what Peter's teaching made it possible for me to appreciate and absorb, and so part of what makes me continuously grateful for his example.

1. The Rules of the Game

As I noted earlier, it is central to Hacker's reading of the analogy between language and games that it is designed to draw us away from the assumption that the role of rules in language is akin to that of rules in a calculus (an assumption to which Wittgenstein himself was strongly attracted in earlier phases of his thinking). In particular, it is meant to break with the assumption that the rules of language constitute a system of computational rules—rules that add up to a single, utterly rigid and complete whole, covering all possible cases of their application. On Hacker's account, Wittgenstein's 1931 breakthrough consists in seeing that any such assumption amounts to dogmatism about what a rule of language must be; but to overcome that dogmatism, it suffices to recognize that language is 'loosely governed by rules that do not try (absurdly) to budget for all conceivable eventualities'.[4] What the shift in analogy from calculus to game does not put in question is the idea that language is a rule-governed activity.

But when one examines the texts that Hacker himself cites as he charts Wittgenstein's registration of, and initial reflection upon, this insight, one might think that the full ramifications of this shift in objects of comparison reach further, or at least that Wittgenstein's position on the matter is harder to pin down—perhaps even more subject to internal tensions—than Hacker's interpretation fully brings out. Here, for example, is what Wittgenstein has to say in MS 113, 30v:

[N]o-one will deny that the study of the nature of rules of games must be useful for the study of grammatical rules, since *some sort* of similarity undeniably obtains. It is on the whole better to reflect on rules of games without any fixed opinion or prejudice about the analogy between grammar and game, but merely to be driven by the sure instinct that there is here a kinship. And here again, one should simply report what one sees . . .[5]

There seem to be two rather different lines of thought struggling for dominance in this passage. According to the first, there simply *must* be some sort of similarity between grammatical rules and rules of games—the instinct that there is a kinship here is sure and undeniable; according to the second, it is better to reflect on the comparison without any fixed opinion or prejudice about what it might teach us, better simply to report what one sees even if what one sees is that one's initial instinct was misdirected or importantly misleading. I am here reminded of the famous passage in section 66 of the *Investigations*, where Wittgenstein urges us not to say or think that there *must* be something in common to all instances of games, but rather simply to look and see whether there is or not. Section 52 is also relevant:

If I am inclined to suppose that a mouse has come into being by spontaneous generation out of grey rags and dust, I shall do well to examine those rags very

---

[4] Hacker, WUM I, 50.   [5] Quoted in Hacker, WUM I, 50.

closely to see how a mouse may have hidden in them, how it may have got there and so on. But if I am convinced that a mouse cannot come into being from these things, then this investigation will perhaps be superfluous.

But first we must learn to understand what it is that opposes such an examination of details in philosophy.   (PI, 52)

Both these later passages suggest that what opposes a simple recognition of the detailed reality of things in philosophy is a conviction that things must be a particular way, that they cannot be otherwise. In their light, one might see in the 1931 remarks a battle between the desire to look and see what the similarities and dissimilarities between rules in a game and rules of language actually are, and the driven conviction that there must be some important similarities. Or perhaps more charitably, one might say that Wittgenstein is struggling to ensure that his instinct here does not prevent him from accurately describing the degree and nature of the kinship he actually sees—from allowing for the possibility that it may take a form, and a degree, other than his initial expectations would suggest.

It is therefore worth emphasizing that the first lesson Wittgenstein himself draws from the comparison between language and a game is articulated in a passage from MS 112, 95v–96r, which is an ancestor of PI, section 83:

We can easily imagine people amusing themselves in a field by playing with a ball so as to start various existing games, but playing many without finishing them and in between throwing the ball aimlessly into the air, chasing one another with the ball and bombarding one another for a joke and so on. And now someone says: the whole time they are playing a ball-game and following definite rules at every throw.

And is there not also the case where we play and—make up the rules as we go along? And there is even one where we alter them—as we go along.   (PI, 83)

Is the point of this analogy simply to suggest that the rules of language are indefinite, that is, looser and more flexible than the rules of a calculus; or does it rather suggest that at least some of our uses of language manifest a fluidity of a kind that amounts to their not being governed by rules at all? Hacker's summary of Wittgenstein's point, offered as an introduction to the ancestor of this passage from the *Investigations*, could be interpreted in either way: 'here there are no strict rules. There is, rather, a fluid use.'[6]

---

[6] Hacker, WUM I, 50.

But the point he emphasizes immediately after quoting the passage seems to come down in favour of the former interpretation, referring as it does to a 'conception of language . . . as loosely governed by rules that do not try to budget for all conceivable eventualities'.[7] And yet the final remark Wittgenstein makes in the passage that Hacker's remark presents itself as summarizing, seems rather to emphasize the latter interpretation. 'We can say: let's investigate language in respect of its rules. If here and there it has no rules, then *that* is the result of our investigation.'[8] In these remarks at least, Wittgenstein is not prepared to allow even his own sense that games and grammar must be rule-governed (even if loosely and flexibly so) to prevent him from looking and seeing whether language always matches his preconception of it.

It certainly seems clear in the *Investigations* that Wittgenstein is concerned to emphasize—in the light of a variant upon his imagined language-game with coloured squares (PI, 48)—that, insofar as language is rule-governed, even governed by a definite rule, 'what we call a rule of a language-game may have very different roles in the game' (PI, 53).

Let us recall the kinds of case where we say that a game is played according to a definite rule.

The rule may be an aid in teaching the game . . . Or it is an instrument of the game itself.—Or a rule is employed neither in the teaching nor in the game itself; nor is it set down in a list of rules. One learns the game by watching how others play. But we say that it is played according to such-and-such rules because an observer can read these rules off from the practice of the game—like a natural law governing the play.—But how does the observer distinguish in this case between players' mistakes and correct play?—There are characteristic signs of it in the players' behaviour. Think of the behaviour characteristic of correcting a slip of the tongue.   (PI, 54)

And later, in a more figurative register, as part of his discussion of the sense in which one might understand and hence be guided in one's reading by a text, Wittgenstein invites us to consider the sheer variety of ways in which we experience ourselves as being guided, and thereby the sheer variety of activities each of which might (in the right context) count as being guided:

You are in a playing field with your eyes bandaged, and someone leads you by the hand, sometimes left, sometimes right . . .

---

[7] Hacker, WUM I, 50.   [8] Quoted in Hacker, WUM I, 50.

Or again: someone leads you by the hand where you are unwilling to go, by force.

Or: you are guided by a partner in a dance; you make yourself as receptive as possible, in order to guess his intention and obey the slightest pressure.

Or: someone takes you for a walk; you are having a conversation; you go wherever he does.

Or: you walk along a field-track, simply following it. (PI, 172)

In short, whether the rule involved is definite or indefinite, there is a variety of cases of rule-following behaviour. Might one also say that there is a variety of cases in which word-use does not exhibit normativity of the kind that the analogy between language and games might lead us to expect? To put things another way, what kinds of fluid use of language might correspond to what the ball-players are up to in section 83 between the rule-governed passages of their play?

When contesting compositional theories of meaning in his essay 'Contextual Dicta and Contextual Principles', in the same volume of the commentary, Hacker mentions three uses of language that he thinks will escape such theorists' reliance upon rigid and complete calculi-like rules: word-clusters and analogical relations, figurative meaning and metaphor. My suggestion is that these three uses might equally well be thought of as escaping the control of rules altogether.

Take metaphorical and figurative uses of language first. Hacker rightly points out that our language is run through with verbal pictures that quickly become regular linguistic currency ('flashes of insights, sparks of wit, flights of fancy'); then he goes on to say:

The phenomenon . . . is ubiquitous, and there are no general principles (as opposed to *ad hoc* enumeration of cases) which yield a set of generative rules that show how such-and-such combinations of words are generated from such-and-such elements, and others debarred. However, *ad hoc* enumeration does not show that we are dealing with ambiguity *simpliciter*, since the relevant associations are not coincidental.[9]

The passage is condensed, and it is in particular unclear to me whether or not 'ad hoc enumeration of cases' is meant to encompass an explanatory dimension. But suppose we assume that it does: even if we can explain retrospectively why a particular verbal picture was coined and found

---

[9] Hacker, WUM I, 178.

acceptable, and furthermore explain how they are to be used in their new context, we do not thereby provide a principle of any kind (let alone a general, rigid or inflexible one) for the successful generation of such pictures. And yet such figurative projections of words can be found intelligible or not, in the absence of any standards of correctness, by other speakers.

A similar point might be made about metaphorical uses of language. Once again, Hacker rightly emphasizes the centrality of such uses to our life with words—they cannot be dismissed as merely poetic, secondary or derivative in comparison with, say, literal descriptive uses of language; words used metaphorically do not have a different meaning from their customary ones, but they cannot be explained by explaining what those meanings are, and then citing a specific mode of word-combination. ' "Architecture is frozen music" would not be thus explained, but it resonates powerfully and is readily grasped. If it had to be explained, the explanation would be analogical, and if someone did not understand it, he would be exhibiting a form of meaning-blindness.'[10] Once again, then, understanding such uses of language is not just not a matter of grasping calculus-like rules; it does not seem to be rule-governed at all.

Hacker's concluding reference to meaning-blindness points us to another dimension of language use that transcends governance by a rule: secondary uses of words, of the kind discussed extensively in Part II, section 11 of the *Investigations*. In this domain, grammatical investigations cannot be conducted by recalling grammatical rules; rather, one's willingness (or lack of it) to go along with a certain projection of a word amounts to a kind of primitive linguistic reaction (analogous to the repertoire of primitive prelinguistic responses without which primary uses of words would not be assimilable by learners of language). I have tried to demonstrate elsewhere how central to Wittgenstein's conception of language, and so of ourselves as inheritors of language, this phenomenon is.[11]

Hacker also connects metaphorical uses of words with analogical forms of explanation, and thereby returns us to the first linguistic phenomenon on his list—that of word-clusters and analogical relations. For example, we speak of animals running, taps running, rivers running, paint running,

---

[10] Hacker, WUM I, 179.
[11] Cf. part I, sections 42–50 of my *Inheritance and Originality* (Oxford: Oxford University Press, 2001).

stains running and routes running (from A to B), and of politicians running (for office); Hacker says that the expressions in such a cluster are related by analogy, but that it is not always obvious (to say the least of it) that the meaning of a given expression within a cluster can always be represented as derived by a set operation from one another, because the analogies involved are neither regular nor predictable, and there is no way of circumscribing the operative similarity. In fact, Hacker goes so far as to say that even 'if there is any hidden regularity that an ingenious linguistic theorist might discover, it is just that: a regularity, not a rule that we use to guide us or invoke to explain what a phrase means'.[12]

Opinions may, of course, differ about how pervasive such word-clusters are, and hence how dependent upon analogical relations our use of language may be—although it is noteworthy that Hacker himself says that 'Wittgenstein stressed the pervasive role of analogy in language',[13] and that when Stanley Cavell attempts to sketch Wittgenstein's vision of language as such, it is exactly such modes of projection of words that he treats as emblematic (his central example, in chapter VII of *The Claim of Reason*, is the way we move from feeding a lion to feeding a meter to feeding our pride[14]). To that extent, Cavell might wish to resist labelling the phenomenon as a 'word-cluster', insofar as that might be taken to imply that each point along the projection carves out a distinct meaning of (or way of meaning) the given word, as opposed to unfolding or articulating its distinct meaning.

Perhaps further evidence in favour of seeing such phenomena as central to Wittgenstein's thinking is to be found in the fact that, as Hacker himself is careful to note, Wittgenstein's way of introducing the very term 'language-game' in section 7 of the *Investigations* suggests that it is itself a kind of word-cluster. For it picks out three analogically related linguistic phenomena or dimensions of language: primitive games with words of a kind which are or might be used to teach children how to speak; more primitive uses of language than our own; and any and all uses of words, when viewed as woven into patterns of activity. Once invited to do so, we don't have any difficulty in seeing how the term 'language-game' might apply to all three cases, and so in understanding

---

[12] Hacker, WUM I, 178.   [13] Hacker, WUM I, 177.
[14] Oxford: Oxford University Press, 1979.

how Wittgenstein and we might go on to use the term; but it is not as if existing patterns of explaining and employing the terms 'language' and 'game' self-evidently authorize such a conjoined projection of them. In short, the very idea of a language-game seems to draw upon the very powers of language that it may (if used without due care and attention) itself help to occlude.

However that may be, Hacker has here identified yet another dimension of language use that appears not only to confound the calculus model of linguistic normativity, but to put serious pressure on the very idea that such ways with words might helpfully be thought of as governed by rules at all—at least if that is taken to involve the thought that the grammar of a word licenses certain uses of it and excludes certain other uses, unless and until a new grammatical rule is introduced to determine a new use for it. For how exactly would that model apply to 'running' or 'feeding'? When we go on from talking of a lion running to talk of a river running and then of a route running (from A to B), are we in each case forging a new set of grammatical rules (and so a new language-game) with the word, and thereby changing its meaning at every point of the projection? Or is it rather part of what it is to be a word (part of the grammar of the word 'word') that it be capable of bearing up under such unpredictable projections into new contexts, and so part of understanding it that one be willing and able to keep up with its unfolding adventures in the world, and so with the world's unpredictable unfolding of itself?

Suppose these aspects of language use, taken together with the sheer variety of ways in which other aspects of language might be said to be governed by definite rules, or even by loose and flexible ones, at the very least lead us to be less confident about how much philosophical light is cast by the suggestion that language is (in its essence or by its very nature) a rule-governed activity. It is not obvious that doing so would lead us to withdraw our initial investment in the idea of grammar's autonomy, and so of the distinctive power of grammatical investigation. For giving a less prominent role to the idea of rules in this context would hardly open the door to a competing conception of word-projection as essentially descriptive of reality, and so could not help those who wish to reduce grammatical investigation to no more than the first word in philosophy by asking whether a word's grammar might misrepresent reality. It might, however, lead us to tell a more complex story about the ways in which a word's grammar and the reality it reveals to us are related, of the kind to which I have adverted above.

2. Games, Language and Normality Conditions

A key purpose of the analogy between speaking a language and playing a game, on Hacker's account, is the prominence that the analogy gives to context:

Like any other game, a language-game is 'played' in a setting. Wittgenstein's stress on the context of the game appears to be motivated by the wish to bring to the fore elements of linguistic activities which, while not obviously involved in the explanation of the meaning of constituent expressions . . . are nevertheless pertinent to their meaning. At its most general the notion of context encompasses the presuppositions of meaning. If the context were significantly different, the game would not be played, for it would be pointless. Every game has its normality conditions, the obtaining of which are presupposed by the game.[15]

The central thrust of this passage is to distinguish between the internal structure of the language-game, understood as essentially given by the rules for employing its constitutive words, and the utility or point of playing it in a given set of circumstances, and to suggest that when those circumstances differ significantly from what is normal, then it would be pointless to play the game, although it would not be impossible to do so. In other words, a clear distinction is to be drawn between the game itself and the conditions under which it is played; in abnormal conditions, the rules of the game are not (so to speak) falsified, nor do they suffer any kind of internal disruption, but the point of following them evaporates.

The most obvious place in which something like this distinction is drawn in the *Investigations* is sections 240–1:

Disputes do not break out (among mathematicians, say) over the question of whether a rule has been obeyed or not. People don't come to blows over it, for example. This is part of the framework on which the workings of our language is based (for example, in giving descriptions).

'So you are saying that human agreement decides what is true and what is false?'—It is what human beings *say* that is true and false; and they agree in

---

[15] Hacker, WUM I, 61.

the *language* they use. That is not agreement in opinions but in form of life. (PI, 240–1)

To talk of such agreement in applications of a rule as part of a framework on which our language is based certainly implies that, as it were, the base and the structure erected upon it are essentially distinct phenomena. And by pressing this distinction, Hacker is able to contest, for example, many of Norman Malcolm's ways of defending his claim that rule-following is (for Wittgenstein, and in fact) an essentially communal phenomenon. For even in the case of admittedly shared language-games, the distinction allows Hacker to locate the role of agreement in the base or the framework of our workings with language, rather than allotting it a constitutive role in the work itself.

An implication of Hacker's more general remarks about this distinction is, however, that while we *could* play a given language-game in the absence of its normal base or framework, we would not do so, because it would be pointless. One might say: the internal coherence or integrity of the language-game would be unaffected, but its utility would not. And Hacker generalizes this point in volume 2 of the commentary:[16]

Thus, for example, if the colours of objects changed incessantly, so that we never saw unchanging colours, there would be little or no use for our language-games with colours . . . Again, if putting the same object on a pair of scales gave different readings on every occasion, the point of weighing would be lost . . .[17]

The example of weighing occurs in section 142 of the *Investigations*, in a more specifically mercantile context:

It is only in normal cases that the use of a word is clearly prescribed; we know, are in no doubt, what to say in this or that case. The more abnormal the case, the more doubtful it becomes what we are to say. And if things were quite different from what they actually are—if there were for instance no characteristic expression of pain, of fear, of joy; if rule became exception and exception rule; or if both became phenomena of equal frequency—this would make our normal language-games lose their point.—The procedure of putting a lump of cheese on a balance and fixing the price by the turn of the scale would lose its point if it frequently happened for such lumps to suddenly grow or shrink for no obvious reason.   (PI, 142)

---

[16] Hacker, *Wittgenstein: Rules, Grammar and Necessity* (Oxford: Blackwell, 1985).
[17] *Wittgenstein: Rules, Grammar and Necessity*, 229.

As Cora Diamond has suggested, Wittgenstein's way of putting his point allows for a rather different way of understanding it from the one that Hacker emphasizes.[18] For Wittgenstein does not say that the procedure of selling cheese by weight would lose its point if lumps of cheese frequently but unpredictably grew or shrank; he says that putting a lump on a balance and fixing a price according to the number on the scale would lose its point. In other words, he at least holds open the possibility that, in such abnormal circumstances, what would (in normal circumstances) count without question as selling cheese by weight would no longer so count; and—to go further than Wittgenstein explicitly does—one might wonder whether it would even count as fixing the price of the cheese. For the number called out by the shopkeeper would patently not be the price of a certain amount of cheese; so is it the price of that particular lump? What makes it one and the same lump through its shrinkings and expansions? How would one compare prices in two different cheese-shops, or between two different types of cheese? How would one calculate the cost of living in terms of such prices, and so work out the pay-rise one might need to continue to feed one's family?

The point is this: the very same sequence of actions that in one context counts as selling cheese by weight will, in a very different context, have either a very different significance or no obvious significance at all (just as it isn't a matter of course that a person making a mark in a diary, regardless of the circumstances, is making a note of anything whatever (PI, 260)). And this suggests that the distinction Hacker draws between the language-game itself and the circumstances of its employment may not be as clear as he seems to assume—that the base or framework of the game is not so much a presupposition or precondition of its pointful employment but rather partly determinative of whether or not that specific game (as opposed to another, or to none at all) is being played. It is only in normal circumstances that this kind of behaviour counts as playing that particular game; it is not that in abnormal circumstances there would be no point in playing it (playing what?). Since this point would seem to be just as true of games as of language-games, we cannot say that the analogy between speaking a language and

[18] 'Rules: Looking in the Right Place', in D.Z. Phillips (ed.), *Wittgenstein: Attention to Particulars* (London: Macmillan, 1989), 12–34.

playing a game occludes this insight. It is rather that the connection that the analogy points to (between a game and its context) is in fact rather closer (more internal) than even Wittgenstein's figurative articulations of that relationship—in terms of framework and object framed or base and (super)structure—would seem to allow. And it might very well be that fully acknowledging this point would not so much provide ammunition for either side in such controversies as those between Malcolm and Hacker over the communal nature of rule-following, but rather reinforce Hacker's instinctive sense (often expressed in my hearing) that getting involved in such controversies is the real false step, philosophically speaking.[19]

3. 'Language-Game' as a Family Resemblance Concept

What exactly are the implications of the fact that, since Wittgenstein explicitly characterizes both 'language' and 'game' as family resemblance concepts, then the term of philosophical art created by their conjunction may well inherit that characterization? One conclusion that it patently does not, in and of itself, license is the idea that a language consists of a family of language-games. For to say that 'language' is a family resemblance concept tells us that the term picks out a variety of phenomena that will resemble one another in a variety of overlapping ways, but which need not have a common attribute or set of attributes. As Wittgenstein puts it: 'I want to say: It is *primarily* the apparatus of our ordinary language, of our word-language, that we call language; and then other things by analogy or comparability with this' (PI, 494).

By such analogical extensions, we might talk not only of German and English as languages, but of computing languages, the language of fashion, the dance-language of honeybees, and so on. In short, to talk of family resemblance is to talk of the structure of a concept, not the structure of any given phenomenon to which the concept applies.

Nevertheless, as Hacker points out, Wittgenstein's complex and varied use of the concept of a language-game at once resists and invites the thought

---

[19] For more on this point, cf. part I, sections 33–5 of my *Inheritance and Originality*.

that a natural language such as English might be illuminatingly viewed as an assemblage of language-games, insofar as its range of application includes both (what Hacker calls) invented and natural language-games.

On the one hand, Wittgenstein declares that the primitive language-games with which the text of the *Investigations* is studded are invented objects with which aspects or fragments of our language might usefully be compared:

Our clear and simple language-games are not preparatory studies for a future regularization of language—as it were first approximations, ignoring friction and air-resistance. The language-games are rather set up as *objects of comparison* which are meant to throw light on the facts of our language by way not only of similarities, but also of dissimilarities.

For we can avoid ineptness or emptiness in our assertions only by presenting the model as what it is, as an object of comparison—as so to speak, a measuring-rod; not as a preconceived idea to which reality *must* correspond. (The dogmatism into which we fall so easily in doing philosophy.)   (PI, 130–1)

On this understanding, it is vital for the avoidance of philosophical confusion even among those committed to employing Wittgensteinian terms of art that they recognize that language-games are a philosophical artefact designed to further certain philosophical goals, and not a pre-existing component of the linguistic reality that their careful use might allow us better to understand. On the other hand, Wittgenstein also repeatedly uses the term 'language-game' to designate fragments of our actual linguistic practices, not to designate inventions with which a fragment of our actual linguistic practices might be compared. He speaks, for example, of lying, telling, giving orders, reporting an event, confessing a motive—even of forming and testing hypotheses, or constructing an object from a description—as language-games. And perhaps most famously, he articulates his own philosophical approach in terms that similarly imply that language-games are constituents of a language:

When philosophers use a word—'knowledge', 'being', 'object', 'I', 'proposition', 'name'—and try to grasp the *essence* of the things, one must always ask oneself: is the word ever actually used this way in the language-game which is its original home?—

What *we* do is to bring words back from their metaphysical to their everyday use.   (PI, 116)

Hacker offers us a way of understanding how Wittgenstein might be led from the first of these methodological declarations to the second.

If the similarities between the artificial language-games which Wittgenstein invented and such a fragment of language are sufficiently striking and extensive, it is natural to extend the term 'language-game' by applying it also to the fragment itself.[20]

As a diagnosis, this seems compelling. But is it also a sufficient justification? More precisely, should we not be a little more anxious about the very real possibility of being misled by such an extension into doing exactly what Wittgenstein (in another mood or frame of mind) warns us will produce only dogmatism, confusion and emptiness—namely taking an object of comparison as a first approximation to the reality with which it is being compared?

Rush Rhees famously thought that there were two very real dangers in thinking of a language as an assemblage or totality of language-games.[21] The first is that it invites a comparison between saying something and making a move in a game; but for Rhees, if words were equivalent to pieces in board-games, and if understanding the meanings of words really were exhausted by grasping rules for their use, then they could not form the medium of conversational exchanges. For understanding how to converse—how to follow the development of a conversation, how to make a pertinent or telling contribution to it, how to re-direct its focus, how to acknowledge the relevance of another's contribution without agreeing with it, how to recognize when it has reached a dead-end or when a little further persistence will bring it to an illuminating resting-place—understanding all this is not something that can be reduced to the application of a body of rules, or fruitfully compared with learning how to make moves in a (or at least in many kinds of) game. This kind of understanding is essentially responsive both to the subject-matter of the conversation and to the individual contributions of those participating in it; but moves in chess do not have a subject-matter, and do not give any individual player the logical room to give expression to what they bring to a game from

---

[20] Hacker, WUM I, 63.

[21] He first expressed those worries in his essay 'Wittgenstein's Builders'; but they are given a far more detailed articulation in his *Wittgenstein and the Possibility of Discourse*, ed. D.Z. Phillips (Cambridge: Cambridge University Press, 1998). The next few paragraphs of this essay draw on chapter 1 of my *The Conversation of Humanity* (Charlottesville, Va.: University of Virginia Press, 2007).

their experience outside it. If being able to speak involves being able to converse, then it is not just a matter of applying words in accordance with criteria, of making linguistic moves, or of doing things with words.

R hees is equally concerned to block the thought that language as a whole should be thought of as a collection or family of distinct but inter-related language-games. If it were so viewed, the family resemblance structure of the concept of a 'language-game' might be held to imply that there is something wrong with the question 'What does it mean to say something?' or 'What is the unity of language?' For why should we expect there to be any such unity in any given collection of language-games, in the fundamentally various ways we speak or do things with words? Wasn't this assumption precisely what led the author of the *Tractatus* astray, compelling him to seek the will-o'-the-wisp of the general form of the proposition, and to attribute to ordinary language the structural unity of a calculus? And doesn't the author of the *Investigations* repeatedly find that philosophical confusions result from a conflation or crossing of language-games—a failure to respect differences of use, and hence of meaning? By contrast, R hees not only thinks that there *is* something that might be called the unity of language; he believes that trying (and failing) to get this unity into focus has been *the* characteristic business of philosophy since its inception, and hence that any conception of language that occludes the question of its unity thereby threatens not only the historical unity, but also the deepest concern, and even the ultimate point, of the enterprise of philosophy as such.

This is where the notion of 'conversation' finds a second major point of application in R hees's thinking; for his claim is that the various different forms of human discourse and practice relate to one another in the same way as various contributions to a conversation relate to one another. In other words, the unity of language is the unity of a dialogue; the various modes of human discourse about things interlock intelligibly with one another, and the sense that each makes is both constituted by and constitutes the sense of these interconnections. As R hees puts it: the generality or unity of language is the generality or unity of a form of life.

Part of what R hees is driving at is already implicit in the ways in which one participates as an individual in specific conversations. Two builders discussing how best to solve a construction problem will bring to bear an understanding not only of construction techniques, but also of the economic and political contexts within which they and their employer are working (which option is cheaper, and how much additional expense matters here and now), the kind of building under construction (a house, a church, a factory), and thereby an understanding of the particular activities that go on in such a building, and their relation to other activities in the culture more generally, and so on. The conversation might be about this building project, but it will draw upon the participants' understanding of the bearing of a variety of other domains and concerns upon this particular practical problem; and in the absence of a grasp of those interlocking considerations, the conversation would lose any proper grip on its subject-matter.

What this exemplifies is the way in which the various aspects or dimensions of human social life are interwoven with one another. The same phenomenon is also exemplified at what one might call the disciplinary level of culture—the level at which particular domains of human inquiry and activity are rendered systematic and reflective. On the one hand, especially since the Enlightenment and its concern for the autonomy of both individuals and cultural spheres, we have tended to think of the domains of politics, morality, religion, art, history, physics, astronomy and so on as essentially distinct, possessed of a particular internal logic and purpose that separates them from even cognate domains, and that might itself be the subject of systematic study. On the other hand, whenever human beings try to make sense of a particular phenomenon, we find that any of these disciplines may have a contribution to make to that project.

Pretty much any issue that is of interest to us will have its historical, political, moral, technological and scientific, social and cultural aspects and implications, and so can be properly understood only by seeing how each of these aspects and implications bear upon the others; and this means that it forms a fit subject for conversation between those well-versed in a variety of forms of human inquiry—between historians, scientists, political theorists, sociologists, literary critics and others. Each participant will bring her own particular understanding and expertise to the conversation; but each can learn from what the others bring to that conversation, and may even alter her understanding of her own enterprise as a result; and each can in principle grasp that the others are capable of making a significant contribution to the task of better understanding the subject-matter of the conversation. This is the individually mediated cultural analogue of what Rhees calls the kind of understanding that is capable of growth—of a deepening that finds expression in one's ability to see how things hang together: both the various distinctive modes of human understanding of our life in the world and the various aspects of that life itself.

At this kind of level, Rhees's image of a conversation foregrounds his sense that the various branches of human culture have a bearing on one another, that their distinctive concerns and methods nevertheless can and do interlock intelligibly with each other; and he encourages us to see this as both a reflection and an exemplary instance of the fact that their subject-matter—any aspect of reality whatever that bears upon and is engaged by the forms of human life in the world—itself manifests a dialogical unity, each of its aspects capable of bearing intelligibly on the others. This is what Rhees means when he claims that language makes sense insofar as living makes sense. And he further thinks that, if our forms of life with language, and hence language itself, have a dialogical unity, then so must philosophy, and for two reasons.

The first is that, like any other aspect of systematic human inquiry, philosophy is internally differentiated and unified in a dialogical way. Just as history comprises many branches and sub-disciplines, some of which grow towards as well as from branches and sub-disciplines of other forms of human inquiry, so too does philosophy. And just as work in one branch of history will bear upon other branches, so work in one area of philosophy will bear upon work in another area; and a deepening understanding of either discipline will manifest itself in an ability to recognize, activate and elaborate such dialogical relations. And even those who deny in some specific case that one branch of philosophy has any bearing on an issue addressed by another branch are thereby showing that it would make sense to think the reverse, and so that the question of how one branch bears upon another or fails to is always there to be asked.

From Rhees's point of view, this kind of unity is particularly to be expected in philosophy (more so than in other internally differentiated and dialogically unified disciplines) because of its distinctive mode of generality. One familiar way of understanding the philosophical enterprise is as raising questions about any and every aspect of human forms of life in the world—questions which concern that which is taken for granted within a particular domain of discourse and activity, and hence which cannot be answered from within it without begging the question itself. The philosopher of science might question the validity of inductive reasoning; but since all scientific inquiry presupposes its validity, no scientific result or procedure can possibly answer the philosophers' question. Or the philosopher of history might ask what we mean by the reality of the past; no historical inquiry can answer that question, because it will take the reality of its subject-matter for granted.

One might say, then, that philosophical inquiry is essentially parasitic on the existence of the various forms of human understanding of, and inquiry into, reality; it is, in other words, a mode of discourse whose subject-matter is the various forms of human discourse. And if, as Rhees claims, those forms of human discourse manifest an essentially dialogical unity, then so must the various forms of distinctively philosophical discourse; if our life with language and so language itself have a dialogical unity, then so must the aspect of our (life with) language that takes that life as its distinctive concern. Conversely, if one holds that philosophical discourse has no dialogical unity, that amounts to saying that its subject-matter has no such unity; it amounts to assuming that language and hence our life with language do not manifest any interlocking intelligibility of the kind that might be a possible object of the kind of understanding that can grow and deepen (or fail to). To adapt Rhees's claim that I cited earlier: if living makes sense, and hence language makes sense, then so must philosophy; and if philosophy does not have this kind of sense, then neither will language, or the human form of life with language.

Hence, Rhees characterizes philosophy as 'discourse about the possibility of discourse'—a characterization that has two key implications. First, it acknowledges that philosophy is itself a kind of discourse, one of the many and various ways in which we talk about things; hence philosophy must itself stand in dialogical relations with other modes of discourse. It does not stand outside the dialogical unity that is one of its central preoccupations; rather, what it has to say about that dialogical unity is a contribution to it and an exemplification of it. After all, if it were not, how would it hang together with the other dimensions of our life with language? How otherwise could philosophy have a non-accidental or non-contingent, a genuinely intelligible, relation to the rest of our form of life?

Philosophy must, then, be a potential conversation partner for other disciplines—such as history, literature, science—not only in the sense that it may have specific things to say about the presuppositions of those disciplines, but also in that they may have something of their own to say about matters that are distinctively of interest to philosophy. This possibility is realized in, for example, the work of Stanley Cavell—when he claims that what is taken up in philosophy as scepticism is taken up in literature as tragedy, or when he finds that psychoanalysis and philosophy each have an interest in manifestations of the human wish to deny the human, or when he sees in the history of Western philosophy a perennial preoccupation with a distinctively perfectionist concept of the self and its world that has its equally perennial moral and religious conceptions. To acknowledge such themes as potential topics for conversation is precisely not to conflate or collapse these various disciplines and modes of discourse, each with their own resources and presumptions, into one another. It is to recognize each of these cultural, ethical, religious and psychoanalytical traditions as genuinely other to philosophy—that is, as requiring acknowledgement as much for their differences from, as for their resemblances to, a distinctively philosophical perspective.

The second implication of Rhees's characterization is that philosophy is not only concerned with the conditions for the possibility of any specific mode of human language, but also with the possibility of discourse as such. It cannot be concerned only with particular modes of discourse, as if each might have its distinctive, local kind of sense and yet have no intelligible bearing on any other mode of discourse, as different contributions to a conversation hang together; for each such discourse is what it is partly in virtue of its specific location in the more general field of discourse, and its specific connections with other such modes of discourse. Philosophy must, in short, concern itself with, be struck by, the sheer possibility of speech—the human ability to say not just any one of a bewildering variety of things, but anything at all, about reality.

I noted earlier that Peter Hacker has not shown any sign in his writing of having found these kinds of claim about language, speech, philosophy and human forms of life—or at least Rhees's ways of advancing them—to be terribly convincing or important. But supposing for a moment that they are worth taking seriously, how far can we say that Hacker's way of handling Wittgenstein's concept of a language-game, and specifically of natural language-games, would prevent us from articulating or developing them?

We should probably begin by noting that Hacker's way of handling the notion has some of the same ambivalence that is evident in Wittgenstein's own. On the one hand, he is sometimes careful to stress the purely analogical nature of the connection between language and playing games—as when he says: 'insofar as we are to conceive of a language and speech as akin to a motley of language games and playing them . . .'.[22] On the other, his turns of phrase more commonly dispense with such caution: a few pages earlier in the same essay, we are straightforwardly told that '[a] language is a motley of language-games', and that '[o]ne cannot say how many different language-games must coexist to constitute a language'.[23] To this extent, the idea of language-games as natural seems to play a more central role in Hacker's Wittgensteinian vision of language than the idea of them as invented—as philosophical artefacts. One might say that, in this respect, Hacker risks offending against the very principle he forcefully articulates elsewhere—namely, that the legitimacy of the transition from the latter to the former application of the term 'language-game' is always conditional upon the extent of actual similarity between an invented language-game and some given fragment of our language. But does this mean that he succumbs to the temptations against which Rhees sets his face?

As I noted earlier, Hacker specifically warns us that speaking a language is no more playing a game than making a move in a game is equivalent to performing a speech-act; so he does explicitly register the first of Rhees's anxieties, even if he makes nothing in particular of the idea of conversation as a central part of speaking. And with respect to the second—the question of the unity of language—Hacker is careful to stress that 'while one game is not interwoven with another . . ., the various language-games we play *are* systematically interconnected'.[24] On the other hand, the issue here is not whether or not our language and speech form a whole, but rather what kind of whole they form. And the only kind of unity that Hacker appears to acknowledge here is that in which one language-game might be more or less directly connected with another—as one event about which one might give a report may be the giving of an order, just as one thing one might order another to do is to give a report. The notion of a conversational or dialogical unity of the kind that interests Rhees is just not registered; and *a fortiori* the idea of philosophy as discourse about the possibility of such discursive unity makes no appearance.

How significant these absences may be, philosophically speaking, is plainly a matter for argument. It seems clear that, in tending rather more systematically towards one facet of Wittgenstein's understanding of

---

[22] Hacker, WUM I, 54.   [23] Hacker, WUM I, 51.   [24] WUM I, 53.

the significance of his language-game method than the other, Hacker's philosophical procedures are less likely to accommodate any significance that might reside in these reaches of Rhees's and Cavell's thinking. But what reassures me is the fact that it is not at all obvious that the alterations in those procedures needed to make such accommodations possible would put at risk the many and various insights they already permit us to appreciate. For in wanting to go on from Peter's work in ways that he is not inclined to explore, I certainly do not want to leave behind the philosophical riches he has uncovered in reading Wittgenstein his way, with such exemplary attentiveness and rigour, over a lifetime.

Wittgenstein's Ethics: Boundaries and Boundary Crossings

HANS OBERDIEK

> My whole tendency and, I believe, the tendency of all men who ever tried to write or talk Ethics or Religion was to run against the boundaries of language.
>
> Wittgenstein, 'Lecture on Ethics'

1. The Ethics of Wittgenstein and Wittgenstein's Ethics

Wittgenstein led a tumultuous internal life, one lived with white-hot intensity, marked by deep concern, especially about his moral character. He placed great demands on students and friends, but nothing like the extraordinary demands he placed on himself. If he was often hard on others, he was always much harder on himself. The 'duty of genius' drove him into the depths of philosophy—which turned out to be in front of our eyes if we could but see it!—but never allowed him much satisfaction, other than in the knowledge that his mistakes and infelicities were at least in pursuit of deep philosophical understanding. Self-satisfaction in a philosopher was, to Wittgenstein, intolerable: far better to be a philosopher dissatisfied than a fool satisfied. But in addition to his exacting and unending duties as a philosopher, there were equally exacting and unending self-imposed *moral* duties. These included his philosophical duties—how could they not?—but extended to every aspect of life, in thought, will, and deed. He was a man of great moral seriousness and an unrelenting truthfulness and rejection of guile or affectation.

Wittgenstein knew a wide range of moral emotions and virtues, but especially, I think, those that exact from one the most: self-reproach and courage. His diary entries are filled with a sense of his own inadequacies,

not only as a philosopher, but also as a man. Wittgenstein was, as Peter
Hacker remarked to me, 'a connoisseur of self-torment'. One example
will suffice. Writing to Paul Engelmann in 1921 about his perceived (and
perhaps real) failure as a teacher of Austrian village children, Wittgenstein
stated:

I am one of those cases which perhaps are not all that rare today: I had a task, did
not do it, and now the failure is wrecking my life. I ought to have done something
positive with my life, to have become a star in the sky. Instead of which I remained
stuck on earth, and now I am gradually fading out. My life has really become
meaningless and so it consists only of futile episodes. The people around me do
not notice this and would not understand; but I know that I have a fundamental
deficiency.[1]

Wittgenstein's directness and honesty in his interactions with Russell,
Moore, and Frege are surely admirable, as was his extraordinary courage
during the Great War as a forward observer for an artillery unit—for which
he was multiply decorated for bravery. Perhaps at no time in his life did
Wittgenstein feel more alive—and more wish to live: 'Yesterday I was shot
at. I was scared! I was afraid of death. I now have such a desire to live. And
it is difficult to give up life when one enjoys it.'[2] Facing death was, if only
in small measure, a test of his worthiness as a man as well as his worthiness
as a thinker, as if to place in the hands of God or fate the question whether
he was worthy to live. If we know anything about Wittgenstein, we should
know that neither his moral emotions nor virtues would take more typical
forms: he was far too complicated for that.

   This is true as well of his own moral stance, which was highly personal.
Wittgenstein was taken with Otto Weininger's *Sex and Character*, which he
read as a schoolboy.[3] Weininger held that 'all duty is duty to oneself', so it
comes as no surprise when he writes: 'Logic and ethics are fundamentally
the same, they are no more than duty to oneself. They celebrate their union
by the highest service to truth, which is overshadowed in one case by error,

---

[1] P. Engelmann, *Letters from Ludwig Wittgenstein with a Memoir* (Oxford: Oxford University Press,
1967), 114–15.
[2] MS 103, 27.7.16. Quotation taken from Ray Monk, *Wittgenstein: The Duty of Genius* (London:
Jonathan Cape, 1990), 146. But then Wittgenstein immediately adds self-reproach: 'This is precisely
what "sin" is, the unreasoning life, a false view of life.'
[3] Otto Weininger, *Geschlecht und Charakter* (Vienna: Braumüller & Co., 1903); trans. as *Sex and
Character* (London: William Heinemann, 1906); quotations are from this translation.

in the other by untruth.'⁴ This doesn't mean, however, that Wittgenstein interpreted Weininger in an entirely egocentric way. While at the Russian front in 1916, Wittgenstein admonished himself: 'Help yourself and help others with all your strength. And at the same time be cheerful! But how much strength should one need for oneself and how much for the others? It is hard to live well!! But it is good to live well.'⁵ While Wittgenstein took issue with much of Weininger's *argument*, he clearly embraced many *dicta*,⁶ including 'Truth, purity, faithfulness, uprightness, with respect to oneself: these give the only conceivable ethics.'⁷

Wittgenstein's personal ethics were, like Weininger's, Kantian in being categorical, yet, if anything, even more demanding than Kant would have required and certainly more eccentric. For Wittgenstein set himself moral standards of truthfulness, humility, courage, and uprightness that *no one* could meet. And yet at the same time his moral commitments were existential in the sense that there isn't any hint that they should be universalizable or generalizable. We find in Wittgenstein's own moral stance an echo of Martin Luther's: 'Here I stand: I can do no other.' The difference, of course, is that Martin Luther thought that his stance was informed by God's will, and presumably applied to all, at least to all Christians; Wittgenstein thinks that any justification of a religious or any other kind is illusory.

Why this is so we will explore below, and the reasons run deep in Wittgenstein's thought, especially as found in the *Tractatus* and the 'Lecture on Ethics'. Here it is enough to observe three things. First, more than for many philosophers, the ethics of Wittgenstein the man and Wittgenstein the philosopher are deeply intertwined. Not inextricably, perhaps, but certainly profoundly so. One can study the moral views of utilitarians, for instance, and wonder what the authors are like in life, and not be

---

⁴ *Sex and Character*, 96.
⁵ MS 103, 30.3.16. Quoted in Ray Monk, *Wittgenstein: The Duty of Genius*, 138.
⁶ Regarding Weininger, Wittgenstein wrote to G.E. Moore: 'It isn't necessary or rather not possible to agree with him but the greatness lies in that with which we disagree. It is his enormous mistake which is great' (quoted in Monk, *Wittgenstein*, 313).
⁷ Weininger, *Sex and Character*, 96. Looking back, it is hard to see what Wittgenstein found of value in Weininger's thought, though certainly others found things of value too: August Strindberg, for example, was an enthusiast. Others were much more critical, but even so, many of them thought that the book was a 'must read'. Wittgenstein read Weininger at the height of the 'cult' of Weininger—but that doesn't explain why he still thought it worth reading—and recommending to others—in mid-life.

surprised to find them as markedly different from each other as were
Jeremy Bentham, James and J.S. Mill, and Henry Sidgwick. But when one
looks at Wittgenstein's reflections on ethics, one feels the presence of the
man close at hand. This might account in part for the limited appeal of
his ethics: in comparison with Kantianism, for instance, distinguishing the
man from his ethics seems more problematic.

Second, although Wittgenstein does not think that there is much to *say*
about ethics, as we shall see, this doesn't imply that it is of little importance:
indeed, quite the opposite. Ethics—along with aesthetics and religion—is
of *profound* significance. That there are no propositions of ethics or that
one's moral commitments lack compelling reasons for others shows only
that ethics is neither part of science nor of logic. After philosophical issues in
language, logic, and metaphysics, nothing preoccupied Wittgenstein more
than how *he* should live his life—and how miserably bad he was at doing
it well.

Third, while there is an 'early' and 'late' Wittgenstein on language,
logic, and metaphysics, there isn't a 'later Wittgenstein' when it comes
to ethics. For while Wittgenstein's thought on *theoretical* subjects moved
well beyond the *Tractatus* and the 'Lecture on Ethics' (when it did not
abandon them altogether), there is nothing that suggests his thinking
about ethics left the confines of his earlier work, though it would surely
have had to. The 'saying/showing' distinction, for example, that is so
distinctive about his ethical views in the *Tractatus* disappears with barely
a trace in the *Investigations*. Yet there is no indication that he subjects
ethics to the penetrating analysis that he applies to logic, language, and
metaphysics.

If we use Kant's division of reason into *theoretical* and *practical*, Wittgenstein's *philosophical* preoccupation lay in the former. His deepest
philosophical insights concern logic, language, mind, and questions that
were the traditional domain of epistemology and metaphysics, not *practical*
reason. As a result of various challenges to *Tractatus* doctrines, he was
forced to rethink them. Why, then, didn't he rethink his views on ethics? We can only speculate. In part it might be because he took on the
Kantian division, and only his views on matters pertaining to theoretical
reason seemed to him to be in need of radical reworking. But in part,
too, I believe that he found his categorical, existential picture of ethics
compelling, even without the philosophical scaffolding of the *Tractatus*.

That Wittgenstein did not rethink his views in this regard is a great pity. For while there is something mesmerizing about his Tractarian ethics—as there obviously is about the *Tractatus* more generally—his ethical thought is largely confined by the limitations of that work. This is unfortunate, because I believe that Wittgenstein's later work provides resources for a fruitful approach to clear thinking in and about ethics. The sensibility revealed in the *Investigations* and *On Certainty* would allow us to explore possibilities not permitted by the limits imposed by the *Tractatus* without losing sight of the fact that ethics is neither a branch of science nor of logic. Or so I shall argue.

2. Boundary Setting: *Tractatus* and 'Lecture on Ethics'

Wittgenstein agrees with Weininger that logic and ethics are one and the same, but he provides an altogether different explanation for the 'sameness': namely, ethics and logic are both 'higher' than science and 'transcendental'. In these two respects aesthetics and religion are also higher and transcendental.[8] They are higher in the sense that our commitments cannot be *said*, but only *shown*. As used by Wittgenstein, what is shown doesn't capture anything *in* the world, but provides a lens, as it were, through which we see the world, and so applies with necessity. In this sense, and this sense only, ethics, aesthetics, and religion are like Kantian categories. If ways of seeing the world were able to be *said*, then they could be expressed *within* the world, but this is just what they cannot be. Logic differs from ethics and aesthetics in that it draws limits to the linguistic expression of thought. It does not draw limits to thought itself, Wittgenstein explains, 'for in order to be able to draw a limit to thought, we should have to find both sides of the limit thinkable (i.e. we should have to be able to think what cannot be thought.)' (TLP, Preface, 3). Ethics, aesthetics, and religion *show* themselves in actions, attitudes, and in works of art. A shopkeeper *shows* his honesty in never contemplating cheating his customers, as seeing it as ethically impossible—not in subscribing to a moral principle such as the categorical imperative. Indeed, 'subscribing to a principle' would be just another way of showing one's commitments, though undoubtedly not as effectively.[9]

Ethics, aesthetics, and religion are transcendental in the quasi-Kantian sense that they try to express—through action, attitudes, and art—what cannot be otherwise: all are viewed *sub specie aeternitatis*—from the standpoint of eternity.[10] I say 'quasi-Kantian' because ethics does not consist in synthetic judgments known *a priori*: ethics for Wittgenstein lies 'outside the world' and therefore cannot be expressed in propositions. And this is so because (according to the *Tractatus*) propositions provide a picture of reality that is either true or false. But logic, ethics, aesthetics, and religion do not depict possible states of affairs, so cannot be expressed as propositions. They lack *sense*, in Wittgenstein's vocabulary. Scientific truths can be *said* in the form of propositions that such and such is the case. The price, of course, is that true scientific propositions are 'lower' and 'accidental' (*zufällig*). They are lower in that they can be *said*; they are accidental in that what they picture could have been otherwise. The sense in which ethics could not have been otherwise will be explored below.

This brief summary, however, does not tell us much about how and why Wittgenstein thinks of ethics as he does. In what follows I shall largely put to one side his remarks concerning logic, aesthetics, and religion, though religion is especially closely linked with his views regarding ethics, at least in the *Tractatus* and in the 'Lecture on Ethics', which was written in 1929, when he had not yet broken with the central claims of the *Tractatus*. I will begin with Wittgenstein's views as expressed in these two texts. Remarks made in letters and conversation are also pertinent, though here one treads lightly, as they would not have been subject to the kind of care Wittgenstein would have given them even in written work not intended for publication. They are pertinent, however, because almost nothing Wittgenstein wrote or said pertaining to philosophy was casual or 'off the cuff'.

---

[9] The 'saying/showing' distinction is a subject of much controversy among Wittgensteinians. My own view is that what can only be shown represent *insights* for Wittgenstein and not something to be discarded because not sayable. But I can't enter into that controversy here. See Hans-Johann Glock's entry 'Saying/Showing' in his generally useful *A Wittgenstein Dictionary* (Oxford: Blackwell, 1996), 331–5. See also Peter Hacker's 'Was he Trying to Whistle it?', in Peter Hacker, *Wittgenstein: Connections and Controversies* (Oxford: Clarendon Press, 2001).

[10] 'The work of art is the object seen *sub specie aeternitatis*; and the good life is the world seen *sub specie aeternitatis*. This is the connexion between art and ethics' (NB, 7). This Schopenhauerian thought has echoes in Stoic thought as well.

So much of what Wittgenstein says about ethics in the *Tractatus* and 'Lecture on Ethics' has an air of mystery, if not paradox, right from the beginning of his discussion of ethics at 6.4 (though most of the stage-setting occurs earlier). Why, for instance, must the sense of the world lie outside the world (6.41)? Why, if a good or bad exercise of the will alters the world, can it be only at the limits of the world it alters—but not also alter the facts (6.423)? And what does Wittgenstein mean by 'the happy man'—and how, if one's will cannot alter the facts, does his world differ from that of the unhappy man?[11] Equally if not more importantly, how can it be the case that we make ethical judgments, yet such judgments are both senseless and worthy of one's deepest respect?

To see the difficulties, it will be helpful to explore Wittgenstein's own (and rare) example taken from his 'Lecture on Ethics' of 1929:

Supposing that I could play tennis and one of you saw me playing and said, 'Well, you play pretty badly' and suppose I answered 'I know, I'm playing badly but I don't want to play any better,' all the other could say would be 'Ah, then that's all right.' But suppose I had told one of you a preposterous lie and he came up to me and said, 'You're behaving like a beast' and then I were to say 'I know I behave badly, but then I don't want to behave any better,' could he then say 'Ah, then that's all right'? Certainly not; he would say 'Well, you *ought* to want to behave better.' Here you have an absolute judgment of value, whereas the first instance was one of a relative judgment.[12]

The passage is puzzling at almost every level. Why is it 'all right' to play badly? One's playing partner and even one's opponent usually care very much how one plays! Why would one not want to play better? Why play at all? One might reasonably say 'I'm playing about as well as I can, and the extra time and effort I'd have to expend in getting any better isn't worth it, given other valuable things in my life.' Perhaps all Wittgenstein is doing is telegraphing that there are other reasons for playing a game: e.g., to get exercise or enjoy the outdoors.

Playing tennis has value primarily for those who play it, so it is relativized to their interests. And activities may have comparatively little or great value.

---

[11] It is clear that Wittgenstein *desperately* wanted a happy life. He is often misquoted as saying, on his deathbed, 'Tell them I had a happy life.' In fact, he said that he had had a 'wonderful' life, and whatever *that* means, it is clearly not the same as a *happy* life.

[12] LE, 5. (The work was originally given as a lecture to the Heretics Society, Cambridge University, in 1929.)

Consider the activity of doing philosophy. It, too, has value primarily (though not exclusively) for those who engage in it, so it is relativized to interests and context. It is inconceivable, however, that Wittgenstein would have given the same relaxed answer to someone who said he knew he did philosophy badly but didn't care! If one engages in philosophy, Wittgenstein adamantly felt, one should strive to do one's best, and if one's best is less than stellar, then one should give it up. But whether games or philosophy or other activities have little or great value does not seem to be a matter of their *relative* value, but one of the degree of value they have. Something of great *intrinsic* value can have little *relative* value in certain contexts. When value is relative it is so because it is relative to interests and context.

At the next level, surely no one has ever told a preposterous lie simply because he didn't want to behave any better, as if telling the truth were somehow (like playing tennis might be) exhausting or that he was an indifferent truth-teller and that was good enough for him. Finally, why would one say to the person who doesn't care that he told a preposterous lie that he 'ought to want' to behave better? Why does the interlocutor care what the liar *wants*? Desires and wants are part of empirical psychology for Wittgenstein, and thus seem out of place as the objects of censure. Surely the interlocutor should say 'You ought not tell preposterous lies.' Period. So it is a puzzle why Wittgenstein lets in empirical matters here.

So let's begin again to get a better grip on what Wittgenstein seems to have had in mind in thinking of ethics as issuing in absolute judgments. The phrases 'a good tennis player', 'a good pianist', and even 'a good philosopher' employ a use of 'good' that is attributive. In the case of a 'good pianist' we mean, Wittgenstein says, '... that he can play pieces of a certain degree of difficulty with a certain degree of dexterity'. He also says that if it is *important* for me not to catch cold, then '... I mean that catching a cold produces certain describable disturbances in my life'[13] and if I say this is the right road '... I mean that it's the right road relative to a certain goal' (LE, 5). All of these judgments of value, Wittgenstein claims, are relative in the sense that they are a 'mere statement of facts' and can therefore be put in a descriptive form that loses all appearance of

---

[13] In *The Varieties of Goodness*, which will be discussed later, G.H. von Wright distinguishes these cases, calling the first kind *technical* goods and the second kind *instrumental* goods (or, as in this case, evils). G.H. von Wright, *The Varieties of Goodness* (London: Routledge & Kegan Paul, 1963).

value: 'Instead of saying "This is the right way you have to go to get to Granchester", I could equally well have said, "This is the way you have to go to get to Granchester in the shortest time"' (LE, 6).

Wittgenstein's point is that non-ethical values are relative to conventional standards, interests, or aims. In relation to standards developed and adhered to in the West, Glenn Gould was a good (indeed great) pianist and Roger Federer is a good (indeed great) tennis player. And it is a fact that if one catches cold, then one cannot work efficiently, just as it is a fact that the shortest way to get to Granchester is *this* way. Wittgenstein is getting at differences between, say, a straight road and the right road: whatever my interests, something can be both a road and straight, but only ties to human interests can make it the *right* road. Nor can someone press piano keys and be a good pianist independently of reference to human interests; e.g., in hearing pieces played with dexterity, grace, and musical imagination. And so to the tennis player: a bad tennis player is one who doesn't meet a certain humanly developed and sustained standard, but if he doesn't care, why should we?

Not so in ethics, which are absolute. He hints at what he means in the 'Lecture on Ethics' when he asks what we could possibly mean by the expression '*the* absolutely right road'.

I think it would be the road by which *everybody* on seeing it would, *with logical necessity*, have to go, or be ashamed for not going. And similarly the *absolute good*, if it is a describable state of affairs, would be one which everybody, independent of his tastes and inclinations, would *necessarily* bring about or feel guilty for not bringing about. And I want to say that such a state of affairs is a chimera. No state of affairs has, in itself, what I would like to call the coercive power of an absolute judge.   (LE, 7)

This peculiar passage contains many clues to how Wittgenstein sees ethics. First, we experience ethical claims as a *necessity*, but not a *logical necessity*. Martin Luther's 'Here I stand; I can do no other' expresses a necessity, but not a logical necessity. What kind of necessity, then? Wittgenstein doesn't say, but it appears to be one that either structures or is part of what structures one's response to the world. Contrary to both Kant and Mill, then, morality is not so much a guide to conduct as a way of structuring one's moral response to the world. That is, we don't ask, 'I know this would be lying, but may I do so?' There isn't the lie *and* the question of whether to tell it. An analogy might help. For Wittgenstein, there isn't the act and then the question of whether it is sinful, but the recognition that 'This is a sinful act—and hence not to be done.' One needn't take up Christianity, of course, but if one does, then man will be seen as fallen and in need of redemption.

Ethics cannot have an 'end' such as human flourishing. If it did, Wittgenstein seems to think, it would lie in the province of social sciences, and would vary with the state of our confidence in those sciences. Unlike relative values, ends in ethics cannot be abandoned because there are none to abandon or embrace. Instead, there is a way of *seeing* the world. Now how one sees the world can change, but then it isn't that one has *abandoned* anything, but, rather, that a certain way of seeing the world *vanishes*—and another stands in its stead.

But couldn't ethics vanish altogether? It might seem so. And if so, it would be a world in which everything was possible and nothing prohibited. Such radical amoralism, however, would be hard to sustain. Nothing would be pure—nor impure; nothing honest—nor dishonest; no activity would be worthless—nor worth doing or caring about, either. To see the world as utterly material would be to see a world destitute of meaning. In such a world there can be no place for ethics—or deep aesthetic and religious meaning, either. A world with only desires for arbitrarily chosen ends to move one would seem to press against the boundary of intelligibility. Not only would there be nothing to *say*, but nothing to *show*—except life's emptiness. Wittgenstein could not countenance this possibility. *Our* world is one we *must* experience in moral terms: we can never get *beyond* good and evil. We are already beyond the bounds of sense when we see the world as ethical. We cannot get beyond *that*.

The passage, second, makes clear that ethics doesn't *describe* a state of affairs (hence does not consist in propositions) and yet is independent of anyone's tastes, interests, or needs, for the latter are empirical, and so part of the world. Third, ethics *does* express absolute judgments such that if we fail to live up to them we feel shame or guilt. This, he thinks, we wouldn't feel regarding so-called relative values.[14] Finally, we experience ethical claims as if they have 'the coercive power of an absolute judge'. It is

---

[14] Wittgenstein would no doubt grant that I can be embarrassed that I'm such a bad golfer, but not that I can be ashamed of my lack of talent. Perhaps I should be ashamed that I never tried harder to improve, but that would seem to move the matter into the realm of the ethical.

not that the judgments *restrain* us, like handcuffs, but that they *constrain* us, like *modus tollens*. We can, of course, resist doing the right thing just as we can fail to reason logically. But, Wittgenstein suggests, when we do, it is as if we are unconscionably resisting the coercive power of a judge, logical in one case, moral in the other.

If this is on the right track, then what is the man who remonstrates with the liar doing? He surely isn't telling him anything he doesn't *know*, because ethics isn't a matter of knowledge: there are no true or false propositions of ethics. Nor is he appealing (though it might appear that way) to what the liar wants. He is forcefully reminding him, I think, of the liar's own commitments—or the commitments of any decent human being. In this sense, it would be like reminding a devout Catholic that—given that he sees the world a certain way—he ought to attend Mass. It is not optional, not up to one's interests, wants, or needs—whether to attend Mass.

But isn't becoming or remaining Catholic 'optional'? Wittgenstein would have thought it absurd to 'shop around' for a congenial religion *or* a congenial ethics. *Either* the total picture 'grabs' one, as it were, so that one can't help but see the world a certain way—or it doesn't. One can, of course, be put in a position so that the picture eventually exercises its grip, which is why religions insist on a certain upbringing. A child can be made to feel guilty for this and ashamed for that so that at some stage the child sees it as necessary to avoid this and that, and as 'behaving like a beast' if one does. At some point, one just comes to see the world a certain way. Or not. No one, however, can be *argued into* it or shown *evidence* of the power of either a religious or ethical outlook. Wittgenstein suggests that anyone who perceives ethics or religion as 'optional' has already lost both.

Even within the confines of Tractarian doctrine, however, Wittgenstein's example is problematic. For he appears not to distinguish three questions: how are standards of excellence in sports, art, etc. established? Can they be subject to reasoned criticism and improvement? How ought one to act with respect to them? To the first question the answer is 'by tradition and convention'. Yet this must be distinguished from the road example. For the best way to Granchester doesn't depend on conventions, but directly on interests and needs. The fastest way is *this* way, the *shortest* way is that way. True, in a certain society the *scenic* road might always be regarded as the best way to get anywhere, and what is scenic might be thought to rest on tradition or convention. Even so, this doesn't address the second question, which is odd, since Wittgenstein *rejected* some conventional standards of excellence in art as decadent. He thought, moreover, that most of what passed for good philosophy was rubbish, too. Surely he had reasoned criticism of each, often penetrating and convincing. To the third question Wittgenstein's clear answer is that if we do not *want* to conform to standards, then we cannot be subject to ethical criticism because the values these standards embody are relative. I suggested above that this isn't so. A critical case for Wittgenstein would have been the practice of doing philosophy. For him, clearly, there were conventional standards of doing philosophy well (that we should jettison) and non-conventional standards that one ought to live up to, or abandon philosophy altogether.

Given that he does not disentangle these three questions, we can see why Wittgenstein would not wish to assimilate all questions of ethics to those of standards of excellence in sport or art. For while the outward *form* of words might be the same when criticizing one's performance at tennis or truth-telling, the logic is radically different. For someone who tells preposterous lies doesn't do so because he or she does not tell the truth well, as if this required some special technique or training. Telling the truth requires *resolve*. That alone, however, won't get you far in sport, art, or philosophy if you lack talent, technique, and training. Further, if I am weak and lack resolve, this doesn't get me off the moral hook. It is reasonable to say 'I lack dexterity, so I've given up any hope of playing the piano well', but not 'I lack resolve, so I've given up on telling the truth.' To tell the truth is a *categorical demand* of an imperious judge. The problem, of course, is that the judge isn't Kantian reason or Humean psychology. The command to do what is right issues from each of us as a groundless categorical imperative. The grounds cannot be Humean because nothing outside us, Wittgenstein thinks, can influence one's personal ethical stance. And the grounds cannot be Kantian, because reason cannot generate them. And the grounds cannot be Aristotelian, because that would make ethics hostage to human nature. Ethical injunctions thus appear to us as groundless, as ineffable commands beyond the bounds of sense.

According to the *Tractatus*, 'You ought to try to behave better' is not a proposition; it is a *judgment*. But the judgment is expressed in language that, strictly speaking, appears to be without sense. 'You ought to try to behave

better' is, of course, a sentence in English. But in the *Tractatus* Wittgenstein
sees such sentences as *themselves* expressing (not stating) one's admiration or
aversion to the object of judgment. In terms of justification, Wittgenstein
could not ground the judgment in the will. For although in the *Tractatus*
there is a distinction between, say, thinking that *p* and willing that *p*,
empirically speaking, phenomenal willing is just another empirical fact and,
moreover, not within one's control.[15] So absolute judgments cannot get
into the world *this* way.

At this stage of Wittgenstein's thought, ethical judgments structure our
response to the world. Notice that it is the *speaker* who upbraids the liar
in Wittgenstein's example and the *speaker* who lets the excuse for the bad
tennis playing slide. So it is how the speaker—the 'agent' as I shall call
him—responds to the world that matters. And this provides an answer to
how Wittgenstein himself would have responded to someone who said
that he knew he did philosophy poorly, but didn't care. Someone who
said such a thing would surely have been met with a stern rebuke: 'You
ought (to want) to do philosophy better (or give it up).' The *only* way in
which this is unlike other examples of absolute value judgments is that
no one needs to do philosophy. But then we see that what will count
as an absolute ethical judgment for Wittgenstein depends *solely* on the
agent's way of seeing the world. That is, depending on the agent, 'You
ought (to want) to play tennis well (or play the piano well or do science
well)' could have the categorical absoluteness Wittgenstein requires for
ethics. Wittgenstein provides no criteria for determining the *content* of the
ethical—e.g., promoting human welfare, living in accord with nature or
the categorical imperative. Instead, it depends *entirely* on how the agent
responds to the factual world, the senseless but profound lens through
which one makes sense of it.

One implication is that the person subject to the agent's rebuke can,
for all Wittgenstein says in the *Tractatus* or 'Lecture on Ethics', *reject* the
rebuke. Only if one responds to the world as does the agent must one
accept it. There cannot be any reasons why one *must* see the world in any
particular way. There is an added layer of complexity to Wittgenstein's

---

[15] Wittgenstein rejects this conception of willing in the *Investigations*. There he brings home to us
that the relationship between willing and doing isn't like that between swinging a hammer and driving
a nail, but an *internal* relation. He thus rejects the empiricist account of willing as an experience and his
earlier idea of willing as an ineffable force lying outside the world (see PI, 611 and 620).

views here. About some matters—such as lying and other matters of 'moral purity'—Wittgenstein would hold in utter contempt those who tolerate lying in themselves. At the same time, one need not see the world through the eyes of, say, a devout Catholic. Even here, however, Wittgenstein takes an especially rigid stance that doesn't appear to be explained or justified anywhere. It is this. While a person need not see the world through the eyes of a Catholic, if someone *professes* to do so, then we are entitled to rebuke that person for not attending Mass regularly. Nominal Catholics—nominal *anything*—he had no time for. But this tells us more about Wittgenstein than anything that the *Tractatus* or 'Lecture on Ethics' necessitates. Justification, where it has a use in ethics, can occur only within a stance that itself comes from *outside* the world with respect to particular judgments *within* that stance. *Given* that one is a Catholic, for example, then one behaves badly in failing to attend Mass regularly; given that one is not Catholic, the question of attending Mass does not even arise. And the same is true of a more straightforward ethical stance. If one sees the world through purely utilitarian eyes, then *of course* one is not justified in preferring the well-being of one's friends and family to that of strangers, unless it can be shown that this will lead to the greater good. So we cannot escape seeing the world in ethical terms, but as to the question of *which* way one sees the world—and acts in it—Wittgenstein cannot speak, and so must remain silent. The ineffable provides the frame of the ethical but it cannot provide its content.

Let's return again to the central claims of the *Tractatus* as they pertain to ethics. The ethical sense of the world lies outside the boundaries of sense, and *must* do so, because otherwise ethics would be transformed into something descriptively true or false and relative to conventions and interests. Ethics would lose both its necessity and the deep and abiding respect it deserves. A good or bad exercise of the will alters the world, moreover, as to the stance one takes to the world, not as a way of importing value into the world: 'I can only make myself independent of the world—and so in a certain sense master it—by renouncing any influence on happenings' (NB, 5.7.16). Now *obviously* if I behave well or badly I make a difference in the world. But what Wittgenstein means, I think, is that my behaving well or badly doesn't make the world a better or worse place—for that would be to put value *into* the world. To put it in a way that a positivist might, from an *empirical* perspective, a preposterous lie has such and such consequences; e.g., because of the deliberate untruth Smith makes an investment that leads to his financial ruin. For the positivist, furthermore, one's *attitudes* towards lying are just more facts about the world to be uncovered by social science. For Wittgenstein, on the other hand, there is something *like* Kant's 'noumenal self' at work here. I say 'something like' because for Wittgenstein such a notion is nonsense, inexpressible, and thus ineffable. Wittgenstein, in short, is prepared to grant that there could be a complete description of the world that would, perforce, not mention the willing subject—the agent who wills not to lie or to live in purity.

To the objection that if an experience seems to have 'absolute or ethical value and importance', then these words 'don't mean nonsense' Wittgenstein responds with a flourish:

Now when this is urged against me I at once see clearly, as it were in a flash of light, not only that no description that I can think of would do to describe what I mean by absolute value, but that I would reject every significant description that anybody could possibly suggest, *ab initio*, on the ground of its significance. That is to say: I see now that these nonsensical expressions were not nonsensical because I had not yet found the correct expressions, but that their nonsensicality was their very essence. For all I wanted to do with them was just to go beyond the world and that is to say beyond significant language. My whole tendency and, I believe, the tendency of all men who ever tried to write or talk Ethics or Religion was to run against the boundaries of language.

What is even more revealing, however, is the object of Wittgenstein's concern:

This running against the walls of our cage is perfectly, absolutely hopeless. Ethics so far as it springs from the desire to say something about the ultimate meaning of life, the absolute good, the absolute valuable, can be no science. What it says does not add to our knowledge in any sense.   (LE, 11–12)

Science and ordinary factual judgments, which make sense, have no room for absolute (as opposed to relative) value. There can be no room *in* the world, however, for absolute value, for ethics. It must therefore be pushed outside the world onto a subject who is not, as Wittgenstein says in his *Notebooks*, part of the world but a presupposition of it (NB, 2.8.16). The world isn't good or evil, only the willing subject. Good and evil, Wittgenstein writes in his *Notebooks*, are not properties of the world, but predicates of the subject. Writing a few days later, he states, 'What is good and evil is essentially the I, not the world' (NB, 5.8.16). At the same time we are to live happily, despite, Wittgenstein says, 'the misery of the world' (NB, 13.8.16).

Something has gone badly awry here. The boundaries of language against which we futilely but inevitably rush—the cage from which we cannot escape, although we cannot stop trying—end up tying Wittgenstein in knots. For while Wittgenstein avoids the dead-end of logical positivism regarding ethics, the austere doctrine of the *Tractatus* cannot, in the end, make what he says there and in the 'Lecture on Ethics' coherent. Recall that the world is just a world of facts, a world without good and evil. The bearer of good and evil is the willing subject, but that subject is not part of the world. Yet the agent who acts is not just the empirical subject that can be studied by the social and physical sciences, but the subject—a living human being—who strives to live honestly, courageously, and so on. As such, the subject *intends* to make a difference in the world, and a difference of a certain *kind*. That is, the subject, at least the subject who strives to act ethically, must respond to *ethically charged* situations in the world. Facing enemy fire, as Wittgenstein bravely did, is a situation in which many are tempted to cut and run. It is a situation that *cries out* for a courageous response, which is why one feels guilt and shame when one doesn't heed the cry.

David Wiggins makes a similar point. We might grant, he says, that:

The conception of good or bad is our invention; but whether *situations, practices, acts, actions* etc. are good or bad depends not on our conceptions but on what the situations themselves are. Do these situations, practices, etc.—or do they not—fall under this or that concept that our conceptions aim at? That is the question which, by inventing these conceptions, we have made it possible for ourselves to ask. It is up to us that the question is there. But the *answer* is not up to us.[16]

The point is similar but not identical to the one I wish to make. For while I agree with Wiggins, I want to add: *we need to bring practical reason to bear to determine the proper content of the answer*. As Aristotle long ago pointed out, it isn't courage but foolhardiness to respond to a situation of

---

[16] David Wiggins, 'Wittgenstein on Ethics and the Riddle of Life', *Philosophy*, 79 (2004), 382, n. 14. I have found this thoughtful and profound discussion of Wittgenstein's ethics immensely helpful in understanding his ethics and its difficulties.

danger by taking foolish risks. So the 'willing subject' must think through how to act in *this* world, this world of fact, in such a way that his or her ethical commitments are realized. Of course, at one level, actions can be described in the language of science: a man on a horse shouted 'charge' and one body of men advanced on another. But once we conceive of what happens as two *armies* facing each other in a *war* led by *generals* who have the *responsibility* to order their troops into battle, we then can't effect the clear and clean distinction Wittgenstein seems intent on making. The italicized words in the previous sentence point to our understanding of such situations as ethically charged, as crying out for certain responses. The wise and courageous general knows when to advance, when to hold his ground, and when to beat a strategic retreat. We can grant, if we wish, that good and evil are initially predicated of the willing subject, but then the subject frames the world in evaluative terms—and not just relative value in Wittgenstein's sense—and responds to that world as an *agent* with practical reason and whatever practical wisdom such agents acquire. If a general acts in a cowardly manner, then cowardice and fault enter the world as surely as does the military disaster and the broken bodies.

I conclude that ethics doesn't run up against the boundaries of language—of sense—but rather that *Wittgenstein* found himself running up against the boundaries of the *Tractatus*. Clearly, he found this to be true when he rethought what he had said about language, mind, logic, and metaphysics in the 1930s and later, but there isn't much evidence, I think, that he thought he needed to rethink what he said about ethics in his early work. In any case, both the *Investigations* and other writings—especially *On Certainty*—would have provided an approach to ethics as distinctive as marks his later writings generally.

3. Boundary Crossings

Had he different interests and, perhaps, a different character, Wittgenstein might have called on the resources of the *Investigations* and—had he lived longer—his last thoughts as recorded in *On Certainty* to think about ethics anew. Doing so would not have required him to alter all his own categorical moral judgments, though some might have been more difficult to maintain than others. Why Wittgenstein didn't reconsider his views on ethics when he did so on so much else must remain something of a mystery. He wrote a bit more about religion than about ethics, and some speculate that his views on ethics became absorbed into his views on religious belief and practice. That, however, seems unlikely. There is a revealing passage in *Culture and Value*, where Wittgenstein discusses predestination, with special emphasis on the doctrine that some are chosen in advance to go to a 'good place' after death and others 'to the place of torment'. He closes his brief discussion with this remark: 'Teaching it could not constitute an ethical upbringing. If you wanted to bring someone up ethically while yet teaching him such a doctrine, you would have to teach it to him *after* having educated him ethically, representing it as a sort of incomprehensible mystery.'[17] Of course, it doesn't follow that one could never embed the teaching of ethics within a set of religious doctrines, but the remark does indicate that he didn't conflate ethics and religion.

In the end, I don't think there is a convincing explanation of why Wittgenstein did not reconsider his views on ethics. Given his philosophical inventiveness, he would surely have provided something rich and provocative. Instead, he left only a few scattered remarks, as well as Rush Rhees's notes on a discussion of ethics with Wittgenstein.[18] Although this is interesting, I see no trace of any *development* of Wittgenstein's thought on or about ethics from the time of the 'Lecture on Ethics'. So in what follows I can hope only to show a way of developing the insights of the *Investigations* and *On Certainty*.

Throughout his life Wittgenstein saw philosophy as an activity aimed at clarifying language and thought. This is already clearly prefigured in the *Tractatus* at 4.112: 'Philosophy is not a body of doctrine but an activity. A philosophical work consists essentially in elucidations.' These two core claims remain unchanged. We need to elucidate 'elucidation', however, if we are to see how someone who embraced the later Wittgenstein might

---

[17] CV, 81. The remark was made in 1949. My attention was drawn to this passage in Cyril Barrett's *Wittgenstein on Ethics and Religious Belief* (Oxford: Blackwell, 1991), 228. Barrett, like me, finds all the purported explanations of why Wittgenstein ignored sustained reflection on ethics to be based on 'scanty evidence'. He conveniently lists them for us: 1. Wittgenstein had lost interest in ethics. 2. His views had not changed, but it was not necessary to say this, as he had said all he had to say and had nothing to add. 3. His thinking on ethics had been absorbed into his views on religious belief. 4. He had abandoned his earlier account of ethics. 5. He had adopted a new, relativistic account of ethics consonant with his notions of language-games and forms of life, but it was not necessary to talk about it explicitly (Barrett, *Wittgenstein on Ethics and Religious Belief*, 227).

[18] Rush Rhees, *Discussions of Wittgenstein* (London: Routledge, 1970).

have proceeded—and to learn how at least one student of Wittgenstein *did* proceed. What need elucidating for the later Wittgenstein are concepts as they are embedded in language as it manifests itself in various lived social practices. Recall that in the *Tractatus* itself Wittgenstein acknowledged that even sentences without 'sense' (according to the picture theory) can nonetheless have perfectly legitimate uses. Mathematical equations and tautologies in particular license transitions from one statement to another, and therefore each plays an indispensable role in argument and proofs. So the strict boundary set up in the *Tractatus* was already breached. This concession—along with the abandonment of the picture theory—provides Wittgenstein with an opening for elucidations of many other concepts, e.g., colour concepts. In saying that 'Pink is a colour', for instance, we are saying no more than we would if we said that 'pink' is a colour word rather than, say, a personal name. In saying that 'Red is darker than pink' we aren't reporting a *discovery* about red and pink, but giving a partial elucidation of the meanings of 'red' and 'pink'. These are, for Wittgenstein, *grammatical propositions*—i.e., sentences used to express a rule for correct use of terms as they (typically) appear in the language games in which they find a use. In a highly qualified sense, then, grammatical rules might be said to have an explanatory function. It is crucial, of course, not to misunderstand Wittgenstein here. For such explanations are not causal but explanations of the ways in which we use terms. Further, explanations of this sort don't involve providing a 'theory' of anything. Explanation of meaning is instead tightly linked with linguistic understanding that, in turn, links with correct use in a language-game.

Philosophy when properly conducted, accordingly, consists largely in elucidating grammatical propositions and showing how doing so either resolves or dissolves philosophical problems. But isn't it all, then, just about words and nothing else? What is mistaken in this question is '. . . and nothing else'. For in grasping grammatical rules we are also, and crucially, learning how to make moves within our various lived practices. When we grasp that 'Pink is a colour' and 'Red is darker than pink' we grasp not only something about 'pink', 'red', and 'darker than' but about *colours*. But isn't this to confuse grammatical rules with empirical findings? No: it is to distinguish between them. Science discovers how a prism refracts light, but not that red is darker than pink. It cannot do the latter not because the scientific task is so difficult, but because it isn't a task for science at all. Wittgenstein sometimes expresses this distinction as a contrast between *rules of* our language-games (grammatical propositions) and *moves within* our language-games that accord with these rules (PI, 251). In *On Certainty* he grants that the distinction isn't sharp or necessarily unchanging, but that doesn't make the distinction useless. That a boundary isn't sharp doesn't mean that there isn't one. Nor does the fact that a *particular* proposition might shift from empirical to grammatical mean that *all* can, and certainly not all at once. Any particular empirical proposition, he says, '. . . can be transformed into a postulate—and then it becomes a norm of description'.[19] Even if there were such a shift, however, it would not mean that the grammatical was *continuous* with science. It would mean only that what was framed became, instead, part of the frame. More generally, Wittgenstein opposed the naturalistic trend—so widespread among philosophers in America since Quine—that philosophy is continuous with science. That only makes philosophers into scientists *manqués*.

The point that I wish to make here is that most of what Wittgenstein says about rules governing the correct use of colour words and thus the language-games in which we talk about colours applies equally to terms found in ethics and axiology more generally.

G.H. von Wright has done just this in *The Varieties of Goodness*.[20] He shows the fruitfulness of challenging philosophical dogma (such as the distinction between *normative ethics* and *meta-ethics*) while attending to terms as we use them in thinking about good, duty, and justice. He is especially acute at showing how a *field* of concepts interconnects.[21] In ethics, he notes:

. . . conceptual investigations . . . are a quest for grounds or standards, whereby to judge of good and bad and duty. To have such standards is important to our orientation in the world as moral agents. As we shape our standards for judging of

---

[19] OC, 321. Yet Wittgenstein quickly adds: 'I am suspicious even of this. The sentence is too general . . . .It sounds all too reminiscent of the *Tractatus*.' Yet Wittgenstein also says that '. . . the river-bed of thoughts may shift. But I distinguish between the movement of the waters on the river-bed and the shift of the bed itself; though there is not a sharp division of the one from the other. But if someone were to say "So logic too is an empirical science" he would be wrong. Yet this is right: the same proposition may get treated at one time as something to test by experience, at another as a rule of testing.'

[20] Von Wright, *The Varieties of Goodness*. Much the same could be said about von Wright's other great work, *Norm and Action: A Logical Inquiry* (London: Routledge & Kegan Paul, 1963).

[21] This is what Peter Hacker, following Peter Strawson, calls 'connective analysis'. See Hacker, *Connections and Controversies*.

good and bad and duty differently, we shape the conceptual frame of our moral judgments differently. It does not necessarily follow that the judgments too will be different, although they *may* be. But the grounds on which the judgments are based will be different, and therewith their meaning. Our moral 'point of view' will be different.[22]

Here we see a way forward beyond the boundaries imposed by Wittgenstein in the *Tractatus* and 'Lecture on Ethics'. For while in *theoretical* inquiry our concern is primarily, if not solely, with the structure of our conceptual scheme and of grammatical relations among its elements,[23] in *practical* inquiry we seek 'to judge of good and bad and duty' because it is important 'to our orientation in the world as moral agents'. We begin with conceptual analysis, then, but always with an eye not only to elucidating the 'grammar' (or conceptual aspects) of moral notions, but also to judging what is good and bad and constitutes our duty (and responsibility, obligation, etc.). Here not everything need remain as it was before. This approach is not only *continuous* with ordinary moral reflection, but *integral* to it. While distinctions can be made for various purposes, separation is out of the question.

A few examples from *The Varieties of Goodness* must suffice. After distinguishing between *instrumental* and *technical* goodness, von Wright inquires into the good of man: 'Of what kind of thing or being can it be said that it has a good?' While lubrication can be beneficial *for* a car and dropping a watch can be bad *for* it, 'A being, of whose good it is meaningful to talk, is one who can meaningfully be said to be well or ill, to flourish, be happy or miserable'.[24] Terms such as 'happiness' and 'welfare' are attributes of beings of whom it is meaningful to say that they have a *life*. There are other qualifications and borderline cases that von Wright considers (e.g., Does a nation have a life?), but from a *Wittgensteinian* perspective the essential point is that the claim that happiness and welfare attach only to beings of whom it is meaningful to say that they have a life is a *grammatical* claim, not a contingent scientific truth we have somehow discovered.

---

[22] Von Wright, *The Varieties of Goodness*, 6.

[23] See Peter Hacker, 'Philosophy: A Contribution, not to Human Knowledge, but to Human Understanding', forthcoming in Royal Institute of Philosophy lecture series (2007–8), for a detailed and sustained defence of this way of viewing the task of theoretical philosophy.

[24] Von Wright, *The Varieties of Goodness*, 50.

Among beings who have a life, von Wright argues, man is peculiar in
two respects, to one of which I wish to draw attention here. Just as creating
nests is natural to birds, creating a vast array of social units is natural to man.
What is special about these units—as opposed to social units of non-human
animals—is that they presuppose a *normative* order. That is, they specify
how one *may* or *must* conduct oneself. These 'covenanted' social units, as
von Wright calls them, are *conceptually* (i.e., grammatically) related to the
good *of* human beings. As such they provide a central problem for social,
political, and legal philosophy: namely, how to understand and justify
authority.[25]

In discussing the good of human beings, von Wright draws numerous
subtle distinctions between a variety of nested concepts: i.e., happiness,
well-being, pleasure, welfare, and the beneficial. Here I want to draw
attention to the way von Wright distinguishes *happiness* from *welfare*.
Clearly, they are sometimes used as synonyms, but they typically point in
different directions. Happiness, von Wright claims, is allied to (not identical
with) pleasure, and through it to such notions as enjoyment, gladness, and
liking. But:

Happiness has no immediate logical connexion with the beneficial. Welfare again
is primarily a matter of things beneficial and harmful, i.e., good and bad, for the
being concerned. As happiness, through pleasure, is related to that which a man
enjoys and likes, in a similar manner welfare, through the beneficial, is connected
with that which a man wants and needs.[26]

There are other differences that von Wright notes. Happiness is more like
a 'state' (or state of affairs) than welfare is, for one can become happy, be
happy, and cease to be happy, and, like an end, happiness can be achieved.
Welfare doesn't have these same connections to events in time. But a major
logical difference between them is their relation to causality:

Considerations of welfare are essentially considerations of how the doing and
happening of various things will causally affect a being. One cannot pronounce on
the question of whether something is good or bad for man, without considering

---

[25] The other respect in which humans are peculiar among beings who have a good is that we
distinguish between body and mind, so that we can speak of the good (or bad) of each. I will not
pursue this here. Clearly, von Wright does not understand this distinction as giving rise to a Cartesian
picture of body and mind.

[26] Von Wright, *The Varieties of Goodness*, 87.

the causal connexions in which this thing is or may become embedded. But one can pronounce on the question whether a man is happy or not, without necessarily considering what were the causal antecedents and what will be the consequences of his present situation.[27]

Despite these logical (again, grammatical) distinctions, it doesn't follow that the concepts of happiness and welfare are unconnected. Von Wright admits that the connections aren't altogether clear to him. But what he does say is, I think, illuminating in showing how one might proceed in doing ethics: 'Welfare (the good of a being) is, somehow, the broader and more basic notion . . . .It is also the notion which is of greater importance to ethics and to a general study of the varieties of goodness.'[28] If this is broadly correct, we see how through the kind of conceptual analysis that Wittgenstein initiated we can become clearer not only about how the field of various concepts interconnect, but provide guidance as to where to look when doing substantive ethics. That is, if von Wright is on the right track, then as we think about ethical problems—including problems in political philosophy—we'll look *away* from happiness and more to welfare. This doesn't, of course, *by itself* provide us with substantive ethical prescriptions. That will require us moving yet further afield, but still, I believe, within the field of philosophy. Or it will stay within the field *provided* that philosophy—at least in its practical employment—isn't limited solely to grammatical remarks. We've seen how von Wright already crosses that border when he insists that welfare is 'of greater importance' to ethics than happiness. This cannot be a conceptual point, but is a perfectly proper substantive point made within the field of philosophy.

Von Wright's discussion of 'happiness' also makes numerous conceptual points in the service of better understanding our moral life. Consider, for example, the ascetic ideal of life. According to it, the safest road to happiness is to have as few wants as possible, thus minimizing the chances of frustration and maximizing those of satisfaction. Ideally, the ascetic conceives happiness as the total abnegation of all desire. But this, argues von Wright, is a *crippled* view of happiness because it makes a *logical* (i.e., grammatical) mistake: namely, '. . . the mistake of regarding happiness as the *contradictory*, and not the *contrary*, of unhappiness'.[29] The

[27] *The Varieties of Goodness*, 88. [28] *The Varieties of Goodness*, 88.
[29] *The Varieties of Goodness*, 94.

contrary of happiness, von Wright notes, is unhappiness or misery. By escaping frustration one escapes unhappiness or misery—but it doesn't follow that one will be happy! Striving to desire nothing—if that is not contradictory—might purify the soul, but if taken as an ideal of human happiness, then it is *mistaken*, and thus not a path one ought, *ethically*, to pursue. We see here how it is possible to move *seamlessly* from conceptual analysis to substantive ethical claims.

These are just a few of many instances where von Wright makes conceptual points in the service of providing us moral insight. There are many more. After a discussion of intention, to give another example, von Wright notes an asymmetry in the difference between morally good and bad intention in acting:

> The intention in acting is morally good, if and only if, good for somebody is intended for its own sake and harm is not foreseen to follow for anybody from the act; and the intention in acting is morally bad, if and only if, harm is foreseen to follow for somebody from the act.[30]

Only if the harm was intended, von Wright adds, would it be true that one's intention was not only morally bad but morally malicious. Now the asymmetry here is a logical (grammatical or conceptual) point. *What* constitutes 'good for somebody', however, is a substantive matter. Must we now slide into simple moralism? Is philosophy inquiry here at an end?

I see no reason to think this. Recall that von Wright is inquiring into the good of man. We could equally inquire into the good of polar bears and rightly conclude that global warming is bad for them. For the shrinking ice cap and warm water make it much more difficult for polar bears to survive, let alone thrive. Confining polar bears in cages is also bad for them because it curtails their natural need to exercise vigorously. These are not difficult evaluative judgments. Why should it be impossible to make them in the case of man? Well, we are, we might say, more complicated, and our 'natural habitat' is more varied. No doubt. But that means only that the variety of ways in which we can flourish, the conditions under which we can thrive, vary widely. Still, while different ways of life will impose different duties and license different evaluative judgments, not everything goes.

---

[30] *The Varieties of Goodness*, 128.

Clearly, if we are to inquire into what is good and bad for polar bears we have to know something about them. Similarly, if we are to inquire into the good of man we will have to say something about human beings. If polar bears could easily shed their fur or lie contentedly for hours in confined spaces, then neither global warming nor cages would be particularly bad for them. Similarly, if human infants took a few weeks or months to mature, then the kind of nurturing provided by families would not be needed. Indeed, it is unlikely that families, nuclear or extended, would have even come into being. But human infants take years to mature, so family life *or something like it* is good for human development. So, too, when families don't nurture in appropriate ways it is bad for human development and so bad for humans. It is within the lived practice of family life that we come to understand, through generations of experience, more or less effective ways of raising children.

The Wittgenstein of the 'Lecture on Ethics' would have been dismissive of such value judgments, thinking them 'relative' and reducible to descriptive propositions. I've argued that his position is problematic even within the strictures of the *Tractatus*. But once Wittgenstein himself abandons central doctrines of his earlier work there is no reason to follow him in excluding such judgments from the 'ethical'.

We can, indeed, capitalize on the *latest* Wittgenstein, the reflections that took up his final days and were published as *On Certainty*. Not only are their conceptual claims in ethics to be made, but they are made against a backdrop of certainties. What is incontrovertible is neither *intuitions* nor matters of *knowledge*. Certainties, Wittgenstein writes, have a stamp of incontestability: 'Dispute about other things; *this* is immovable—it is the hinge on which your dispute can turn' (OC, 655). One might have an intuition—that is, an inkling, a hunch, a pre-critical belief—that, say, stem cell research can (or cannot) be justified. But it isn't an intuition that it is bad for children to be deprived of love and emotional support any more than it is an intuition that it is bad for polar bears to be deprived of room to romp and ice floes on which to take refuge from drowning. These are matters immune to doubt and therefore knowledge claims, too. If faced with someone who actually rejected the claim that children need love and emotional support to develop one would not know how to speak to such a person, any more than one would know how to speak to a person who truly rejected the proposition that the world has existed for hundreds of years.

To say that it is incontrovertibly bad for children to be raised without love and emotional support is, of course, not to answer many questions about what shape that needs to take: different cultures will have worked out different ways of providing this. Those that don't wither and die.[31] To say, moreover, that it is a moral certainty—'a hinge around which disputes can turn'—does not mean that reasons why moral certainties are certain cannot be given. Still, it is more likely that the reasons given won't be as persuasive as the certainty itself. To change the metaphor to another Wittgenstein uses, such certainties are the river-bed within which our ordinary moral reasoning flows.

In *On Certainty*, it is true, Wittgenstein never extends his remarks to moral or ethical knowledge. But there is no reason *not* to extend them beyond narrowly epistemic matters. Epistemically speaking, we can take a number of things beyond the reach of doubt: e.g., that the world existed before one was born and that $12 \times 12 = 144$. The hinge metaphor occurs earlier in *On Certainty*:

...the *questions* we raise and our *doubts* depend on the fact that some propositions are exempt from doubt, are as it were like hinges on which those turn. That is to say, it belongs to the logic of our scientific investigations that certain things are *in deed* not doubted.....If I want the door to turn, the hinges must stay put.   (OC, 341−3)

Ethical reflection depends, I believe, on moral certainties as well as on how these play out in understanding the good of man in varied human 'experiments in living'. *I* cannot doubt that children need love and emotional support to develop normally any more than *I* can doubt that inflicting pain on people for fun is deeply immoral. How I come to acquire these certainties (whether through learning, experience, or reflection) doesn't alter their incontrovertibility. There is simply no room for doubt here. These are two of many hinges on which the door of morality turns.

[31] Colin M. Turnbull, *The Mountain People* (New York: Simon and Schuster, 1972). If Turnbull is to be believed, the Iks (through no fault of their own) descended into a Hobbesian hell in which children were nothing but a burden to be ignored.

But now it will be objected that I am employing *both* an Aristotelian approach to understanding what is good for man stemming from the *Investigations* (through von Wright) *and* an approach found in *On Certainty*. And indeed this is true—except that there is no inconsistency or even tension in doing so. First, Wittgenstein is much closer to Aristotle in the way he thinks than first meets the eye. Further and more pertinent here, I would say that someone with Wittgensteinian sympathies can happily grant his affinity with Aristotle on ethical matters, especially his functional account about what constitutes the good of man. True, Aristotle doesn't emphasize various points as *grammatical* as such, but it isn't too hard to see Aristotle drawing conceptual distinctions throughout his philosophical writings.

Where Wittgenstein and Aristotle *do* differ is in the fact that Aristotle begins with the best opinions of the best men. Although not in any way foundational, these opinions provide Aristotle with reasons for making sure that something isn't overlooked, and that is fine as far as it goes. A proposition such as 'Being in great pain is bad for a human individual' is surely *also* a matter of enlightened opinion, but it functions differently from a Wittgensteinian perspective: it is something that it makes no sense to doubt, something no moral reflection could possibly disturb. It is bedrock. But of course there is no inconsistency between holding this and holding a number of other propositions: e.g., that to be unable to feel pain *at all* is also bad for human beings and that sometimes the infliction of pain, even great pain, is morally justifiable.

This is not to say, either, that moral certainties and an Aristotelian approach can't conflict. It will very much depend on what one thinks is beyond the reach of doubt. For knowing what is good for human beings only points to reasons for action and doesn't, by itself, establish duties or rights or resolve puzzles about social justice. Many of our duties and responsibilities will be dependent on our embedded social relationships. If my student is in need of some special attention, then it is I who should give it, not just anyone: it is a responsibility I have, not a right the student has against the world. Part of our finding ourselves embedded in 'covenanted' social units entails specific rights, duties, and responsibilities—but also their limits. Further, the social units can themselves be subject to moral criticism on various grounds. All this remains to be done, but I think someone who finds the *later* and *latest* Wittgensteinian approach to philosophy congenial can find elements within it to extend to ethics and axiology generally.

Once 'hinges' are in place, once we have a 'river-bed', then we can reason morally taking into account human welfare (well-being), happiness, and duty. We can, for example, inquire into the conditions, responsibilities, and implications of friendship. This will be partly conceptual—what friendship *is*—but also will involve contestable reasons about its concrete, substantive implications of friendship.[32] We can also inquire, more narrowly, into what we owe to each other, not as friends, but as fellow human beings. All of this requires Wittgensteinian conceptual map-making. But borders that Wittgenstein erected in the *Tractatus* can be crossed, and once we have our map—which is no mean objective—we can explore the terrain in good conscience.

---

[32] 'The better part of one's life', said Abraham Lincoln, 'consists of friendships.' Surely my own life has been enriched beyond measure by my good fortune of friendship with Peter Hacker.

The Lessons of Life: Wittgenstein, Religion and Analytic Philosophy

JOHN COTTINGHAM

1. Introduction

Philosophy is as fashion-prone as any other human enterprise, and it is perhaps no surprise that Wittgenstein's influence has recently suffered something of an eclipse in the anglophone philosophical world. This may well be a natural 'rebound' reaction against the climate of that substantial chunk of the twentieth century when much of philosophy was dominated by his approach to the subject. It may also be a result of a certain cautious, academic tidy-mindedness, which is wary of work that is sweeping enough to resist neat dissection within the burgeoning technical specialisms of current 'mainstream' philosophy. Or, thirdly, it may be due to the rise of a scientistic vision of philosophy—the view that philosophers should 'either...adopt and emulate the method of successful sciences, or...operate in tandem with the sciences, as their abstract and reflective branch'.[1] Sigmund Freud, who has a good claim to rank alongside Ludwig Wittgenstein as the most original philosophical (in the broad sense) thinker of the twentieth century, certainly seems to have suffered as much as Wittgenstein from all three of the damaging trends just noted: his methods are not such as to appeal to the devotees of modern experimental science as *the* model for human cognitive endeavour; his insights are wide enough in scope to resist narrow disciplinary boundaries; and his ideas have succeeded in infusing our intellectual culture for long enough to make many people want to turn the page and move on.

---

[1] Brian Leiter, *The Future for Philosophy* (Oxford: Clarendon Press, 2004), 2–3.

Whatever the reasons, Wittgenstein, like Freud, figures far less in the current citation indexes of analytic philosophy than anyone even slightly acquainted with the extraordinary richness of his thought might have been led to expect. I ought to add, right here at the outset, that I count myself as one whose acquaintance with the Wittgensteinian corpus is by professional standards only a little more than slight. In a volume devoted to honouring a supremely accomplished Wittgenstein scholar, who has done more than anyone else to reveal the riches of his thought, I am all too conscious of my inadequate qualifications for the present task. My rashness can be explained only by my admiration for Peter Hacker's work and my awareness of how much I have learnt from him; I can also plead, by way of excuse for entering territory he knows so much better than I, the fact that Wittgenstein's views on religion have not, to my knowledge, been a topic to which he has devoted any systematic commentary.

Apart from the general eclipse I have already referred to, Wittgenstein has, in the particular case of his philosophy of religion (if that is not too grand a term for a scattered, if highly fertile, collection of remarks), suffered the additional fate of being subject to a hostile pincer movement from theistic philosophers on one flank and atheistic ones on the other. On the atheist side, opponents of theism, or those suspicious of its intellectual credentials, have been keen to close off a soggy 'non-cognitivist' escape-route which they have taken Wittgenstein to be offering to the beleaguered believer—an escape route that would place Christian belief 'beyond historical and scientific criticism'.[2] On the theist side, Christian analytic philosophers have in recent years wanted to defend the epistemic respectability of their religious beliefs head on.[3] They have done so, moreover, in a robustly realist mode: in reaction to the non-cognitivist

---

[2] Compare John Hyman: '[Wittgenstein's] avowed aim . . . is to explain how concepts such as sin, redemption, judgement, grace and atonement can have an indispensable place in an individual's or a community's way of life; and to show how we can resist assimilating the use of these concepts to hypotheses, predictions and theoretical explanations. But I suspect that behind this is "the great cry of 'I would like to believe, but unfortunately I cannot'", and an intense desire to place Christian faith beyond criticism, or rather, beyond the criticism that it depends on scientific errors and historical falsehoods—in other words, to protect a faith he himself was unable to share' (John Hyman, 'Wittgenstein', in P. Draper and C. Tagliaferro (eds.), *A Companion to Philosophy of Religion* (2nd edn, Oxford: Blackwell, forthcoming).

[3] Classic examples are Richard Swinburne, *The Existence of God* (Oxford: Oxford University Press, 2nd edn, 2004), and Alvin Plantinga, *Warranted Christian Belief* (Oxford: Oxford University Press, 2000).

line adopted by several admirers of Wittgenstein, most notably the late D. Z. Phillips, these theists have insisted that the religious believer must unapologetically be prepared to advance truth claims, rather than resting content with scrutiny of the internal structure of religious 'language games' or practices.[4]

So Wittgenstein's influence on the philosophy of religion, along perhaps with his philosophical influence generally, appears for the moment to be on the wane. In this essay I shall nevertheless argue that his ideas, properly understood, would richly repay the continued attention of philosophers interested in religion.[5] I shall also suggest that it is important not to be put off by certain received interpretations of Wittgenstein's philosophy of religion, which (I shall maintain) are mistaken, or at least fail to grasp important insights he has to offer about the nature of religious allegiance. For those who wish to defend the respectability of religious belief, Wittgenstein turns out on further examination to be a far more promising ally, philosophically speaking, than is generally supposed. As for those for whom (as was the case with Wittgenstein himself) religious faith is not a viable option, his ideas may at least help to illuminate the nature of the door which they take to be shut.

---

[4] D. Z. Phillips, inspired by Wittgenstein's ideas about language games, often stressed that if we want to understand religious talk we should resist pontificating about the 'reality' of God, and instead address ourselves to the more modest task of clarifying the grammar of religious concepts. 'Theological realism', objected Phillips, 'often indulges in philosophy by italics. We are told that we could not worship unless we believed that God *exists*. We are told that we cannot talk to God unless he is *there* to talk to. And so on. But nothing is achieved by italicising these words. The task of clarifying their grammar when they are used remains' (*Wittgenstein and Religion* (London: Macmillan, 1993), 35). Contrast the position taken by Christopher J. Insole in his *The Realist Hope* (Aldershot: Ashgate, 2006), which is a sustained attack on anti-realism in the philosophy of religion (a position which my predecessor in the philosophy chair at Reading, A. G. N. Flew, used to refer to as 'Swansea obscurantism'). For Insole, there is something fundamentally evasive about all attempts to duck the question of God's reality. For however closely we investigate the internal structure of a particular language game, or a given system of epistemic beliefs and practices, there is a separate question about the truth of our beliefs. And truth, Insole insists, is determined by 'what is the case' or 'the way things are', independently of human cognition (pp. 1–2). It should, however, be noted in fairness to Phillips, that on his interpretation Wittgenstein is not saying that realism is a correct analysis of ordinary beliefs, and non-realism of religious beliefs. He is saying that *both* realism and non-realism are 'idle talk' (Phillips, *Wittgenstein and Religion*, 35).

[5] There exist very many such philosophers, covering a wide spectrum of believers, agnostics, sceptics and atheists. This perhaps (just) needs saying, in the light of the fact that a recent collection of state-of-the-art articles devoted to surveying the 'important agendas for philosophy's future' has no room for a chapter concerned with religion, and indeed does not contain a single index entry under any of the headings 'God', 'religion', 'faith' or 'spiritual' (see Leiter, *The Future for Philosophy*, 2–3).

2. Wittgenstein's Position

In a lucid summary of Wittgenstein's views on religion, Hans-Johann Glock identifies, it seems to me, three main strands running through the various surviving texts and notes. First, religious discourse is *autonomous*: it does not compete with science or technology, but 'constitutes a *sui generis* grammatical system'. Second, religious beliefs are given meaning and content via their role in the *practice or 'form of life' of the believer*. Third, religious language is *non-descriptive* and *non-cognitive*: 'religious statements do not describe any kind of reality, empirical or transcendent, and do not make any knowledge claims', but instead have a purely expressive function.[6] I should like to postpone for the moment the third, non-cognitivist, aspect, since that is the most problematic, and begin by saying a few words about the first two features.

3. Religion not a Rival to Science

That religion involves a sui-generis form of discourse, not to be construed as competing with science, does indeed appear to be a consistent theme in Wittgenstein's thinking about religion. It is strikingly present, for example, in his 'Remarks on Frazer's *The Golden Bough*'. Wittgenstein believed that the anthropologist James George Frazer had committed a fundamental error in his account of ritual practices by construing them in scientific or rationalistic terms, as aimed at the production of certain effects.[7] Highly relevant here is the distinction made by Wittgenstein between *faith* and *superstition*. Superstition, unlike faith, 'springs from fear and is a sort of false science' (CV, 82). Thus Wittgenstein would say, I think, that baptism of a child, if accompanied by the belief that this is an efficacious procedure for making the child's life more lucky or more successful, is mere superstition—a kind of primitive pseudo-technology. If we want to ensure the best opportunities for the child's health and success, we are far better off turning to the methods of science (for example modern medicine). But if the baptism is an act of joyful affirmation and thanksgiving for the new

---

[6] H.-J. Glock, *A Wittgenstein Dictionary* (Oxford: Blackwell, 1996), s. v. 'Religion'.
[7] For a detailed discussion of this, see Jacques Bouveresse, 'Wittgenstein's Critique of Frazer', *Ratio*, 20 (2007), 357–76, reprinted in J. Preston (ed.), *Wittgenstein and Reason* (Oxford: Blackwell, 2008).

life—what Wittgenstein called a 'trusting' (*ein Vertrauen*, CV, 82)—then it is a genuine manifestation of religious faith.

This distinction is an important one, because it partly disables a common attack mounted by atheist critics of religion, most famously by Freud, namely that religious behaviour characteristically stems from helplessness and the need for protection against natural threats—'the majestic, cruel and inexorable powers of nature'.[8] Once that premise is granted, it would be a short step to conclude that religion is increasingly likely to become obsolete as science learns to alleviate those threats. The general line is prefigured in David Hume, who argues that what prompts humans to turn to God is 'the ordinary affections of human life' such as the dread of misery and the terror of death.[9] The implication is the same as Freud's: religion is an illusion born of helplessness and fear.[10]

No doubt many religious adherents have, over the ages, turned to ritual practices in a desperate attempt to avert disaster. But assimilating all religious behaviour to that pattern is surely a crude over-simplification. When St Paul encouraged his followers to bear adversity with the cry that 'neither death nor life nor . . . any other creature shall be able to separate us from the love of God' (Romans 8:38), he cannot have meant to advance the glib claim that a few well-chosen prayers would keep us out of trouble. The Jewish scriptures, in which he was so well versed, are packed with stories of terrible trials suffered by innocent believers, of heroic goodness often crushed by the forces of tyranny and oppression. So Paul's point cannot be to advocate a slick piece of pseudo-technology, but must involve a rather more subtle understanding of the nature of faith.[11] The extraordinary

[8] Sigmund Freud, *Civilization and its Discontents* [*Das Unbehagen in der Kultur*, 1929], in *The Penguin Freud Library*, Vol. 12 (London: Penguin Books, 1985), 195.

[9] David Hume, *The Natural History of Religion* [1757]. For further discussion of these Freudian and Humean themes, see Michael Palmer's fascinating study *Freud and Jung on Religion* (London: Routledge, 1997).

[10] It is important to note that an 'illusion', in Freudian usage, is not necessarily erroneous. Freud at one point explicitly concedes this, distinguishing 'illusion' from 'delusion' (though his terminology is not always consistent). Cinderella may have the fantasy that a prince will come and marry her—and in a few cases it may actually happen. But Freud argues that it is characteristic of illusions in his sense that they are held without regard for rational justification; further, they characteristically stem from (indeed are generated by) the wishes or needs of the believer. And again the conclusion is all too clear: religion is something we need to grow out of. See Freud, *The Future of an Illusion* [*Die Zukunft einer Illusion*, 1927], *The Penguin Freud Library*, Vol. 12, 213. Cf. Palmer, *Freud and Jung on Religion*, Ch. 3.

[11] See further J. Cottingham, 'What Difference Does it Make? The Nature and Significance of Religious Belief', *Ratio*, 19 (2006), 401–20, and in J. Cottingham (ed.), *The Meaning of Theism* (Oxford: Blackwell, 2007), 19 ff.

remark in the Hebrew Bible 'though he slay me, yet will I trust in him' (Job 1:4) seems, in a similar way, to vindicate Wittgenstein's distinction: the language looks much more like an expression of *Vertrauen* than an attempt at superstitious manipulation.[12] In short, those who dismiss religion as a primitive attempt to control a hostile world, now superseded by the more efficient methods of modern science, seem to be relying on a crude caricature of religion—one that may match the intentions of some religious practitioners, but which will not survive serious scrutiny of a great deal of mainstream religious discourse. This part of 'Wittgensteinian apologetics', then, seems to me still in very good shape.

4. The Importance of Praxis

Let me now turn to the role of practices and forms of life in religious discourse. Wittgenstein's emphasis on praxis is often interpreted as implying the following kind of claim: 'Religious belief should not be understood as assent to a doctrine or doctrines, but rather as involvement in a certain set of practices.' But putting it this way runs together two points, which I think should be sharply distinguished. To deny that assent to doctrines is involved in being religious takes us straight into the non-cognitivist camp. That may or may not be a tenable position, and it may or may not be Wittgenstein's position, but we have agreed to postpone discussion of this until later on. The Wittgensteinian emphasis on praxis may, however, be construed as neutral or silent on the cognitivist versus non-cognitivist issue, and directed instead at making the point that the meaning and content of religious beliefs cannot be understood in isolation from the practices and forms of life of the believer. That point seems to me a very plausible one.

Wittgenstein's interest in 'forms of life' (*Lebensformen*), was, I take it, in part a 'holistic' reaction against the atomistic approaches to meaning observable in his own earlier work (TLP) and also (in a different way) in

---

[12] A riposte of a broadly Freudian kind would be to say that language like that of Paul or Job reflects massive self-deception, or a subconscious attempt at self-compensation in the face of misfortune and failure. Such deflationary 'wishful thinking' explanations cannot of course be dismissed out of hand, though it is a matter for legitimate scepticism whether they offer a sufficiently powerful mechanism to explain the trust and hope that seem to be reflected in such passages (many other scriptural and other examples could be given).

some versions of the verificationism proposed by the logical positivists in the first half of the twentieth century. In a famous thought-experiment in his celebrated paper 'Elimination of Metaphysics', Rudolph Carnap took an imaginary isolated word ('teavy'), and asked how it could possibly count as meaningful unless one was able to provide precise empirical criteria for its application; the implied interlocutor was supposedly driven to admit that without such criteria the concept of 'teaviness' must be discarded as meaningless. Carnap then triumphantly proceeded to suggest that the same argument must apply to the term 'God'.[13]

The corrective that Wittgenstein (by implication) offers to such strategies is to insist that the speaking of language is 'part of an activity or of a form of life' (PI, 23). Our language games are interwoven with a web of non-linguistic activities, and cannot be understood apart from the context that gives them life. These, I assume, are by now fairly uncontroversial points; and, again, they offer some solid ground for the religious apologist. As I have argued elsewhere,[14] analytic philosophers are often prone to use the 'fruit-juicer' method when approaching modes of thought of which they are sceptical: they require the clear liquid of a few propositions to be extracted for examination in isolation from what they take to be the irrelevant pulpy mush of context. Yet to demand an answer to the yes/no question: 'Do you or do you not believe that P?', where P stands for a statement or series of statements in one of the creeds or some other doctrinal summary, often tells us surprisingly little about how a religious worldview informs someone's outlook. A juice extractor does not, as might at first be supposed, give us the true essence of a fruit; what it often delivers is a not very palatable drink plus a pulpy mess. Someone who has tasted strawberries only via the output of a juicer, and has firmly decided 'this is not for me', may turn out to have a radically impoverished grasp of what it is about the fruit that makes the strawberry lover so enthusiastic.

The point can be especially relevant when 'Do you or do you not?' questions are fired off by an external scrutineer in a misguided attempt to 'settle' what it is that the believer subscribes to. Consider for example 'Do

---

[13] Rudolf Carnap, 'The Elimination of Metaphysics through Logical Analysis of Language' [*Überwindung der Metaphysik durch logische Analyse der Sprache*, 1932], trans. Arthur Pap, in A. J. Ayer (ed.), *Logical Positivism* (New York: Free Press, 1959), 60–80.

[14] See J. Cottingham, *The Spiritual Dimension* (Cambridge: Cambridge University Press, 2005), Ch. 1, and Ch. 5 (on which the next two paragraphs draw).

you or do you not believe that the Bread is transubstantiated into the Body of Christ?', when asked 'externally' by someone who has heard of this Catholic doctrine about the Mass, and wants to sort out whether Bloggs 'really believes' it. The reason why either answer, positive or negative, will almost certainly be unenlightening is that questions involving this kind of religious language are quite unlike scientific questions of the form 'Do you or do you not believe that gold is soluble in hydrochloric acid?' Even in the scientific case, of course, a good deal of contextual background is needed in order to understand the meaning of such a question. But in the religious case, the complications are multiplied because of the multi-layered nature of the discourse involved. Someone who is committed to a doctrine like the transubstantiation is almost certainly so committed because of the role that certain sorts of language about the Eucharist play in her religious praxis, and because her grasp of the language and liturgy of the Eucharist puts her in touch with multiple levels of rich significance, each of which resonates with powerful moral and spiritual aspects of her worldview.[15] Insisting on the question 'But does the wine actually change into blood?' *appears* to cut to the chase, eliminate evasion and ambiguity, and focus on what is 'really' believed. But in the context of a 'cold', no-nonsense question from an external scrutineer who is largely ignorant of the multiple levels of meaning just indicated, the yes/no question functions like the strawberry juicer: isolating the propositional liquid from the contextual pulp does not make for a properly informed evaluation of the belief's content. For the religious believer, 'signs' such as the bread and wine of the Eucharist[16] can function

---

[15] A caveat: nothing here said about symbols and the importance of praxis need be taken to imply a retreat from a real and genuine truth claim. Of course, when questions like 'But do the bread and wine *really* change?' are put, the questioner is often insisting on having an answer to what he or she takes to be the damaging question of whether there is any actual physical change—where 'actual' and 'physical' are taken to be more or less equivalent. Yet, as Michael Dummett has persuasively argued, it is a mistake 'to conceive of metaphysical reality after the model of physical reality' ('The Intelligibility of Eucharistic Doctrine', in W. J. Abraham and S. W. Holtzer (eds.), *The Rationality of Religious Belief* (Oxford: Clarendon Press, 1987), 247). In the light of this kind of misunderstanding, those who give different answers to the kind of yes/no question just described may more often than not turn out to be talking at cross purposes. This may be one way of interpreting the sense of Wittgenstein's reported remark that those who disagree about whether there will be a last judgement are not in fact contradicting each other (LC, 53).

[16] For the term 'signs' as used of the bread and wine of the Eucharist, see *Catechism of the Catholic Church* (New York: Doubleday, 1995, rev. 1997), §1333. For an interesting account of Aquinas's view of the sacraments as a kind of sign, see Mark Jordan, 'Theology and Philosophy', in N. Kretzmann and E. Stump (eds.), *The Cambridge Companion to Aquinas* (Cambridge: Cambridge University Press, 1993), Ch. 9.

as, in William Wainwright's phrase, 'a medium for fuller, riper knowing'. Insistence on yes/no answers to literalistically construed questions is a way of mangling what lies at the core of this kind of knowing; it is a denial of the unique power such signs have to capture the mystery and complexity of our human experience of the world.[17]

These last few remarks take us beyond anything Wittgenstein himself ventures to discuss in connection with religion, but they are, I think, consistent with, and supported by, his persuasive thesis about the inter-weaving of language and practice. 'It is characteristic of our language that the foundation out of which it grows consists in steady forms of life, regular activity. Its function is determined above all by the action which it accompanies' (CE, 404). Philosophical critics of religion are often prone to think they can evaluate religious claims on the basis of only a cursory grasp of their meaning. It does not of course follow that a richer contextual examination of the practices that give life to religion will end up *vindicating* those claims; that question is left open. But without a proper grasp of meaning, which in turn requires a preparedness to investigate context and praxis, the evaluation of truth cannot even get off the ground. It seems to me that the quality of much contemporary philosophy of religion would be greatly improved if that lesson alone, profoundly Wittgensteinian in spirit, were thoroughly digested.

5. 'Wittgensteinian Fideism'

I turn now to the third of the three features commonly taken to be central to Wittgenstein's approach to religion, namely his supposed view that religion discourse does not make knowledge claims. On this view, religious language is non-cognitive—not descriptive of any supposed facts, bur rather expressive of a certain commitment. This view, or elements of it, is often discussed under the label 'Wittgensteinian fideism',[18] though in fact 'fideism' is not a particularly helpful term, since it covers a

---

[17] Here I partly follow the phrasing of David Cooper, *Metaphor* (Oxford: Blackwell, 1986), 219; the phrase 'medium for a fully and riper knowing' comes from William Wainwright (cited by Cooper, though with some reservations). Compare Wainwright, *Reason and the Heart* (Ithaca, NY: Cornell University Press, 1995).

[18] As noted by Glock, *A Wittgenstein Dictionary*, 320.

spectrum of positions, which need to be disentangled if confusion is to be avoided.

The word 'fideism' was apparently first used by French Protestants in 1870s as a term of approval, but has since widely acquired a pejorative connotation (particularly among Catholic writers), as implying an over-reliance on faith at the expense of reason.[19] The classic account of the relationship between reason and faith was given by Thomas Aquinas, who maintained that the two are complementary. Some religious beliefs (for example, belief in the existence of God) can, he argued, be established by 'natural reason', while other beliefs (including those in the 'revealed truths' of Christianity such as the Incarnation and the doctrine of the Trinity) cannot be reached by reason, but require faith. For Aquinas, there is a harmony between reason and faith, since both types of truth are worthy of our belief. Moreover, he taught that even the truths of natural reason may sometimes be accepted on faith—for example, by those who do not have the time or resources to follow the relevant arguments.[20]

Notice that there is nothing 'non-cognitivist' in any of this. Truths of faith are just as much truths as truths of reason; it is simply that the method of their acquisition may be different. Aquinas's emphasis on reason and faith as complementary is anticipated by Augustine and Anselm, though both these earlier thinkers take it that faith is in some sense prior to reason. The subtitle of Anselm's *Proslogion* is *fides quaerens intellectum* ('faith seeking understanding'). Anselm's starting point is his unquestioned belief in God, which he takes to be a pre-requisite for embarking on the meditation that will establish God's existence by rational reflection: 'credo ut intelligam' ('I believe in order that I may understand': *Proslogion* (1077–8), ch. 1). The Anselmian approach owes much to Augustine's reflections on the slogan 'nisi credideris, non intelliges'—'unless you have believed you will not understand' (based on the inspired if questionable Septuagint rendering of a verse of Isaiah (7:9): 'ean mê pisteusête, oude mê synête').[21] Again, these

---

[19] For more on this, see Alistair Mason, 'Fideism', in A. Hastings, A. Mason and H. Pyper (eds.), *The Oxford Companion to Christian Thought* (Oxford: Oxford University Press, 2000), 240–1.

[20] *Summa contra Gentiles* [1260], I, 4.

[21] The rendering is questionable inasmuch as the original Hebrew may simply mean (as the New Revised Standard Version has it) 'If you do not stand firm in faith, you shall not stand at all.' For Augustine's reflections on the verse in question see *Contra Faustum Manichaeum* [AD 400], Book IV. For a critical exposition of the 'faith seeks understanding' programme in Christian philosophical theology, see Paul Helm, *Faith and Understanding* (Edinburgh: Edinburgh University Press, 1997).

early reflections on the importance of faith are fully compatible with a strictly cognitivist account of religious truth—and indeed both Augustine and Anselm do famously go on to offer rational arguments designed to establish and justify their beliefs in the existence of God.

Although it does not imply any retreat from cognitivism, the line taken by Augustine and Anselm, and indeed by Aquinas himself, does certainly admit that religious allegiance depends on more than the rational evaluation of truth claims, and to that extent their view of religious allegiance may all be said to have a 'fideist' component. In stressing the importance of faith (in Latin *fides*), they are stressing something over and above mere rational assent to a set of doctrines; for *fides*, like its Greek counterpart *pistis*, always connotes a stronger volitional component than simple assent—some further element of trust and commitment. As one moves towards more extreme forms of fideism, such as that of Søren Kierkegaard, the volitional element becomes stronger and stronger. 'Faith does not need proof,' asserted Kierkegaard in one of his famous purple passages, 'indeed it must regard proof as its enemy.'[22] And he went on to insist that

Christianity is spirit, spirit is inwardness, inwardness is subjectivity, subjectivity is essential passion, and in its maximum an infinite, personal, passionate interest in one's eternal happiness . . . If I wish to preserve myself in faith, I must constantly be intent on holding fast the objective uncertainty, so as to remain out upon the deep, over seventy thousand fathoms of water, still preserving my faith.[23]

Clearly Wittgenstein had read Kierkegaard, and clearly he was strongly influenced by him.[24] He shares with Kierkegaard the view that passionate commitment is central to what makes someone religious. He thought, with Kierkegaard, that there was something 'ludicrous' in attempting to shore up the reasonableness of religious belief in the light of dispassionate scrutiny of the evidence (LC, 58). But this in itself does not make him (or Kierkegaard for that matter) a non-cognitivist. One may maintain that Christianity involves passionately holding fast to *x*, and also that *x* cannot be rationally or objectively demonstrated; but this is quite compatible with holding that *x* is, or entails, a certain proposition or propositions, and that

[22] S. Kierkegaard, *Concluding Unscientific Postscript* [*Afsluttende Uvidenskabelig Efterskrift*, 1846], trans. D. F. Swenson (Princeton, NJ: Princeton University Press, 1941), 31 (from Book I, Ch. 1).

[23] *Concluding Unscientific Postscript*, 182 (from Book II, Part II, Ch. 2).

[24] See further Hyman, 'Wittgenstein'.

to be a Christian entails subscribing to the truth of that proposition (or those propositions). The upshot is that critics who wish to criticize Wittgenstein for advocating a non-cognitivist view of religion are not entitled to use the 'Kierkegaardian' flavour of many of his remarks as ammunition to support their hostile interpretation. And as for the general point that religious faith characteristically involves a willingness to trust, and to commit oneself in advance of rational scrutiny of arguments or detached evaluation of the evidence, if this is 'fideism', it is something that, with varying degrees of emphasis, may be found throughout Western philosophy of religion, from Augustine and Aquinas through Pascal down to Kierkegaard and William James.[25] Indeed, it goes back to the very earliest times, to the story of the doubting apostle Thomas, whose eventual act of passionate commitment made a mockery of his prior insistence that various empirical confirmatory tests would be needed to make him a believer.[26]

It is of course a separate question whether trust prior to evidence is an epistemically respectable procedure. Blaise Pascal famously urged us to make a religious commitment, and engage in religious forms of life, *in order to* generate belief in God—and hence in due course achieve salvation.[27] But whatever one makes of this recommendation, it does, I think, contain an underlying insight that does not depend on the somewhat quirky logic of Pascal's wager. For there are many areas of life where it is perfectly proper and sensible to make a commitment in advance of established belief, in the hope that evidence *further down the line* will emerge, which will retrospectively justify one's having made that commitment. Embarking on an intimate personal relationship is often like this—one takes the plunge

[25] Aquinas, the master architect of rational philosophical theology, wrote the famous line 'praestet fides supplementum sensuum defectui'—'faith makes up the deficiency of the senses' (from the hymn *Pange lingua* [1260]). Blaise Pascal is equally famous for his dictum 'le coeur a ses raisons que la raison ne connaît point'—'the heart has its reasons of which reason is quite unaware' (*Pensées* [1670], ed. L. Lafuma (Paris: Seuil, 1962), no. 423). Compare no. 424: 'C'est le coeur qui sent Dieu et non la raison. Voilà ce que c'est que la foi'—'It's the heart, not Reason, that senses God: that is what faith is.' See also William James, *The Will to Believe* (New York: Longmans Green, 1897), Ch. 1.
[26] According to the story, Thomas's eventual allegiance did not hinge on his ever, in the event, performing the test he had previously specified, namely 'putting his finger in the print of the nails' (John 20: 24–9).
[27] 'You want to cure yourself of unbelief, and you ask for remedies: learn from those who were hampered like you and who now wager all they possess. These are people who know the road you would like to follow; they are cured of the malady for which you seek a cure; so follow them and begin as they did—*by acting as if they believed*, by taking holy water, having masses said, and so on. In the natural course of events this in itself will make you believe, this will train you.' Pascal, *Pensées*, no. 418.

and bestows one's trust without prior certification that the trust is justified. Not only is this possible, but often it is perfectly rational. For without the vulnerability and openness generated by such acts of trust, loving relationships would never develop in the first place. Cold insistence on prior assurance is the best way to close off the possibility of a relationship taking root; in Martha Nussbaum's telling phrase, it is a 'stratagem of flight'.[28] Willed commitment without scientific assessment of evidence, should not, then, be condemned as inherently irrational.

The upshot of our discussion in this section is that Wittgenstein's 'fideistic' emphasis on the importance of passionate commitment in religion emerges in much better shape than many of his critics are apt to suppose. It takes its place in a long tradition of Western religious thought that underlines the importance of trust and openness in the spiritual life. Moreover, it need not, in itself, imply a non-cognitivist view of religious discourse. And it is also worth noting that it harmonizes with one of Wittgenstein's most persuasive themes—the need to look at each domain of human discourse in its own terms, without trying to assimilate its rules and methods to those of modern science.[29]

6. 'Wittgensteinian Expressivism'

It is now time to look at some more troublesome Wittgensteinian texts on religion, so far ignored, which seem to point firmly in a non-cognitivist direction. The most striking example comes in *Culture and Value*: 'it appears to me as though a religious belief could only be (something like) passionately committing oneself to a system of reference' (CV, 73). The implication here seems to be that belief, in the normal sense of the term, namely assent to a proposition with a certain cognitive content, drops out of the picture completely in Wittgenstein's conception of religious faith; it reduces simply to the volitional act of committing oneself. This has called forth some pointed criticism. Hanjo Glock, for example, observes: 'a religious belief cannot simply amount to committing oneself to a religious

[28] Martha Nussbaum, 'Love's Knowledge' [1988], reprinted her book of the same title (Oxford: Oxford University Press, 1990). For further discussion of this theme, see Cottingham, *The Spiritual Dimension*, Ch. 1.

[29] Cf. Bouveresse, 'Wittgenstein's Critique of Frazer,' *passim*.

life, since the belief will typically be part of the reason for making such a commitment'.[30] Similarly John Hyman: 'if I have and retain [this kind of] commitment, my belief that God exists will typically be among my *reasons* for doing so'.[31]

The 'typically' in both these formulations is presumably there to guard against the objection that one *can* make a commitment in the absence of a belief. This is certainly possible; as we have just seen, Pascal urged us to make commitments *in order* to generate a (not yet held) belief. Nevertheless, the point made by Glock, Hyman and others does succeed in pointing to a genuine worry. To say that a religious belief just *is* a commitment appears to sidestep the question of *justification* in a problematic way.[32] Commitments, though it may be psychologically possible to make them in the absence of prior beliefs, seem to presuppose, for their validity, the truth of the beliefs logically required by the nature of the commitment. If I commit myself to a loved one, or to God, my commitment will lose its justification if the object of my commitment turns out not to exist, or to be wholly unworthy of my commitment.

It has, however, been persuasively argued by Severin Schroeder that, contrary to the common reading of the key sentence in *Culture and Value*, Wittgenstein is not proposing a *purely* expressivist construal of credal statements.[33] In saying that religious belief '*can only* be a passionate commitment', he may simply be underlining the *inescapability* of a passionate, volitional element; he need not be saying that what is involved in the belief is *merely* the commitment—as if nothing else, no cognitive or doxastic elements, were entailed. On the question of phrasing and nuance, Schroeder seems to me clearly right. To say, for example, 'this remark can only have

---

[30] Glock, *A Wittgenstein Dictionary*, 323.

[31] J. Hyman, 'The Gospel according to Wittgenstein', in R. Arrington (ed.), *Wittgenstein and Religious Belief* (London: Routledge, 2001), 10. Compare also John Searle: 'When ordinary people pray it is because they think there is a God up there listening. But whether or not there is a God listening to their prayer isn't itself part of the language game. The reason people play the language game of religion is because they think there is something outside the language game that gives it a point.' Searle, 'Wittgenstein', in B. Magee, *The Great Philosophers* (London: BBC Books, 1987), 344–5.

[32] In a later article, Hyman reformulates his earlier objection by distinguishing how religious beliefs are *formed* from how they are *justified*. His revised argument is that beliefs cannot be commitments, since the latter need to be justified by the former (Hyman, 'Wittgenstein').

[33] S. Schroeder, 'The Tightrope Walker', *Ratio*, 20 (2007), 442–63; reprinted in Preston (ed.), *Wittgenstein and Reason*. I am most grateful to Severin Schroeder, not just for what I have learnt from this and other writings of his, but also for kindly commenting on an earlier draft of the present paper, and providing many helpful comments and corrections.

been malicious' does not imply that it was malicious *and nothing else*; it does not, for example rule out its being true, or self-interested, or timely, or funny. What is more, and quite apart from this, there are, as Schroeder points out, many passages where Wittgenstein makes it quite explicit that belief *is* involved in religious commitment. In the very next sentence following our key dictum, he goes on to say, 'Hence, although it is *belief*, it is a way of living, or a way of judging life' (CV, 73).[34] There is evidence, moreover, that Wittgenstein would have liked to commit himself to Christianity, but felt unable to make the commitment because he *could not bring himself to assent to the required beliefs*—for example a belief in the last judgment (CV, 38).[35]

A further text often cited in favour of a non-cognitivist interpretation of Wittgenstein's view of religious belief is his remark that the assertion (i.e., in the ontological argument) that God's essence guarantees his existence 'really means ... that what is here at issue is not the existence of something [*daß es sich hier um eine Existenz nicht handelt*]' (CV, 82). It would be unwise, however, to read non-cognitivism into this, unless we propose to construe the most mainstream Catholic theologian, Aquinas, as a non-cognitivist. For on the standard conception found in Aquinas, God is not an individual being at all, not an 'entity' alongside the other entities in the world, but is rather the source of all being.[36] In other words, it is not as if the theist's inventory of the universe includes some extra item that is absent from the atheist's list. So far from seeming outrageously non-cognitivist or anti-realist, Wittgenstein's remark that in discussing God we are not dealing with 'eine Existenz' would seem entirely unproblematic to many orthodox theologians.[37]

[34] It is sometimes difficult to render in English the precise nuances of sentences like these, since the German word *Glaube* covers both belief and faith—something that caused problems for my translator when I recently presented a paper in Berlin on the theme of 'Idolatry, Faith and Belief' (Katholische Akademie, in association with Humboldt-Universität, Berlin, November 2006). I am grateful for the helpful comments received on that occasion, especially from Christoph Halbig and Martin Knechtges, which have helped me in my thinking about the present paper.

[35] This and other evidence is cited by Schroeder in 'The Tightrope Walker'.

[36] God is 'outside the realm of entities, as a cause that pours forth every entity in all its variant forms' ('extra ordinem entium existens, velut causa quaedam profundens totum ens et omnes eius differentias'). *Commentary on Aristotle's 'Peri Hermeneias'* [*Sententiae super Peri Hermeneias,* 1270–1], I, 14. Quoted in B. Davies, *Aquinas* (London: Continuum, 2002), 74. The divine simplicity, as Davies also explains, precludes talk of God as an individual (*Aquinas*, Ch. 7). See further Cottingham, 'What Difference Does it Make?'

[37] See for example Herbert McCabe, *Faith within Reason* (London: Continuum, 2006), *passim.*

Belief in God must, to be sure, lie at the centre of any theistic worldview. But it is worth noting that many of the analytic philosophical critics of theism (and a good many supporters too) appear to have a crude and distorted picture of what this means. 'May the Force be with you!' say the characters in the film *Star Wars*, implying that the Deity is a mysterious occult power who will assist the believer in achieving all sorts of successes. But much Christian theology is adamant in rejecting as idolatrous any conception of God as an active power within the universe. As the Dominican thinker Herbert McCabe put it, God is not a specific cause of events in the world: 'a hurricane leaves its thumbprint on the world, but God does not leave any such thumbprint.' Thus the famous argument from design turns out in McCabe's view to be 'silly', since you cannot pick out features of the world and proceed to attribute them to divine creation. What God does is to make the difference between existing and non-existing; and it is this 'elusive metaphysical notion' that is at the heart of true religious belief, not the simplistic and anthropomorphic notion of a cosmic designer: 'So far as the kind of world we have is concerned, the atheist and the theist will expect to see exactly the same features.'[38]

To those who prefer to dismiss religion from a safe distance, it may come as something of a surprise to see what practising theists such as McCabe actually say about God. There are many other examples. Blaise Pascal, a devoutly Christian philosopher, was quite blunt about our human inability to grasp either 'what God is or that he is'.[39] We might add, taking our cue from many writers in the long-standing 'apophatic' tradition of Christian thought,[40] that this does not have to be understood as merely an epistemic

[38] McCabe, *Faith within Reason*, 75–6. Compare Wittgenstein's own comment: 'God does not reveal himself in the world...It is not *how* things are in the world that is mystical, but *that* it exists' (TLP, 6.432, 6.44). (I am grateful to Hanjo Glock for drawing my attention to this parallel.)

[39] 'If there is a God, he is infinitely beyond our comprehension, since having neither parts nor limits he bears no relation to us. We are thus incapable of knowing either what he is or if he is.' Pascal, *Pensées*, ed. Lafuma, no. 418.

[40] ' "Apophaticism" is the name of that theology which is done against the background of human ignorance of the nature of God. It is the doing of theology in the light of the statement of Thomas Aquinas...that "we do not know what kind of being God is" (*Summa theologiae* I, q12, a. 13 ad 1). It is the conception of theology not as a naïve pre-critical ignorance of God, but as a kind of acquired ignorance, a *docta ignorantia* as Nicolas of Sues called it in the fifteenth century. It is the conception of theology as a strategy and practice of unknowing, as the fourteenth century English mystic called it [in *The Cloud of Unknowing*], who, we might say invented the transitive verb-form "to unknow" in order to describe theological knowledge in this deconstructive mode. Finally, "apophaticism" is the same as what the Latin tradition of Christian called the *via negativa*, the "negative way"... Apophasis is a Greek neologism for the breakdown of speech, which in the face of the unknowability of God falls

limitation, like our inability to grasp certain mysterious features of the cosmos such as the paradoxical nature of quantum particles. Rather it can be seen as an ontological barrier, stemming from the very being of God, whose nature is beyond the furthest limit of our thought. The theologian Jean-Luc Marion, whose apophaticism is particularly radical, would even baulk at the term 'ontological', since its normal connotations evoke the idea of the *nature* or *essence* of God. For Marion argues, in effect, that any attempt to determine the 'essence' or 'nature' of the ineffable God is simply a form of idolatry.[41] Anselm's celebrated formulation is also highly significant here: God is not the 'greatest conceivable being', but is 'id quo nihil maius cogitari potest'—'that than which nothing greater can be thought'. Like a necessarily receding horizon, God eludes the limits of our thought, so that any claim to bring him within the horizon of our human conceptions would be self-refuting: the purported achievement would be the best possible evidence that what had been brought within the horizon was not God, but a mere 'god'—an idol.

There is no space here to evaluate the coherence or otherwise of this kind of theology in which rational argument is intermingled with an acknowledgement of the mystical. For the present purpose, it will suffice to remember that Wittgenstein himself was clearly attracted in his early writings by what we have seen to be a fairly mainstream theological notion—the idea of religion as related to the domain of the ineffable (TLP, 6.522).[42] So far from retreating to a flabby form of non-cognitivism, it seems to me likely that his later thinking about religion preserves the central idea that our language about God cannot be construed as having straightforward propositional content (in the *Tractatus* sense), or

infinitely short of the mark.' Denys Turner, *The Darkness of God* (Cambridge: Cambridge University Press, 1995), 19.

[41] 'God cannot be seen, not only because nothing finite can bear his glory without perishing, but above all because a God that could be conceptually comprehended would no longer bear the title "God". It is not much to say that God remains God even if one is ignorant of his essence, his concept, and his presence—he remains God only on condition that this ignorance be established and admitted definitively. Every thing in the world gains by being known—but God who is not of the world, gains by not being known conceptually. The idolatry of the concept is the same as that of the gaze, imagining oneself to have attained God and to be capable of maintaining him under our gaze, like a thing of the world. And the Revelation of God consists first of all in cleaning the slate of this illusion and its blasphemy.' Jean-Luc Marion, 'In the Name', in J. D. Caputo and M. J. Scanlon (eds.), *God, the Gift, and Postmodernism* (Bloomington: Indiana University Press, 1999), 34.

[42] 'Es gibt allerdings Unaussprechliches. Dies zeigt sich, es ist das Mystische' ('There are indeed things that cannot be put into words. They *make themselves manifest*. They are what is mystical').

as asserting the existence of an item in the world. But none of this entails a radically non-realist conception of religious discourse; it is simply that we need to be careful to avoid assimilating the reality of God to the reality obtaining within the 'world'—the reality possessed by contingent things, or, in Wittgensteinian parlance, whatever happens to be 'the case'. Being religious is not a matter of proposing explanatory hypotheses about the world of a scientific or quasi-scientific kind, but rather of passionate commitment to a certain system of reference, a certain framework for interpreting the world. But this goes beyond *mere* expressivism, since adopting the framework in question does imply belief in God. It is, moreover, a framework that it may be reasonable, or at least not unreasonable, to adopt. In the next and final section of this essay, I shall attempt to unpack the crucial claims in these last three sentences, which lead us to what I take to be the heart of Wittgenstein's conception of religion.

7. Religion as a Framework of Interpretation

A religious person commits him or herself, according to Wittgenstein, 'to a system of co-ordinates' ('zu einem Koordinatensystem'). A variant reading has the more general phrase 'a system of reference' ('einem Bezugssystem') (CV, 73). What this means, according to John Hyman, is that the religious person makes a passionate commitment to the use of certain concepts. And just as, for example, the metric system cannot be verified, neither can a system or framework of religious concepts. 'A system of co-ordinates is . . . an intellectual apparatus we use to construct truths and falsehoods; it cannot itself be either true or false.'[43] There is a parallel here with the case of ethics, of which Wittgenstein's mature view appears to be that 'to make [ethical judgments] is to adopt a certain framework of action and justification, which itself cannot be justified'.[44]

  In so far as these observations may be taken to imply that Wittgenstein's view of religion is a non-cognitivist one, it seems to me they may be misleading. It is perfectly true that a system of reference or a system of measurement (for example the metric system) cannot itself

---

[43] Hyman, 'Wittgenstein'.   [44] Glock, *A Wittgenstein Dictionary*, s. v. 'Ethics'.

be called true or false in the sense that a given measurement within the system ('this stick is two metres long') may be true or false. The metric system does not itself belong in the complete set of true propositions expressing metric measurements; rather it is a framework that generates the possibility of such measurements. And it is also true that many advocates of the metric system are passionately committed to it. But none of this means that the metric system cannot be a perfectly valid and rationally defensible framework for dealing with the world. If we divide human language (somewhat artificially) into the cognitive and the affective, with the domain of rationally and epistemically justifiable modes of discourse on the one side, and mere arbitrary or entirely subjectively motivated expressions of emotion on the other, then the metric system and the decision to adopt it surely belong firmly in the former camp. To avoid misunderstanding, I should add that I do not mean here to challenge the general importance of the Wittgensteinian distinction between true or false statements within a system, and the structure of the system itself that makes such true or false statements possible. I simply wish to insert a caveat against the possible use of the label 'non-cognitive' in this context, if this is taken to imply that the adoption of a framework is something wholly arbitrary and beyond rational criticism or evaluation.

It is important to note in this connection that, as Hyman himself has pointed out, 'some systems are more useful, convenient and easy to understand and apply than others'.[45] This goes a good way to dispelling the otherwise damaging implication that to describe religious allegiance as commitment to a system of reference puts such commitment beyond rational evaluation. Moreover, there is, it seems to me, one further suggestive point about the comparison of religious faith to a 'reference system', which also pushes things in a more 'cognitivist' direction. Although a system of co-ordinates 'cannot itself be true or false' (as Hyman rightly notes), the adoption of such a system does nevertheless itself *presuppose* certain truths—for example, the actual reality of the standard posited by the system (the paradigm 'metre bar', or the properties of light in the more sophisticated redefined standard now used). In the same way, a religious 'system of reference' can be said to have cognitive implications (by

---

[45] 'The Gospel According to Wittgenstein', 8.

presupposing that supreme creative reality without which the system would make no sense), as well as being, for those who adopt it, a valuable and rationally defensible way of making sense of human life (though 'rationally defensible' here would not, as with the metrical case, be understood primarily in scientific and technological terms, but rather in moral and spiritual terms).

Wittgenstein's central insight, and it seems to me one with profound implications, is that the primary function of a religious outlook is to provide a framework for understanding and interpreting the world in which we find ourselves. The religious adherent confronts the same world as the atheist—a world of pain and suffering, a world of finitude and mortality, with all the fragility of goodness which that implies—and yet holds fast to a 'system of reference' which allows those potentially terrifying or depressing features to be viewed through the eyes of faith and hope. Does that phrase 'holds fast' imply a view of religion that tries to insulate it from all contact with evidence or argument? Certainly Wittgenstein dismissed the idea that something like the Resurrection could be established or refuted by appeal to a 'historic[al] basis in the sense that the ordinary belief in historic[al] facts could serve as a foundation' (LC, 57).[46] I take Wittgenstein's underlying point here to be the crucially important one that the role of evidence in religious commitment is entirely different from that which it occupies on the 'Humean' model—a dispassionate scrutiny of empirical probabilities based on past instances (the model which made Hume dryly observe that 'the Christian religion not only was at first attended with miracles, but even at this day cannot be believed by any reasonable person without one').[47] The kind of evidence which, for the believer, supports faith is not evidence assessed from a detached standpoint, but experience that is available only as a result of certain inner transformations. Saying this does *not* imply some kind of subjectivism about religious truth; it merely makes the point that there may be some truths

---

[46] Peter Winch's translation is slightly off target here (as indicated by my suggested addenda within square brackets). Compare the following piece of dialogue from that master of English nuance, John Le Carré (the context is that the spymasters are trying to muzzle the press to damp down any scandal about the murder of one of their agents): 'Yes, sir, an "extinct case of purely historic concern'', sir,' Strickland went on into the telephone . . . 'Am I on target there Oliver?'. '*Historical*', Lacon corrected him irritably. 'Not *historic* concern. That's the last thing we want.' *Smiley's People* (London: Pan Books, 1980), 45.

[47] David Hume, *An Enquiry concerning Human Understanding* [1748], Section X.

whose *accessibility conditions* include certain requirements as to the attitude of the subject.[48]

To introduce the idea of a special kind of evidence requiring the need for 'inner transformation' may look to some people like a fallback position—a hastily devised escape route for the beleaguered modern theist who has been forced by Humean and other Enlightenment critics of religion to abandon the straightforward factualism about, for example, the Resurrection that characterized the simpler, if more naïve, devout faith of the past. In a stimulating recent study, however, the theologian Sarah Coakley has convincingly shown that even if we go back to earliest times, to the New Testament narratives, we find the need for inner 'epistemic transformation' presented as a prerequisite for witnessing the Resurrection. The story in Matthew does not (as a modern spin doctor might perhaps do) enhance the dossier with overwhelming 'objective' evidence, but adds the telling phrase 'but some doubted' even in the very sentence that reports the Galilee appearance (Matthew 28:17). The narrative in John of the appearance in the locked room on the Sunday after Easter suggests that 'some change in one's normal demands for perceptual evidences' were needed to recognize the risen body (John 20:24–8). And the Emmaus story in Luke implies that 'a narrowly noetic investigation would take one *nowhere* in this quest', and that 'evidences of the heart . . . could not be neglected if Christ-as-risen were to be apprehended' (Luke 24:28–35).[49]

In Wittgensteinian terms, we may say that these early disciples seized passionately upon a new framework of interpretation: what had seemed the total failure of a horrible and humiliating execution was now perceived as the prelude to the triumphant proclamation of a message of hope. But does

---

[48] For more on the idea of 'accessibility conditions', see Cottingham, 'What Difference Does it Make?' Compare also Cottingham, *The Spiritual Dimension*, Ch. 5: '[S]uch experience does not qualify as "evidence" in the sense that it is available for impartial assessment or repeatable experimentation. As in many areas of human existence, it evades such detached scrutiny, since it is the fruit of a living commitment. But that does not mean it can be dismissed as "merely subjective". A lifetime of musical discipline may enable the committed musician to discern profundities and beauties of musical form that are in large part quite literally inaccessible to the novice; but that does not mean that they are mere idiosyncrasies of subjective feeling. On the contrary they are genuine responses to a transpersonal reality—it simply takes a lifetime of the appropriate *askesis* to acquire the capacity to appreciate them. And so it may be with spiritual experience' (pp. 138–9).

[49] Sarah Coakley, *Powers and Submissions: Spirituality, Philosophy and Gender* (Oxford: Blackwell, 2002), 140. Coakley's discussion includes an insightful chapter entitled 'Wittgenstein and Resurrection Epistemology' to which I am indebted in this part of the paper.

this kind of interpretive shift involve no cognitive change—no change in belief contents? This would surely be an implausible position, since the early disciples, and subsequent Christians, in adopting such a framework, surely *did* shift their beliefs: with the new framework went a return from despair to faith in God, and a belief that his power was manifested in the risen Christ. Wittgenstein was unable to embrace the framework, since, as he himself observed, he was unable to make the belief shift (CV, 51). *But he did believe the belief shift could occur.* This is clearly shown by one of his most pregnant remarks: 'Life can educate one to a belief in God' (CV, 86).

8.   Coda: Life can Educate one to a Belief in God

Let me close with what seems to me a powerful example from Tolstoy of the phenomenon to which Wittgenstein pointed, of being 'educated by life to a belief in God'. Konstantin Levin, husband in the relatively secure marriage portrayed in *Anna Karenina* as a counterpart to the eponymous heroine's ill-fated one, has been waiting for his pregnant wife Kitty, who is long overdue, to give birth. After a troubled night, punctuated with a protracted argument triggered by his wife's anxious jealousy (Levin has come in late after an evening drinking at his club, followed by a visit with friends to the house of the captivating but emotionally disturbed Anna), the labour suddenly begins. Levin is at once in torment.

'Kostya, please don't be frightened, it's nothing. I'm not afraid at all,' she said, seeing his frightened face, and she pressed his hand to her breast, then to her lips.

He hastily jumped out of bed, unaware of himself and not taking his eyes off her, put on his dressing gown . . . Her flushed face, surrounded by soft hair coming from under her night-cap, shone with joy and resolution.

However little unnaturalness and conventionality there was in Kitty's character generally, Levin was still struck by what was uncovered to him now, when all the veils were suddenly taken away and the very core of her soul shone in her eyes. And in that simplicity and nakedness she, the very one he loved, was still more visible. She looked at him and smiled, but suddenly her eyebrows twitched, she raised her head, and quickly going up to him, took his hand and pressed all of herself to him, so that he could feel her hot breath on him. She was suffering and seemed to be complaining to him of her suffering . . .

'I'm going to the doctor now. Do we need anything else? Shall I send for Dolly?'

'Yes, yes, Go, go', she said quickly, frowning and waving her hand at him.

He was going into the drawing room when he suddenly heard a pitiful, instantly fading moan from the bedroom. He stopped and for a long time could not understand.

'Yes, it's she,' he said to himself and, clutching his head, he ran down the stairs.

'Lord, have mercy, forgive us, help us!', he repeated words that somehow suddenly came to his lips. And he, an unbeliever, repeated these words not just with his lips. Now, in that moment, he knew that neither all his doubts nor the impossibility he knew in himself of believing by means of reason, hindered him in the least from addressing God. It all blew off his soul like dust. To whom was he to turn if not to Him in whose hands he felt himself, his soul and his love to be?[50]

All sorts of dismissive interpretations of this passage may occur to the sceptical mind. Perhaps Levin is so beside himself with anxiety that he goes against his better judgement and indulges in a superstitious ritual that he rationally knows can do no good.[51] But that deflationary reading will not survive serious scrutiny of the text and its full context. Levin has always loved Kitty, but previously in a fierce, possessive and somewhat controlling way that made him genuinely miserable when (earlier in the novel) he thought his suit would not be successful. At the start of the crucial episode of her confinement he has lapsed into a sort of complacency: the earlier torments of courtship are over, and Kitty is now his devoted wife, happily involved in her domestic pursuits and preparation for impending motherhood. But now Levin's perceptions undergo a radical shift. As the pangs of labour begin to shake her, and he is confronted with the mysterious process of childbirth, and the very real danger that process poses to her own life, he sees for the first time her true beauty and integrity. In that moment, his heart is opened to the mystery and fragility and wonder and terror of life and of love, and he begins to pray. His

[50] Leo Tolstoy, *Anna Karenina* [1873–7], trans. R. Pevear and L. Volokhonsky (London: Penguin, 2001), Part VII, Ch. 13.

[51] Tolstoy, with typical honesty, shows Levin later in the novel raising just this doubt to himself. But he eventually dismisses the doubt as a piece of bad faith. 'He could not admit that he had known the truth then and was now mistaken . . . because he cherished his state of soul of that time, and by admitting that it had been due to weakness he would have profaned those moments.' (*Anna Karenina*, 787; from Part VIII, Ch. 9).

decision could never have been arrived at by cold scrutiny of the evidence; indeed, Levin knows in himself the 'impossibility in himself of believing by means of reason'. But only a religious framework is now adequate for interpreting the momentous truths to which his heart has now been opened. He prays to God, and repeats the words 'not just with his lips'. He believes.

It is important to underline that what Levin undergoes is not a 'religious experience' in the sense of a vision of angels or other supernatural influences, but rather a certain opening of the heart, and an associated heightening of moral awareness. Tolstoy, with great delicacy and a keen insight into the nature of the religious journey, resists the temptation to present the reader with a neat 'once for all' moment of change. Further anxieties, further intellectual agonizings, and further deepenings of moral and emotional awareness, are needed in order to consolidate Levin's new-found faith. At the close of the novel he is able to declare to himself: 'This new feeling hasn't changed me, hasn't made me happy or suddenly enlightened, as I dreamed—just like the feeling for my son. Nor was there any surprise. And faith or not faith—I don't know what it is—but this feeling has entered into me just as imperceptibly through suffering and has firmly lodged itself in my soul.'[52] Life has educated him to a belief in God.

The moral, perhaps, for analytic philosophers and others who have agonized over the 'the great cry of "I would like to believe but unfortunately I cannot"' is that their problem can never be resolved in the study. By drawing on Wittgenstein's subtle analysis of religious allegiance, we have perhaps been able to see a little more clearly just why this should be so. Konstantin Levin was able to make the religious commitment, with its associated belief shift, partly because he had been inducted as a child into forms of religious praxis which had made the framework he embraced accessible to him, and given it shape and significance. The other necessary condition for his conversion, also a form of education, was the 'education' provided by 'life'—the actual structure of the perception-changing experiences he underwent during his wife's confinement and in the phase of his life that followed it. For Wittgenstein himself, things were not so easy: neither his upbringing nor the course of his life had quite equipped him to take such a step. Given that, he may have been being unduly hard on

---

[52] *Anna Karenina*, 817; from Part VIII, Ch. 19.

himself in an enigmatic comment from a manuscript of 1937, which it is perhaps not too fanciful to see as a characteristically harsh self-judgement on his inability to enter the promised land that he had marked out with such clarity: 'The *edifice of your pride has* to be dismantled. And that means frightful work' (CV, 30).[53]

---

[53] 'Das *Gebäude Deines Stolzes* ist abzutragen. Und das gibt furchtbare Arbeit.' I am most grateful to John Hyman and Hanjo Glock for perceptive comments on an earlier draft of this paper. Their reactions have been most encouraging, even though I know I have failed to convince them on certain points.

Hard and Easy Questions about Consciousness

JOHN DUPRÉ

Introduction

After a quiet period for much of the twentieth century, presumably reflecting the influence of various forms of behaviourism, in recent years philosophical writing on consciousness has reached epidemic proportions. A well-known philosophical website[1] lists almost a thousand online articles on the philosophy of consciousness, and no doubt there are another thousand not so available. This writing has, however, had a quite peculiar focus. A founding document of recent philosophical studies of consciousness is Thomas Nagel's classic article 'What is it Like to be a Bat?'[2] The almost universally accepted answer to this question nowadays is that although there is definitely something it is like to be a bat, it is extraordinarily difficult, perhaps impossible, to say exactly what this is. More difficult still is the problem of explaining how this ineffable something could somehow have resulted, as it is almost universally agreed it must, from the merely mechanical operations of the brain. This latter conundrum, in particular, has come to be known as the Hard Problem of consciousness—in contrast with the apparently 'Easy Problem'[3] of understanding the relevant mechanical operations of the brain—and has provided the motivation for a great deal of the philosophical work I have mentioned.

---

[1] <http://consc.net/online.html>. This website is maintained by David Chalmers, who is credited with naming the Hard Problem mentioned below. Despite this potentially partial source, I think it fairly represents the concentration of philosophical effort in the area.

[2] T. Nagel, 'What is it Like to Be a Bat?', *Philosophical Review*, 83 (1974), 435–50.

[3] These terms appear to have originated in a much admired paper by David Chalmers at the 1994 conference 'Toward a Science of Consciousness' in Tucson, which inaugurated a biennial series of meetings that has continued to the present.

Of course there are quite different kinds of academic work also directed to the topic of consciousness. I shall touch briefly, for example, on the work of psychologist Merlin Donald, who as well as offering some illuminating ideas about how we should understand the place of consciousness in our mental economies has little time for the Hard Problem. The Hard Problem, he remarks, is 'nothing more than a local squabble between members of a species who are already able to represent what they know or don't know in words. The thing that really needs explaining is how a particular species (humans) came to be able to have such squabbles in the first place.'[4] The question [of] what consciousness does, and thereby how it might have evolved, seems an obviously promising one. But the devotees of the Hard Problem have actually tended to rule out this approach, since they take the (unconscious) whirring of neural cogs as being sufficient to explain everything that humans can do, and consciousness therefore to be no more than an epiphenomenal gloss on this real neurological action.[5] Consciousness is defined as being subjective, and the physicalism embraced by most contemporary philosophers holds that science—which is confidently expected to explain everything—is objective. So there is no room for consciousness to do anything or explain anything.

Donald's account of the human mind, of the central role within it of consciousness, and of what the latter should help us to explain has more to commend it than merely the acknowledgement that it might explain something. For example, and contrary to a line being very effectively promulgated by evolutionary psychologists, he notes the remarkable flexibility of the human mind, and the consequent possibility of recognizing the great changes—evolutionary changes, even—that have happened to human minds in the last few millennia. As well as elaborating these points, Donald eloquently explains the still insufficiently unappreciated extent to which our minds are a product of the unparalleled complexity of our cultures, and acknowledges how much of what our minds enable us to do depends on the existence of resources external to the individual mind.[6] The centrality of consciousness to understanding the capacities of the human mind is,

[4] M. Donald, *A Mind So Rare: The Evolution of Human Consciousness* (New York: W. W. Norton, 2001).

[5] See D. Chalmers, *The Conscious Mind: In Search of a Fundamental Theory* (New York: Oxford University Press, 1996), 160.

[6] On the preceding points, see also my *Human Nature and the Limits of Science* (Oxford: Oxford University Press, 2001).

indeed, the main point of Donald's book (2001), and this role is defended specifically against those philosophers who have treated consciousness as non-existent or epiphenomenal and inefficacious.

I think Donald's defence is convincing. One of my objectives in the present essay is to understand better the origins of the curious idea that consciousness might be a fortunate accident, something we could manage perfectly well without, an idea that is central to the dominant place of the Hard Problem and related matters in philosophical discussions of consciousness. One way of understanding this strange state of affairs, I shall argue, is to see that much of this discussion of consciousness remains mired in problems from the seventeenth century that we should by now have left behind. After this critical discussion, I shall more briefly recommend for philosophical consideration a concept relatively neglected by philosophers, but one that is central to Donald's account of consciousness, attention. But before we can begin to address the question what is the function of consciousness or, relatedly, how consciousness might have evolved, we need to reach some understanding of what it is that has this function or, presumably, evolved: there is not even much agreement what consciousness is. No doubt this is one reason why philosophers have taken such an interest in the topic.

The Hard Problem

One natural starting point would be the following thought. At any moment there are some things of which I am actively conscious and others of which I am not; and many of those things of which I am not conscious are things of which I could be conscious if I attended to them or brought them to mind. There are presently a large number of objects within my visual field—tables, chairs, books, piles of paper, etc.—and if a book fell off the shelf or a pile of paper blew over, it would immediately attract my attention. However, my consciousness is entirely absorbed by my computer screen or, occasionally, owing to my impoverished typing skills, by my fingers and the keyboard. The vast majority of things I know or believe are not currently present to my mind, and there are many aspects of my immediate environment to which I am paying no attention. There are obvious questions, both empirical and conceptual, about the nature, function and consequences of this feature of the mind, questions that also have clear relevance to discussions of the evolution of consciousness. I shall return briefly to these important and interesting questions later in this essay.

However, by far the largest part of this enormous literature addresses a cluster of issues responding to what is widely seen as the deep philosophical problem about consciousness, the Hard Problem mentioned above. Indeed, so deep is this problem felt to be that some philosophers have declared that it is in principle insoluble and must be accepted, somewhat in the manner of parts of Catholic theology, as a mystery.[7] I mentioned that the Hard Problem is generally formulated as concerning the way in which the phenomena of consciousness could arise from the occurrence of 'merely' physical, mechanical processes, specifically processes in the brain.[8] This Hard Problem of consciousness is understood as concerning the very possibility of conscious experience in a material universe and indeed has led some philosophers, most notably David Chalmers, to embrace a kind of dualism.[9]

The Hard Problem concerns what is often called phenomenal consciousness. In a recent survey article, Uriah Kriegel defines the extent of the problem as follows: 'Phenomenal consciousness is the property [that] mental states, events and processes have when, and only when, there is something it is like for their subject to undergo them, or be in them.'[10] One should already find this heady stuff. 'There is something it is like to F' is an unusual form of words, and that there should be a property that attaches to the mental state if, and only if, there is something it is like to undergo it, is even more peculiar. More of this later.

I have referred to this as a cluster of problems, and indeed there are a number of similar problems of this kind widely discussed. As I have mentioned, the canonical source of the 'something it is like' talk, is Thomas Nagel's famous paper 'What is it Like to be a Bat?' As David Chalmers puts it, 'In [the] central sense of "consciousness", an organism

---

[7] Colin McGinn, *Consciousness and its Objects* (Oxford: Oxford University Press, 2004).

[8] I should note, in passing, that I am deeply suspicious of the description of the brain as mechanism, though this concept is now being rethought by some philosophers in ways intended to make it more congenial to the nature of biological, and especially neurological, processes (see e.g. P. K. Machamer, L. Darden and C. F. Craver, 'Thinking about Mechanisms', *Philosophy of Science*, 57 (2000), 1–25). It does, however, further illustrate the extent to which much of this philosophical discussion is still conducted in the terms of the seventeenth century.

[9] See especially Chalmers, *The Conscious Mind*.

[10] Uriah Kriegel, 'Consciousness, Theories of', *Philosophy Compass*, 1 (2006), 58–64.

is conscious if there is something it is like to be that organism, and a mental state is conscious if there is something it is like to be in that state.'[11] Chalmers proposes reserving the word 'consciousness' for the sense assumed in this problem and referring to the various 'easy' problems as concerning awareness. These latter, including, for example, the ability to discriminate aspects of the environment, the ability to report on one's mental states, the ability to control behaviour and the difference between being awake and asleep, are easy because, as he judges, they seem suited to the standard empirical methods of cognitive science. By contrast, according to Chalmers and many others, we have no idea how to go about investigating the Hard Problem.

Defusing the Hard Problem

One might mention in passing that the easy problems are a remarkably diverse bunch, and certainly do not look all that easy—I shall return to some of these later. But it is the Hard Problem with which I shall mostly be concerned here. And, to get straight to the point, my suggestion is that the Hard Problem, as it has generally been formulated, is not a problem at all; indeed most formulations of it, bluntly put, make little or no sense. I certainly should not claim to be the first person to have made such a claim. One notable instance, and one to which the following discussion will be greatly indebted, is a contribution to this philosophical industry by Peter Hacker in a paper entitled 'Is there Anything it is Like to be a Bat?', and expanded considerably as part of the important book that Hacker coauthored with the distinguished neuroscientist Max Bennett.[12] This paper, with characteristic acuity and wit, confirmed my intuition that Nagel's question, or at least the predominant reaction to it, was deeply confused.

A glance at Google Scholar suggests that Hacker's 2002 paper was entirely ignored by the philosophical consciousness community. The book

---

[11] D. Chalmers, 'Facing up to the Problem of Consciousness', *Journal of Consciousness Studies*, 2 (1995), 200–19.

[12] P. M. S. Hacker, *Philosophy*, 77 (2002), 157–74; M. R. Bennett and P. M. S. Hacker, *Philosophical Foundations of Neuroscience* (Oxford and Malden, Mass.: Blackwell, 2003). Another person suspicious of the Hard Problem, though for quite different reasons, is Daniel Dennett (see his *Consciousness Explained* (London: Little, Brown, 1991)).

with Bennett has, on the other hand, been quite widely discussed though mainly by psychologists and neuroscientists rather than philosophers. It did, however, give rise to a session at the 2005 Eastern Division meeting of the American Philosophical Association, at which it was criticized by Daniel Dennett and John Searle, and this, in turn, has led to a book in which Hacker, Bennett, Dennett and Searle debate the issues further.[13] So it may be that the kinds of problems that Hacker so clearly explained in 2002 will have some impact on this burgeoning field. One objective of this essay will be to try to contribute to such an outcome. I shall also reflect a little on why the kinds of arguments Hacker marshalled appear to have had so little effect on most contemporary philosophizing and, from there, reflect briefly on the nature of the proper relation between philosophy and science.

So what were these arguments? Hacker asked, as the title of his 2002 paper indicates, whether there was anything it is like to be a bat. As the impact of Nagel's original paper shows, the expression 'what it is like to be a bat' has immediate resonance with many readers. However, there is an immediate and obvious ambiguity. Does the question ask what it is like for a person—say myself—to be a bat, or what it is like for a bat to be a bat? The problem with the first reading is that it is quite impossible to see how I could be a bat—and if I couldn't be a bat, there is nothing it would be like for me to be one.

One might reflect, in this context, on Kafka's famous story about a man waking up to find that he had turned into a cockroach. Of course he had really done nothing of the sort. He had perhaps grown a shiny carapace, six legs and a pair of antennae, all of which, though no doubt biologically impossible, is surely imaginable. But no cockroach lies in bed recalling that the day before it had been human. The reflections that Gregor Samsa enters into after this appalling discovery make it quite clear that he feels, more or less, like himself; it is just that horrible things have happened to his body. A human who really turned into a cockroach or a bat would no longer be a human, and hence would not be able to experience what it is like for a human to be a bat: there is fairly clearly no such thing (logically no such thing) as a human having the experience of a beetle or a bat. The

<hr />

[13] M. R. Bennett, D. C. Dennett, P. M. S. Hacker and J. Searle, *Neuroscience and Philosophy: Brain, Mind, and Language* (New York: Columbia University Press, 2007). As Akeel Bilgrami notes on the dust-jacket, to persuade Dennett and Searle, widely known as philosophical antagonists, to join forces in their opposition to your views is a remarkable achievement in philosophical controversy.

importance of this point is just that the intuitive attraction of the question, 'What is it like to be a bat?' surely derives in part from the (inevitably failed and confused) attempt to imagine (oneself) being a bat. The attempt is confused because if one really became a bat one would surely no longer be oneself.

So it seems that what is at issue must be what it feels like for a bat to be a bat. But this is also a problematic question, and in so far as it makes sense at all, it doesn't make the sense intended by Nagel and his philosophical successors. One can very well describe what it is like to be a bat: you live in a cave or a belfry hanging upside down and flying out at night to catch insects, or eat fruit, or whatever, depending on what kind of bat you are. Moreover, as was famously described by Donald Griffin, you find your way about using a kind of sonar. But of course that isn't what the questioner wants to know. In fact anything it is possible to say about what it is like to be a bat will, in so far as it is intelligible by both speaker and hearer, fail to satisfy the intended request. If it can be said and understood, it is something objectively describable, not the subjective and indescribable thing we are looking for.

In normal parlance, the question 'What is it like to be a bat?'—for a bat to be bat, that is—calls for the kind of answer which I just sketched, but which evidently misses the questioner's intent. One intends, perhaps, to ask, what it feels like to be a bat, but then it is again rather doubtful whether there is any answer: it takes a little work, at any rate, to convince me that there is something—surely not just one thing—it feels like to be me. Now it is true that there is a perfectly good form of question 'What is it like for an X to be a Y?' To take one of Hacker's examples, we might ask, 'What is it like for a woman to be a soldier?', expecting to be told of the particular difficulties and perhaps advantages that face a woman in the military life. And in fact the perfectly sensible question 'What is it like to be soldier?' could be taken as equivalent to the question 'What is it like for a person to be a soldier?', an expansion we omit because the class of possible soldiers we had in mind is so obvious as not to require specification. But one restriction on this form of question appears to be that X cannot be the same as Y. 'What is it like for a soldier to be a soldier?' seems decidedly odd (for certainly no one besides a soldier could be a soldier), and is surely at best an eccentric way of posing the question 'What is it like (for a person) to be a soldier?' And this, just as with the normal understanding of the question 'What is it like to be a bat?', seems to call simply for a straightforward description of the characteristic patterns, activities and experiences of the soldier's life.

We might, of course, go on to ask—presumably a soldier—what it *felt like* to be a soldier. To which he, or she, might reply, for instance, 'Wonderful! I'm so proud to be serving my country', or 'Horrible, I'm constantly afraid that I may be called upon to kill people', etc. As Hacker reminds us, there is a perfectly standard and unmysterious question about what it feels like to experience something, but again this is equally clearly not what the philosophical questioner is looking for. It is true that we can't ask the bat what it feels like to be a bat, but this does nothing to restore the mystery, for if it were, *per impossibile*, to answer 'Wonderful, it's such a fantastic sensation to soar down on unsuspecting and delicious mosquitoes', we would have had an answer no more puzzling than those imagined for the soldier. Even if the bat could speak, it could no more tell us what it is like to be a bat than I could tell you what it is like to be John Dupré—in the sense imagined by the consciousness theorist.

The reason for this, I have been suggesting, is quite straightforward: there is no such thing. Indeed, much of this 'what it is like' talk seems a perfect illustration of what is sometimes referred to as the fallacy of reification. From the possibility, sometimes, of saying what it is like to have particular experiences, we conclude that there is something that this is like, and we then try to characterize this entity. But the entity is no more than an unwanted consequence of some linguistic sleight of hand. There are many things to say about being a bat, but the description of some indescribable internal phenomenal quality is not among them.

It is no surprise that these hypothetical feelings-like do not do any-thing—this is of course why they are so hard to track down. Indeed, not doing anything might almost be their defining quality. This is the premise of what is sometimes said to be the most compelling argument for phenom-enal consciousness, the notorious zombie argument. The zombie argument proposes that there could be creatures like us in every respect, but lacking any phenomenal consciousness. They talk and act just like humans but, so it is said, inside is only darkness. They have no phenomenal consciousness and there is nothing it is like to be a zombie. Since we are not zombies—it is apparently brilliantly lit inside *our* heads—we are faced with the problem of saying exactly what it is that distinguishes us from zombies. And this, it is claimed, is the problem of phenomenal consciousness.

Qualia

Rather than confront zombies directly, let me say something about the most crucial kind of thing that we are supposed to have in our heads, but that zombies lack, qualia. Qualia, a central part of the stock in trade of philosophers grappling with the Hard Problem, have, it seems, two very different philosophical genealogies. On the one hand, and in the context of the present debates over consciousness, they are the things it is like to have particular perceptual experiences. As Ned Block puts it: 'Qualia include the ways things look, sound and smell, the way it feels to have a pain and, more generally, what it's like to have experiential mental states.'[14] But they also have an ancestry in theories of perception dating from the seventeenth-century way of ideas and leading to twentieth-century sense-data theories. In this tradition sense-data, for example, were the direct objects of perception. One did not see red objects 'directly', but rather inferred their existence from red sense-data. For many reasons these theories of perception have been abandoned. J. L. Austin's critique of the theory in *Sense and Sensibilia* was only the most brilliant such exercise.[15] No doubt some of the philosophical accounts of perception that have replaced sense-data theories have equally serious difficulties, but that is not my concern here. My present point is that these two histories give one a plausible account of how we got to the present philosophical orthodoxy. Although sense-data no longer serve their original central function, that of providing an account of perception, their existence has not come to seem any less plausible. Not least because it is probably the best understood area of neuroscience, scientifically minded philosophers are generally inclined nowadays to discuss perception in terms of reflectances, light waves and neural processing. The sense-data that used to serve an essential purpose in this area hang around as unemployed nomological danglers, forlornly hoping for a new function. Where once they were the objects of perception, now they are a brilliant but useless sideshow to perception.

The ontology remains the same; only the roles played by the various entities have changed. On the past view the mind's eye perceived the

---

[14] N. Block, 'Qualia', in S. Guttenplan (ed.), *A Companion to Philosophy of Mind* (Oxford: Blackwell, 1994).

[15] Oxford: Oxford University Press, 1962.

sense-datum, and on the basis of this perception the mind reached conclusions about the external world and thence made appropriate decisions about behaviour: my mind's eye sees an image of a lamp-post increasing rapidly in size, and instructs the limbs to change direction to avoid walking into the real lamp-post that caused this image. Nowadays we are inclined to see the brain as doing all this without any help from the poor mind. The brain processes light rays reflected from the lamp-post and it sends the orders to the limbs to change direction. The image has no work to do in this picture, which is why it seems mere luck that we did not, like zombies, find ourselves without any. All they do is light up the insides of our heads—which is no doubt a good thing as the life of a zombie seems distinctly dull—but the only things there are to see inside our heads, unfortunately, are the light sources themselves.

So am I suggesting that there isn't really anything it is like to see red, say? Not exactly. For a start, a literal interpretation of this question might invite the remark that seeing red is a bit like seeing orange, only less yellow—though it is doubtful whether there is any point in saying this, except perhaps to someone wholly colour-blind. But in fact—and here again I follow Hacker—the usual expectation when one asks 'What is it like to perceive X?' is some kind of emotional evaluation. Thus, what is it like to smell coffee? Delicious. Or, what is it like to smell the latrines? Disgusting. And so on. Apart from lacking the philosophical depth generally expected of answers to such questions, this interpretation suggests that for many percepts there is nothing it is like to perceive them. As I walk down the street and perceive, and thus avoid colliding with, the lamp-post I have no emotional response to it at all. Which is why, of course, I am unlikely to be asked, on successfully negotiating this length of street, 'What was it like to see the lamp-post?'

Despite the lack of depth, these banal answers to 'What is it like?' questions have one overwhelming advantage. They point to the efficacious nature of these qualities of experience. The delicious smell of the coffee may be instrumental in moving me rapidly towards the kitchen whence it emanates. The foul smell of the latrines may discourage me from volunteering for latrine duty. And no doubt my association of certain experiences with pleasurable or unpleasurable feelings or emotions will sometimes motivate much more complex trains of action designed to reproduce the experiences with which these feelings have been associated in the past. From this point of view there is no mystery about there being something some perceptions or sensations are like, nor as to the efficaciousness of these associated feelings or emotions.

But of course theorists of consciousness are not much moved by such remarks. As I have described, they do not answer the hard, deep problem that is thought to be at stake. For surely, even if our language annoyingly has difficulty in formulating the question that has the right kind of answer, there really are those things it is like to be a bat or see red. Another classic thought experiment to reinforce this intuition is the inverted spectrum. Might it not be the case that the way red things look to me, say, might be the same as the way blue things look to you? Contemporary qualia theorists generally do think of this as a perfectly conceivable possibility: my red quale might be indistinguishable from your blue quale. It is admittedly too bad that there is no way of finding out. But we can't find out what's going on outside our lightcone either, and that doesn't mean that nothing is.

The first thing I want to note about this argument is that it confirms the continuity of these views of perception with those of the seventeenth century. Suppose we ask which are the primary bearers of colours: objects in the world, or entities of some kind in the mind? Clearly the seventeenth-century philosophers thought the latter. Locke, for example, thought that physical objects were, literally, colourless.[16] An alternative and more defensible view is that colours pertain to things, and only derivatively to such mental entities as afterimages or imagined scenes. Green is the colour of grass, not the colour of some private quale that grass, if I am lucky, will correctly match.[17] Of course, I could have some peculiar neural condition such that tomatoes looked blue—they might look the colour of the sky, for instance. But that I might be born with experiences of blue invariably connected to experiences of (what everyone else experienced as) red is an unintelligible hypothesis. For 'experiences of blue' can mean only the

---

[16] At any rate, colours as they pertain to objects are powers to produce sensations in our minds, and generally Locke identifies the colour with the sensation rather than the power. Forthright versions of such a view are far from uncommon today. No less an authority on perception than Richard Gregory, for instance, is quoted as saying, 'one . . . projects colours onto objects—they're not, of course, themselves coloured' (in S. Blackmore, *Conversations on Consciousness* (Oxford: Oxford University Press, 2005), 107.)

[17] Anyone to whom this is not obvious will need to refer to the classic arguments especially in Wittgenstein's *Philosophical Investigations*. The private internal quale as the definitive sample of a colour is of course a standard example of the kind of postulate the private language argument shows to be incoherent.

experiences produced by observing blue things. Might the qualia theorist think of colours as applying equally, and in just the same way, to mental and external entities? In that case it would, I suppose, be a matter of good luck that when we saw red things they gave rise to red rather than blue qualia. The absurdity of this supposition is enough, I hope, to show that we must see colours as primarily qualifying either internal or external entities. If the latter, then the inverted spectrum problem cannot arise: red images are just images the colour of tomatoes and suchlike. Hence it appears that contemporary defenders of inverted spectra are committed to the idea that colours are primarily tied to internal entities, which explains my suggestion that they have remained remarkably true to the seventeenth-century way of thinking. On a more contemporary understanding that colours are in the first place attributes of objects, the inverted spectrum doesn't arise. And at the same time one central intuition behind the existence of qualia is defused.

A natural response to all of this might be to ask whether, if there are no qualia, or 'what-it-is-likes', we are no different from zombies. Zombies, after all, are just like us except that they lack phenomenal consciousness. If there is no such thing as phenomenal consciousness in the intended sense, then it appears that we are indeed just like zombies. Of course, I have not said that we are not conscious, so the real question is whether there is anything that the zombie could be missing and that we possess, that would nevertheless leave it able to do all the things described in the so-called easy problems. What I have said so far shows just that phenomenal consciousness is not an adequate conception to establish the difference between us and zombies or, therefore, the coherence of the possibility of zombies.

A first point worth noting, in relation to the familiar characterization of zombies as being 'dark inside', is that on the whole it doesn't seem to me that it is light on the inside of my head. In bright daylight, it seems to me that the light is on the outside, and in pitch dark it seems dark both inside and outside. It is customary to respond to the apparent externality of perceptions by adverting to hallucinations and suchlike. But of course hallucinations are, perhaps even by definition, somewhat similar to perceptions. My hallucination of a pink elephant does not appear to be inside my head, not least but not only because my head isn't big enough to contain an elephant. One might, as a last resort, consider phenomena such as afterimages, or possibly the stars that people are said to see following a sharp blow to the head, which might perhaps be described with reference to internal lights, though even apart from tending to be on the dim side, my own experience of such things is that they seem to be located, if anywhere, just in front of the eyes.

But returning to the more standard case, would it seem dark *outside* to a zombie? My immediate thought is that if a zombie were just like us except that it was dark outside, it would keep bumping into and stumbling over things, which most of us do only rarely. If a zombie were, apart from the inside lights, just like us, in broad daylight it would seem to it to be light outside—as evidenced by the ease with which it avoided bumping into things and, for that matter, its tendency to report, if asked, that it was light. I would say that just like us it would be neither light nor dark inside; provided perception is understood as a relation to external rather than internal objects, lightness and darkness are qualities of the external world rather than the internal. A more productive response to the zombie argument, then, is to provide a more adequate account of consciousness than that centred on qualia and the like, and thereby demonstrate that to be indistinguishable from us zombies would need to have an interesting and sophisticated form of consciousness.

Consciousness and Attention

Having easily disposed of the so-called Hard Problem, the Easy Problem will hardly be so easy to solve. The important point so far is just that the 'easy' problems will not be merely hard but impossible to solve if they are seen as intertwined with a network of imaginary entities and 'what-it-is-likes'. So this essay so far should be seen as a bit of routine Lockean underlabouring, clearing the ground for better-directed scientific investigation. The point of Lockean underlabouring is to allow the construction of sounder and more useful edifices that can replace the inadequate ones whose rubble the underlabourers have disposed of. I cannot hope here to build any sort of useful edifice. I shall, though, make a suggestion as to one promising site for such an erection.

David Chalmers has offered several examples of what he considers easy problems about consciousness—easy, he says, because 'There is no real issue about whether *these* phenomena can be explained scientifically. All of them are straightforwardly vulnerable to explanation in terms of computational or neural mechanisms.' His examples are: the ability to discriminate, categorize and react to environmental stimuli; the integration of information by a cognitive system; the reportability of mental states; the ability of a system to access its own internal states; the focus of attention; the deliberate control of behaviour; and the difference between wakefulness and sleep.[18]

This is a motley bunch, and one question one might begin with is the variable extent to which these are really problems about consciousness. The ability to discriminate, categorize and react to environmental stimuli, for example, poses a wide variety of questions, but none that obviously has a lot to do with consciousness. At the neurological level it is an area in which a great deal of progress in understanding has been achieved; at the psychological and philosophical level there is much to be said about what discriminations we are able to make, and what we are doing when we categorize on the basis of such discriminations. That we are conscious—i.e., in this context, aware—seems to be a background assumption of such issues rather than a central aspect of the research. At the other extreme the difference between wakefulness and sleep is pretty clearly connected to consciousness, since in one case one is conscious and in the other not, but the interesting functional question here is presumably about the value of not being conscious—sleeping—rather than of consciousness.

My last remark points to an everyday sense of 'consciousness' that has little to do with the epiphenomenal hangers on of 'phenomenal' consciousness. In this sense consciousness is perhaps analogous to the classic Humean understanding of freedom: the important point is what it takes not to have it—being asleep, in a coma, lost in a daydream. In this sense, consciousness means awareness, sensitivity to one's surroundings, and of course its absence doesn't entail that the mind is empty (as the daydream, or more standard dream in sleep, illustrates). There is a further question, then: whether the person unconscious in this sense is also lacking in mental activity—a tragically vital question concerning some people in persistent comas.

Putting worries about zombies on one side, there is of course no difficulty in deciding whether, in this sense, a person (or one of many kinds of animal) is conscious, though it may certainly be a very difficult thing

---

[18] Chalmers, 'Facing up to the Problem of Consciousness', 201.

to understand the neurological processes that make such consciousness possible. No philosophical mystery seems to present itself. Whether or not it is mysterious, I think we can find among Chalmers's 'easy' problems an issue that really is philosophically fundamental, and which has probably been a major victim of neglect consequent on the obsession with philosophical consciousness. This is the question of attention. And here I again link up with Donald, in whose account of the function of consciousness attention is of central importance.

In comparison with qualia and what-it-is-likeness, attention has received negligible recent philosophical discussion.[19] Though it is quite widely discussed by cognitive psychologists I have been able to track down only a handful of explicitly philosophical discussions. A few of these derive from the phenomenological tradition and especially from Husserl. A handful of papers by analytic philosophers seem mainly concerned with the relation of attention to phenomenal consciousness. There is also some discussion of whether consciousness and attention are coextensive, with psychological evidence adduced to suggest that there are subtle differences between the two.[20] This question will not concern me here, not least because a satisfactory answer to it would presumably require an uncontentious definition of consciousness.

I propose instead to offer a comparative perspective. Unlike the elusive question of what it is like to be a bat, there is no difficulty at all (in principle) in saying what bats can and do attend to. And it is not a novel observation that a fundamental aspect of an organism is the set of features of its environment that an organism can discriminate. For most organisms, surely, this is closely connected to the ways in which the organism can interact with its environment, an idea commemorated in J. J. Gibson's concept of affordance, a feature of an organism's environment that it can perceive and that affords a possibility of action. The set of things to which an organism can attend is a fundamental determinant of its relation to the external environment.

---

[19] In the website to which I referred in n. 1 above, there is a heading for 'Attention and Consciousness' but only under the subheading 'Science of Consciousness'; there are fifteen entries, half the number on zombies. A noteworthy exception is a recent book by John Campbell (*Reference and Consciousness* (Oxford: Clarendon Press, 2002)), though Campbell's main aim is to provide insight into reference.

[20] See e.g. V. G. Hardcastle, 'Attention versus Consciousness: A Distinction with a Difference', *Cognitive Studies: Bulletin of the Japanese Cognitive Science Society*, 4 (2007), 56–66.

We should be careful not to stretch our terms too far. We do not say that the plant attends to the sunlight, though its ability to respond to sunlight, whether simply by photosynthesizing or by more actively reorientating its leaves is certainly a comparable feature of its relation to its environment. The swimming of a bacterium up a chemical gradient is probably more similar to the activity of the phototactic plant than to human consciousness. One reason why we do not say that the plant is attending to the light is that it could hardly refrain from doing so. Attention is something that can focus on one thing rather than another, that can wander or be impressive in its steadiness. A plausible scale of behavioural complexity would be a measure of the range of features of the environment that offered affordances or that were potential foci of attention. And it is clear that in this regard humans vastly exceed the complexity of any other organisms.

In case this last were open to doubt, I should just point out that one reason why humans have so many possible objects of attention is that they make them. Modern humans live in an environment containing great numbers of things that have been put there by other humans, living or dead, precisely for the affordances, possibilities of action, that they can offer. The process of becoming a mature human requires, among much else, learning to recognize and make use of many of these artefacts. To gesture towards another wide range of relevant considerations, there is no doubt that human language plays an essential role (or perhaps a variety of roles) in facilitating the production, maintenance and exploitation of the diverse salient features that characterize human environments. And it is a familiar but fundamental point that language enables us to carry our attention beyond the confines of the immediate environment to things that are absent and even merely possible or abstract.

The present point of all this is that the more diverse becomes the range of items of potential interest in the environment, the more interesting and difficult becomes the problem of deciding on what feature of the environment attention should be focused. There is surely no simple answer to this question. Much of the philosophy of decision, of the will (its freedom and its weakness), of intention and planning and so on, addresses problems that arise as humans confront the variety of possibilities for action made possible by the almost indefinitely diverse salience of their engineered and theorized environments. This seems to me a good direction from which to approach the uniqueness and continuity of humans and other animals:

all animals are intimately related to their environments by the features of the environment that are relevant to their activities. These are the features that they perceive and the points at which they act on the environment. Humans have increased the diversity of such features to a degree that is incomparably greater than that of other animals: this is one way of seeing why the attempt to apply simple models of psychological evolution, such as are the stock in trade of evolutionary psychologists, tends to produce a simplistic caricature of human behaviour. The primitive precursor of human attention, I am tempted to say, comes into being when attention can be focused on one thing rather than another—when there is choice. And if attention is what is important about consciousness, this perspective will also capture the common intuition that while most vertebrate animals exhibit some degree of consciousness, the stereotyped and rigid behavioural routines of many instincts don't meet this standard.

I noted that attention is central to Merlin Donald's account of the human mind. Donald focuses on the factors that make possible the diversity of salient features of human environments, language and culture, and the argument that learning, which is of course absolutely essential in mastering language and finding one's way around a complex human culture, is wholly dependent on conscious attention. So the ability to attend, to focus the mind, both is a prerequisite for acquiring the behavioural complexity that is uniquely human, and is essential for dealing with the complexity of behavioural possibilities that this learning process makes possible. I hope this cursory summary doesn't suggest that I think that understanding the nature of such mental attention, let alone describing the neurological structures that (in part) make it possible, is a simple task. It will, nevertheless, be simpler if we focus on the actual content on which this attention is directed—objects in the world, cultural practices and suchlike—rather than on the ineffable feelings that are alleged somehow to accompany these contents.

Language, Science and Philosophy

I want to conclude with some reflections on a quite different kind of question: what is the role of philosophy in addressing topics such as the present one? The arguments I have been considering that the notion of phenomenal consciousness does not make sense appeal to claims about the functioning of language. I remarked, for instance, that the question 'What is it like to see red?', in so far as it had a meaning at all, did not have the one assumed by many consciousness theorists. How is such a claim to be substantiated? Even if there were a definitive list of correct uses of words, might it not be quite legitimate for someone to introduce a new, more or less technical, usage for some particular theoretical purpose? This difficulty can easily be exaggerated. The meaningfulness of most sentences is not controversial. 'That flower is red' makes sense, while 'The number nine is red' does not; these are not dubious intuitions but mundane, if slightly esoteric, banalities.

But even this doesn't quite get to the point. Dennett criticizes Hacker for relying on his linguistic intuitions with no apparent awareness of the difficulty linguists have experienced in formulating linguistic rules.[21] Consider once again the question 'What is it like to be a bat?' It is not a simple question whether, according to the philosopher's intuition, this sentence makes sense. Indeed, if there were a vote among philosophers it seems likely that most would vote in its favour. It is not, on the other hand, a sentence that wears its everyday meaning on its face. It might derive its meaningfulness from analogy with other similar and more familiar questions, or it might be given an explicit definition or explanation in some philosophical context. As a matter of fact, however, neither in Nagel's classic paper nor in the flood of derivative philosophical work is it felt necessary to provide such an explicit introduction. It is quite clear, on the contrary, that it is taken to have a familiar and well-understood meaning. In evaluating the meaningfulness of this form of words Hacker takes the appropriate line of exploring superficially similar sentences and considering in some detail how these are actually used. As I have described, this investigation fails to disclose an appropriate meaning

---

[21] Dennett in M. Bennett, D Dennett, P. Hacker and J. Searle, *Neuroscience and Philosophy: Brain, Mind and Language* (New York: Columbia University Press, 2007). Dennett, as I noted, has his own qualms with qualia, and the attacks in question concern Hacker's objections to attributing mental states to brains and their parts. However, the arguments in question can equally well be considered with reference to the present issue.

for the original question. This is a more complex form of argument than merely weighing the sentence on one's linguistic palate and declaring it to be sense or nonsense. One might, I suppose, suggest that any philosophical argument depends on intuitions about the meanings of the sentences employed in developing the argument. But this hardly serves as an all-purpose refutation of all philosophical arguments. Rebutting Hacker's (and my) arguments would require the hard work of explaining where his linguistic intuitions have gone astray and why, and then explaining what are the genuine conditions of use of the forms of word in dispute.

Contrary to an occasional knee-jerk reaction that is sometimes induced by what is derided as 'ordinary language' philosophy, then, there is nothing wrong in principle with the methodology Hacker employs, and which I have endorsed by imitation, for questioning the views of philosophers and scientists studying the mind. This is consistent with Hacker's view, much criticized by Dennett and Searle, that philosophy is about distinguishing sense from nonsense, and science is about distinguishing truth from falsehood, and consequently that the two have essentially distinct, non-overlapping subject matters.[22] Ironically enough, a similar view might be seen as implicit in the views of philosophers such as David Chalmers on phenomenal consciousness. Apparently this issue needs some serious philosophical work before it can be passed on to the scientists for empirical resolution. For Chalmers this empirical resolution, when the time comes, appears to be a relatively routine if no doubt time-consuming activity; it is, compared with the 'hard' philosophical problem, 'easy'. No one can doubt that scientists, given time, will sort out the details. This all fits with what was once a very standard story: all problems start out as philosophy, but at a certain point in history enough conceptual clarity is reached in a given area of enquiry for it to be handed over to the scientists. Thus physics in the seventeenth century, chemistry in the eighteenth, biology and psychology in the nineteenth.

I am not persuaded, however, that it is useful to draw such a sharp line between science and philosophy. There are of course major differences in

---

[22] Dennett and Searle, in Bennett et al., *Neuroscience and Philosophy*, 79 ff. and 122–40.

training, skills and quotidian practice; but I don't think that problems can be unequivocally divided into one category or the other. This is not because I want to make a radical Quinean denial of any distinction between truths of logic and truths of fact. But I do think that most intellectual work, whether in philosophy or science, requires the confrontation of both kinds of problem. The close, and sometimes productive, engagement between many contemporary philosophers of science and practising scientists is, I believe, an appropriate reflection of the interconnections between philosophical and empirical questions.[23]

Successful science, I think, requires good philosophy, not just as a foundation that, once constructed, can be left to take care of itself, but as part of a continuing contribution to the advancement of science. Of course this doesn't mean that every lab needs a resident philosopher (though perhaps that wouldn't be so bad); conceptual work is just part of what many scientists do. Contrary to the now declining philosophical tradition that saw scientists as engaged in a quest for laws, biologists, at least, talk far more about concepts. (In fact they almost never talk about laws.) The question whether a concept is useful is simultaneously a question whether it applies coherently to the appropriate range of known cases, and whether it guides a productive programme of further empirical research. (An example of a concept whose usefulness remains subject to some such dispute is that of affordance, which I have used earlier in this essay.) It is distinctive of work in the philosophy of biology that it is very much concerned with the coherence of such concepts, but it would make no sense to explore this question without attempting to understand the empirical work that they had facilitated. Understanding what a scientific concept means requires understanding how it is used; and, typically, scientific concepts are used in formulating, implementing and reporting programmes of scientific work. Often scientific concepts are used in a variety of very different contexts as, for example, the concept of 'gene', which guided both the Mendelian studies of inheritance that flourished in the first half of the twentieth century and continue today,

---

[23] I should perhaps add that I do not assume that empirical questions are strictly the preserve of science, and I do not believe that so-called folk knowledge should, as many scientifically minded philosophers suppose, be assumed to be ignorant and ungrounded.

and the molecular genetics that developed during the second half of the last century. There is an interesting debate among philosophers whether this is a regrettable situation that should be rectified by philosophical intervention or, rather, as is increasingly often proposed, it is a productive ambiguity that promotes the interchange of ideas between related fields of enquiry.[24] At any rate, it is clear that it would be impossible to address such a question without detailed consideration of the investigative practices in which the term is used. Indeed, the collaboration between Bennett and Hacker, providing respectively authoritative scientific and philosophical expertise, seems to me exemplary of the kind of interaction between science and philosophy that is characteristic of the best current philosophical contributions to science.

One aim in offering this cursory discussion of the contemporary methodology of philosophy of science is to note its striking contrast with the philosophical discussions of qualia, zombies and the internal life of bats that I described earlier in this essay. Far from being grounded in a serious consideration of scientific practice, these phenomena, it is widely agreed, are beyond the reach of any investigative practice that we can yet imagine. Since they are imagined as ineffectual and generally unobservable epiphenomena, this lack of empirical input is of course not surprising. What is evidently not adequately appreciated is that it is not merely that we have no scientific account of qualia and the like, but that we have no proper grounding for these things in our pre-scientific (but nonetheless empirical) picture of the world. It seems to me that there is a real danger that insisting on an impassable divide between the conceptual and the empirical might actually encourage the pursuit of this vacuous quasi-philosophical enterprise. A hypothesis borne out by both Dennett's and Searle's response to Bennett and Hacker's book is that Hacker's commitment to this divide is

---

[24] A sophisticated argument for the usefulness of a degree of flexibility in central scientific concepts, with special reference to the concept of a gene, is H.-J. Rheinberger, 'Gene Concepts: Fragments for the Perspective of Molecular Biology', in P. Beurton, R. Falk and H.-J. Rheinberger (eds.), *The Concept of the Gene in Development and Evolution* (Cambridge: Cambridge University Press, 2000), 219–39. An analysis of the problems that can arise from conflation of different gene concepts, thoroughly informed by contemporary molecular biology, is L. Moss, *What Genes Can't Do* (Cambridge, Mass.: MIT Press, 2003). A prominent example of the growing movement in 'empirical philosophy' is the Representing Genes project led by Karola Stotz and Paul Griffiths, which investigates the diverse uses of the concept of gene by contemporary scientists. See K. Stotz, P. E. Griffiths and R. Knight, 'How Scientists Conceptualise Genes: An Empirical Study', *Studies in History and Philosophy of Biological and Biomedical Sciences*, 35 (2004), 647–73.

liable to provide one excuse for refusing to take his important philosophical arguments seriously. If this is so, I offer myself as one piece of evidence that one can find these arguments entirely persuasive even in the context of a more muddled and inchoate vision of the relation of science to philosophy.[25]

[25] I'm very grateful to John Hyman and Hans-Johann Glock, whose comments on an earlier draft led to many improvements. An early version of the paper was presented to a workshop on the Basic Functions of Consciousness hosted by the research group on 'Funktionen des Bewusstseins' at the Berlin-Brandenburgische Akademie der Wissenschaften, and I am also grateful to participants at that meeting for various helpful comments.

Cognitive Scientism

ANTHONY KENNY

How Many Kinds of Proposition?

Once upon a time it was easy to classify propositions. There were analytic propositions, true in virtue of their meaning, and there were synthetic propositions that contained information about the world. All analytic propositions were known a priori; empirical propositions, known a posteriori, were all synthetic. Out of respect for Kant philosophers would inquire whether any propositions were synthetic a priori, but commonly the question was raised only to be answered in the negative.

In the latter part of the twentieth century the tidy dichotomy—analytic a priori vs synthetic a posteriori—came under attack from two opposite directions. In 1951 Quine's 'Two Dogmas of Empiricism' sought to undermine the analytic/synthetic distinction, replacing it with a continuum of propositions of varying degrees of entrenchment in the web of our beliefs. In 1969 there appeared Wittgenstein's *On Certainty*, which drew attention to an important class of propositions which appeared to be neither analytic nor empirical. Instead of two packages of propositions, we were offered either a single package or three packages.

Quine denied that analyticity could be defined in terms of synonymy or necessity, and he rejected the idea that a sentence was synthetic if it could be verified or falsified by experience. It is not single sentences, he argued, but whole systems—which include mathematics and logic as well as geography and history—that are verified or falsified. 'Our statements about the external world face the tribunal of sense experience not individually but only as a corporate body . . . A conflict with experience at the periphery occasions readjustments in the interior of the field. Truth values have to be redistributed over some of our statements.'[1] We cannot single out a class of analytic statements which remain true whatever happens; no statement—not even a law of logic—can be totally immune to revision.

Wittgenstein, by contrast, explored the no man's land between the analytic and the synthetic—propositions such as 'motor cars don't grow on trees' and 'a man cannot live if his head is cut off' (OC, 273–4, 279). Such propositions seem very different from the theorems of a priori disciplines such as logic and mathematics, and yet it would be foolish to try to verify or falsify them by empirical research. 'Propositions of the form of empirical propositions', Wittgenstein wrote (later preferring the expression 'statements about material objects'), 'and not only propositions of logic, form the foundation of all operating with thoughts' (OC, 401). Such propositions, as he put it, stand fast for us.[2]

Though Wittgenstein increased, while Quine reduced, the number of classes of propositions, the two philosophers agree on many points. Wittgenstein, like Quine, was a holist. 'Our knowledge', he wrote, 'forms an enormous system. And only within this system has a particular bit the value we give it' (OC, 410). He came close to saying that there was no sharp boundary between propositions of logic (rules) and empirical propositions (OC, 319–20). And, like Quine, he raises the question whether there are any propositions that are immune to revision in the face of new facts.

'Would it be unthinkable', he asks, 'that I should stay in the saddle however much the facts bucked?' (OC, 616). But whereas Quine says that unexpected facts might force us to redistribute truth values across the field of our knowledge, Wittgenstein's response is: 'Certain events would put me into a position in which I could not go on with the old language game' (OC, 617). A proposition, on this view, would not change from true to false; but we might give up using it. To adapt an example Wittgenstein gives elsewhere: I weigh something, and announce the result. But if it later transpires that successive weighings of the same object, on various scales, produce wildly irregular readings, then I do not declare the earlier

---

[1] *From a Logical Point of View* (Cambridge, Mass.; Harvard University Press, 1953), 140.

[2] The trichotomy that Wittgenstein introduced into the classification of propositions is not easy to reconcile with his second-order remarks on the nature of philosophical theses, as I have complained in my paper 'Philosophy States Only what Everyone Admits', in E. Ammereller and E. Fischer, *Wittgenstein at Work* (London: Routledge, 2002), 173–82.

measurement was wrong; rather, I give up any trust in the language game of assigning weights.

Hesitantly, Wittgenstein was prepared to agree that 'any empirical proposition can be transformed into a postulate—and then become a norm of description' (OC, 321). There can also, we may note, be change in the other direction—as is shown by the proposition 'no man has ever been on the moon', which Wittgenstein notoriously gave as an example of something that stands fast for us. 'If we are thinking within our system, then it is certain that no one has ever been on the moon. Not merely is nothing of the sort ever seriously reported to us by reasonable people, but our whole system of physics forbids us to believe it' (OC, 208). Nowadays, of course, it is a matter of straightforward empirical inquiry to ascertain how many men have been on the moon.

Science vs Philosophy

These features bring out the similarities between the teachings of Quine and Wittgenstein.[3] But despite these resemblances, the two philosophers have a quite different conception of the nature of philosophy. For Quine and his followers there is a continuum between science and philosophy, between physics and metaphysics, between empirical psychology and philosophy of mind. For Wittgenstein, science and philosophy are two totally different activities, science being concerned with information and explanation, philosophy with description and understanding. The distinction was something that Wittgenstein upheld constantly throughout his life, right from his insistence in the *Tractatus* (4.112) that philosophy was not a body of doctrine but an activity of clarification.

In the *Blue Book* Wittgenstein wrote, 'Philosophers constantly see the method of science before their eyes, and are irresistibly tempted to ask and answer questions in the way science does. This tendency is the real source of metaphysics, and leads the philosopher into complete darkness' (BB, 18). Later, he wrote that the essential mark of metaphysics was its obliteration of the distinction between factual and conceptual investigations (Z, 458).

---

[3] Other resemblances have been usefully catalogued in Peter Hacker's *Wittgenstein's Place in Twentieth-Century Analytic Philosophy* (Oxford and Cambridge, Mass.: Blackwell, 1996), 189–93.

A particular sentence might be used at one time to express a rule and at another to state a fact; but since it is the use, rather than the sequence of words, that is significant, this does nothing to call in question the radical difference between the two kinds of investigation. If this is so, then Quine's form of holism is, for Wittgenstein, metaphysical in the bad sense: it is an attempt to do philosophy with the methods of science.

At the present time scientistic metaphysics is most prevalent in the study of the mind: many neuroscientists, psychologists and philosophers champion a programme of cognitive science whose goal is precisely to amalgamate the philosophy of mind with the scientific investigation of the brain. Philosophical practitioners of cognitive science often explicitly identify themselves as Quineans, just as critics of the programme take their stand on the philosophy of Wittgenstein.

Philosophical Foundations of Neuroscience by Max Bennett and Peter Hacker[4] is the most significant contribution to philosophy of mind in recent years. It examines thoroughly and carefully the pretensions of cognitive science to have superannuated philosophical psychology. It shows how the writings of some of the most prominent proponents of the new discipline are infected throughout with philosophical confusion. Those who scorn our ordinary concepts of thought, intention, and reasons as relics of a folk psychology are engaged, as Bennett and Hacker show, in sawing off the branches on which any scientist exploring the neurological basis of the mind must have to sit. Bennett and Hacker's book demonstrates that the insights of Wittgenstein, so far from being antiquated by recent developments, remain of the utmost importance in the philosophy of mind. In this essay I simply wish to express—in slightly different language—my agreement with the conclusions of Bennett and Hacker, and then to enter a modest demurrer to one of Wittgenstein's more arresting proposals.

Patent vs Latent Cartesianism

Contemporary investigation of the nature of the human mind customarily starts with a renunciation of Cartesian dualism. This is so, whether the investigator is Quinean or Wittgensteinian. Wittgenstein himself rarely

---

[4] Oxford and Malden, Mass.: Blackwell, 2003.

mentions Descartes—one of the few exceptions is a passage in the *Blue Book* (BB, 69) where he says that misunderstanding of the use of 'I' creates the illusion that we use this word to refer to something bodiless, which has its seat in our body. 'In fact', he continues, '*this* seems to be the real ego, the one of which it was said "Cogito ergo sum"'. But Wittgenstein's argument against private ostensive definition is, in effect, the most thoroughgoing critique of Cartesianism ever propounded. Cognitive scientists, on the other hand, while rejecting the dualist idea of the mind as a separate substance, retain many of Descartes's crucial assumptions.

In the first place, they accept Descartes's demarcation between the mental and the material. For Aristotelians before Descartes the mind was the faculty, or set of faculties, that set off human beings from other animals. Dumb animals and human beings shared certain abilities and activities: dogs, cows, pigs and humans could all see and hear and feel, they had in common the faculties of sensation. But only human beings could think abstract thoughts and take rational decisions; they were marked off from the other animals by the possession of intellect and will, and it was these two faculties that essentially constituted the mind. Intellectual activity was in a particular sense immaterial, whereas sensation was impossible without a material body.

For Descartes and for many others after him the boundary between mind and matter was set elsewhere. It was consciousness, not intelligence or rationality, that was the defining criterion of the mental. The mind, viewed from this standpoint, is the realm of whatever is accessible to introspection: the mental includes not only human understanding and willing, but also human seeing, hearing, pain and pleasure. This conception of the mind, though I call it Cartesian, should not be regarded simply as an aberration of continental philosophy: it was shared by the British empiricists, and it is shared to-day by many Anglo–American philosophers and scientists.

Cognitive scientists not only accept that consciousness is the mark of the mental; they also accept a Cartesian/empiricist notion of what consciousness is. Consciousness is considered as an object of introspection: something we can observe when we look within ourselves, something that has a purely contingent connection with its expression in speech and behaviour, something to which we ourselves have direct access, but which others can learn of only indirectly, through accepting our verbal testimony or making causal inferences from our physical behaviour.

'Consciousness', in the writings of such theorists, acquires a special sense. Without any philosophical commitment one can use the word as a general term to cover those faculties and activities, such as the senses and sensation, that are peculiar to humans and animals. But in the Cartesian tradition the word is intended to stand for some feature, directly observable only by introspection, that is common to all those activities, and in virtue of which alone they are entitled to be called 'conscious activities'. Such a usage is open to many objections, the chief of which is that there is no such common feature. Some recent philosophers have tried to identify such a feature as the possession of a 'qualitative feel': if something is an object of consciousness then there is a certain way in which it feels like to have it. In the tenth chapter of *Philosophical Foundations of Neuroscience* Hacker and Bennett have definitively disposed of the myth of the qualitative feel as a universal feature of consciousness.

An Aristotelian Account of the Mind

What does a non-Cartesian account of the mind look like? If the mind is not a substance, what is it? The mind is a capacity. (That, as Wittgenstein would say, is a grammatical remark.) The mind is a comprehensive ability to acquire abilities. It is the capacity to acquire linguistic and symbolic skills, which are themselves abilities of a certain kind. Abilities and capacities are individuated by their possessors and their exercises, but they are distinct from both. The possessor of an ability is what *has* the ability: in the case of the mind, the human being whose mind it is. It is I, and not my mind, who know English and am exercising this ability in writing this essay. An ability is a more or less enduring state, while the exercise of an ability will be a datable event or process. The mind lasts a lifetime while its exercises are our thoughts and projects and the other items of our mental lives.

A capacity is clearly something distinct from its possessor and from its exercise, but it must also be distinguished from a third thing, which we may call its *vehicle*. Consider the capacity of whisky to intoxicate. The vehicle of this capacity to intoxicate is the alcohol that the whisky contains: it is the ingredient in virtue of which the whisky has the power to intoxicate. The vehicle of a power need not be a substantial ingredient like alcohol, which can be physically separated from the possessor of the power, though it is in such cases that the distinction between a power and its vehicle is most obvious (one cannot, for example, weigh the power of whisky to intoxicate as one can weigh the alcohol it contains). Take the less exciting power which my wedding ring has of fitting on my finger. It has that power in virtue of having the size and shape it has, and size and shape are not modal, relational, potential properties in the same way as *being able to fit on my finger* is. They are not the power, but the vehicle of the power. A vehicle is something concrete, something that can be located and measured. An ability, on the other hand, has neither length nor breadth nor location. This does not mean that an ability is something ghostly: my front-door key's ability to open my front door is not a concrete object, but it is not a spirit either.

The notion of a vehicle, as I have explained it, is an extension of Aristotle's exploration of the differences between actuality and potentiality. The vehicle of a power is the abiding actuality in virtue of which a substance possesses a potentiality which finds expression in transitory exercises. This underlying actuality may be an ingredient, or a property, or a structure. The identification of the actuality provides an explanation of the possession of the power or active potentiality.

Molière mocked at physicians who explained that opium put people to sleep because it had dormitive power. The statement was philosophically correct, but medically vacuous. The connection between a power and its exercise is not a causal one like that linking smoking and cancer. The job of the physicians was to look for the vehicle of the power, not to hypostatise the power itself, treating it as a substance in its own right. The vehicle was identified when the soporific ingredient of opium was discovered to be morphine.

The following question may be raised. Pure morphine puts people to sleep just as opium does, so surely their soporific powers have the same vehicle. It would seem to follow that in the case of morphine the agent and the vehicle are one and the same thing. This would in effect reproduce the quack pharmacology at a lower level—only now it is the morphine rather than the opium that has the dormitive power.

Such an objection rests on a misunderstanding of the Aristotelian frame-work. Actualities and potentialities are, for Aristotle, stratified. Something that is a potentiality with respect to a particular exercise may itself be an actuality of a more primitive potentiality. Aristotle's favourite example is the knowledge of a language. This is a potentiality, exercised in the actual, episodic use of the language. But it is itself an actuality, a skill acquired on the basis of the underlying human, species-specific, capacity for language learning.

The same system of stratification can be applied to the vehicles of powers. Morphine is the vehicle of opium's dormitive power because it is the abiding ingredient that explains opium's ability to put people to sleep. But it is not its own vehicle precisely because the statement that morphine always contains morphine, while true, provides no explanation of its soporific qualities. To discover the vehicle of these powers, one has to move to a different level, to morphine's molecular structure and its relationship to the anatomy of the animal brain.[5]

Two Kinds of Reductionism

In every age philosophers have been tempted to blur the distinctions between powers and their exercises and their vehicles. There is a perennial tendency to reduce potentialities to actualities. There are two kinds of reductionism: one reduces abilities to their exercises, the other reduces abilities to their vehicles. Hume, who said that the distinction between a power and its exercise was frivolous, was an exercise-reductionist. Descartes, who identified the powers of bodies with their geometrical properties, was a vehicle-reductionist.

Philosophical errors about capacities show up particularly vividly when they occur in the philosophy of mind. Applied in this area, exercise-reductionism is behaviourism: the attempt to identify mind with its particular exercises in behaviour. Applied in this area, vehicle-reductionism becomes materialism: the reduction of our mental capacities to the parts and structures of our bodies in virtue of which we possess them, and in particular to our brains. The identification of mind and brain is a category mistake, because the brain is a material object and the mind is a capacity.

---

[5] When, many years ago, I introduced the notion of *vehicle* I said that the connection between a power and its vehicle could be either necessary or contingent: 'It is a conceptual truth', I wrote, 'that a round peg has the power to fit into a round hole' (*Will, Freedom, and Power*, Oxford: Blackwell, 1975, 10). To allow that the relationship between vehicle and power could be anything but an empirical matter was an error, and inconsistent with other things I have repeatedly said elsewhere.

The mind is the capacity to acquire intellectual abilities. The possessor of human mental capacities is neither the mind nor the brain but the human being.

'Only of a human being', Wittgenstein wrote, 'and what resembles (behaves like) a human being can one say: it has sensations; it sees; is blind; hears; is deaf; is conscious or unconscious' (PI, 281). This does not mean that Wittgenstein is a behaviourist: he is not identifying experience with behaviour, or even with dispositions to behave. The point is that what experiences one can have depends on how one *can* behave. Only someone who can play chess can feel the desire to castle; only a being that can discriminate between light and darkness can have visual experiences.

The relation between experiences of certain kinds, and the capacity to behave in certain ways, is not a merely contingent connection. Wittgenstein made a distinction between two kinds of evidence that we may have for the obtaining of states of affairs, namely *symptoms* and *criteria*. Where the connection between a certain kind of evidence and the conclusion drawn from it is a matter of empirical discovery, through theory and induction, the evidence may be called a *symptom* of the state of affairs; where the relation between evidence and conclusion is not something discovered by empirical investigation, but is something that must be grasped by anyone who possesses the concept of the state of affairs in question, then the evidence is not a mere symptom, but a *criterion* of the event in question. Such is the relation between scratching and itching, between crying and pain.

Exploiting the notion of *criterion* enabled Wittgenstein to steer between the Scylla of dualism and the Charybdis of behaviourism. He agreed with dualists that particular mental events could occur without accompanying bodily behaviour; on the other hand he agreed with behaviourists that the possibility of ascribing mental acts to people depends on such acts having, in general, a behavioural expression.

If it is wrong to identify the mind with behaviour, it is even more mistaken, according to Wittgenstein, to identify the mind with the brain. Such materialism is in fact a grosser philosophical error than behaviourism because the connection between mind and behaviour is a more intimate one than that between mind and brain. The relation between mind and behaviour is a criterial one, something prior to experience; the connection between mind and brain is a contingent one, discoverable by empirical science. Any discovery of links between mind and brain must take as its starting point the everyday concepts we use in describing the mind, concepts which are grafted on to behavioural criteria.

It is conceivable that when my skull is opened after my death it will be found to contain nothing but sawdust. Of course it would be astonishing, nay miraculous, if this were to be the case. But if *per impossibile* it happened it would not cast any doubt on my having had a mind, known various languages, and written a number of books. This shows that the relationship between mind and brain is not a conceptual one. Aristotle, no mean philosopher of mind, had a wildly erroneous notion of the nature of the brain.

Wittgenstein gives 'I have a brain' as an example of a proposition that stands fast and cannot be doubted. 'Everything speaks in its favour, nothing against it. Nevertheless it is imaginable that my skull should turn out empty when it was operated on' (OC, 4; cf. also OC, 118, 159). It is not just a strange coincidence that every man whose skull has been opened had a brain. 'I am sure that my friend hasn't sawdust in his body or in his head, even though I have no direct evidence of my senses to that effect' (OC, 281).

The Homunculus Fallacy

Developments in the philosophy of mind since Wittgenstein have shown that it is possible to combine the errors of materialism with those of dualism. One of the standard dualist misunderstandings of the nature of the mind is the picture of mind's relation to body as that between a little person or homunculus on the one hand, and a tool or instrument or machine on the other. This misunderstanding is compounded if we assign the role of homunculus to the brain, identifying it, as materialists do, with the mind so conceived.

What is wrong with the homunculus fallacy? In itself there is nothing misguided in speaking of images in the brain, if one means patterns in the brain, observable to a neurophysiologist, that can be mapped on to features of the visible environment. What is misleading is to take these mappings as representations, to regard them as visible to the mind, and to say that seeing consists in the mind's perception of these images. The misleading aspect is that such an account pretends to explain seeing, but the explanation reproduces exactly the puzzling features it was supposed to explain.

Peter Hacker and Max Bennett prefer to call the fallacy 'the mereological fallacy'—they point out that it is a fallacy that can be committed in connection with a mechanism like a clock no less than in connection with an animal such as a human being.

> We called the mistake 'mereological' because it involves ascribing to parts attributes that can intelligibly be ascribed only to the wholes of which they are parts. A form of this error was pointed out around 350 BC by Aristotle, who remarked that 'to say that the soul is angry is as if one were to say that the soul weaves or builds. For it is surely better not to say that the soul pities, learns or thinks, but that a man does these' (De An. 408b12–15). . . . Our primary concern was with the neuroscientific cousin of this, namely the error of ascribing to the brain—a part of an animal—attributes that can be ascribed literally only to the animal as a whole . . . In Aristotelian spirit we now observe that to say that the brain is angry is as if one were to say that the brain weaves or builds. For it is surely better to say not that the brain pities, learns or thinks, but that a man does these. Accordingly, we deny that it makes sense to say that the brain is conscious, feels sensations, perceives, thinks, knows or wants anything—for these are attributes of animals, not of their brains.[6]

Sometimes cognitive scientists write as if the relation between mind and brain was that the mind made inferences from events in the brain and nervous system. This is a form of the homunculus fallacy, and it was explicitly rejected by Wittgenstein.

> An event leaves a trace in the memory: one sometimes imagines this as if it consisted in the event's having left a tract, an impression, a consequence in the nervous system. As if one could say: the nerves too have a memory. But then when someone remembered an event, he would have to infer it from this impression, this trace. Whatever the event does leave behind in the organism, *it* isn't the memory.   (RPP I, 220)

When something is recorded on a tape, the alteration in the tape is not a memory, and when the tape is played it is not remembering.

---

⁶ P. M. S. Hacker, Max Bennett, Daniel Dennett and John Searle, *Neuroscience and Philosophy* (New York: Columbia University Press, 2007), 131–2.

Aristotelianism in Excess?

Not all cognitive scientists go so far as explicitly to identify the mind with the brain, but all seek a parallelism between mental and physical events. Wittgenstein rejected this. 'Nothing seems more possible to me', he wrote 'than that people some day will come to the definite opinion that there is no copy in either the physiological or the nervous systems which corresponds to a particular thought, or a particular idea, or memory' (LW I, 504). The history of the mind is not a history of events in the way that the history of the body is. A thought does not have temporal parts as the utterance of a sentence does. Of course, there are such things as mental events and processes—hitting on an idea, or reciting a nursery rhyme in the imagination—but such events and processes are what they are because of the abilities from which they issue and which provide their background.

The true task of neuroscience is to investigate the vehicles of mental abilities. It is in this investigation that the scientific advances of the last century have been achieved. But we may pose a fundamental question. Is it the case that every mental ability does have a physical vehicle? We might think that this is something certain—a certainty parallel to our knowledge that we do not have sawdust in our heads. But Wittgenstein does not agree.

No supposition seems to me more natural than that there is no process in the brain correlated with associating or with thinking; so that it would be impossible to read off thought processes from brain processes . . . It is perfectly possible that certain psychological phenomena *cannot* be investigated physiologically, because physiologically nothing corresponds to them. I saw this man years ago: now I have seen him again, I recognize him, I remember his name. And why does there have to be a cause of this remembering in my nervous system? . . . Why should there not be a psychological regularity to which *no* physiological regularity corresponds? If this upsets our concept of causality then it is high time it was upset.   (Z, 608–10; cf. RPP I, 903–6)

So Wittgenstein is willing to countenance a case of causality between psychological phenomena that is unmediated physiologically. He is anxious to say that this does not amount to the 'admission of the existence of a soul *alongside* the body, a ghostly, spiritual nature' (RPP I, 906). The entity that does the associating, thinking and remembering is not a spiritual substance, à la Plato and Descartes, but a corporeal human being. But this passage seems to envisage the possibility of an Aristotelian soul or entelechy, which operates with no material vehicle, a formal and final cause to which there corresponds no mechanistic efficient cause.

Since the time of Galileo it has been a presumption of science that every power has a vehicle, that to every potentiality for the future there corresponds a present actuality. It is this presumption that Wittgenstein is here calling in question. He is undoubtedly correct that there is nothing conceptually incoherent in the idea of a capacity existing without a material vehicle, but one must ask whether, and if so when, it can be reasonable for science simply to give up the quest for a vehicle. I share the queasiness about this passage that is widespread even among Wittgenstein's admirers. Much of history suggests that scientific progress is made by inquiring into the vehicles of capacities, rather than by treating capacities such as dormitive powers as the basic building blocks of science. Maybe Wittgenstein is right that, in Aristotelian terms, there may be formal and final causes in the absence of efficient and material ones. Perhaps there can: but one cannot help worrying whether Wittgenstein may here be adopting towards contemporary neuroscientists the attitude that renaissance Aristotelians adopted to Galileo.

Knowing How To and Knowing That

DAVID WIGGINS

I

Gilbert Ryle maintained that knowing how [to V] and knowing that [p] were distinct, not the same thing.[1] The first was not reducible to the second. They represented different aspects or powers of mind. It was a long-standing, deep-seated, intellectualist mistake to assimilate them, he said. In the last decade, relatively few philosophers have taken Ryle's part,[2] but I shall.

Some who doubt Ryle's contention are impressed by the point that there are cases where knowing some ordinary fact appears to be all that is needed in order to put one into a position to do something. (I shall say something about that towards the end.) Others argue that knowing how to V is always a matter of knowing the way to V, where knowing the way to V is knowing propositionally that such and such is that way. Against both kinds of critic, I shall argue that the Rylean contention is simply correct.

---

[1] See *The Concept of Mind* (London: Hutchinson, 1949), chapter 2, recapitulating his 'Knowing How and Knowing That', *Proceedings of the Aristotelian Society*, 46 (1945–6), 1–16.

[2] I know of three who have been sympathetic to Ryle: (1) Jennifer Hornsby in 'Semantic Knowledge and Practical Knowledge I', *Proceedings of the Aristotelian Society*, supplementary volume 79 (2005), 107–30; see especially notes 16 and 17; (2) David Wiggins, 'That which is Inherently Practical: Some Brief Reflections', in Fátima Evora *et al.* (eds.), *Lógica e Ontologia: Insaios em Homenagem a Balthazar Barbosa Filho* (São Paulo: Discurso Editorial, 2004), 461–71; (3) Ian Rumfitt, 'Savoir faire', *Journal of Philosophy*, 100 (2003), 158–66, an article which seeks, among other things, to remind Ryle's critics what Ryle's actual claim was—first and foremost, that is, a claim in the material or metaphysical mode, not the formal or the grammatical mode.

2

First, certain misconceptions need to be dissipated. To say that knowing how to V and knowing that p represent or manifest different determinable powers of mind and the second cannot subsume the first is not to say that these powers can be activated separately or to deny that they have manifold relations of interdependence. It is only to say that they are not the same power and neither can be resolved into the other.[3] At risk of labouring the obvious, let us be as clear as possible about this. If I say that being a baker and being a lifeboat pilot are distinct occupations/avocations, I do not mean that nobody is both. Similarly, if I say that being a cricketer and being a footballer are distinct pursuits, I am not denying that anyone followed both. As almost everybody once knew, Denis Compton (1918–1997) played for England at both games.

Lest it appear that, by giving examples overlapping the area of competences, I make confusion or beg some question or other, I must urge that the point just made is a formal and perfectly general one. Here is another example. Aquatic creatures can be classified as fresh-water, as estuarine (at home in brackish water), or as saline. These are distinct and different characteristics. It does not count against the distinctness of the characteristics that some creatures fall under more than one of them. Salmon and eels are so equipped that they fall under all three. Again, being an omnivore and being a scavenger are distinct properties, despite the fact that some animals are both and despite the fact that certain single pieces of behaviour by a given animal may qualify as part of the case for counting that animal as an omnivore or as a scavenger or as both.

3

Once so much is made clear, it will be evident that Ryle is in a position not merely to allow but also to assert that, in their full distinctness,

[3] In *The Nature of Knowledge*, APQ Library of Philosophy (Totowa, NJ: Roman and Littlefield, 1982), 14, Alan R. White says that Ryle says that knowing how and knowing that are 'essentially different'. That is one way of saying what Ryle says, but Ryle's point is best made (as he made it) without a detour through the 'essences' of the powers of the mind or of competences.

knowing how to and knowing that need one another. Over and over again, we may be unable to exercise practical knowledge without some relevant piece of propositional knowledge. (Where the fuse box or trip-switch is located, for instance, or the stopcock.) Frequently moreover, and more interestingly, the improvement of practice may depend on simply scientific/theoretical/propositional discoveries. Think of dentistry or surgery.

That is one sort of dependence. But there is also an opposite dependence. A ship's pilot who is retained to bring large ships safely to anchorage in a difficult harbour can say, on the basis of his experience, that, when the wind is from the north and the tide is running out, the best way to avoid the hazardous sandbank is to steer straight for such and such a beacon until one is well past a certain bend in the channel and.... Here propositional knowledge reposes upon practical knowledge. In the same spirit, but in an ethical connection, I have argued that, just as the various branches of the practical are keyed to the internal purposes of this or that craft or skill or art, so we can conceive of the ethical as keyed to certain internal purposes—namely the unforsakeable human purposes which support (however contestably) our understanding of 'must', 'ought', 'needs', 'forbidden',[4] etc. Here too we can expect an understanding that is inherently practical to give voice to propositional declarations that can be assessed (by one who properly grasps their sense, which presupposes the said purposes) as true or false. Such declarations are the step-children (if I may borrow Ryle's metaphor) of a certain way of being or trying to be and answerable as such to that way of being.

4

Before defending the appearances or going further afield, it may be worth dwelling a little longer, as a proper understanding of Ryle's thesis may safely encourage, on the constant back-and-forth between knowledge that rests upon the practical and knowledge which rests on the propositional.

[4] See my *Ethics: Twelve Lectures on the Philosophy of Morality* (London Penguin, 2006), 358–9. Compare Aristotle, *Nicomachean Ethics*, 1143a25–b14.

Consider land measurement, where one supposes that, early on in their efforts to survey the lands about the Nile, the ancient Egyptians discovered that two suitably placed 3-4-5 triangles form a rectangle. In the time that has elapsed since then, countless discoveries in geometry and trigonometry have greatly enhanced techniques of land surveying and of mapping the surface of the earth. Such discoveries have transformed the practical competencies of the surveyors and map makers who do the work on the ground. Again, consider music. In the beginning, the musical arts led to the discovery of mathematical truths concerning the octave and some other intervals. Thousands of years later, the discovery of the frequency ratio for the semitones that gives the most euphonious equal tempering of the musical scale diversified and transformed the practical and compositional possibilities within music.

5

On a Rylean view, this back-and-forth between the practical and the propositional and the propositional and the practical, so far from undermining the contrast between the two kinds of knowledge, only makes one eager to understand better the powers (the determinable competences) of the mind that make it possible. To Ryle's critics, on the other hand, it appears that the sheer multiplicity of phenomena such as those just instanced discredits the very idea of seeing them as grounded in the two determinables that Ryle distinguishes. Such critics will be deaf to his protests against the pseudo-philosophical intellectualism that discounts the distinctive contribution of knowing-how-to. Here though are Ryle's own words:

Philosophers have not done justice to the distinction which is quite familiar to all of us between knowing that something is the case and knowing how to do things. In their theories of knowledge they concentrate on the discovery of truths or facts, and they either ignore the discovery of ways and methods of doing things or else they try to reduce it to the discovery of facts....I want to turn the tables and to prove that knowledge-how cannot be defined in terms of knowledge-that and further, that knowledge-how is a concept logically prior to the concept of knowledge-that. I hope to show that a number of notorious cruces and paradoxes remain insoluble if knowing-that is taken as the ideal model of all operations of intelligence. They are resolved if we see that a man's intelligence or stupidity is as directly exhibited in some of his doings as it is in some of his thinking.[5]

6

Is it integral to Ryle's position that, in every back-and-forth of the kinds instanced in section 3, the mass of knowledge that agents exercise should be resolvable into bare knowings-how and knowings-that?

A parallel question suggests itself. If someone says, with Hume, that benevolence and self-love give rise to distinct and different motivations, are they committed to think that, for every occasion of someone's doing some act, it must be possible in principle cleanly to apportion the motivation for doing it between the concern for the good of others and the concern for the good of oneself? And, if that is not possible, does this imply that there is really no such thing as a motivation of *genuine* benevolence?

Here lie some of the oldest confusions in philosophy, confusions not yet concluded despite Hume's masterly discrimination of the distinct tendencies of benevolence and self-love. Even now these spill out into life itself. To cynics who delight in this sort of confusion, I commend especially from the last paragraph of Hume's appendix 'On Self-Love':

[W]here is the difficulty in conceiving . . . with benevolence and friendship . . . that, from the original frame of our temper, we may feel a desire of another's happiness or good, which, by means of that affection, becomes our own good, and is afterwards pursued, from the combined motives of benevolence and self-enjoyment?[6]

7

To conceive benevolence and self-love as coeval and distinct forces within the hurly-burly of human motivation does not commit one to say that

---

[5] 'Knowing How and Knowing That', paragraphs 16–17. As regards the claims that Ryle enters at the end of the quotation, claims I do not discuss here, see, for instance, paragraph 20 and the use Ryle makes there of Lewis Carroll's Tortoise and Achilles paradox.

[6] David Hume, *Enquiry Concerning the Principles of Morals*, Appendix II, last paragraph. Compare my *Twelve Lectures*, 36–44.

genuine benevolence/concern for the good of others always works within a principle of action from which all wants of the agent himself are rigorously excluded. But, if the multiplicity and inward interconnectedness of the hurly-burly of human motivation are no obstacle to making sense of benevolence and self-love as coeval and distinct, then *mutatis mutandis* why cannot knowing that something is the case and knowing how to do something be similarly distinctly conceived, even where (on the ground, so to speak) the back-and-forth we have been describing excludes winnowing them cleanly apart?

In countering cynicism and conceptual confusion, it helped Hume to have examples by which to show forth the simplest kind of benevolence.[7] If Ryle had been challenged to show forth similar simplest cases of knowing-how-to, he might have begun by claiming that, among the huge variety of things human beings do, there have to be *some* that they can come to do otherwise than on the basis of learning that such and such is the way they are done. He might have said that these are among the things we learn to do by habituation and practice; and that when we do them, we do them directly and not on the basis of information about how they are done.

The regress arguments that Ryle offered for some such conclusion now have few converts. Here though is a recent variant:

[E]ven a limited goal usually takes a more than one-step procedure to achieve . . . . Even where only a one-step procedure is called for, more than one piece of procedural knowledge may be required. Thus, to take a well-worn example, someone may know how to illuminate the room—by pressing that light switch; and know how to press that light switch—by using their finger appropriately. Here *one can φ by ψ-ing* and *one can ψ by χ-ing*; and ψ-ing and χ-ing will both be things an agent does intentionally if she exercises such knowledge of how to φ. Sometimes a whole series of procedural facts need to be known to get something done: *One can φ by ψ-ing and χ-ing* and *One can ψ by χ-ing* and *One can χ by ω-ing*, and . . . . There are potential regresses here. But it must be possible to halt them. For we surely do not require indefinitely much procedural knowledge in order to get anything done. Thus some things—at the end of these 'by'-chains as it were—must be done without possession of knowledge of procedures. These are things the agent does 'directly'. They are basic things, in one sense of that action-theoretic notion. They are things which we are inclined to say that the agent *is able to simply do* . . . . We can do, and may have reason to do, a very great

---

[7] See Hume, *Enquiry*, Appendix II; see also Appendix III, second paragraph.

deal more than we are able to simply do; but our doing these other things requires procedural knowledge that we can put into practice. Practical knowledge, when it has been learned and not forgotten, is what enables an agent to get started, as it were.[8]

Any such argument, as Ryle foresees,[9] is likely to provoke (what he called) a 'not unfashionable shuffle'. In confrontation with the things simply done which Hornsby speaks of and the 'simple' competences by virtue of which we do them, a philosopher tempted to make the intellectualist shuffle may suggest that, even though the agent has no 'explicit' knowledge that such and such is the way to do them, he has 'implicit' knowledge of it.

Three points may be made about this. The first is a countersuggestion: that, in the case of something I can simply do, if I am to be credited with the implicit knowledge that such and such is the way to do it, then isn't this putative implicit knowledge something owed to my competence to do it, not the other way about? Doesn't the regress argument just quoted show that, with simple acts, it has to be?

Secondly, where an agent got himself explicit knowledge that such and such was the way to do that simple thing, he still might bungle.[10] Indeed, getting that explicit knowledge might precisely undermine a previously ready and existing competence. Or will it be part of the opponent's doctrine of implicitness to add that it is 'best for practical purposes' that the knowledge-that which is in question be not explicit? If so, then on the intellectualist view why should that be so?[11]

Thirdly, every worked-out account that I know of implicit knowledge depends crucially at some point on practical knowledge.[12]

---

[8] Hornsby, 'Semantic Knowledge', 113–15; see also 116, footnote 17.

[9] 'Knowing How and Knowing That', paragraph 2.

[10] Compare Ryle, 'Knowing How and Knowing That', paragraph 24[0].

[11] A more interesting implicitist stance would of course be an anti-intellectualist position insisting with Ryle on the non-subsumability of knowing-how-to within knowing-that. Often, it will say, when we know more than we can say, what we know is not simply propositional.

[12] Consider, for instance, Leibniz's account of the *clear* (i.e. operational/effective) but *indistinct* (i.e. not articulate) knowledge by virtue of which someone recognizes reliably enough a kind of plant or animal (say) without being able to say what they go by in putting the name to it. (See 'Meditations on Cognition, Truth and Ideas', in *Die philosophischen Schriften von Gottfried Wilhelm Leibniz*, ed. C. I. Gerhardt, (Berlin: Weidmannsche Buchhandlung, 1875–90), IV, 422.) If or when a person with clear indistinct knowledge gets to the point where he or she can start to enumerate the marks of the plant or animal, his or her more distinct new knowledge is 'the step-child' (as Ryle would say) of the recognitional capacity. It is this practical capacity which is the starting point. Someone who was less good at catching on in the business of putting names to thing-kinds pointed out to him or her would

8

Fashionable (and further) shuffles apart, there is one larger and even more important point that needs to be made on Ryle's behalf.

In opposition to Ryle, Alan White claimed that to know how to V is to know the way to V; that this entailed being 'able to say or show' the way to V ('which includes knowing the manner, means and methods, where these are appropriate'). Such knowing the way to V, he insisted, was knowing propositionally that such and such was the way to V.

Sensing that some difficulty lurks here, Hacker and Bennett cannily qualify White's claim. They are careful to say that the way to do something 'is *often* to know and to be able to say or show that it is done thus and so'.[13] That leaves open, of course, what is to be said about the other cases—the cases where it seems more natural to construe X's knowing how to V not propositionally but as a matter of X's practical relation to the business of V-ing.

No qualifications such as Bennett's and Hacker's impinge on the account of these matters which has provoked the most discussion in the present decade, namely that of Jason Stanley and Timothy Williamson.[14] They model 'X knows how to V' on the scheme of an indirect question, wherein X is said to know the answer (or an answer) to the direct question 'How is one to V?' They claim that knowing how to V comes down to knowing, of some way w, that w is a way to V and entertaining the proposition that w is a way to V under a practical mode of presentation. Thus Hannah knows how to ride a bicycle if and only if, for some way w (e.g. this way, which she can demonstrate or put on display somehow), Hannah knows that way w is a way for Hannah to ride a bicycle.

be markedly less competent to make the advance towards more distinct (more articulate) knowledge of the distinguishing marks of the thing-kind in question. Concerning clarity and distinctness as Leibniz conceives them, see section II of my 'Three Moments in the Theory of Definition or Analysis: its Possibility, its Aim or Aims, and its Limit or Terminus', *Proceedings of the Aristotelian Society*, 107 (2006–7), 73–109.

[13] See M. R. Bennett and P. M. S. Hacker, *Philosophical Foundations of Neuroscience* (Oxford and Malden, Mass.: Blackwell, 2003), 151. Compare p. 155, where they write that remembering how to do something is '*in many kinds of case* . . . no different from remembering that the way to V is to do such and such (as is obviously the case in remembering how to open a combination lock, how to integrate, how to address the Pope, or how to spell "Edinburgh")'.

[14] See 'Knowing How', *Journal of Philosophy*, 98 (2001), 411–44.

In so far as these proposals are to be understood as standing in opposition to Ryle rather than as doing something else (see section 11 below), their difficulty may be seen by returning to the ship's pilot who is retained to bring ships safely to anchorage in a difficult harbour. (Never mind that old bicycling paradigm.) Consider the advice the pilot offers for the case when the wind is from the north and the tide is running out. The advice does not purport to be complete; it is gathered up from the pilot's own competence and experience; and its whole usefulness presupposes an existing competence of some kind in any recipient who will deploy it. Advice is one thing and a whole procedure for V-ing as a competent performer would V is another thing. Why should we suppose that such a procedure could ever be spelled out and set forth in the way required for there to be a propositional knowable in the form 'w is the way to V'? There is even less reason to believe that there is some simply propositional knowable that spells out the *whole set of complete procedures* which would somehow comprise and exhaust the pilot's competence for every imaginable situation of ship, cargo, tide, wind and weather.

9

Once we appreciate the difficulty of supposing that knowing the way to V (knowing it practically, that is) can be fully accounted for without knowing-how-to-V itself's reappearing as a precondition for w's being identified as the w that verifies the proposition 'w is a/the way by which one Vs'—once we appreciate everything that would be involved in this—examples will multiply.

Think of a small family firm in which the senior partner knows how to ensure that the people who work for the enterprise get on with one another, co-operate, and keep the show on the road. When he retires, there are all sorts of things that he can say to the family member who will succeed him about how he did what he did and what he owed his success to. But he reads these things off his own know-how and experience. The thing that he can't do is to reduce all the things that he practically knows into a finite form of words representing a complete guide or instruction book for his successor. The idea that he himself was implicitly following some such inner instruction book is absurd. There is no proposition, no form of words, that answers to and condenses his way of running the show. When he advises his successor, what he reads off from his experience and know-how isn't to be thought of as a full operating manual for competent performance by the senior partner.

Similarly, think of a general who fights a remarkably successful campaign over a certain terrain. On one unfortunate occasion, where things go wrong, he knows how to save whatever can be saved from the rout that the enemy inflicts upon him. As the campaign progresses, he can say a few things to his adjutant about how he does these things. After he retires, he can even give a lecture at a military college on the basis of his recollections. But nothing he says at the time or later can be turned into a drill for his successors, or into precise instructions. The more complete he tried to make his advice, moreover, the worse things might be for a successor who was sent out later to fight on the same terrain and decided to treat that advice as his complete instructions, as a recipe for success, or as a precise ritual for seeking in the exact Roman manner the favour and good offices of some god of war who might attend to anything extra that might be needed for the commander to win his battle.

10

It is likely that, at this point, Ryle's critic will insist that we are underestimating the resources of demonstration. Cannot the outgoing senior partner say to his successor: 'Well, you were here. Obviously, I can't describe everything. But you saw what I did and we talked about it. *That* is the way—that is one way at least—to run things'? Cannot the general say the same—to his adjutant at least, if not to his lecture audiences? Cannot the ship's pilot say something similar to his trainee or apprentice?

Such a defence, in so far as it is intended to sustain a campaign against Ryle's contentions, imports at least two difficulties. I shall try to state them, so far as possible, in the spirit of Ryle's original exposition.

Doesn't a demonstration that may take up to half a lifetime, is only made possible by the demonstrator's know-how, and depends for its effect on a hearer's incipient know-how, transcend the limits of any propositional knowledge that is to absorb or subsume the practical? In so far as one focuses upon Ryle's thesis, what matters is to keep track of the supposed transposition of knowing-how-to into knowing-that. No residue of knowing-how-to must linger within the result of trying to subsume the province of knowing-how-to within the province of knowing-that. Stanley and Williamson fail that test.

Secondly, as Ryle says, 'however many strata of knowing are postulated' and however we imagine the prolonged demonstration itself being bedded down and supplied to the position occupied by '*w*' in '*w* is a way to V' (the proposition which is supposedly grasped by one whose competence precisely consists in their 'entertaining' it) 'the same crux always recurs that a fool might have all that knowledge without knowing how to perform, and a sensible or cunning person might know how to perform who had not been introduced to the postulated [proposition that "*w* is a way to V"]'.[15]

I I

Reading Ryle as I do, I have concentrated throughout this essay on his anti-intellectualist claims about the impossibility of knowing-that's subsuming knowing-how-to. Strictly speaking, as Rumfitt indicates,[16] such a defence of Ryle can leave open the question of the logical or grammatical form of the English sentence 'John knows how to V'. All the same, however briefly, now let us consider the question: in that sentence does the 'how to' introduce an indirect question arising from the direct question 'How ought one, or how may one best V?'; or does the 'how to' introduce the act or activity in which John is said to be competent? (Or can it do either the one or the other?)

An archetype or paradigm for the first proposal might be the German form 'Johann weiß, wie man eine Gesellschaft leitet', where the verb *wissen* is followed by *wie* + *man* + the third person indicative. (The corresponding direct question is 'Wie leitet man eine Gesellschaft?') Here, for that standard way in German of speaking of competence, the act or activity construal seems very unpromising, and Stanley's and Williamson's propositional model seems virtually compulsory.

Suppose it were shown to be an equally compulsory account of 'knowing how to' in English. What would follow? Would the evidence then be

---

[15] Ryle, 'Knowing How and Knowing That', paragraph 25.   [16] See Rumfitt, 'Savoir faire'.

mounting up against Ryle? No. For, when it is worked out in Stanley's and Williamson's way, the propositional construal effectively concedes the correctness of Ryle's substantive thesis. Or so I claimed. If that is right then all that could be shown by the parallel between the English and German constructions is that the English language, like the German, falls short of being an ideal instrument for exploring and assessing Ryle's philosophy of knowing-how.[17] Maybe there is a better instrument. Linguistic form is an invaluable instrument for the explanation of function and the explanation of function greatly assists in the exploration of the metaphysical. But where one seeks assistance from language, one needs to choose a language which will furnish examples that illustrate rather than blur the point that is in question.

12

But is the Stanley–Williamson construal compulsory for English? The other linguistic form which has beckoned to those who have engaged in controversy concerning 'knows how to V' is the *savoir faire* construction in French. Here *savoir* governs a verb V which is given in the infinitive and connotes a competence to V which is attributed to the subject of the verb. There is no apparent difficulty in construing 'X knows how to run the family firm' in exactly the same way. Moreover, as Ian Rumfitt points out, there are similar infinitival constructions in Latin with *sapere*, in Russian with *imetj*, and in numerous other languages of yet other branches of Indo-European. These constructions serve very well to illustrate Ryle's contention; but they do so best when the contention has been made out—as I claim that it has—in its own terms.

Suppose we take seriously a parallel between *know how to* and *savoir faire* (the parallel which, I confess, I have always taken utterly for granted). Then

[17] Such a conclusion would not be unprecedented. It has been clear for a long time that neither Latin nor Russian furnishes the best range of examples for explicating singular denotation. Neither Latin nor French is the ideal language in which to illustrate the phenomenon of verb-aspect. Estuary English is not the ideal instrument for the discussion of counterfactual possibilities. Finally, given a choice, Russian or Polish is not the ideal language in which to expound or explain Russell's Theory of Descriptions.

we are faced immediately with a complication or a *bifurcation*. However frequently *knows how* may need to be construed as introducing something non-propositional, namely the business of V-ing, no less frequently, whether the verb in the following phrase is finite or infinitival, *knows how* can introduce an indirect question corresponding to a direct question with the same interrogative *how* that we find in 'How did Leander swim from Abydos to Sestos?', or 'How does one open that door?', or 'How to borrow money most cheaply?' So it seems that there is a wide range of indirect questions in *how* which are no different from indirect questions corresponding to *when* ('when to luff?') or *where* ('where to buy a spare bracket for that old Raleigh bicycle?') or *whom* ('whom to ask that question?' or 'whom did she ask to dance the polka with her?').

Why not simply accept that *knows how* takes two different constructions which deliver two discernible senses? It is true that this bifurcation of construction—and the semantic ambiguity which it imports—has been challenged. But one of Rumfitt's signal services to our topic is to have suggested an answer to that challenge and lent independent plausibility to a bifurcation that strikes instinctive Ryleans (among them myself) as entirely easy and inevitable.[18] Having referred to Rumfitt, I shall not paint the lily.

13

As already remarked in section 1, critics of Ryle such as White have made much of the cases of knowing how to spell 'silhouette', knowing how to get from Aberystwyth to Scarborough by train, knowing how to light the grill on this cooker, or knowing how to address the Queen or the Pope or an Archbishop. Examples like this do not fall under the act or activity paradigm that interested Gilbert Ryle. But, as we have just seen, Ryle does not need to say they do. It is well worth noticing, moreover, how often it is a practical competence that is the source of propositional knowledge of these kinds (see again section 3, the second paragraph) or in other cases

---

[18] See Rumfitt, 'Savoir faire', especially 163–5.

how often the propositional knowledge in question is of a kind chiefly useful to a person who already has practical competence. To be told how 'silhouette' is spelled may fill one gap in someone's *general* competence to write or spell.

14

Having known one another but slightly for a decade or two, Peter Hacker and I became friends in the 1990s when we combined in two successive summer terms to organize a seminar about the history of Oxford philosophy. Prior to the seminar, Peter's reservations about me focused mainly on my interest in truth-conditional semantics; mine about him centred on his adversarial attitude towards that and other emergent enterprises. If, in the course of our collaboration,[19] Peter changed his mind about anything it was about me, not about truth-conditional semantics; the things that I came to understand about him were the true width and depth of his knowledge of philosophy, his learning about history, science, and art, and his preoccupation (which it proved we shared) with the environmental, cultural, and academic devastation that is everywhere about us. Above all, I discovered his good nature and the true meaning of the severe and terrifying accusations he was wont to send out against the philosophical world—mostly to the effect that what X or Y or Z had said or written quite simply 'made no sense'. It took me time to grasp this, but for Peter failing to make sense is the ordinary condition of philosophy (and of many other subjects) as done by human beings. Save in the presence of supreme effort, there has to be a presumption that one will often fail to make sense. Even Ryle sometimes failed (though not, I have contended, in 'Knowing How and Knowing That'). Wittgenstein too—even the later Wittgenstein, I boldly venture to assert—failed on occasion.[20] But once we contemplate these precedents, they set us free. Once reassured that not making sense

---

[19] In the seminar, Peter did Hampshire and Strawson; Williams did Collingwood; Peacocke did Berlin; Baker did Waismann; Hornsby did Austin; Hyman did Ryle; Kenny did Anscombe; Mander did Bradley; and I did Ross and Hare.

[20] For instance, so many of his denials essentially involve 'philosophical' uses of words; and all too often these denials, if we heed them, deprive us of things we want to say in an ordinary language uncorrupted—as he would wish—by philosophy. For a word or two more on Wittgenstein and on making sense more generally, see my *Twelve Lectures*, 28.

stands well apart from illiteracy, moral failure, dishonesty, lapse of personal hygiene, dropping a brick, or affirming the consequent, we can take heart and look for small local victories, both in writing and in reading, against the nonsense in which ordinary human nature prompts us so readily and easily to acquiesce.

Action, Content and Inference

JONATHAN DANCY

In this essay I try to make progress with a rather peculiar question: can an action be the conclusion of an inference? My answer to this question is no. But it takes me quite a long time to get to this answer. Probably some readers will feel that the answer is obvious. How could one infer an action? Action is just the wrong sort of thing to be the conclusion of anything worth calling inference. All that inference can do is to take one from belief to belief; it can't take one from belief to action—say, the action of combing one's hair. Unfortunately this is altogether too quick. My question is ambiguous, and its ambiguity sets us a puzzle, and it is a puzzle to which the answer is not obvious, as we will see.

I

There is a familiar distinction between inference-as-process and inference-as-structure. Modus ponens is an example of an inferential structure. An inferrer whose inference has that structure is engaging in a process, that of moving from two beliefs to a third—or, if not exactly that process then some similar one. This process can also be called an inference, and it is an action. Someone who infers is someone who acts. But where such an action is done, there must be premises and conclusions, and these are not actions (at least not normally), nor are they parts of the process that constitutes the inference-as-process. In the ordinary case,

It is a privilege to be able to offer this paper in a volume honouring Peter Hacker, from whom I have learnt an enormous amount, not only in philosophy, but also about how to do philosophy and how not to do it. I wish that I were capable of engaging more directly with one of his many concerns, and brave enough to do so as well. My paper is an attempt to apply some work by Alan White, which I first encountered in Peter's reading group in St John's, to some issues in the philosophy of action. White's question was 'What do we believe'; mine is 'What do we do?'

where we infer beliefs from beliefs, the premises will be things that we believe, and we come to believe the conclusion by recognizing, perhaps only implicitly, an 'inferential' relation between them and the conclusion to which they lead. That we believe these premises is not itself one of the premises; but still the premises must be believed if belief in the conclusion is to result. So there is a process, a move from believings to a new believing, and there is a relation between things believed, which, in the deductive case at least, will have a structure; and both of these things can be called an inference. We can display the structure and set it alongside an account of the process involved, thus getting both of the things that are called inference in one grid. The result might look like this:

Belief	p
Belief	If p then q
Belief	q

This grid has the weakness that it fails to express the direction, or flow, of the inference. But I don't know how to represent that in my grid. Remembering that there is a direction in the process as well as in the structure, one could try this:

Belief	p
Belief	If p then q
So: Belief	So: q

But this isn't very convincing as it stands; there seems to be one too many 'so's. But if we are only allowed one 'so', it is not clear where to put it. Perhaps having two 'so's is all right, so long as we remember that they are different 'so's. Perplexed, I am going to leave the 'so's out from now on. Perhaps an imaginary downward arrow to the left of each grid will suffice.

Someone who starts by believing that p, recognizes that if it is true that p, it must be true that q and so comes to believe that q, is someone who has inferred that q. He has not inferred that q from his beliefs that p and that if p then q. That is, his inference is not of this form:

Belief	I believe that p
Belief	I believe that if p then q
Belief	q

If it had been of this form, it would have been invalid. There is another sense, however, in which it is perfectly proper to say that he has inferred that q from his beliefs, for he has inferred it from things he believes, namely that p and that if p then q.

It is possible to draw an inference without yet forming the belief or accepting that the relevant conclusion is true. We might do this, for instance, when having seen that the conclusion follows from the premises, we decide to ponder the matter awhile in order to decide whether to abandon one of the premises or to accept the conclusion. So there are in fact two actions to be considered: the action of inferring, and the 'action' of coming to believe the conclusion. For the purposes of this essay I am just going to accept that this 'coming to believe' is a perfectly proper sort of action; we can do it, we can do it for reasons, we can decide not to do it but to do something else (abandon one of the premises)—in all these ways it is as active as one could hope to get. But I am not really arguing the point here.

My question is whether an action can be the conclusion of an inference, and in one sense the answer is a clear yes. In fact, there are two actions around, as I have just said: that of drawing the inference and that of coming to accept the conclusion. Both of these could be called 'concluding'. But my question was not about *these* actions. What I want to know is whether we can have an inference whose conclusion is an ordinary action, say that of combing one's hair. Suppose that I comb my hair for the reason that it will make me look more kempt. How might we represent this as an inference? Our grid might start something like this:

Aim	To look more kempt
Belief	If I comb my hair, I will look more kempt
?	?

But it just doesn't seem that there is anything to put on the last line. If I put the action of combing on the left-hand side, where there are some other things that I am happy to think of as actions, nothing remains to be put on the right; and if we put it on the right, it seems that we need something else to put on the left, and nothing suggests itself. The home case, as it were, where we are dealing with beliefs alone, is one where it is easy to see what to put along the bottom line, for where there is belief there is always the thing believed, however we are to understand that vexed phrase, along with the believing of it (sometimes, but unhelpfully, called a propositional attitude). What is more, the force of the inference derives from the relations between the various things believed, the things that appear on the right-hand side. But where the conclusion is an action such as combing one's hair, we seem to be stymied; we don't get the sort of structure we need if we are to carve things up in the way required.

It doesn't matter, for this simple point, how we are to conceive exactly of the 'thing believed'. All that is required is that one try to discover, for an ordinary action such as combing one's hair, some distinction suitably analogous to that between the thing believed and the believing of it, that will enable us to fill in the last two boxes appropriately. And the standard approaches to these issues all seem to agree that there is no such thing to be found. Think of Aristotle's so-called Practical Syllogism. Here is an apparently Aristotelian example:

Belief	Dry food is good for a man
Belief	This chicken is dry food

So: Eats.

It would not make it any better if we complicated the grid—which we could do thus:

Wanted	Appropriate food
Belief	Dry food is good for a man
Belief	This chicken is dry food

The conclusion would still have to be: Eats.

One way of dealing with this situation is to allow that action cannot be inferred—whatever that would mean—but to insist that intention can be. This is effectively the position that John Broome takes in recent work, not yet published, though for rather different reasons than the ones I am considering. Here is an apparently comprehensible grid, which is much helped by understanding an intention to eat as an intention that I eat:

Intention	I eat appropriate food
Belief	Dry food is good for a man
Belief	This chicken is dry food
Intention	I eat this chicken

This is not Aristotelian at all, but it does have the notable advantage that some cases, at least, of reasoning of this sort will have a valid inference on the right-hand side. Here is one:

Intention	I am more kempt
Belief	If not [I comb my hair], then not [I am more kempt]
Intention	I comb my hair

Broome wants to say that cases like this are paradigm cases of practical reasoning, understood as a form of inference. Reasoning never gets more practical than this move from a combination of intention and belief to the formation of a new intention. And the force of the reasoning is effectively the force of modus ponens. (As I said, he has his own reasons for saying this, which I don't accept, but which are not my present concern.) Unfortunately, however, there are some perfectly good examples of very similar reasoning whose force this sort of account cannot capture at all, such as this one:

Intention	I am more kempt
Belief	If I comb my hair, I am more kempt
Intention	I comb my hair

If the force of the previous inference is to be explained by the fact that its right-hand side is modus ponens, this new inference should have no force, since it is a logical fallacy, namely that of affirming the antecedent. But in fact the new inference has a perfectly clear force,[1] as an instance of reasoning to a sufficient, if not a necessary, means. This persuades me that the sort of gerrymandering required to make Broome's approach work, by which I mean all the unintuitive reshaping of the various things on the right-hand side in order to get them to jump through the appropriate logical hoops, is not only awkward (or worse, as I will suggest shortly) but fruitless.

My original question was whether it is possible for an action to conclude an inference. This has turned into the question of how to carve things up so that we have some method of filling in both boxes in the bottom line of our grid, even though we are dealing neither with belief nor with intention, but with action. The obvious strategy, as I have said, is to find, for action, some analogue of the distinction between believing and thing believed. This strategy is not helped by the fact that the distinction between believing and thing believed is deeply disputed. And it might be proposed instead that what is needed is an analogue of the rather different distinction between propositional attitude and proposition as content, where a content is thought of as something distinct from what I have been calling so far a thing believed (which I have been thinking of as something capable of being the case). If an action has a content, in this sense, that content will not be identical with what is done; and that seems right, since after all what is done, the things we do, must be actions, and one action cannot be somehow the content of another one.

It seems to me, then, that there are three possible ways of proceeding, of which the first two construct a notion of *content* that is supposedly capable of playing the role required, without being identical with *what is done*. Of these two ways, the first takes the content of the action to be whatever it is that one knows when one knows what one is doing; the content of the action is the content of the knowledge. The second takes the content of the action to be the content of the relevant intention. (There are those who would say that these two amount to the same thing;[2] I am assuming for present purposes that they are wrong.) The third, and most promising, is not to look elsewhere, to knowledge of action or to intention to act,

---

[1] Or rather, it is perfectly clear that it has a force, though it is of course far from clear how to elucidate that force.

[2] Elisabeth Anscombe and J. O. Urmson spring to mind. See Anscombe, *Intention* (Oxford: Blackwell, 1957) and Urmson, 'Memory and Imagination', *Mind*, 76 (1967), 83–91.

hoping to construct a notion of content here without any suggestion that the content of the action will be what is done, but rather to look directly at the concept of acting itself, and to write some distinction between what is done and the doing of it that is suitably analogous to the distinction between what is believed and the believing of it, leaving the notion of content behind altogether. (The analogy is suitable if it enables us to fill in the grid in such a way that both sides of it make the right sort of sense.) I will spend most of the space remaining to me on this last option, though I will use the distinction between what is intended and the intending of it as a sort of intermediate case between belief and action, when it seems appropriate.

I start with the suggestion that we could take what is known by the agent in knowing what she is doing, and use that to stand as the 'content' of the action, that is, to go in the bottom right-hand corner of the grid, with the action itself on the left-hand side. Now this notion of 'agentual knowledge' is much disputed, and it is hard to be sure quite how one should characterize it. So for present purposes I will be as generous as possible, and allow (what I don't believe) that we are dealing here with ordinary knowledge-that. The thing known could then perhaps stand on the right-hand side as a content for the action, leaving us with something to put on the left-hand side.

But if our model is inference, it will have it that we come to do the action (which stands on the left-hand side) because we see a suitable inferential relation between premises and conclusion. The conclusion is what one knows when one knows what one is doing. But it makes little sense to suppose that one acts because one recognizes that this sort of thing known—that I am Φ-ing—follows suitably from premises about the situation. If it does follow, it seems that I ought to be acting already. That is, the conclusion of the inference should be true *because* I am acting, rather than the action occurring because the agent recognizes some inferential relation between premises and the conclusion that he is acting in a certain way. So I don't see that this first approach delivers the goods.

This criticism also applies to the second approach, which takes the content of the relevant intention to stand on the right-hand side, allowing the action itself to stand on the left. But this approach has its own defects too. First, one might worry that one and the same action may be done with several distinct intentions. Miss Anscombe's example of pumping and poisoning makes the point perfectly well.[3] There are various descriptions of one and the same action, and even if we restrict ourselves to those under which the action was intentional, we will still end up with several. The man was pumping the water *and* poisoning the well *and* killing off that lot inside the house, and she maintained that the pumping *was* the poisoning of the well, and *was* the killing of that lot inside. Can one and the same action have several 'contents' in this way? Belief is not allowed such a luxury; we normally individuate beliefs according to their contents. But perhaps this is not a problem. All that we wanted in the first place was *some* formulation that we could put on the right-hand side, leaving the action itself firmly on the left. The fact that more than one formulation is available should not disconcert us; indeed, for each formulation different reasoning is appropriate, and this is just how it should be.

In the case that Anscombe considers, one and the same action is characterized in terms of the different intentions with which it was done. Unfortunately for the present strategy, however, it is not always possible for the intention with which an action is done to be converted into a new description of the action itself. If I buy a ticket to Scotland, with the intention of going to a conference there next week, the content of that intention does not serve as a suitable 'content' for my action. It is not as if the action of buying the ticket *is* the action of going to the conference, or that I am going to the conference *by* buying the ticket. (I may be making it possible for me to go to the conference, but that is a different matter.) Such cases will have to be excluded somehow, for otherwise some actions will be ascribed inappropriate contents.

But what worries me most is the thought that, for this second approach to work, we have to understand the thing intended as specified by a that-clause rather than in the normal form 'to Φ'. John Broome routinely does this, and thinks of it as innocuous.[4] But I think it is not innocuous at all. There are perfectly good uses of 'intend that p' in English, but the normal ones are when A intends that B should do something or other, perhaps agree to do his share of departmental administration. To convert

---

[3] *Intention*, 37 ff.

[4] See J. Broome, 'Practical Reasoning', in J. Bermùdez and A. Millar (eds.), *Reason and Nature: Essays in the Theory of Rationality* (Oxford: Oxford University Press, 2002), 85–111.

any ordinary intention, intention to Φ, into an intention that one Φ's, seems to involve taking the same attitude to oneself and one's future actions as one takes towards others and their actions when one intends that they will act in this way rather than that, and this distorts the special nature of intending to Φ. If I intend that he Φ's, I might so arrange things that he only has one option, that of Φ-ing. If I intend that I Φ, similar sorts of action might be envisaged in relation to myself, say boxing myself into a corner in such a way that only one choice remains to me, the one that I earlier intended that I would choose—but that seems a very odd approach, and one that seems out of place if my intention is simply to Φ.

Constantine Sandis reminded me that the relation between intention and action is like that between trying and action; I intend to Φ and I try to Φ. But I cannot try that I Φ. The absurdity of supposing that no damage is done to the notion of trying by understanding all attempts as attempts that p seems to me to infect similar attempts to convert intending to Φ into intending that I Φ.

I am encouraged in my reluctance here by thinking about the ways in which other languages treat intention. In French, the notion of intending that p is simply not available. This is perhaps because they have no *verb* equivalent to our 'intend' (the Latin *intendere* having vanished), and make do with the noun *intention*, so that to intend is always to have an intention, 'avoir l'intention *de* faire quelque chose'. In French one cannot have the intention that something is the case, or that something be so; one only has the intention of doing something. If one wants to intend that someone else do something, say that one's son goes into the law, the French expression is 'je le destine à la loi'.

Intending that I do something cannot be expressed in German either. German does at least have a verb *beabsichtigen*. But in the first-person singular, one cannot 'beabsichtigen dass', one can only 'beabsichtigen zu'. So A always intends to Φ, A never intends that A Φ. One can intend, of another person, that that person Φ's; in such contexts, and only there, is 'beabsichtigen dass' acceptable.

All this is in the service of raising suspicion about the 'propositional' expression of intention. There is a distinction between intending to Φ and intending that something be the case, even when that thing is that one Φ's. But still, we might say, 'to Φ' could perfectly well stand as the content of an intention, and thus stand on the right-hand side in the grid:

Intention/aim	To look more kempt
Belief	If I comb my hair, I will look more kempt
Action	To comb my hair

The fact that this doesn't look like modus ponens, nor even like the fallacy of asserting the antecedent, should not disconcert us; we can, and surely should, abandon the aim of trying to get our inferences to look like valid deductive inferences; there are, or at least may be, other sorts of inference for them to be. Things would be no worse if we took 'Φ-ing' rather than 'to Φ' as the content of the intention (helped by the possibility of, and undeterred by the awkwardness of, 'I intend combing my hair'), which would give us:

Intention/aim	Looking more kempt
Belief	If I comb my hair, I will look more kempt
Action	Combing my hair

On these two accounts the 'content' of my action of combing my hair is either 'to comb my hair' or just 'combing my hair'. If these are unfamiliar sorts of content, too bad. The notion of content that we are using here has rather few constraints.

It seems to me, however, that by now these manoeuvres are achieving nothing. The third approach has collapsed into the first. When we look at the sort of content we have constructed, these 'contents' are just what, in doing that action, we were intending to do; but what we were intending to do is normally just what we go on to do—which is either the action itself or the thing done (which is of course also called an action, just as the thing believed is called a belief), but not some third thing thought of as its content. So we might as well have been talking about the action, on the one hand, and what is done on the other. But what does the distinction between the action and what is done amount to?

II

In his magisterial paper 'What We Believe',[5] Alan White draws a distinction between two types of accusative, which he calls 'object-accusatives' and 'intentional-accusatives' (p. 70). In the case of belief, which is his topic, object-accusatives range from people and stories to propositions—though White is of the opinion that propositions make rather strange objects of belief (and I agree with him). The 'intentional-accusative' is the 'that p' that appears in 'S believes that p'. This, according to White, does not specify an object that is believed, even though it does tell us what S believes; we know that 'that p' is not an object-accusative because it doesn't matter to the truth of 'S believes that p' whether 'that p' exists or not. (One reason why 'the proposition that p' is a bogus object-accusative is that the existence of the proposition that p is somehow guaranteed, unlike that of the persons, stories, claims, propaganda and other things that are believed by us. One cannot believe propaganda that does not exist.)

So now: if 'that p' does not specify an object, what is the role of the 'that p' clause in 'S believes that p'? We will have to understand its contribution in some other way. White considers the possibility that the answer to the question 'What do we believe?' might be just 'Nothing'. One way of building that answer up into an explanation, to which he devotes quite a lot of time, starts from the idea that when someone believes that p, there is something that they have, namely the belief that p. This 'belief that p' is an 'internal accusative', apparently; and the suggestion is, as White puts it, that in this expression 'that p' is 'an adjective of internal accusatives and thus might be assigned adverbial force' (p. 81). The 'thus' in this needs some explanation, but I suppose the idea is that an internal accusative is just a grammatical device, a sort of grammatical fiction or expansion of the verb from which we started; and so that adjectives attached to that accusative 'really' function as adverbs attached to the original verb.

White then considers this sort of internal accusative in some detail. He claims that, although when we believe that p we have the belief that p, we do not believe the belief that p; what we believe is always that p, and

[5] A. White, 'What We Believe', in N. Rescher (ed.), *Studies in the Philosophy of Mind*, American Philosophical Quarterly monograph series, 6 (Oxford: Blackwell, 1972), 69–84. Unattributed page references are to this article.

never our belief that p. Similarly, when we discover something we make a discovery (this is the internal accusative for 'discover'), but we do not discover our discovery. 'Believe' and 'discover' are different in this respect from many other verbs that have internal accusatives; we smell smells, we catch catches and we dream dreams.

To give another example, intermediate between belief (White's target) and action (mine): when I intend, I have an intention (internal accusative), but what I intend is not the intention that I have. What I intend is an action, but the intention that I have is not an action—even though we can say such things as 'to marry well—that is my intention'. It is my intention, what I intend, but not the intention that I have.

White's eventual conclusion is that even if there is a way of understanding 'that p' as an adjective of the internal accusative 'belief', this is quite compatible with allowing that 'that p' also names an 'intentional object' which might therefore still serve as the sort of thing picked out by the expression 'what we believe'. He writes, 'It would be ridiculous to argue that just because a man who firmly and sincerely believes in fairies holds a firm, sincere, and in-fairies belief, therefore "fairies" cannot also be the name of what he believes in' (p. 83). So White concludes that even if this story about adverbial force is coherent, it does nothing to sustain what it is supposed to sustain, namely the answer 'Nothing' to the question 'What do we believe?' And he substantiates this point by listing various adjectives that apply to what is believed but not to the belief that, in so believing, one has. For instance, what is believed may be improbable, impossible or about to happen, but the belief can be none of these things; the belief, however, can be yours rather than mine, sensible, tentative, erroneous and subject to revision, while what is believed can be none of these things. The overall message, then, is that the answer 'Nothing' to the question what we believe is not only unsupported but wrong.

My interest is not primarily in what we believe, but in what we do. Still, much of what White says about belief can be equally well said about action. When we talk of 'doing an action', the phrase 'an action' is an internal accusative. When S Φ's, S does an action, the action of Φ-ing. In this, 'of Φ-ing' is an adjective of an internal accusative, and thus might be 'assigned adverbial force'—to use White's expression. But this, if he is right, is quite compatible with allowing that there is an intentional object, the thing done. We are not getting away from that. And such a thing could serve on the right-hand side in my grid.

Or could it? If it is an *intentional object* of action, the question whether it 'exists' should be irrelevant to the truth of 'S did an action'. But can S do an action that somehow doesn't exist? This seems all wrong, whereas similar remarks about what is believed and intended make some sense. One can intend something that does not 'exist', that is, come to pass; but one cannot do such a thing. But this may not be an insoluble difficulty. Perhaps the appropriate analogy here is between belief, which can be of what is not, and knowledge, which cannot—even though there is a sense in which knowledge has an intentional object, a focus of attention, just as belief does. We could perhaps say the same thing about intention. What I intend is what I later do, though qua intended it does not have to exist and qua thing done it does.

However, I don't think that White's conclusions can be applied to the case of action in this last respect. I see no pressure to admit the 'existence' of a thing done in addition to the doing of that thing. There is of course a perfectly good and independent sense of 'something done' which means 'something achieved', some consequence of the action. This I mention only to leave aside. The 'things done' that I am talking about are actions done, not results achieved.

First, even if one allows White's claims about the internal accusatives he considers, there are other models around. When I am asked to give examples of internal accusatives, I tend to offer 'striking a blow' and 'winning a victory'. The verbs 'strike' and 'win' have both internal and external accusatives; we strike people and oil as well as blows, and we win battles and prizes as well as victories; sometimes internal and external accusatives can appear together, as in 'he struck Peter a well-judged blow'. To such cases, White's account of an internal accusative seems not to apply. He writes, 'A host of verbs has both an internal and an external accusative; where the internal accusative is a verbal noun characterizing what is Ved by reference to the Ving of it, but being itself identifiable by reference to the external accusative, that is, what is Ved.' (p. 81). It is hard for me to be sure that I have understood this sentence. White uses an example of bequeathing a house. The house is my bequest, what I bequeath (though I don't bequeath the bequest, I only bequeath the house), and in this case there is something quite substantial, the house that is bequeathed, by reference to which, it seems, the internal accusative is identifiable. There is nothing like this for 'strike a blow'. If Peter is the person struck, we might say that the blow struck is identifiable, distinguished from others, by reference to Peter. But in no way is it true that in 'he struck Peter a blow' the internal accusative characterizes Peter by reference to his being struck. The phrase 'a blow' is not a way of characterizing Peter as struck at all. This is because Peter is not a blow, whereas White's house was a bequest.

Second, it is very tempting to think of doing an action as analogous to striking a blow. The idea is that the noun is a mere device of grammatical convenience. The thing done, unlike a thing bequeathed or discovered, has no more a separate 'existence' than does the blow that is struck. We can attach adjectives to 'the action that he did' in the characterization of behaviour, but we can achieve just the same end by the use of adverbs. Either way we are characterizing how someone behaved, which is to say, what he did. He gave her a vicious kick, or he kicked her viciously (which is different from 'he kicked her, viciously', where 'viciously' is in apposition, not characterizing the manner but the fact of the kicking). He did a courageous thing, or he acted courageously. He struck several blows, or he struck often. He did something unusual, or he acted in an unusual way. These apparent adjectives of internal accusatives have adverbial force, in much the sort of way that White was considering. Their focus is the relevant verb, and they characterize the manner of someone's acting, how they behaved.

There are differences between this model and the one with which White is working. First, one can certainly do the action, even if one cannot believe the belief or bequeath the bequest. Second, the blow struck, having no independent 'existence', is incapable of independent characterization (unlike things believed, bequeathed or discovered); the same, I would say, is true of the action done. Third, the possibility of an intentional object, which as White says remains open in the case of belief, does not seem to remain open in the case of action.

There is of course a risk of over-generalization here. Is it true of every adjective attached to an internal accusative (of my sort) that it can be turned into an adverb attached to the verb? I don't know that I need to pronounce on the matter. Complex cases such as 'he acted in an unusual way, but what he did was not unusual' cause no difficulties; they involve nested adverbs. Still, there may be cases where the language is more comfortable with the use of a noun than of an adverb. There may even be some whether the use of a noun is somehow the only way to do it. All that one would have to say in response to such things is that, still, what is being characterized is the way in which the agent acted.

A summary is in order. We have been trying to make sense of the idea that we might be able to distinguish between a doing and the thing done, in a way analogous to the distinction between a belief and the thing believed. But I am suggesting that though the thing believed can have qualities that the believing does not have—it can be complicated, contradictory, relevant, important and so on—the same is not true of the action and the thing done. If this is so, there is considerable pressure to abandon the idea that just as 'what he believes' names an intentional object capable of its own qualities, so too 'the thing done' names an intentional object of some sort.[6] Nor would it be helpful to think of it as an intentional-accusative—but it isn't an object-accusative either. And if this is so, we have failed in our attempt to find something, or rather two distinct things, to put along the bottom line of the grid that represents practical reasoning.

III

If one looks for other accounts of the relation between the doing and the thing done, one finds very few. But there is one, offered by Richard Cartwright and Jennifer Hornsby. According to Hornsby,

[a]ctions are particulars—unrepeatable things, named by phrases like 'Hyam's setting light to the petrol at two o'clock on the fateful day' and 'my reading this paper now'. *Something done*, on the other hand, is not a particular: things done are named by phrases like 'inflict damage', or 'eat an egg', or 'throw a brick'.[7]

Actions are 'variably describable'; this means that there are different things that can be said about an action, and all are equally descriptions of it, for there is no 'single truth' about what an action is. What is done, however, is not a particular, and there is only one thing that can be said about a thing done. In that sense, its essence exhausts its nature.

---

[6] Let alone an abstract object, as suggested by Jennifer Hornsby.
[7] J. Hornsby, 'On What's Intentionally Done', in S. Shute *et al.* (eds.), *Action and Value in Criminal Law* (Oxford: Oxford University Press, 1993), 55–74, at p. 56.

But if what is done has an essence, and a nature, but is not a particular, what can it be but a universal? And can one *do* a universal? What is more, cannot I say at least some things about things done, such as that they are wrong? And how could a universal be wrong? It might be that all instances of the universal are wrong, and wrong as such; but this would not make the universal itself wrong. And are we to suppose that the action is itself an instance of a thing done, in fact of many things done? If so, the relation between action and thing done is the relation between particular and universal—the same relation as that between object and property. This looks very unconvincing to me.

IV

The conclusion that White draws from his discussion of internal accusatives is rather peculiar. He writes, 'Hence, the fact that "that p" can be an adjective of the internal accusative "belief" is no reason for supposing that it cannot also be the name of the intentional accusative, which expresses what is believed.' (p. 83) This cannot be the right way to put the point, since 'that p' cannot be the name of an accusative, intentional or otherwise; if it is the name of anything, it must be of some kind of object, not of a word of a certain sort. 'That p' could however *be* an intentional accusative (in White's sense), which then would express (or name?) what is believed, just as in the next sentence White suggests that 'fairies' could be the name of what someone believes in. If it is a name, we have a choice to face. We could say that what it names is an intentional object, on the grounds that it is not required that there be fairies for him to believe in them, just as what someone believes, namely that p, may not be so. Alternatively, we could say that in every case where it is not the case that p, 'that p' is an empty name, a name that names nothing. These options are different. Names of the first sort are guaranteed all the success of which they are capable, since the possibility of reference failure does not arise. Names of the second sort are not.

I take White's conclusion to be that even if 'that p' can be understood as an adjective of internal accusatives, still it might be, and in fact is, the name of an intentional object. When asked, then, what is believed when one believes that p, his only answer is 'something which exists when the belief is not mistaken and does not exist when it is mistaken' (p. 83). This is different from the answer 'something, when the belief is not mistaken, and nothing when it is mistaken'.

One could perhaps take the same view about intention: that it, like belief, has an intentional object, one which 'exists' when the intention is carried out and not otherwise. And could we not then say that an action has that same object, the only difference being that if the action has such an object, that object must 'exist'—just as knowledge has the same object as belief, except that for it to be knowledge, the object must 'exist', i.e. (in this case) be true, or be the case?

The answer to this last question is clearly no. The intentional object of the intention is the action intended. That action cannot have itself as its intentional object. However there is a temptation at this point to return to the previously discarded notion of a content. Why should we not say that the *content* of an intention is something of the form 'that I Φ', even though this is not what is intended? And once we are given this, cannot we award the same content to the action intended? I argued previously that we should not be impressed with the form 'I intend that I Φ'; but that says nothing against the claim that someone who says 'I intend to Φ' expresses an intention whose content is that he Φ's.[8] And then, since we are supposing that actions may inherit the content of the intention with which they are done, we can allot the same content to the act of Φ-ing.[9]

Have we yet said anything that tells against this manoeuvre? I think that at this point it is impossible to avoid saying something about what a content is supposed to be. All that we have on the table so far is that the content of a belief is not to be identical with what is believed.

First, however, it is important to point out that the supposed content of intention, 'that I Φ', is not something that could also stand as the content of a belief. To do that, it would have to be of some form such as 'that I will Φ', or 'that I am Φ-ing'. But these things do not look promising as contents for intentions. So we are missing one attractive feature of the notion of content, which is that content can be shared. What I believe can be what he hopes and what she fears. Similarly, my belief, her fear and his

---

[8] In his 'Practical Reasoning', Broome takes it that the content of an intention is a proposition, one of the form 'I will Φ'.

[9] Constantine Sandis pointed out that this approach would deprive completely unintentional actions of any content.

hope can have the same content. But I doubt that an intention can share that content.

This by itself does little to unsettle the idea that 'that I Φ' might be the content of an intention. For that, we need to ask more closely what we are expecting of the notion of content. I think there are two main aspects to be considered. The first is the link with issues of individuation. The second is the link with explanation.

So our obscure question whether intentions have a content can become the following longer but rather less obscure question: Is there some feature of intention, other than the thing intended, that plays a role in the individuation or explanation of intention similar to the role played by what is called 'content' in the individuation or explanation of belief? And if the answer is yes, there will be the follow-up question: Is there some feature of action, other than the thing done, that plays a role in individuation or explanation of action similar to the role played by what is called 'content' in the individuation or explanation of belief and intention?

What is the case when two people have the same belief? We are supposing that the answer to this question is not given by showing when two people believe the same thing, that is, that it is true of both of them that they believe that p. If you believe that you are ill and I believe that you are ill, we believe the same thing; if my belief is true, so is yours. But there is another sense in which we do not have the same belief. We would have the same belief if you believe that you are ill and I believe that I am ill. Let us say in such a case that our beliefs have the same content, though the thing believed is not the same. So 'having the same belief' is ambiguous, and it is disambiguated by distinguishing between identity of content and identity of thing believed. (Do not assume that identity of content is to be understood in terms of identity of proposition.)

Exactly similar things can be said of intention. What is the case when two people have the same intention? First we should ask whether this is even possible. Initially one is tempted to say no; what I intend must be an action of mine, and what you intend must be an action of yours. (This sort of thought depends on the strictures on 'intend that p' in section II above.) If the identity of an intention is given by the conditions under which that intention will be successful, your intention and mine are bound to be distinct. Suppose that we both intend to come joint second in the race. (This is distinct from our both intending to come joint second together.

That would be a special case, a joint intention. I am thinking of a case where our intentions are quite separate.) Our intentions are not identical, because the success conditions for one are distinct from those for the other. Still, we might say, though what we intend is not the same, our intentions may yet have the same content, of this form: I come joint second in the race. (Again, do not assume that this is a proposition. It is not at all clear that it is the same proposition both times, if it is even a proposition at all.)

If this is the right model, it looks as if there are as good reasons for attributing content to intention as there are for attributing it to belief, in addition to the thing intended or believed. Intention can have a content of the form 'I Φ'. And we are supposing that an action of Φ-ing might inherit content of this sort from its intention.

But are we able to draw the same contrast for action as we have used for belief and intention? Is there a distinction between two senses in which two people's actions are or can be identical? The answer to this question is affected by our earlier decision that in 'do an action' the phrase 'an action' is an internal accusative. On this account, doing the same action amounts to no more than acting in the same way. Talk of identity is now harder to impose on the situation, because identity of way is no more than similarity.

Suppose that we are both walking to the top of the hill. What you are doing is what I am doing. Your action is not my action, but this is simply because you are doing one and I am doing the other. The same is true of belief and intention; we may have the same belief or the same intention, but my believing or intending cannot be yours. This is just a difference in agent. The fact that your action is not my action gives us two actions, but not yet two things done. There are no things done of a sort to have identity conditions. All we can say is that we acted in the same way. Are we able to find some dimension of similarity for actions which can only, or best, be expressed using a notion of content analogous to the one we used for belief and intention? I can't see one. We could try contrasting two situations. In the first we both travel to London with my wife, in the second I travel with my wife and you travel with yours. Does this generate two dimensions of identity, two distinct criteria for 'doing the same thing'? All we need say is that your behaviour is similar to mine in different respects in the different situations. If so, the notion of content that we need to use to distinguish different dimensions of identity for belief and for intention does not apply to action.

The other possible role for thoughts about content originates in the explanation of belief. Here our question is whether there is some feature that plays the same role in the explanation of intention, and of action, as the content of a belief plays in the explanation of that belief. Remember again that any role played by what is believed is not allowed to count as a role played by the content of belief. If the notion of content plays no role in explanation beyond that already played by what we believe, this approach falls to the ground. So why should we think that the explanation of belief is sensitive to content in addition to, or besides, the way it is sensitive to what we believe? Ordinarily, if we are trying to explain someone's belief that the bus is about to arrive, we might expect to find ourselves appealing to other beliefs of hers, that it is 3.25, that the bus timetable says that the bus is due at 3.30, and that the buses generally run on time. And I can see no reason why we should think of these other beliefs as anything other than further things that she believes. In the grids that I laid out earlier in this essay, the things on the right-hand side could perfectly well have been things believed.

But we should introduce at this point the sorts of considerations that persuaded us that we need a notion of content in addition to that of the thing believed. My belief that I am ill has the same content as your belief that you are ill, though what is believed in the two cases is not the same. What is believed, therefore, is not essentially first-personal, since in believing that you are ill I believe what you believe when you believe that you are ill. The content of your belief is essentially first-personal, however. And the formation of such a *de se* belief seems to require a distinctive sort of explanation.

The same will apply to all intentions, which if they have a content at all have an essentially *de se* content, which we have been characterizing as 'I Φ'. The explanation of something like this will have to be distinctive, because it will have to have an appropriate focus on the first-personal.

But now again, what about action? Ordinarily our explanation of action is targeted at what is done; we explain someone's action when we explain why she acted in that way. (We can of course seek to explain other things, such as why it was she who did it rather than someone else.) Action is first-personal, but only in the trivial sense that I do my actions and you do yours. Beyond that, return to the contrast between our both travelling to London with my wife and each of us travelling to London with his wife.

There seems to be nothing here that is *de se* in any sense that requires a special explanatory focus. Everything gets sucked into the way in which we acted. I conclude that even if we were to allow intention a content of the form 'I Φ', this would not generate anything worth calling content for action. Actions cannot inherit the content of the intention with which they are done.

This exhausts my attempts to locate a recognizable distinction that will enable us to think of action as the conclusion of inference. The force of practical deliberation will have to be captured in some other way. If it is not inference, what is it? I have an answer to this question, but I leave it for another occasion.[10]

---

[10] Thanks to Constantine Sandis.

P. M. S. Hacker: A Bibliography

A Books*

1. *Insight and Illusion: Wittgenstein on Philosophy and the Metaphysics of Experience*, 321 pp. (Oxford: Clarendon Press, 1972).
   German translation *Einsicht und Täuschung* (Frankfurt am Main: Suhrkamp, 1978).
   Japanese translation (Katsuo Yonezawa, 1981).

1a. *Insight and Illusion: Themes in the Philosophy of Wittgenstein*, revised edition, 341 pp. (Oxford: Clarendon Press, 1986). An extensively rewritten version of A1.
   Repr. with corrections in pb (Oxford: Clarendon Press, 1989).
   Repr. in pb (Bristol: Thoemmes Press, 1997).
   Chapter 7, pp. 179–214, 'Metaphysics as the Shadow of Grammar', repr. in Meredith Williams, ed., *Wittgenstein's Philosophical Investigations: Critical Essays* (Lanham, Md.: Rowman and Littlefield, 2007).

2. *Law, Morality and Society: Essays in Honour of H. L. A. Hart*, 312 pp. (Oxford: Clarendon Press, 1977); co-editor (with J. Raz) and contributor.

3. *Wittgenstein: Understanding and Meaning, Volume 1 of an Analytical Commentary on the Philosophical Investigations*, 692 pp. (Oxford: Blackwell, and Chicago: Chicago University Press, 1980), co-authored with G. P. Baker.
   Published as two paperbacks:
   (a) *Wittgenstein: Meaning and Understanding—Essays on the Philosophical Investigations* (Oxford: Blackwell, and Chicago: Chicago University Press, 1983; repr. 1984, 1988, repr. with corrections, 1992; repr. 2004).
   (b) *Wittgenstein: An Analytical Commentary on Wittgenstein's Philosophical Investigations* (Oxford: Blackwell, and Chicago: Chicago University Press, 1983; repr. 1984, 1988, repr. with corrections 1992, repr. 2004).

3a. *Wittgenstein: Understanding and Meaning, Volume 1 of an Analytical Commentary on the Philosophical Investigations, Part I—The Essays*, 2nd edition, extensively revised (Oxford: Blackwell, 2005); xxiv + 394 pp.

3b. *Wittgenstein: Understanding and Meaning, Volume 1 of an Analytical Commentary on the Philosophical Investigations, Part II—The Exegesis*, 2nd edition, extensively revised (Oxford: Blackwell, 2005); xix + 363 pp.

---

*Paperbacks are cited only in cases in which significant alterations were made for the paperback edition.

4. *Frege: Logical Excavations*, 406 pp. (Oxford: Blackwell, and New York: Oxford University Press, 1984), co-authored with G. P. Baker.
   Chapter 1, pp. 3–29, repr. as 'Prophetic Glimmerings: The New Pythagorean', in H. D. Sluga, ed., *General Assessments and Historical Accounts of Frege's Philosophy* (New York: Garland, 1993), pp. 315–42.

5. *Language, Sense and Nonsense: A Critical Investigation into Modern Theories of Language*, 392 pp. (Oxford: Blackwell, 1984), co-authored with G. P. Baker. Japanese translation (Shohakusha Publishers, 2000).

6. *Scepticism, Rules and Language*, 135 pp. (Oxford: Blackwell, 1984), co-authored with G. P. Baker.
   Russian translation (Moscow: Canon, 2008).

7. *Wittgenstein: Rules, Grammar, and Necessity, Volume 2 of an Analytical Commentary on the Philosophical Investigations*, 352 pp. (Oxford and Cambridge, Mass.: Blackwell, 1985), co-authored with G. P. Baker.
   pb (Oxford and Cambridge, Mass.: Blackwell, 1988; repr. with corrections 1992).

8. *Appearance and Reality: A Philosophical Investigation into Perception and Perceptual Qualities*, 243 pp. (Oxford: Blackwell, 1987).

9. *The Renaissance of Gravure: The Art of S. W. Hayter*, 125 pp. (Oxford: Oxford University Press, 1988), edited, contributed two essays and annotated catalogue.

10. *Wittgenstein: Meaning and Mind, Volume 3 of an Analytical Commentary on the Philosophical Investigations*, 575 pp. (Oxford and Cambridge, Mass.: Blackwell, 1990).
    Repr. (slightly revised) in two pbs:
    Wittgenstein: Meaning and Mind, Volume 3 of an Analytical Commentary on the Philosophical Investigations, Part I—Essays, 271 pp. (Oxford and Cambridge, Mass.: Blackwell, 1993; repr. 1997 (twice), 1998).
    Wittgenstein: Meaning and Mind, Volume 3 of an Analytical Commentary on the Philosophical Investigations, Part II—Exegesis §§243–427, 314 pp. (Oxford and Cambridge, Mass.: Blackwell, 1993).

11. *Gravure and Grace: The Engravings of Roger Vieillard*, 110 pp. (Oxford: Ashmolean Museum and Scolar Press, 1993), edited, contributed the major essay and compiled catalogues.

12. *Wittgenstein: Mind and Will, Volume 4 of an Analytical Commentary on the Philosophical Investigations*, 737 pp. (Oxford: Blackwell, 1996).
    Repr. (slightly revised) in two pbs:
    Wittgenstein: Mind and Will, Volume 4 of an Analytical Commentary on the Philosophical Investigations, Part I—Essays, pp. 289 (Oxford and Malden, Mass.: Blackwell, 2000).

Wittgenstein: Mind and Will, Volume 4 of an Analytical Commentary on the Philosophical Investigations, Part II—Exegesis §§428–693, 462 pp. (Oxford, and Malden, Mass.: Blackwell, 2000).

13. *Wittgenstein's Place in Twentieth Century Analytic Philosophy*, 346 pp. (Blackwell Oxford and Cambridge, Mass.: Blackwell, 1996).

German translation *Wittgenstein im Kontext der analytischen Philosophie*, 634 pp. (Frankfurt am Main: Suhrkamp, 1997).

'Den analytiske filosofiens krise', translation of pp. 264–73 and notes, in *Agora* 3–4 (1999), *Res publica* 46–7 (Engers Boktrykkeri AS, Otta, 1999), pp. 135–51.

14. *Wittgenstein on Human Nature*, 59 pp. (London: Weidenfeld and Nicolson, 1997).

Polish translation *Wittgenstein*, 87 pp. (Warsaw: Wielcy Filozowie, Wydawnictwo Amber, 1997).

Spanish translation *Wittgenstein*, 78 pp. (Barcelona: Grupo Editorial Norma, 1998).

Chinese translation (Taiwan, 1999).

Portuguese translation *Wittgenstein: Sobre a natureza humana*, 61 pp. (São Paulo: Fundação Editora da UNESP (FEU), 1999).

French translation *Wittgenstein*, 91 pp. (Paris: Éditions du Seuil, 2000).

Finnish translation *Wittgenstein*, 77 pp. (Helsinki: Kustannusosakeyhtiö Otava, 2000) pp. 77.

Hebrew translation *Wittgenstein: al teva HaAdam*, 95 pp. (Tel Aviv: Yediot Achronot, Sifrei Hemed, Sifrei Aliyat Hagag, 2001).

Greek translation *Wittgenstein*.

Korean translation *Wittgenstein*, 121 pp. (Seoul: Kungree Press, 2001).

Repr. in Ray Monk and Frederic Raphael, eds., *The Great Philosophers—From Socrates to Turing* (London: Weidenfeld and Nicolson, 2000), pp. 331–68.

15. *Wittgenstein: Connections and Controversies*, 375 pp. (Oxford: Clarendon Press, 2001).

16. *Philosophical Foundations of Neuroscience*, 454 pp. (Oxford and Malden, Mass.: Blackwell, 2003), co-authored with M. R. Bennett.

German translation of sections 14.4–14.5 in D. Sturma ed., *Philosophie und Neurowissenschaften* (Frankfurt am Main: Surhkamp, 2006), pp. 26–42.

17. *Neuroscience and Philosophy: Brain, Mind and Language*, 215 pp. (New York: Columbia University Press, 2007), co-authored with Max Bennett, Daniel Dennett and John Searle, with an introduction and conclusion by Daniel Robinson.

Spanish translation *La natwaleza de la conciencia: cerebro, mente y lenguaje*, 269 pp. (Barcelona: Paidos, 2008).

18. *Human Nature: The Categorial Framework*, 344 pp. (Oxford: Blackwell, 2007).

19. *History of Cognitive Neuroscience*, 320 pp. (Oxford: Blackwell, 2008), co-authored with M. R. Bennett .

B Articles

1. 'Sull'uso di "dovere" ', *Rivista di filosofia* 57 (1966), pp. 175–92.

2. 'Rules, Definitions and the Naturalistic Fallacy', *American Philosophical Quarterly* 3 (1966) (co-authored with G. P. Baker).

3. 'Definition in Jurisprudence', *Philosophical Quarterly* 19 (1969), pp. 343–7.
   Repr. in T. D. Postgate, ed., *The International Library of Critical Essays in the History of Philosophy*, Vol. 2, *Bentham*, ed. G. Postema (Aldershot: Ashgate, 2000).

4. 'Wittgenstein's Doctrines of the Soul in the Tractatus', *Kantstudien* 62 (1971), pp. 162–71.

5. 'Other Minds and Professor Ayer's Concept of a Person', *Philosophy and Phenomenological Research* 32 (1972), pp. 341–54.

6. 'Are Transcendental Arguments a Version of Verificationism', *American Philosophical Quarterly* 9 (1972), pp. 78–85.
   Spanish translation as 'Son los argumentos trascendentales una versión del verificacionismo?', in Isabel Cabrera, ed., *Argumentos trascendentales* (Mexico City: Universidad Nacional Autónoma de Mexico, 1999), pp.115–34.

7. 'Frege and the Private Language Argument', *Idealistic Studies* 2 (1972), pp. 265–87.

8. 'Sanction Theories of Duty', in *Oxford Essays in Jurisprudence*, second series, ed. A. W. B. Simpson (Oxford: Oxford University Press, 1973), pp. 131–70.
   Repr. in Carl Wellman, ed., *Rights and Duties*, Volume 1, *Conceptual Analyses of Rights and Duties* (New York: Routledge, 2002).

9. 'Wittgenstein on Ostensive Definition', *Inquiry* 18 (1975), pp. 267–87.

10. 'Frege and Wittgenstein on Elucidations', *Mind* 84 (1975), pp. 601–9.

11. 'Laying the Ghost of the Tractatus', *Review of Metaphysics* 29 (1975), pp. 96–116.
    An amended version repr. in S. Shanker, ed., *Ludwig Wittgenstein: Critical Assessments* (London: Croom Helm, 1986), Vol. 1, pp. 76–91.

12. 'Critical Notice of *Philosophical Grammar* by L. Wittgenstein', *Mind* 85 (1976), pp. 269–94 (co-authored with G. P. Baker).
    An extensively amended version repr. in S. Shanker, ed., *Ludwig Wittgenstein: Critical Assessments* (London, Croom Helm, 1986), Vol. 1, pp. 323–51.

13. 'Bentham's Theory of Action and Intention', *Archiv für Rechts- und Sozial-philosophie*, 62 (1976), pp. 89–109.
Repr. in T. D. Postgate, ed., *The International Library of Critical Essays in the History of Philosophy*, Vol. 2, *Bentham*, ed. G. Postema (Aldershot: Ashgate, 2000).

14. 'Locke and the Meaning of Colour Words', in *Impressions of Empiricism*, Royal Institute of Philosophy Lectures 9 (1974–5), ed. G. Vesey (London: Macmillan, 1976), pp. 23–46.

15. 'Hart's Philosophy of Law', in P. M. S. Hacker and J. Raz, eds., *Law, Morality and Society: Essays in Honour of H. L. A. Hart* (Oxford: Oxford University Press, 1977), pp. 1–25.

16. 'Semantic Holism: Frege and Wittgenstein', in G. Luckhardt, ed., *Wittgenstein: Sources and Perspectives* (Ithaca: Cornell University Press, 1979), pp. 213–42.

17. 'Substance: The Constitution of Reality', in *Midwest Studies in Philosophy*, Vol. 4: Studies in Metaphysics, ed. P. A. French, T. E. Uehling and H. K. Wettstein (Minneapolis: University of Minnesota Press, 1979), pp. 239–61.

18. 'Wittgenstein aujourd'hui', *Critique* (1980), pp. 690–709 (co-authored with G. P. Baker).
English translation in S. Shanker, ed., *Ludwig Wittgenstein: Critical Assessments* (London: Croom Helm, 1986), Vol. 2, pp. 24–35.

19. 'The Rise and Fall of the Picture Theory of Meaning', in I. Block, ed., *Perspectives on the Philosophy of Wittgenstein* (Oxford: Blackwell, 1981), pp. 85–109.
Revised version in S. Shanker, ed., *Ludwig Wittgenstein: Critical Assessments* (London: Croom Helm, 1986), Vol. 1, pp. 116–35.

20. 'Events and the Exemplification of Properties', *Philosophical Quarterly* 31 (1981), pp. 242–7.

21. 'Wittgenstein', in A. Kasher and S. Lappin, eds., *Modern Trends in Philosophy* (published in Hebrew; Jerusalem: Yachdav, 1982), pp. 205–30 (co-authored with G. P. Baker).

22. 'Events and Objects in Space and Time', *Mind* 91 (1982), pp. 1–19.
Repr. in Roberto Casati and Achille Varzi, eds., *Events*, International Library of Philosophy (Aldershot: Ashgate, 1996).

23. 'Events, Ontology and Grammar', *Philosophy* 57 (1982), pp. 477–86.
Repr. in Roberto Casati and Achille Varzi, eds., *Events*, International Library of Philosophy (Aldershot: Ashgate, 1996).

24. 'The Grammar of Psychology: Wittgenstein's *Bemerkungen über die Philosophie der Psychologie*', *Language and Communication* 2 (1982), pp. 227–44 (co-authored with G. P. Baker).

Repr. in S. Shanker, ed., *Ludwig Wittgenstein: Critical Assessments* (London: Croom Helm, 1986), Vol. 2, pp. 352–72.

25. 'Dummett's Frege or Through a Looking-Glass Darkly', *Mind* 92 (1983), pp. 239–46 (co-authored with G. P. Baker).

26. 'Dummett's Purge: Frege without Functions', *Philosophical Quarterly* 33 (1983), pp. 115–32 (co-authored with G. P. Baker).

27. 'Wittgenstein and the Vienna Circle: The Exaltation and Deposition of Ostensive Definition', *Teoria* 2 (1985), pp. 5–33 (co-authored with G. P. Baker).
    Repr. in S. Shanker, ed., *Ludwig Wittgenstein: Critical Assessments* (London: Croom Helm, 1986), Vol. 1, pp. 241–62.
    An amended version repr. in A15.

28. 'On Misunderstanding Wittgenstein: Kripke's Private Language Argument', *Synthese* 58 (1984), pp. 407–50 (co-authored with G. P. Baker).
    A slightly amended version repr. in A15.

29. 'The Concept of the Truth-Condition', *Conceptus* 17 (1983), pp. 11–18 (co-authored with G. P. Baker).

30. 'Frege', in A. Kasher and S. Lappin, eds., *Modern Trends in Philosophy*, Vol. 2 (published in Hebrew; Jerusalem: Yachdav, 1984), pp. 302–34 (co-authored with G. P. Baker).

31. 'Echte en zogenaamde', *Wisgerig Perspectif op Maatschappig en Wetenschap* 26 (1985–6), pp. 186–97 (co-authored with G. P. Baker).

32. 'Reply to Mr. Mounce', *Philosophical Investigations* 9 (1986), pp. 199–204 (co-authored with G. P. Baker).

33. 'Are Secondary Qualities Relative?', *Mind* 95 (1986), pp. 180–97.

34. 'Dummett's Dig: Looking Glass Archaeology', *Philosophical Quarterly* 37 (1987), pp. 86–99 (co-authored with G. P. Baker).

35. 'Critical Notice: Norman Malcolm — Nothing is Hidden', *Philosophical Investigations* 10 (1987), pp. 142–50.

36. 'Languages, Minds and Brain', in C. Blakemore and S. Greenfield, eds., *Mindwaves* (Oxford: Blackwell, 1987), pp. 485–506.

37. 'The Restoration of the Painted Glass in the Library', *St John's College Notes* (Oxford, 1987), pp. 46–9.

38. 'Language, Rules, and Pseudo-Rules', *Language and Communication* 8 (1988), pp. 159–72.

39. 'Wittgenstein's *Tractatus Logico-Philosophicus*', in Roy Harris, ed., *Linguistic Thought in England 1914–1945* (London: Duckworth, 1988), pp. 60–84.

40. 'Frege's Antipsychologism', in M. A. Notturno, ed., *Perspectives on Psychologism* (Leiden: Brill, 1989), pp. 75–127 (co-authored with G. P. Baker).

41. 'The Last Ditch', *Philosophical Quarterly* 39 (1989), pp. 471–7 (co-authored with G. P. Baker).

42. 'Roger Vieillard', *Print Quarterly* 7 (June 1990), pp. 146–61.

43. 'Le incisioni a colori di Hayter', in Carla Esposito, ed., *Hayter e l'Atelier 17* (Milan: Electa, 1990), pp. 46–56.

44. 'Malcolm on Language and Rules', *Philosophy* 65 (April 1990), pp. 167–79 (co-authored with G. P. Baker).
Repr. in A15.

45. 'Chomsky's Problems', *Language and Communication* 10/2 (1990), pp. 127–48.

46. 'John Buckland Wright at Atelier 17', in C. Buckland Wright, ed., *The Art of John Buckland Wright* (Aldershot: Scolar Press, 1990), pp. 43–50.

47. 'Seeing, Representing and Describing: An Examination of David Marr's Computational Theory of Vision', in J. Hyman, ed., *Investigating Psychology* (London: Routledge, 1991) pp. 119–54.
Italian translation in John Hyman, *La psicologia doppo Wittgenstein* (Rome: Ubaldini, 1994).

48. 'Experimental Methods and Conceptual Confusion: An Investigation into R. L. Gregory's Theory of Perception', *Iyyun: The Jerusalem Philosophical Quarterly* 40 (July 1991), pp. 289–314.

49. 'The Colour Prints of Stanley William Hayter', in Pat Gilmour, ed., *The Tamarind Papers* 14 (1991–2), pp. 31–42, 77.

50. 'Malcolm and Searle on "Intentional Mental States"', *Philosophical Investigations* 15 (1992), pp. 245–75.

51. 'A Portrait of Anne of Cleves', *The Burlington Magazine* 134 (1992), pp. 172–5 (co-authored with C. Kuhl).

51a. 'A Portrait of Anne of Cleves', *St John's College Notes* (Oxford, 1991), pp. 55–61 (co-authored with Candy Kuhl; a longer version of B51).

52. 'Developmental Hypotheses and Perspicuous Representations: Wittgenstein on Frazer's *Golden Bough*', *Iyyun: The Jerusalem Philosophical Quarterly* 41 (1992), pp. 277–99.
Repr. in A15.

53. 'Hayter's Synthesis of Form and Colour', in Duncan Scott, ed., *Twentieth Century Masterprints—Some Atelier 17 Connections* (London: Bankside Gallery, 1992), pp. 15–27.

54. 'Ostensive Definition' and 'Private Language Argument', in J. Dancy and E. Sosa, eds., *A Companion to Epistemology* (Oxford and Cambridge, Mass.: Blackwell, 1992), pp. 315–17, 368–74.

55. 'The Agreement of Thought and Reality', in J. V. Canfield and S. G. Shanker, eds., *Wittgenstein's Intentions* (New York: Garland, 1993), pp. 38–50.

56. 'Roger Vieillard', *The Ashmolean* (1993).
57. 'Synthèse des formes et des couleurs chez Hayter', in *Hayter et l'Atelier 17* (Gravelines: Musée du Dessin et de l'Estampe Original, Arsenal de Gravelines, 1993). (rewritten variant of B53).
58. 'Krassimira Drenska's Magical Museum', in *Geografias de la memoria* (Lisbon: Galeria Trayecto, 1993), pp. 10–15.
59. 'Ludwig Wittgenstein', in R. W. Mason, ed., *Cambridge Minds* (Cambridge: Cambridge University Press, 1994), pp. 142–59.
60. 'Helmholtz's Theory of Perception', in *International Studies in the Philosophy of Science* 9 (1995), pp. 199–214 (issue in honour of Professor Rom Harré).
    Repr. in *Review roumaine de philosophie* 40 (1996), pp. 227–46.
61. 'Wittgenstein and Post-War Philosophy at Oxford', in Jaakko Hintikka and Klaus Puhl, eds., *The British Tradition in 20th Century Philosophy*, Proceedings of the 17th International Wittgenstein Symposium, Kirchberg, 1994 (Vienna: Verlag Hölder-Pichler-Tempsky, 1995), pp. 100–21.
62. 'G. E. M. Anscombe', 'Beetle in the Box', 'Criterion', 'Duck-Rabbit', 'Family-Resemblance', 'Form of Life', 'Grammar, Autonomy of', 'Grammatical Proposition', 'Language-Game', 'Malcolm, Norman Adrian', 'Private Language Problem', 'Samples, Explanation by', 'Winch, P. G.', 'Wittgenstein, Ludwig Josef Johann', 'Wittgensteinians', in Ted Honderich, ed., *The Oxford Companion to Philosophy* (Oxford: Oxford University Press, 1995).
    Entry on Wittgenstein repr. in T. Honderich, ed., *The Philosophers: Introducing Great Western Thinkers* (Oxford: Oxford University Press, 1999), pp. 225–34.
63. 'On Davidson's Idea of a Conceptual Scheme', *The Philosophical Quarterly* 46 (1996), pp. 289–307.
    Repr. in translation in *La Revue du MAUSS* 17 (2001), pp. 311–331.
64. 'Reference and the First-Person Pronoun', *Language and Communication* 16 (1996), pp. 95–105 (co-authored with H.-J. Glock).
65. 'Hayter, Stanley William', in *The Dictionary of National Biography (1986–1990)*, ed. C. S. Nicholls (Oxford: Oxford University Press, 1996), pp. 196–7.
66. 'Wittgenstein and Quine: Proximity at Great Distance', in R. Arrington and H.-J. Glock, eds., *Wittgenstein and Quine* (London: Routledge, 1996), pp. 1–38.
67. 'The Rise of Twentieth Century Analytic Philosophy', *Ratio* 9 (1996), pp. 243–68.
    Repr. in H.-J. Glock, ed., *The Rise of Analytic Philosophy* (Oxford: Blackwell, 1997), pp. 51–76.
68. 'Davidson on First Person Authority', *The Philosophical Quarterly* 47 (1997), pp. 285–304.

Translation in W. Silva Filho, ed., *Donald Davidson* (Rio de Janeiro: DP&A, 2004).

69. 'Critical Notice: Ray Monk, *Bertrand Russell: The Spirit of Solitude*', *Philosophical Investigations* 21 (1998), pp. 55−62.

70. 'Davidson on the Ontology and Logical Form of Belief', *Philosophy* 73 (1998), pp. 81−96.

71. 'Analytic Philosophy—What, Whence and Whither?', in A. Matar and A. Biletsky, eds., *The Story of Analytic Philosophy—Plot and Heroes* (London: Routledge, 1998), pp. 1−32.
Chinese translation in *World Philosophy* 3 (1996), tr. Jiang Yi; repr. in Chen Bo, ed., *Analytic Philosophy—Reviews and Reflections*, tr. by Jiang Yi (Beijing: Sichun Education Publishing House, 2001).

72. 'Davidson on Intentionality and Externalism', *Philosophy* 73 (1998), pp. 539−52.

73. 'La filosofía analítica de la mente', in A. L. Cuenca, ed., *Resistiendo al oleaje: Reflexiones tras un siglo de filosofía analítica*, *Cuaderno Gris* 4 (1999), pp. 139−47.

74. 'Wittgenstein', in R. L. Arrington, ed., *The Blackwell Companion to the Philosophers* (Oxford: Blackwell, 1998), pp. 538−50.
Reprinted in R. L. Arrington, ed., *The World's Great Philosophers* (Oxford: Blackwell, 2003), pp. 316−32.

75. 'Frege and the Later Wittgenstein', in A. O'Hear, ed., *German Philosophy since Kant*, *Royal Institute of Philosophy Supplement* 44 (1999), pp. 223−47.
Repr. in A15.

76. 'Naming, Thinking and Meaning in the Tractatus', *Philosophical Investigations* 22 (1999), pp. 119−34.
Repr. in A15.

77. 'Was he Trying to Whistle it?', in A. Crary and R. Read, eds., *The New Wittgenstein* (London: Routledge, 2000), pp. 353−88.
Repr. with modifications in A15.
French translation in E. Regal, ed., *Wittgenstein état des lieux*, (Paris: Vrin, 2008), pp. 11−63.

78. 'Criteria and the Egocentric Predicament', in Marilyn Friedman, Larry May, Kate Parsons and Jennifer Stiff, eds., *Rights and Reason: Essays in Honor of Carl Wellman* (Dordrecht: Kluwer Academic Publishers, 2000), pp. 7−22.

79. 'Carnap's "Überwindung der Metaphysik', *Deutsche Zeitschrift für Philosophie* 48/3 (2000) pp. 469−86.
Repr. in A15 as 'On Carnap's Elimination of Metaphysics through the Logical Analysis of Language'.

80. 'Eliminative Materialism', in S. Schroeder, ed., *Wittgenstein and Contemporary Philosophy of Mind* (London: Palgrave, 2001), pp. 60–84.

81. 'An Orrery of Intentionality', *Language and Communication* 21 (2001), pp. 119–41.

82. 'On Wittgenstein', *Philosophical Investigations* 24 (2001), pp. 121–30.

83. 'Wittgenstein and the Autonomy of Humanistic Understanding', in R. Allen and M. Turvey, eds., *Wittgenstein: Theory and the Arts* (London: Routledge, 2001), pp. 39–74.
    Repr. in A15.

84. 'When the Whistling had to Stop', in D. O. M. Charles and T. W. Child, eds., *Wittgensteinian Themes: Essays in Honour of David Pears* (Oxford: Clarendon Press, 2001).
    Repr. in A15.

84a. 'Als das Pfeifen verstummen musste', in M. Kross and H. J. Schneider, eds., *Mit Sprache Spielen—Die Ordnungen und das Offene nach Wittgenstein* (Berlin: Akademie Verlag, 1999), pp. 95–117. A shortened version of B84, delivered as a lecture at the Einstein Forum, Potsdam, in November 1996.

85. 'Philosophy', in H.-J. Glock, ed., *A Wittgenstein Reader* (Oxford: Blackwell, 2001).

86. 'Wittgenstein', in A. Martinich and D. Sosa, eds., *A Companion to Analytic Philosophy* (Oxford: Blackwell, 2001), pp. 68–93.
    Repr. in A15.

87. 'Perception and Memory in Neuroscience: A Conceptual Analysis', *Progress in Neurobiology* 66 (2001), pp. 499–543 (co-authored with M. R. Bennett).

88. 'Verstehen wollen', in Joachim Schulte and Uwe Justus Wenzel, eds., *Was ist ein 'philosophisches' Problem:* (Frankfurt am Main: Fischer Taschenbuch Verlag, 2001), pp. 54–71.
    English translation as: 'What is a Philosophical Problem?', *Think* 12 (2006), pp. 17–28.

89. 'Transitive and Intransitive Consciousness', *Revista de filosofie*, 48/3–4 (May–August 2001), pp. 175–97.
    Repr. in A. Botez and B. M. Popescu, eds., *Filosofia conştiinţei şi ştiinţele cognitive (Philosophy of Consciousness and Cognitive Science)* (Bucharest: Cartea Romaneasca, 2002), pp. 147–73

90. 'Strawson's Concept of a Person', *Proceedings of the Aristotelian Society* 102 (2002), pp. 21–40.

91. 'Is there Anything it is Like to Be a Bat?', *Philosophy* 77 (2002), pp. 157–74.
    Repr. in *e-Journal Philosophie der Psychologie* 5 (May 2006).

92. 'The Motor System in Neuroscience: A History and Analysis of Conceptual Developments', *Progress in Neurobiology* 67 (2002), 1–52 (co-authored with M. R. Bennett).

93. 'Wittgenstein, Carnap and the New American Wittgensteinians', *Philosophical Quarterly* 53 (2003), pp. 1–23.

94. 'Functions in Begriffsschrift', *Synthese* 135 (2003), pp. 273–97 (co-authored with G. P. Baker).

95. 'On Strawson's Rehabilitation of Metaphysics', in H. J. Glock, ed., *Strawson and Kant* (Oxford: Oxford University Press, 2003), pp. 43–66.
    Repr. in A15.

96. 'Of the Ontology of Belief', in Mark Siebel and Mark Textor, eds., *Semantik und Ontologie* (Frankfurt am Main: Ontos Verlag, 2004), pp. 185–222.

97. 'Substance: Things and Stuffs', *Proceedings of the Aristotelian Society* 104 (2004), pp. 41–63.

98. 'Turning the Examination Around: The Recantation of a Metaphysician', in E. Ammereller and Eugen Fischer, eds., *Wittgenstein at Work* (London: Routledge, 2004), pp. 3–21.

99. Biographies of J. L. Austin, N. A. Malcolm, L. Wittgenstein, in *Oxford Dictionary of National Biography* (Oxford: Oxford University Press, 2004).

100. 'Übersichtlichkeit und Übersichtliche Darstellungen', *Deutsche Zeitschrift für Philosophie* (2004), pp. 405–20.

101. 'The Conceptual Framework for the Investigation of the Emotions', *International Review of Psychiatry* 16 (2004), pp. 199–208.
    Repr. in Y. Gustafsson, C. Kronquist and M. McEachrane, eds., *Emotions and Understanding* (Basingstoke: Palgrave, 2008), pp. 43–59.

102. 'Of Knowledge and of Knowing that Someone is in Pain', in A. Pichler and S. Säätelä, eds., *Wittgenstein: The Philosopher and his Works* (Bergen: The Wittgenstein Archives, University of Bergen, 2005), pp. 123–56.
    Repr. (Frankfurt am Main: Ontos Verlag, 2006).

103. Emotion and Cortical-Subcortical Function: Conceptual Developments', *Progress in Neurobiology* 75 (2005), pp. 29–52 (co-authored with M. R. Bennett).

104. 'Thought and Action: A Tribute to Stuart Hampshire', *Philosophy* 80 (2005), pp. 175–97.

104a. A variant published in Anton Leist and Holger Baumann, eds., *Action in Context* (Berlin: De Gruyter, 2007).

105. 'Goodbye to Qualia and All What?—A Reply to David Hodgson', *Journal of Consciousness Studies* 12 (2005), pp. 61–6.

106. 'The Art of Hector Saunier', in Chinese catalogue of his prints (2005).

107. 'Passing by the Naturalistic Turn: On Quine's *cul-de-sac*', *Philosophy* 81 (2006), pp. 221–43.

107a. A shortened version published in G. Gasser, ed., *How Successful is Naturalism?* (Frankfurt am Main: Ontos Verlag, 2007).

108. 'Scott Soames's *Philosophical Analysis in the Twentieth Century*', critical notice, *Philosophical Quarterly* 56 (2006), pp. 121–31.

109. 'Language and Cortical Function: From Wernicke to Levelt', *Progress in Neurobiology* 80 (2006), pp. 20–52 (co-authored with M. R. Bennett).

110. 'Gordon Baker's Late Interpretation of Wittgenstein', in G. Kahane, E. Kanterian and O. Kuusela, eds., *Wittgenstein and his Interpreters* (Oxford: Blackwell, 2007), pp. 88–122.

111. 'Analytic Philosophy: Beyond the Linguistic Turn and Back Again', in M. Beaney, ed., *The Analytic Turn: Analysis in Early Analytic Philosophy and Phenomenology* (London: Routledge, 2007), pp. 125–41.

112. 'Human Beings—the Mind and the Body: Wittgensteinian-Aristotelian Reflections', *Proceedings of the 29 International Wittgenstein Conference 2006* (Heusenstamm: Ontos Verlag, 2007), pp. 67–86.

113. 'A Philosophy of Philosophy: Critical Notice of Timothy Williamson's *Philosophy of Philosophy*', *Philosophical Quarterly* 59 (2009).

C Interviews

1. 'An Interview with Dr Peter Hacker on Wittgenstein Studies', *Chinese Philosophical Review* 1/1 (1993), pp. 1–30.

2. '*Entretien*: Dr Peter Hacker on Wittgenstein', *La Lettre de la Maison Française d'Oxford* 2 (1995), pp. 101–10.

3. 'Interview with P. M. S. Hacker' by Dr Angela Botez, *Revista de filosofie* 43 (1996), pp. 479–85.

4. 'Von der Gefahr, Wittgenstein zu vergessen: der Wittgenstein-Forscher Peter Hacker im Gespräch mit Edward Kanterian', *Information Philosophie* 5 (December 2002), pp. 102–15.

5. 'Hirnforschern aufs Maul Geschaut', Interview by Armin Scholtz, *Gehirn und Geist* 5 (2004), pp. 43–5.

6. Interview by Li Hong, *Philosophical Trends* (published by the Chinese Academy for Social Science), (2004), pp. 21–5.

Index